# THE DRAMATISTS GUILD
# RESOURCE DIRECTORY™

# 2010

## The Writer's Guide
## to the Theatrical Marketplace™

## 16th Edition

ISBN 13: 978-1-58510-364-5
ISBN 10: 1-58510-364-0

The Dramatists Guild Resource Directory and The Writer's Guide to the
Theatrical Marketplace are trademarks of The Dramatists Guild.

Cover image © istockphoto / Duncan Walker

This book is published with permission by Focus Publishing/R. Pullins
Company, 311 Merrimac, Newburyport MA 01950 www.pullins.com,
with the expertise of Joshua Faigen of Folio Publishing Services.

10 9 8 7 6 5 4 3 2 1

1109TS

# Table of Contents

# Preface

Welcome to the 16th printed edition of The Dramatists Guild Resource Directory. Each year we add features that we think our members will find important to their lives as dramatists. This year, in addition to the standard submission opportunities and resources, you'll notice that we've added the following:

- A discussion/dissection on synopsis writing
- Ten-minute/short play submission opportunities
- Submission opportunities for artists of color
- Submission opportunities for writers of non-traditional theatre
- A bibliography of books on playwriting and musical theatre writing.

We're continuing to post the Dramatists Bill of Rights (so you'll always know your rights and protections in whatever situation you find yourself in), along with our statement of submission fees, and still provide you a variety of resources if you are looking for further education.

A strong word of advice about this Resource Directory: by the time we go to press, a number of the opportunities listed within these pages will no longer exist, will not have the same staff listed or will not have the same deadline date as printed. It is essential that you verify the information we provide either by going to the Member's Lounge at www.dramatistsguild.com and double-checking the information on our website, or by going directly to the website of the theatre, contest, festival, etc.

When looking for a listing in the index, please know individuals (primarily agents, attorneys, and producers) and opportunities named for individuals (primarily contests) are listed by the first letter of the individual's surname. For easier reference, we have also indicated any deadlines and fees in boldface next to the title of those opportunities that released them.

The organizations listed in the Resource Directory receive hundreds of inquiries, so please be responsible with your submissions.

1. Name the specific program you're interested in, since many groups sponsor multiple programs.

2. Include a self-addressed stamped envelope (SASE) with sufficient postage. Most organizations won't return material without one, while some organizations don't return material at all. You may also include a self-addressed stamped postcard (SASP) to be notified when the organization has received your material – or if they are interested in reading your script. It's always a smart (and economically sound) choice to discover if the organization takes electronic submissions.

3.  Include your contact information in a query letter, since some organizations prefer blind submissions, with no identification on the script itself.

Please review each organization's policies carefully to ensure that all authorial rights are upheld. If you find a listing you believe is inaccurate or misleading, or if you have questions about any listing, write to us here at the Guild. Remember, though, listings by their nature are never complete, and any listing or omission doesn't necessarily constitute approval or disapproval by the Guild, its Council, officers, employees, agents, or affiliates.

Finally, much thanks to Larry Pontius, Roland Tec, Bailey Stark, Joan Miller, Nicholas Herbert, Nick Gandiello, Elizabeth Magee, Ashley Audette, Rebecca Stump, Kelley Hires, Dylan Glatthorn and Linda Leseman for their invaluable contributions to this resource.

Gary Garrison
*Executive Director,*
*Creative Affairs*

# The Dramatist Bill of Rights

The Dramatists Guild is America's professional association of playwrights, librettists, lyricists and composers, with over 6,000 members around the world. The Guild is governed by our country's leading dramatists, with a fifty-five member Council that includes such dramatists as Edward Albee, Stephen Sondheim, John Patrick Shanley, Tony Kushner, Marsha Norman, Lynn Nottage, Emily Mann and Christopher Durang.

Long before playwrights or musical theatre writers join the Dramatists Guild, they often struggle professionally in small to medium-sized theatres throughout the country. It is essential, therefore, that dramatists know their rights, which the Dramatists Guild has defended for nearly one hundred years. In order to protect the dramatist's unique vision, which has always been the strength of the theatre, s/he needs to understand this fundamental principle: dramatists own and control their work.

The Guild recommends that any production involving a dramatist incorporate a written agreement in which both theatres/producers and writers acknowledge certain key rights with each other.

## In Process and Production

1. ARTISTIC INTEGRITY. No one (e.g., directors, actors, dramaturgs) can make changes, alterations, and/or omissions to your script—including the text, title, and stage directions—without your consent. This is called "script approval."

2. APPROVAL OF PRODUCTION ELEMENTS. You have the right to approve the cast, director, and designers (and, for a musical, the choreographer, orchestrator, arranger, and musical director, as well), including their replacements. This is called "artistic approval."

3. RIGHT TO BE PRESENT. You always have the right to attend casting, rehearsals, previews and performances.

## Compensations

4. ROYALTIES. You are generally entitled to receive a royalty. While it is possible that the amount an author receives may be minimal for a small- to medium-sized production, *some* compensation should always be paid if *any* other artistic collaborator in the production is being paid, or if any admission is being charged. If you are a member of the Guild, you can always call our business office to discuss the standard industry royalties for various levels of production.

5.　BILLING CREDIT. You should receive billing (typographical credit) on all publicity, programs, and advertising distributed or authorized by the theatre. Billing is part of your compensation and the failure to provide it properly is a breach of your rights.

## Ownership

6.　OWNERSHIP OF INTELLECTUAL PROPERTY. You own the copyright of your dramatic work. Authors in the theatre business do not assign (i.e., give away or sell in entirety) their copyrights, nor do they ever engage in "work-for-hire." When a university, producer or theatre wants to mount a production of your play, you actually license (or lease) the public performance rights to your dramatic property to that entity for a finite period of time.

7.　OWNERSHIP OF INCIDENTAL CONTRIBUTIONS. You own all approved revisions, suggestions, and contributions to the script made by other collaborators in the production, including actors, directors, and dramaturgs. You do not owe anyone any money for these contributions.

If a theatre uses *dramaturgs*, you are not obligated to make use of any ideas the dramaturg might have. Even when the input of a dramaturg or director is helpful to the playwright, dramaturgs and directors are still employees of the theatre, not the author, and they are paid for their work *by the theatre/producer.* It has been well-established in case law, beginning with "the Rent Case" (*Thompson v. Larson*) that neither dramaturgs nor directors (nor any other contributors) may be considered a co-author of a play, unless (i) they've collaborated with you from the play's inception, (ii) they've made a copyrightable contribution to the play, and (iii) you have agreed in writing that they are a co-author.

8.　SUBSIDIARY RIGHTS. After the small- or medium-sized production, you not only own your script, but also the rights to market and sell it to all different media (e.g., television, radio, film, internet) in any commercial market in the world. You are not obligated to sign over any portion of your project's future revenues to any third party (fellow artist, advisor, director, producer) as a result of a production, unless that production is a professional (i.e., Actor's Equity) premiere production (including sets, costumes and lighting), of no less than 21 consecutive paid public performances for which the author has received appropriate billing, compensation, and artistic approvals.

9,　FUTURE OPTIONS. Rather than granting the theatre the right to share in future proceeds, you may choose to grant a non-exclusive option to present another production of your work within six months or one year of the close of the initial production. No option should be assignable without your prior written consent.

10. AUTHOR'S CONTRACT: The only way to ensure that you get the benefit of the rights listed above is through a written contract with the producer, no matter how large or small the entity. The Guild's Department of Business Affairs offers a model "production contract" and is available to review any contracts offered to you, and advise as to how those contracts compare to industry standards.

We realize that making demands of a small theatre is a difficult task. However, you should feel confident in presenting this Bill of Rights to the Artistic Director, Producer, Literary Manager, or university administrator as a starting point for discussion. At the very least, any professional in the dramatic arts should realize that it is important for writers to understand the nature of their work—not just the artistic aspects, but the business side, as well—and that they stand together as a community, for their mutual benefit and survival, and for the survival of theatre as a viable art form in the 21st century.

# Suggested Formatting for Plays and Musicals

Included in this document are suggested formats for plays and musicals drawn from suggestions of distinguished dramatists, literary managers, teachers of dramatic writing, producers, professional theatres and publishers. It is the Guild's belief that these formats present a standard that will work for most professional opportunities. A few additional elements to consider:

1.  Formatting works towards two purposes: easy reading and the ability to approximate the performance time of the written story. For plays, we've given you a traditional and a more modern format to choose from. Admittedly, not all stories or styles of writing will work within a standard format. Therefore, use your better judgment in deciding the architecture of the page.

2.  There is an industry standard (though some may say old-fashioned) of using the 12-point Courier-New font; we've also noted that Times New Roman is used in more modern formatting. With the proliferation of computers and word-processing programs, there are literally hundreds of fonts to choose from. Whatever your choice, we recommend that you maintain a font size of 12 points – thereby assuring some reliable approximation of performance time.

3.  Though you wrote the story, someone has to read it before anyone sees it. Therefore, make your manuscript easy to read by employing a standard format with clearly delineated page numbers, scene citations and act citations. Headers and footers are optional.

4.  If you're using a software program, such as Final Draft, to format your work, be aware that you have the ability to create your own format in these programs that can be uniquely named, saved and applied to all of your manuscripts.

5.  Usually, between the title page and the first page of the story and/or dialogue, there is a page devoted to a character break-down. What's important to note on this page is the age, gender and name of each character. Some dramatists write brief character descriptions beside each name.

6.  While it is cost-effective for both xeroxing and mailing, realize that some institutions prefer that you don't send double-sided documents. We recommend that you inquire about preference.

7.  There is no right or wrong way to signify the end of a scene or act. Some writers do nothing but end the scene; others write "black out", "lights fade down", "End Act 1" or some other signifier that the scene or act has concluded.

8.  The binding margin should be 1.5 inches from the edge. All other margins (top, bottom, right) should be 1.0 inch from the edge.

## Sample Title Page

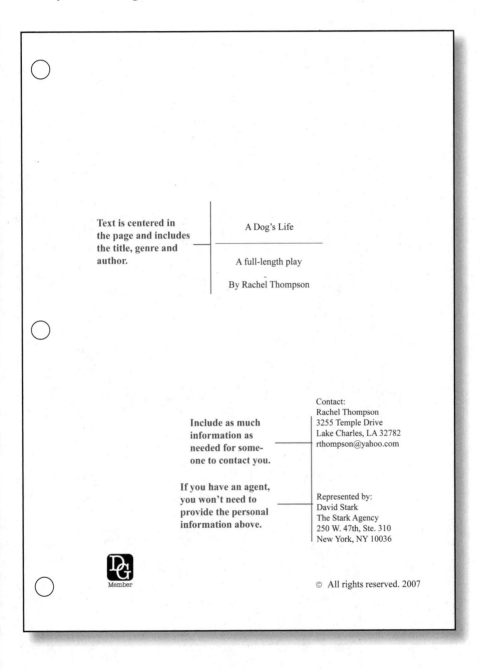

Text is centered in the page and includes the title, genre and author.

A Dog's Life

A full-length play

By Rachel Thompson

Include as much information as needed for someone to contact you.

Contact:
Rachel Thompson
3255 Temple Drive
Lake Charles, LA 32782
rthompson@yahoo.com

If you have an agent, you won't need to provide the personal information above.

Represented by:
David Stark
The Stark Agency
250 W. 47th, Ste. 310
New York, NY 10036

Member

## Traditional Play Format

From Tennessee Williams' *Not About Nightingales*

Essential page numbering**
16.

                                        BOSS
                              (removes cover from basket)

**Dialogue begins 1.5 inches from left side to account for binding. Dialogue is single-spaced.**

Speak of biscuits and what turns up but a nice batch of homemade cookies! Have one young lady – Jim boy!

                      (Jim takes two.)

**Stage action is indented 3 inches from left; put in parenthesis. A blank line is inserted before and after.**

                                          BOSS
Uh-huh, you've got an awful big paw, Jimmy!
                              (laughs)

**Dialogue extends to 1.0 inch from right margin**

Show the new Arky-what's-it to Miss Daily news – or is it the Morning Star? Have a chair! I'll be right with you –
                            (vanishes for a moment)
Sweat, sweat, sweat's all I do these hot breezy days!

                                        JIM
                              (sotto voce)
He thinks you're a newspaper woman.

**Stage action reliant on the proceeding dialogue is indented to the left of the character name.**

                                        BOSS
Turn on that fan.
                            (emerging)
Well, now, let's see –

                                        EVA
To begin with I'm not –

**Character name in all caps; in the center of the page.**

                                        BOSS
You've probably come here to question me about that ex-convicts story in that damned yellow sheet down there in Wilkes county – That stuff about getting Pellagra in here – Jimmy, hand me that sample menu!

**Standard font for this formatting is 12.0 point, Courier New.**

                                        JIM
She's not a reporter.

                                        BOSS
Aw. – What is your business, young lady?

**Stage action is indented 3.0 inches from left margin and enclosed in parentheses.**

                              (She opens her purse and spills
                              contents on floor.)

**There are many ways to paginate your play, from the straightforward numerical sequence of 1, 2, 3 to an older format of I-2-16, (meaning Act 1, Scene 2, Page 16).

## Modern Play Format

From Tennessee Williams' *Not About Nightingales*

Essential page
numbering

16.

**BOSS**

You've probably come here to question me about that ex-convicts story in that damned
yellow sheet down there in Wilkes county – That stuff about getting Pellagra in here
– Jimmy, hand me that sample menu!

Dialogue begins
1.5 inches from
left side to
account for
binding. Dialogue
is single-spaced.

**JIM**

She's not a reporter.

Character name
in all caps; in the
center of the page.

**BOSS**

Aw. – What is your business, young lady?

**EVA**

I understand there's a vacancy here. Mr. McBurney, my landlady's brother-in-law,
told her that you were needing a new stenographer and I'm sure that I can qualify
for the position. I'm a college graduate, Mr. Whalen, I've had three years of business
experience – references with me – but, oh – I've – I've had such abominable luck
these last six months. – the last place I worked – the business recession set in they
had to cut down on their sales-force – they gave me a wonderful letter – I've got it
with me.

Dialogue extends
to 1.0 inch from
right margin

She opens her purse and spills contents
on floor.

**BOSS**

Anybody outside?

Stage action begins
in the center of the
page and scans to
the right margin. A
blank line is inserted
before and after.

**EVA**

Yes. That woman.

**BOSS**

What woman?

Standard font for
this formatting is
12.0 point, New
Times Roman.

**EVA**

The one from Wisconsin. She's still waiting –

**BOSS**

I told you I don't want to see her.

(talking into phone)

How's the track, Bert? Fast? Okay.

Stage action reliant
on the proceeding
dialogue is indented
to the left of the
character name.

Sailor Jack's mother, MRS. BRISTOL, has
quietly entered. She carries a blanket.

**MRS. BRISTOL**

I beg your pardon, I – You see I'm Jack Bristol's mother, and I've been wanting to
have a talk with you so long about – about my boy!

## Musical Format

From *APPLAUSE*, Book by Betty Comden, Adolph Green.
Music by Charles Strouse, Lyrics by Lee Adams

Essential page numbering**
56.

Dialogue begins 1.5 inches from left side to account for binding. Dialogue is single-spaced.

Character name in all caps; in the center of the page.

Stage action is indented 3 inches from left; put in parentheses. A blank line is inserted before and after.

Dialogue extends to 1.0 inch from right margin

Stage action reliant on the proceeding dialogue is indented to the left of the character name.

KAREN
(to Margo)
Margo, you've been kicking us all around long enough. Someone ought to give *you* a good swift one for a change!

(She leaves.)

EVE
Miss Channing . . . if I ever dreamed that anything I did could possibly cause you any unhappiness, or come between you and your friends . . . please believe me.

MARGO
(in a low, weary voice)
Oh, I do. And I'm full of admiration for you.
(stands, approaches Eve)
If you can handle yourself on the stage with the same artistry you display off the stage . . . well, my dear, you are in the right place.

(She speaks the following lines as the music
of <u>WELCOME TO THE THEATRE</u> begins.)

Welcome to the theater, to the magic, to the fun!

(She sings.)

WHERE PAINTED TREES AND FLOWERS GROW
AND LAUGHTER RINGS FORTISSIMO,
AND TREACHERY'S SWEETLY DONE!

NOW YOU'VE ENTERED THE ASYLUM,
THIS PROFESSION UNIQUE
ACTORS ARE CHILDREN
PLAYING HIDE-AND-EGO-SEEK . . .

SO WELCOME, MISS EVE HARRINGTON,
TO THIS BUSINESS WE CALL SHOW,
YOU'RE ON YOUR WAY
TO WEALTH AND FAME,
UNSHEATH YOUR CLAWS,
ENJOY THE GAME!
YOU'LL BE A BITCH
BUT THEY'LL KNOW YOUR NAME
FROM NEW YORK . . . TO KOKOMO

WELCOME TO THEATRE,
MY DEAR, YOU'LL LOVE IT SO!

Stanzas are separated by a blank line and distinguish themselves by dramatic thought and/or changes from verse to chorus to bridges, etc.

Lyric are in all CAPS, separated line to line by either musical phrasing and/or the rhyming scheme and clearly indented from the left margin.

For duets, or characters singing counter-point, create two columns side by side, following the same format here.

**There are many ways to paginate your play, from the straight forward numerical sequence of 1, 2, 3 to an older format of 1-2-16, (meaning Act 1, Scene 2, Page 16).

## The Submission Letter and Production Resume

Though there is no right or wrong way to write a letter of introduction to your work, realize an effective submission letter should be short, professional and with just enough information so the reader knows you've submitted exactly what was called for in the solicitation. And while it's tempting to entice the reader to want to read the script with an overly expressive narrative in your submission letter, consider that this is the first exposure to your writing (of any kind) that will be read by someone in the producing organization . Be mindful, then, how you represent yourself on paper, and allow your play or musical to speak for itself.

A common question is often asked when writers construct a production resume: what do you do if you don't have a lot of readings or productions to list on your resume? Whatever you do, don't misrepresent yourself; don't say you've had a reading or a production of a play at a theatre that you haven't had. You'll eventually be found out and look worse than someone who has a thin resume. If you don't have a lot of production experience with your writing, write a brief synopsis of each of the plays you've written, cite any classes or workshops you've taken as a playwright and detail any other experience you have in the theatre (as stage manager, director, actress, dramaturg, etc.). People are more likely to be sympathetic to you being young in the theatre than they are to you being someone who misrepresents themselves.

A more accomplished playwright's resume should list the productions or readings of plays (by theatre and date), awards, grants, writers colonies attended, workshops, festivals invited to and any special recognition received as a writer. Give the reader a sense of the whole of your writing career, including memberships in theatre groups, professional organizations and related writing work. Include your address and phone number at the top or bottom of your resume, cover sheet of your play and obviously on the return envelope. Again, there are any number of variations on how to construct a writer's resume, but a template to inspire your thinking can be found on the following page.

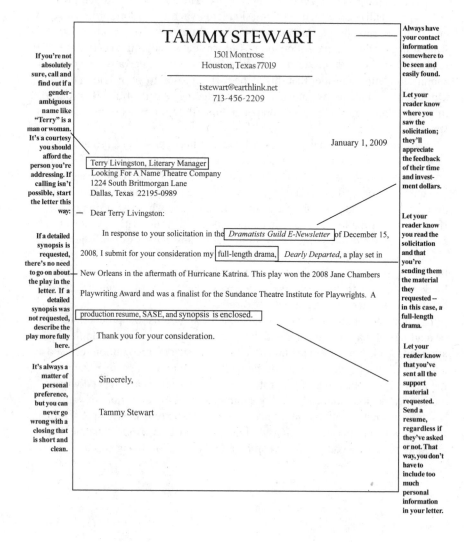

# TAMMY STEWART

1501 Montrose
Houston, Texas 77019

tstewart@earthlink.net
713-456-2209

January 1, 2009

Terry Livingston, Literary Manager
Looking For A Name Theatre Company
1224 South Brittmorgan Lane
Dallas, Texas  22195-0989

Dear Terry Livingston:

In response to your solicitation in the *Dramatists Guild E-Newsletter* of December 15, 2008, I submit for your consideration my full-length drama, *Dearly Departed*, a play set in New Orleans in the aftermath of Hurricane Katrina. This play won the 2008 Jane Chambers Playwriting Award and was a finalist for the Sundance Theatre Institute for Playwrights. A production resume, SASE, and synopsis  is enclosed.

Thank you for your consideration.


Sincerely,


Tammy Stewart

---

**Left margin notes:**

If you're not absolutely sure, call and find out if a gender-ambiguous name like "Terry" is a man or woman. It's a courtesy you should afford the person you're addressing. If calling isn't possible, start the letter this way:

If a detailed synopsis is requested, there's no need to go on about the play in the letter. If a detailed synopsis was not requested, describe the play more fully here.

It's always a matter of personal preference, but you can never go wrong with a closing that is short and clean.

**Right margin notes:**

Always have your contact information somewhere to be seen and easily found.

Let your reader know where you saw the solicitation; they'll appreciate the feedback of their time and investment dollars.

Let your reader know you read the solicitation and that you're sending them the material they requested – in this case, a full-length drama.

Let your reader know that you've sent all the support material requested. Send a resume, regardless if they've asked or not. That way, you don't have to include too much personal information in your letter.

14

# Tammy Stewart

tstewart@earthlink.net
713-456-2209
1501 Montrose
Houston, Texas 77019

## PRODUCTION HISTORY

***Dearly Departed*** (full-length drama)

| | |
|---|---|
| Winner, Jane Chambers Playwriting Award | July 2008 |
| Finalist, 2008 Sundance Theatre Institute for Playwrights | May 2008 |
| Early scenes published in *The Best Stage Scenes of 2008*, Smith & Krause, Inc. | April 2008 |

***Forty-Love, Roger*** (full-length comedy)

| | |
|---|---|
| Winner, Arthur W. Stone New Play Award | September 2007 |
| Hedgerow Theatre Company, Summer Showcase Series, Staged Reading | June 2007 |
| Miranda Theatre, New York City, Off-Off Broadway Equity Showcase | May 2007 |

***Maddie Makes a Madness*** (10-minute play)

| | |
|---|---|
| Finalist, Actors Theatre of Louisville, National Ten Minute Play Contest | December 2007 |

***Daily Puppy Dot Com*** (10-minute play)

| | |
|---|---|
| Summer Shorts Festival, Miami, Florida | May 2006 |
| Turnip Theatre Festival, New York City, Equity showcase | January 2006 |
| Published in *Ten On Ten: The Best Ten Minute Plays of 2006*, Focus Publishing | |

## AWARDS

| | |
|---|---|
| Residency, MacDowell Colony | January 2003 |
| Texas State Foundation for the Arts, Artist Grant | January 2002 |
| The Young Playwrights Award, Texas Education Theatre Association | May 1998 |

## MEMBER/ASSOCIATIONS

Dramatists Guild of America, Associate Member
Minneapolis Playwrights Center
Writers Focusing Writers, Houston, Texas
Scriptwriters, Houston, Texas

## EDUCATION

| | |
|---|---|
| MFA in Playwriting, University of Houston (with Edward Albee, Lanford Wilson) | May 2002 |
| BFA in Acting, The University of Michigan | May 2000 |

# Synopsis Writing

Whether we love writing a synopsis or hate writing a synopsis of our most recent work (and most of us belong to the latter group), one thing has become abundantly clear: we have to do it and it must be done extremely well. Why? The number of theatres requesting a synopsis as an introduction to our work has increased dramatically over the last decade and there is nothing to suggest that trend wlll reverse itself.

To help our members understand the purpose, craft and pitfalls of writing a synopsis (after all, there is no real instruction to speak of anywhere), we've included liberally edited highlights from a synopsis seminar held in New York in the spring of 2009. On the panel was Linda Chapman (Associate Artistic Director, New York Theatre Workshop), Morgan Jenness (Abrams Artists Agency), Jeni Mahoney (Artistic Director, Seven Devils Playwrights Conference) and Nancy Golladay (BMI Lehman Engel Musical Theatre Librettists Workshop). The panel was moderated by Roland Tec, the DG Director of Membership.

ROLAND TEC: A film that I wrote and directed opened in New York about a month and a half ago. In the six weeks leading up to the opening of the film, I probably rewrote the synopsis of the film about half a dozen times. Luckily, I had a very patient publicist who would accept these e-mails from me rewriting the synopsis every other week. Finally my phone rang and he said, "Roland, I have to tell you something, and I hope you won't be upset. Every time you rewrite the synopsis, it gets more and more bland." I think it's important for us to remember that describing our own work can be the most difficult thing. We can sometimes be our own worst enemies because we have all sorts of baggage connected to what we've created.

One of the most important things we can do for ourselves as writers is surround ourselves with trusted souls who can be a sounding board for this sort of work: the packaging and describing of our work. Tonight we have four great examples of some really generous and smart souls who can help us begin to talk about how to describe what one has written.

Linda S. Chapman as Associate Artistic Director of the New York Theatre Workshop has helped support the work of hundreds of local artists through the company's myriad development programs. She's worked as a director, as a performer, and as a playwright.

Nancy Golladay is a faculty member of the BMI Lehman-Engel Musical Theatre Workshop, where she moderates the librettists group. Nancy too has an eclectic background. She has worked as a literary consultant to a whole slew of festivals and still evaluates musical submissions to them and to various commercial producers.

Next is Jeni Mahoney. Jeni Mahoney is a playwright. Her work has been produced or workshopped all over the country, at theatres such as The Lark and Rattlestick. She is the founding artistic director of Seven Devils Playwrights Conference. Seven Devils has an open submission policy. They review all plays submitted, not just synopses. They read the whole play. Jeni is also co-artistic director of id Theater and was recently named head of the playwriting program at Playwrights Horizons Theater School.

Last but not least, we have Morgan Jenness. Morgan is an agent who reads and adores the people who write new work. This may be traced, in part, to Morgan's background. She worked for years at the New York Shakespeare Festival and Public Theater in the literary department. She also held the position Linda now holds at New York Theatre Workshop as Associate Artistic Director. Morgan is often called upon to offer guidance and inspiration on various aspects of new play development from coast to coast.

Let's start with Morgan. I'm wondering if you could talk a little bit about how the synopsis functions in your life as an agent.

MORGAN JENNESS: I think it's important to define a synopsis. The standard is a synopsis that is a page or half a page long. It talks about the details of the story – what we call the plot. There's a wonderful quote by E.M.Forster, which distinguishes between story and plot – that a story is, "what happens," and a plot is what's really going on in the story - why it happens. He says, "A story is: the queen died and then the king died. And the plot is: The queen died and the king died of grief.”…I find that it's really effective if in about four lines you describe the DNA, the spine, the heart of your play. It's not defining the plot. It's defining what it really is.

…They're very hard to write. They're also incredibly useful to write because they help the writer define what the spine of their play is. And it's not reductive. People say, "How can I reduce my play to four lines?" Well, it's not. It's the spine, the heart, the DNA. Is there a line in your script that holds the DNA of the play? Sometimes you can include that…And, it's a tease. It doesn't give away the plot at all. It's a teaser that makes someone want to read a play.

…One of the issues playwrights have is how their plays are marketed by the theatres that produce them. If you have a clear idea and synopsis, you can have more control over how the play is talked about. Sometimes the play is talked about in a way that doesn't prepare the audience for it and sets up an entirely wrong expectation for the play. It also, quite frankly, shows up in reviews. Critics will actually pull that language that's been in the marketing. If the work has been somewhat defined by the playwright really understanding their intentions, then I think you're off to a better start.

JENI MAHONEY: I think that when a synopsis or a blurb is misleading, especially when it is going out to people who are about to see or read the play, it can create false expectations...It's important, just like a headshot has to really look like an actor, the synopsis has to really be a portrayal of the play as much as possible. I was trying to condense my idea of what I do with the synopsis, and what I came up with was, "Trying to convey the spirit and the tone of a play through action in as short as a period as possible."

The quote that I always use is: "I would have sent you a shorter note, but I didn't have the time." It takes a lot of time...I think it can be a really productive tool as part of development. We actually view it as part of the development process. At Seven Devils we ask people not to submit synopses. That's one of my little pet peeves; I think if someone does not ask for a synopsis, I would not send them one. There's a tendency to read a synopsis if it's in front of you, even if you didn't ask for it. I'm not for sending it unless they're asked for and definitely not putting it in the binding of your script.

NANCY GOLLADAY: There are two fates that generally befall musicals in process. Either they never get finished, or the people writing the musical (let's assume it's a team of three) end up writing three different shows. As a result, it's very useful when you're first putting together your collaboration to work on a synopsis together as a means of being sure that you're literally all on the same page. You all understand what the show is. You understand who your leading character is, the tone that you're aiming for, and the narrative and frame that you're going to put it into. I would say there is a difference between something you call a pitch, and something you call synopsis. A pitch is more what Morgan was talking about. It's whetting the appetite of someone to read further, to read the entire piece. A synopsis for musical theatre writers is really more of a tool, it's like a preliminary outline.

LINDA CHAPMAN: Well, I suppose we read between 2,000 and 3,000 scripts a year. We accept submissions of the full script through agents and managers. So the synopses come by way of people who don't have representation yet. We will accept a one page synopsis and ten pages of the author's choice. And we receive those without any other prior knowledge. I suppose we probably get maybe another 500 plus synopses.

JENI MAHONEY: (For this panel) I e-mailed Larry Loebell and asked him if I could use the synopses that we worked on (at Seven Devils), which are the last two. He said, "Sure, that would be great. By the way, if you really want something fun, here's what I was using before we started talking." That's the initial synopsis.

## SYNOPSIS EXAMPLE

### Girl Science

by Larry Loebell

**Initial Synopsis:**

Dr. Johanna Vernon, a still-active and eminent 80-year-old PhD limnologist (water biologist) is interviewed for a biography by her grand niece, Dr. Lois Allen, a well-regarded up-and-coming academic historian whose field is history of science. Lois views her aunt as one of the "forgotten women of science" and worthy of a memoir. Her aunt is not so sure. As a reluctant participant at first, and then more and more willingly, Johanna reveals details of her past to Lois, including stories from her seemingly charmed childhood. But was it? As Lois learns more about Johanna's girlhood, she forms a thesis about a tragic event – the drowning of a teenage friend of her aunt's — that she believes haunts and inspires Johanna to excel in her field. However, a deeper secret lurks beneath the surface. Meanwhile, Lois, untangling herself from a personal and professional relationship with her former mentor, discovers how careers are made and unmade by a word.

*Girl Science* explores the clash of generations and our understanding of conflicting ideas of scientific and practical progress. What does it mean to be useful? To be good? Is personal history a useful lens to understanding the present? Who has the final say on how to interpret history?

**Festival Draft Paragraph:**

Dr. Johanna Vernon, an eminent biologist, is interviewed for a biography by her grand niece, Lois Allen, an up-and-coming historian. Lois views her great aunt as one of the "forgotten pioneers of science." As a reluctant participant at first, and then more willingly, Johanna tells Lois stories from her seemingly charmed girlhood. But was it? As Lois's researches Johanna's past, she uncovers a startling tragedy which, when revealed, changes both women's lives.

**Festival Final Paragraph:**

Lois, an up-and-coming historian, selects her great aunt Johanna, an eminent biologist and "forgotten pioneer of science," as the subject for her new book. Reluctant at first, Johanna soon relents, sharing stories from her seemingly charmed girlhood. But was it? When Lois's work inadvertently reveals the startling and tragic truth, both women's lives are changed forever.

\* \* \* \* \*

JENI MAHONEY (continued): With the second description, he had really tried to take what was in the initial synopsis and break it down a little bit. If you look at the initial synposis, some things are very clear. Getting rid of some of the excess didn't really take anything away from the core of the play in the first paragraph.

...What I'm trying to do when I start looking at a synopsis is to make it active, even making the questions active. I think that the questions asked in this final paragraph of the initial synopsis were too cerebral to me. But, in the festival draft, he did a good job of getting rid of some of the extra details about each of the characters that you could really condense into one simple gesture. What was really interesting to me (and this is why it's good to work with another person on your synopsis) is the festival draft was written from the point of view of Johanna, this forgotten scientist. To him, I think, she was the most interesting character, in terms of what she did scientifically. But, to someone just reading it, she wasn't the one taking the action initially at the top of the play. So, the first thing I wanted was to turn around and give the first action of the play to Lois. She's the one who's actually taking the action. That was a big switch between the second and third synopsis. It also allowed us to make it more active. Johanna is being interviewed, which is rather passive. And we don't know what she's being interviewed for. But, when we switched it to Lois, it was all about, "Lois has to make this book happen." It became much more active immediately — the difference between being a "reluctant participant," and just being reluctant is significant. It's a little shift, but it makes a huge difference in terms of the idea of what they are. There is a difference between, "as Lois researches Joanna's past" and "Lois' work reveals." I also wanted to move the idea of the reveal closer to the beginning of the sentence.

MJ: That's a fabulous example. It's active. It identifies the character who holds the main dramatic action. It has reversals and brings in suspense. It has an emotional quality.

RT: That last paragraph is the kind of trap that I feel I always fall into when I talk about my own work. I start talking on this plane that's thematic and intellectual. I've got all these ideas and it gets in the way of "what the hell is going on in the piece." Which is what people are really interested in, I think.

Let's look at something very different now: a musical proposal for *Groundhog Day*. Many of us probably know the film.

## SYNOPSIS EXAMPLE

## Groundhog Day

Based on the screenplay by Danny Rubin and Harold Ramis
Synopsis © Jack Lechner and Lawrence Goldberg 2002

### The Story:

Based on the 1993 movie starring Bill Murray, *Groundhog Day* is the story of Phil Connors, an arrogant TV weatherman who dreams only of escaping the small-time incompetents he feels surround him. Phil travels to the idyllic small city of Punxsutawney to report on Groundhog Day, where celebrity-rodent Punxsutawney Phil will either see his shadow or not. Phil is working with a new crew: producer Rita and cameraman Larry, who take an instant dislike to Phil and his high-handed ways.

At 6 am on the morning of February 2nd, a clock radio wakes Phil at his bed-and-breakfast in Punxsutawney. He dodges the greetings of his Landlady and his fellow lodgers, but out on the street he meets high school classmate Ned Ryerson, a pushy insurance salesman. Phil extricates himself from Ned's clutches, elbowing a homeless Beggar in the process. He joins Rita and Larry in the town square, where the populace is happily celebrating Groundhog Day, and does his report. An unexpected blizzard strands the team in Punxsutawney. With nothing better to do, Phil hits on Rita, who rebuffs him.

At 6 am the next morning, Phil wakes up to the same radio broadcast. Puzzled, he walks downstairs and is greeted in the same manner by the same people as yesterday. In the snowless street, Ned Ryerson buttonholes him again, and he finds the same celebration in the town square. Everything happens again. For days. Somehow, he's repeating the same 24 hours in an unending loop. When Phil finally unburdens to Rita at the diner, she thinks he's losing his mind. One night he goes bowling with three local Losers who are just drunk enough to believe him. One of them suggests that there's an upside to Phil's predicament: No consequences!

Giddy with freedom, Phil learns to enjoy himself. After numerous crimes and seductions, Phil trains his sights on Rita. She guilelessly describes her idea of the perfect guy, and he takes on the trappings of that guy until he achieves one beautiful day with Rita. But before he can seduce her, she catches on to his act and slaps him. He tries again, but now he's forcing it, and the slap comes earlier. And earlier. And earlier.

Despair sets in. No future also means no hope. Phil has an epiphany: Maybe if he stops the groundhog from seeing its shadow, his long winter of the soul might end. He kidnaps the groundhog and drives it over a cliff — but is back in his bed the next morning. Phil tries to kill himself in dozens of other ways, but nothing works. He's cursed.

Phil wants Rita to believe him. So he tells her about every event about to happen in the diner, even predicting a dropped plate. For the clincher, he tells her about herself. Intrigued, Rita spends the day with Phil to observe. When he apologizes for having been a jerk, Rita points out that his situation might not be a curse — how many people have an unlimited amount of time to learn something, or to do something they love? Phil and Rita spend the night together, chastely, and while she sleeps he vows to become worthy of her.

The next day — which is of course the previous day — Phil has a sense of purpose. He gives money to the beggar. He takes piano lessons. He learns ice sculpture. He hugs Ned Ryerson instead of punching him. After what must be decades, Phil is a new man. His report from the town square becomes a poetic masterpiece that brings tears to Rita's eyes. Now Phil's typical day is: rescuing a kid from a tree, fixing a flat tire, saving the Mayor from choking. Phil performs a virtuoso keyboard solo at that night's big party, and Rita is amazed by the affection the entire town has for him. At the party's bachelor auction, the bidding for Phil is fierce — and Rita wins. They go to bed that night, and Phil feels genuinely happy. When he wakes up the next morning, Rita is still there! He's transcended his predicament by realizing his untapped potential as a human being. Phil is free to continue his life at last — with Rita. In Punxsutawney.

**About our show:**

*Groundhog Day*, like *The Music Man*, is about a man's encounter with an entire town. To bring that town convincingly to life, we plan a Broadway-scale musical with full cast and orchestra. To translate the time transitions of the story, we see the show staged on a revolve — so when the day rolls around again, it literally rolls around. The main sets will be the hotel where Phil stays, the diner to which he continually returns, and the town square where he encounters most of the people.

Our hero is a heel who redeems himself; a city slicker who learns to appreciate the simple pleasures of small town life; a womanizer who falls deeply in love; a cynic who opens his heart. Phil was played memorably by Bill Murray in the original film, and we have hopes that we might persuade him to repeat the role on stage. The female lead, Rita (played in the movie by Andie MacDowell), should be a virtuoso singer-actress like Rebecca Luker or Melissa Errico, to provide the musical chops our leading man may not possess.

We'll further dramatize Phil's predicament with modular song fragments that repeat throughout the show in unexpected combinations. We'll also craft musical and theatrical equivalents of the jump cuts that work so well to convey the passage of time in the film. The brilliance of the film is that its profound themes are cleverly concealed within the form of a romantic comedy. We hope to attain the same balance in our musical.

\* \* \* \* \*

NANCY GOLLADAY: This example is courtesy of Jack Lechner and Lawrence Goldberg who wrote it as part of their second year at the BMI workshop...And what you look for in this kind of material is the ability of the collaborators to actually pull off what they're taking on.

In the first paragraph you get the journalistic "who, what, when, and where" of the show. Then very quickly, in the second paragraph, you get into why we care. It's a guy who's a fish out of water, and it's going to be a redemption story.

One of the things that they do very well in this sample is capture the tone. The tone of the synopsis matches the tone of the show, the kind of droll comedy that you're going to get. You know it's going to be slightly skewed, slightly what one would call screwball, and somewhat romantic.

But, all the while, there's something very serious at the bottom of it. They keep reverting to that. And, you'll notice they don't withhold the ending. You reveal the ending. And, I'm sure that if a CD existed for this project, you would hear that some of these phrases in the synopsis would track nicely with the music. There would be songs with a title or hook something like, "No Consequences" or, "Tomorrow Rolls Around Again."

So, you want to make it as clear and as easy for them as possible to link together your demo music with what they see in the synopsis and what they have read in the script.

If your synopsis is chronological, you want the songs to be in the same chronology. If you talk about "the boy" in your synopsis, you don't want to suddenly start talking about "Tony" on your CD label.

*Video of this complete seminar can be found in the Members Lounge at www.dramatistsguild.com*

# The DG Statement on Submission Fees

The Dramatists Guild of America denounces the practice by festivals, play contests and educational events of charging excessive fees to dramatists who submit their work. Any request for submission fees should be accompanied by a complete explanation of how those fees are to be spent. The Guild also insists that contests and festivals announce the names of all finalists and winners to all participants.

It is important that members understand that submission fees are not the norm and, when required, the festival should offer something significant in return for the writer's investment, such as a large cash prize, a residency or a production. Reading fees are in no case acceptable, as most festivals receive that money from other grant sources. In no case should playwrights have to pay to simply have their work read.

The Guild also strongly disapproves of a festival's placing any encumbrances on the work as a result of the play being chosen a finalist or a participant. Any future participation in the life of the play must be earned by the festival by producing the work, and should never be granted by the writer without consultation with the Guild. If the festival expects any subsidiary income from the plays, that information should be stated clearly in all of the organization's printed and electronic materials related to the event.

The Council of the Guild feels that its members should be made aware of all legitimate opportunities available to them, and so we have listed in this section those particular contests and festivals that charge fees and have provided explanations regarding how their submission fees are spent, as well as full disclosure of any encumbrances they place on a selected writer's work, when offered by the sponsor.

# Career Development Professionals

## ACCOUNTANTS

**Kimerling and Wisdom**
29 Broadway, #1412,
New York, NY 10006
Tel: (212) 986-0892
Ross Wisdom
    Est. 1970. Partners: Noah Kimerling,
    Ross Wisdom.

**Marks Paneth & Shron LLP**
622 3rd Ave., New York, NY 10017
David R. Marcus
Tel: (212) 503-8833
dmarcus@markspaneth.com
http://www.markspaneth.com
    Est. 1907. David R. Marcus, CPA,
    MBA, JD.

**Spielman, Koenigsberg and Parker
(SKP)**
888 7th Ave., Fl. 35, New York, NY 10106
Richard Koenigsberg
Tel: (212) 452-2510; Fax: (212) 453-2594
rkoenigsberg@skpny.com
    Est. 1955. Partners: Melvin Spielman,
    Richard Koenigsberg, Gary Parker,
    Lawrence Spielman.

April 17, 2008
From the Desk of Gary Garrison

## AGENCY

*(Reprinted from the e-newsletter)*

On the average, I get three to four phone calls or emails a day that go something like this: *"I need an agent. I know everyone needs an agent, but I <u>really need</u> an agent. Why can't the Guild help get me an agent or a director or anyone who can help promote my work? And why can't the Guild get more theatres to respond to playwrights and new plays? We need more opportunities!"* Look, I just want to get square with you once and for all: we are a member-service and advocacy organization. And while I don't want to downplay the importance for some of you to be professionally represented by an agent (or your work placed in a theatre), it is not one of the mandates of this organization to help you secure representation or production.

It doesn't matter what anyone has to say about writers and agents, the truth is having an agent is perceived — right or wrong — as a benchmark of success that comes with certain positive opportunities and a healthy amount of validation. The desire in most of us, then, is never likely to go away. But if you really want to pursue the agent thing, I want you to take a good, honest look at simple facts and figures to help you make sense of what's ahead of you.

1.  The numbers: talking to my colleagues here at the Guild, and then making a few phone calls around town to some very respectable agents, to our best estimation there are approximately thirty-five agents dedicated to promoting dramatic writing for the theatre. That's thirty-five agents *total* — throughout the whole country — that represent every playwright you know by name, and then the many hundreds you don't know (yet). The simple numbers alone show the odds are against most of us having an agent.

2.  Most agents that I've spoken with are rarely interested in representing a single piece of work and are far more interested in representing (and helping you grow) a body of work. To approach an agent to represent a single play or musical is not likely to get you anywhere. Agents, like all theatre business people, are as interested in the present as they are the future.

3.  Twenty years ago, maybe even ten years ago, a hit production of a play or a musical and a good *New York Times* review (or any major newspaper review) would almost ensure that you'd have an agency knocking at your door. That's not true any longer; there's a glut of material and writers out there that remain unrepresented.

4.  Theatre, like most arms of the entertainment industry, is ageist.

Jeeeeez, Gary, did you have to be so…honest? In a word, yes, because so many of us are singularly obsessed about getting an agent. Are there exceptions to any of the points above? Of course there are exceptions; that's what makes this life interesting. Can you have a productive, successful career in the theatre without professional representation? You bet, and a heck of a lot of people do.

*Please understand that we provide a list of working literary agents as a convenience for you – nothing more. By listing these agents (which is not a comprehensive list), we do not intend to suggest that they are seeking new clients or that we are particularly endorsing them as agents. Unless indicated otherwise, send a query and synopsis to one agent at a time.*

# AGENTS

**Abrams Artists Agency**
275 7th Ave., Fl. 26, New York, NY 10001
Sarah L. Douglas, Charles Kopelman
Tel: (646) 486-4600
literary@abramsartny.com
www.abramsartists.com/literary.html
   Agents: Sarah L. Douglas, Charles
   Kopelman, Beth Blickers, Morgan
   Jenness, Maura Teitelbaum, Kate
   Navin, Ron Gwiazda. **Application.**
   What to Submit: query, synopsis,
   SASE. Material Must Be: We do not
   accept any unsolicited materials, and
   we are only accepting new clients by
   professional recommendation. How To
   Submit: professional recommendation.

**Ann Elmo Agency**
305 7th Ave., New York, NY 10165
Letti Lee
Tel: (212) 661-2880; Fax: (212) 661-2883
   Staff: Mari Cronin, Letti Lee.
   Response Time: 2 mos. **Application.**
   What to Submit: query, SASE.

**Ann Wright Representatives**
165 W. 46th St. 10th Fl.,
New York, NY 10036
Dan Wright
Tel: (860) 264-0147
danwrightlit@aol.com
   Est. 1961. Response Time: 5/15/10.
   Style: all styles. **Application.** What
   to Submit: query letter (note theme
   addressed), submissions returned with

SASE. Material must be: unoptioned,
unpublished, unproduced. How to
Submit: invitation only.

**Barbara Hogenson Agency, Inc.**
165 West End Ave., #19-C,
New York, NY 10023
Barbara Hogenson
Tel: (212) 874-8084; Fax: (212) 362-3011
   Est. 1994. Response Time: 2 mos.
   What to Submit: query, synopsis.
   How to Submit: professional
   recommendation, email only.

**Beacon Artists Agency**
120 E. 56th St., #540,
New York, NY 10022
Patricia McLaughlin
Tel: (212) 736-6630
beaconagency@hotmail.com
   Style: all styles. **Application.** What
   to Submit: query letter, synopsis, 10-
   pg writing sample. How to Submit:
   professional recommendation.

**Bernard Liebhaber Agency**
352 Seventh Ave., New York, NY 10001
Bernard Liebhaber
Tel: (212) 631-7561; Fax: (212) 637-7592
bernardliebhaber@verizon.net

**The Bohrman Agency**
8899 Beverly Blvd., #811,
Los Angeles, CA 90048
Caren Bohrman

Tel: (310) 550-5444
Agents: Caren Bohrman. Style: all styles. **Application.** What to Submit: query, No phone queries, SASP. How to Submit: professional recommendation, no unsolicited.

**Bret Adams Ltd.**
448 W. 44th St., New York, NY 10036
Ben Coleman
Tel: (212) 765-5630; Fax: (212) 265-2212
bcoleman@bretadamsltd.net
www.bretadamsltd.net
Est. 1953 Staff: Bruce Ostler, Mark Orsini; Natasha Sinha (literary); Margi Rountree, Ken Melamed, Michael Golden (acting). Style: all styles, comedy, drama, musical, no screenplay. **Application.** What to Submit: query. How to Submit: professional recommendation.

**Eric Glass Ltd.**
25 Ladbroke Crescent, London, UK
Janet Glass
Tel: (420) 722-9950; Fax: (420) 722-9622
eglassltd@aol.com
Style: all styles. **Application.** What to Submit: synopsis, 30-pg writing sample, submissions returned with SASE. How to Submit: professional recommendation.

**Farber Literary Agency Inc.**
14 E. 75th St., #2-E, New York, NY 10021
Ann Farber
Tel: (212) 861-7075; Fax: (212) 861-7076
farberlit@aol.com
www.donaldfarber.com
Est.1990. Staff: Ann Farber, Donald C. Farber, Seth Farber. Response Time: 1 mo. **Application.** What to Submit: query, synopsis, full script, SASE. Material must be: unproduced.

**Fifi Oscard Agency, Inc.**
110 W. 40th St., Ste 703,
New York, NY 10018
Peter Sawyer
Tel: (212) 764-1100; Fax: (212) 840-5019
agency@fifioscard.com
www.fifioscard.com

Est. 1956. Literary Staff: Carolyn French, Carmen LaVia, Kevin McShane, Peter Sawyer.

**Gage Group Inc.**
14724 Ventura Blvd., #505,
Sherman Oaks, CA 91403
Martin Gage
Tel: (818) 905-3800; Fax: (818) 905-3322
gagegroupla@gmail.com
Est. 1975. Agents: Martin Gage, Arthur Tortezky, Gerry Kuck. Response Time: 3 mos. **Application.** What to Submit: query, submissions not returned. Material must be: unoptioned, unpublished. How to Submit: professional recommendation.

**Gersh Agency Inc. [NY]**
41 Madison Ave., Fl. 33,
New York, NY 10010
Joyce Ketay
Tel: (212) 997-1818; Fax: (212) 391-8459
Agents: John Buzzetti, Seth Glewen, Joyce Ketay, Carl Mulert, Phyllis Wender, Scott Yoselow. **Application.** What to Submit: query, SASE. How to Submit: professional recommendation.

**Graham Agency**
311 W. 43rd St., New York, NY 10036
Earl Graham
Tel: (212) 489-7730
Style: no adaptation, no translation. **Application.** What to Submit: query, SASE. Author Must Be. resident of US.

**GSK Talent (Grant, Savic, Kopaloff)**
6399 Wilshire Blvd., #415,
Los Angeles, CA 90048
Tel: (323) 782-1854
contact@gsktalent.com
www.gsktalent.com
Agents: Susan Grant, Ivana Savic, Don Kopaloff.

**Harden Curtis Associates**
850 7th Ave, #903, New York, NY 10019
Mary Harden
Tel: (212) 977-8502
www.hardencurtis.com

Est. 1995. Staff: Mary Harden (Pres.),
Diane Riley (Agent), Scott Ewards
(Agent), Diana Glazer (Assistant).
Response Time: 2 mos. Style: all
styles. **Application.** What to Submit:
query. How to Submit: professional
recommendation.

**International Creative Management
(ICM) [UK]**
4-6 Soho Sq., London, UK
Tel: 44-20-7432-0800
books@icmtalent.com
www.icmtalent.com/lit/lit.html
    Talent & lit agency.

**International Creative Management
(ICM) [NY]**
825 8th Ave., New York, NY 10019
Tel: (212) 556-5600
books@icmtalent.com
    Talent & lit agency. Staff: Patrick
Herold, Buddy Thomas. **Application.**
How to Submit: invite.

**International Creative Management
(ICM) [CA]**
10250 Constellation Blvd.,
Los Angeles, CA 90067
Tel: (310) 550-4000
books@icmtalent.com
www.icmtalent.com
    Talent & lit agency.

**The Joyce Ketay Agency**
630 Ninth Ave., #706,
New York, NY 10036
Joyce P. Ketay
Tel: (212) 354-6825; Fax: (212) 354-6732
    MERGED WITH GERSH 1/9/06.
Staff: Joyce P. Ketay, Carl Mulert..
Response Time: 5/15/04. Style:
all styles. **Application.** What to
Submit: query letter (note theme
addressed), submissions returned with
SASE. How to Submit: professional
recommendation.

**Judy Boals Inc.**
307 W. 38th St., #812,
New York, NY 10018
Judy Boals
info@judyboals.com

www.judyboals.com
    Agents: Judy Boals. Response Time:
1 mo. **Application.** What to Submit:
query, SASE. How to Submit:
professional recommendation.

**Kerin-Goldberg Associates**
155 E. 55th St., #5-D,
New York, NY 10022
Charles Kerin
Tel: (212) 838-7373; Fax: (212) 838-0774
kgatalent@nyc.rr.com
    Est. 1989. Staff: Ron Ross, Ellison
Goldberg, Chris Nichols. **Application.**
What to Submit: query, SASE.
Material must be: unproduced. How to
Submit: invite.

**The Marton Agency, Inc.**
1 Union Sq. W., #815,
New York, NY 10003
Tonda Marton
Tel: (212) 255-1908; Fax: (212) 691-9061
info@martonagency.com
    Staff: Tonda Marton, Anne Reingold.
Specializes in brokering foreign-
language rights to US theater works.
Promotes plays to associates abroad,
generally after a production has been
mounted in the US.

**Paradigm**
360 Park Ave. S., New York, NY 10010
Tel: (212) 897-6400
www.paradigmagency.com
    Agents: William Craver, Lucy Stille,
Jack Tantleff. Response Time: 6 mos.
**Application.** What to Submit: query,
SASE. Material must be: unoptioned,
unpublished, unproduced. How to
Submit: professional recommendation.

**Peregrine Whittlesey Agency**
279 Central Park West,
New York, NY 10024
Peregrine Whittlesey
Tel: (212) 787-1802; Fax: (212) 787-4985
pwwagy@aol.com
    **Application.** What to Submit: query,
SASE. Material must be: unoptioned.
How to Submit: professional
recommendation.

**Phoenix Artists**
321 W.44th St. Ste. 401,
New York, NY 10036
Gary Epstein
Tel: (212)-586-9110; Fax: (212)-586-8019
phoenixartistsinc@yahoo.com
> **Application.** How to Submit: Query
> letter.

**Robert A. Freedman Dramatic Agency, Inc.**
1501 Broadway, #2310,
New York, NY 10036
Marta Praeger
Tel: (212) 840-5760; Fax: (212) 840-5776
> Est. 1917. Response Time: 4 mos.
> What to Submit: query, SASE. How to
> Submit: invite.

**The Shukat Company Ltd.**
340 W. 55th St., #1A,
New York, NY 10019
Tel: (212) 582-7614
staff@shukat.com
> Style: all styles. **Application.** What
> to Submit: query letter (note theme
> addressed), 30-pg writing sample,
> submissions returned with SASE. How
> to Submit: unsolicited.

**Soiree Fair Inc.**
133 Midland Ave., #10,
Montclair, NJ 7042
Karen Gunn
Soireefair@yahoo.com
www.soireefair.com
> Est. 1995. Style: comedy, drama.
> **Application.** What to Submit: query,
> synopsis. Author Must Be. resident
> of US. Material must be: unoptioned,
> unpublished, unproduced. How to
> Submit: professional recommendation.

**Susan Gurman Agency, LLC**
245 West 99th St., Suite 24A,
New York, NY 10025
Tel: (212) 749-4618; Fax: (212) 864-5055
assistant@gurmanagency.com
www.gurmanagency.com
> Est. 1993. Response Time: 1 mo.
> **Application.** What to Submit: Letter
> and resume only. How to Submit:
> professional recommendation.

**Talent Representatives, Inc.**
1040 1st Ave., Suite #307,
New York, NY 10022
Tel: (212) 752-1835
> **Application.** What to Submit:
> submissions returned with SASE.
> How to Submit: professional
> recommendation.

**William Morris Agency**
1325 6th Ave., New York, NY 10019
Tel: (212) 586-5100
http://www.wma.com
> Staff: Val Day, Peter Franklin, Biff
> Liff, Roland Scahill, Jack Tantleff,
> Susan Weaving.

**Writers & Artists Agency [CA]**
8383 Wilshire Blvd., #550, Beverly Hills,
CA 90211
Tel: (323) 866-0900
info@wriart.com

# ATTORNEYS

**Beigelman, Feiner & Feldman, P.C.**
100 Wall St., 23rd Floor,
New York, NY 10005
Ronald Feiner, Esq.
Tel: (212) 230-1300; Fax: (212) 230-1090
rfeiner@bfflaw.com
Bfflaw.com

**Brooks & Distler**
110 E. 59th St., Fl. 23,
New York, NY 10022
Marsha Brooks, Esq.
Tel: (212) 486-1400; Fax: (212) 486-2266

**Coblence & Associates**
200 Park Ave. S., #910,
New York, NY 10003
Patricia Crown, Esq.
Tel: (212) 593-8389; Fax: (212) 358-9058
pcrown@coblence.com
www.coblence.com
    Est. 1981. Formerly Coblence &
    Warner.

**Cohen & Grossberg**
770 Lexington Ave., New York, NY 10065
David Grossberg
Tel: (212) 688-6940; Fax: (212) 755-4199
    Est. 1955.

**Cowan, DeBaets, Abrahams &
Sheppard LLP**
41 Madison Ave., Fl. 34,
New York, NY 10010
Frederick P. Bimbler, Esq.
Tel: (212) 974-7474; Fax: (212) 974-8474
fbimbler@cdas.com
www.cdas.com

**Da Silva & Da Silva**
502 Park Ave., #10-G,
New York, NY 10022
Albert Da Silva

**Law Office of Gary N. DaSilva**
111 N. Sepulveda Blvd., #250,
Manhattan Beach, CA 90266
Tel: (310) 318-5665; Fax: (310) 318-2114
mail@garydasilva.com

**David H. Friedlander, Esq.**
81 Park Dr., Mount Kisco, NY 10549
David H. Friedlander, Esq.
Tel: (914) 241-1277; Fax: (914) 470-2244
david@dfriedlander.com
www.dfriedlander.com

**Dumler & Giroux**
488 Madison Ave., #1703,
New York, NY 10022
Leigh A. Giroux, Esq.
Tel: (212) 759-4580; Fax: (914) 967-8418

**Fitelson, Lasky, Aslan, Couture and
Garmise**
551 5th Ave., #605, New York, NY 10176
Jerold Couture
Tel: (212) 586-4700; Fax: (212) 949-6746
dramalex@aol.com

**Franklin, Weinrib, Rudell & Vassallo
PC**
488 Madison Ave., New York, NY 10022
Elliot H. Brown
Tel: (212) 935-5500; Fax: (212) 308-0642
ehb@fwrv.com
www.fwrv.com

**Gordon P. Firemark, Esq.**
Theatre & Entertainment Law,
10940 Wilshire Blvd, 16th Floor,
Los Angeles, CA 90024
Gordon P. Firemark Esq.
Tel: (310) 443-4185; Fax: (310) 477-7676
gfiremark@firemark.com
www.firemark.com
www.theatrelawyer.com

**Graubart. Law Offices of Jeffrey L.
Graubart, P.C.**
350 W. Colorado Blvd., #200,
Pasadena, CA 91105
Tel: (626) 304-2800; Fax: (626) 304-2807
info@jlgraubart.com
www.lawyers.com/entertainmentlaw
    Est. 1970.

**Jay Julien, Esq.**
1501 Broadway, #1609,
New York, NY 10036
Jay Julien
Tel: (212) 221-7575; Fax: (212) 221-7386

**Law Offices of Bartley F. Day**
1001 S.W. Fifth Ave., suite 1100,
Portland, OR 97204
Bartley F. Day
Tel: (503) 291-9300; Tel: (503) 291-0165;
Fax: (503) 292-8462
allmedia@hevanet.com

**Law Office of John J. Tormey III, Esq.**
217 East 86th St., PMB 221,
New York, NY 10028
John L. Tormey III
Tel: (212) 410-4142; Tel: (845) 735-9691;
Fax: (212) 410-2380
brightline@att.net
www.tormey.org

**Law Offices of Lloyd J. Jassin**
1560 Broadway, #400,
New York, NY 10036
Lloyd J. Jassin
Tel: (212) 354-4442; Fax: (212) 840-4124
jassin@copylaw.com
www.copylaw.com
    Est. 1991.

**Lazarus & Harris LLP**
561 7th Ave., Fl. 11, New York, NY 10018
Tel: (212) 302-5252; Fax: (212) 302-8181
www.lazhar.com

**Manatt, Phelps & Philips LLP**
11355 W. Olympic Blvd.,
Los Angeles, CA 90064
Fred Bernstein
Tel: (310) 312-4166; Fax: (310) 312-4224
fbernstein@manatt.com
www.manatt.com

**McLaughlin & Stern**
260 Madison Ave., New York, NY 10016
Alvin Deutsch, Esq.
Tel: (212) 448-1100; Fax: (212) 448-0066
adeutsch@mclaughlinstern.com
www.mclaughlinstern.com
    Est. 1898.

**Paul, Weiss, Rifkind, Wharton & Garrison**
1285 Ave. of the Americas,
New York, NY 10019-6064
John Breglio, Esq.
Tel: (212) 373-3000; Fax: (212) 757-3990
mailbox@paulweiss.com
www.paulweiss.com

**Peter S. Cane, Esq.**
410 W. 24th St., New York, NY 10011
Tel: (212) 922-9800
peter@canelaw.com

**Robert Perlstein**
1501 Broadway, suite 703,
New York, NY 10036
Robert S. Perlstein Esq.
Tel: (212) 832-9951; Fax: (212) 831-9906
rspesq@judgedee.net

**Robinson, Brog, Leinwand, Greene, Genovese & Gluck**
1345 6th Ave., New York, NY 10105
Richard M. Ticktin
Tel: (212) 203-4053; Fax: (212) 956-2164
rmt@robinsonbrog.com
www.robinsonbrog.com

**Ronald A. Lachman**
2002 Wilshire Blvd., #510,
Santa Monica, CA 90403
Tel: (323) 655-6020; Fax: (323) 655-6099
ronnielock@aol.com

**Sendroff & Baruch, LLP**
1500 Broadway, #2001,
New York, NY 10036
Mark D. Sendroff, Esq.
Tel: (212) 840-6400; Fax: (212) 840-6401
msendroff@sendroffbaruch.com
www.sendroffbaruch.com
    Staff: Mark Sendroff, Jason Baruch,
    Eric S. Goldman.

**Steiger. Law Office of Susan J. Steiger, Esq.**
60 East 42nd St., 47th floor,
New York, NY 10165
Tel: (212) 880-0865; Fax: (212) 682-1965
sjsteigs@yahoo.com
    Est. 1982.

**Stern. Law Office of Miriam Stern**
303 E. 83rd St., Fl. 20,
New York, NY 10028
Miriam Stern, Esq.
Tel: (212) 794-1289
   Attorney represents writers, producers,
   directors and other creative elements
   involved in producing theater.
   **Application.** What to Submit:
   Telephone inquiry before sending
   material. How to Submit:
   recommendation, Telephone call.

**Volunteer Lawyers for the Arts (VLA)**
1 E. 53rd St., Fl. 6, New York, NY 10022
Elena M. Paul, Esq.
Tel: (212) 319-2787 ext. 1
Fax: (212) 752-6575
vlany@vlany.org
www.vlany.org
   Est. 1969. Leading provider of
   pro bono legal and mediation
   services, educational programs and
   publications, and advocacy to the
   arts community in NYC area. Thru
   public advocacy, VLA frequently
   acts on issues vitally important to the
   arts community in NYC and beyond.
   Based on client's finances. Author
   Must Be: under certain income ceiling.

# COMMERCIAL PRODUCERS

**Araca Group**
260 W. 44th St., #501,
New York, NY 10036
Amanda Guettel
Tel: (212) 869-0070; Fax: (212) 869-0210
creative@araca.com
www.araca.com
   Est. 1997. Matthew Rego, Michael
   Rego and Hank Unger are principals.
   Wicked, The Wedding Singer, 'night
   Mother, The Good Body, Urinetown,
   Frankie and Johnny in the Clair de
   Lune, Match, Debbie Does Dallas,
   The Vagina Monologues, The Laramie
   Project. **Application.** What to Submit:
   full script, audio, SASE. How To
   Submit: agent.

**Emanuel Azenberg**
250 W. 52nd St., New York, NY 10019

**Boyett Ostar Productions**
745 5th Ave., #3500, New York, NY 10151

**Cameron Mackintosh Inc.**
1650 Broadway, #800,
New York, NY 10019
Shidan Majidi

Tel: (212) 921-9290; Fax: (212) 921-9271
   Mary Poppins, Les Miserables,
   The Phantom of the Opera, Oliver!,
   Oklahoma!, My Fair Lady, The
   Witches of Eastwick, Miss Saigon,
   CATS. **Application.** How to Submit:
   agent, submission only.

**Carole Shorenstein Hays Prods.**
**(CSHP)**
1182 Market St., San Francisco, CA 94102
Duffy Anderson
   Est. 2006.

**Dodger Properties**
311 W. 43rd St., #602,
New York, NY 10036
Tel: (212) 575-9710
info@dodger.com
www.dodger.com
   Est. 1978. Jersey Boys. **Application.**
   How to Submit: agent.

**Frankel-Baruch-Viertel-Routh Group**
729 7th Ave., Fl. 12, New York, NY 10019
Richard Frankel
Tel: (212) 302-5559
info@rfpny.com

www.rfpny.com
Est. 1985. Principals: Richard Frankel,
Tom Viertel, Steven Baruch, Marc
Routh. Young Frankenstein, Hairspray,
The Producers, The Fantasticks,
Sweeney Todd Tour.

**Harold Prince**
10 Rockefeller Plaza, #1004,
New York, NY 10020

**Jane Harmon Associates**
One Lincoln Plaza, #280, 20 W. 64th St.,
New York, NY 10023
Jane Harmon
Tel: (212) 362-6836; Fax: (212) 362-8572
harmonjane@aol.com
Est. 1979. Associates: Valentina Fratti,
Jill Alexander. Response Time: 4-6
wks. Style: drama/comedy, no musical.
**Application.** What to Submit: query,
synopsis, SASE. Material must be:
preferably unoptioned, unpublished.
How to Submit: agent, professional
reccomendation, unsolicited.

**Koslow Productions**
225 Rector Pl., New York, NY 10280
Pamela Koslow
Formerly Wavecrest Prods. Jelly's
Last Jam, Jane Eyre. Material must
be: unoptioned, original. **Application.**
How to Submit: agent.

**Lisa Dozier Productions**
New York, New York
Lisa Dozier
Tel: (917) 470-0246
lisadozier@gmail.com
www.lisadozierproductions.com

**Margery Klain**
2107 Locust St., Philadelphia, PA 19103
Margery Klain
Tel: (215) 567-1512; Fax: (215) 567-2049
mklain1011@aol.com
Est. 1985. A Shanya Maidel,
Mountain, Das Barbecu, Broadway
Opus. Staff: Matthew Klein. Response
Time: 2 mos. **Application.** What
to Submit: query, SASE. Material
must be: unoptioned. How to Submit:
professional recommendation.

**Margo Lion Ltd.**
246 W. 44th St., Fl. 8,
New York, NY 10036
Rick Hayashi
Tel: (212) 869-1112; Fax: (212) 730-0381
office@margolionltd.com
www.margolionltd.com
Hairspray, Caroline, or Change, The
Cryptogram, Angels in America,
Jelly's Last Jam, The Wedding Singer.
Response Time: 1 yr. **Application.**
What to Submit: synopsis, 10-pg
sample, audio, SASE. How to Submit:
agent (prefer electronic, to be green).

**Nederlander Organization**
1450 Broadway, Fl. 6,
New York, NY 10018
Charlene Nederlander
Tel: (212) 840-5577; Fax: (212) 840-5577
www.nederlander.com
Est. 1912. **Application.** How to
Submit: agent.

**New Time Productions**
311 W. 43rd St., #305,
New York, NY 10036
Lauren Doll
Tel: (212) 265-9659; Fax: (212) 956-0498
sarah@newtiimeproductions.com
www.new. Timeproductions.com
Est. 1998. Equity Broadway, Off-
Broadway, MSUA., Radio Golf, Faith
Healer, Brooklyn, Squonk, Electra,
On the Waterfront, The Norman
Conquests. **Application.** What to
Submit: query, SASE. How to Submit:
agent, email preferred.

**Rick Hobard**
234 W. 44th St., New York, NY 10036
Tel: (212) 354-8797

**Rodger Hess Productions Inc.**
1501 Broadway, Ste. 2302,
New York, NY 10036
Tel: (212) 719-2233
Est. 1973.

**Shubert Organization**
234 W. 44th St., New York, NY 10036
D.S. Moynihan
www.shubertorg.com

Est. 1900. Amour, The Blue Room, Closer, Amy's View, The Ride Down Mt. Morgan, Dirty Blonde, Dance of Death, Passing Strange. **Application.** How to Submit: agent.

**Stephen Pevner, Inc.**
382 Lafayette St., Fl. 8,
New York, NY 10003
Stephen Pevner
Tel: (212) 674-8403

**Stewart F. Lane**
36 W.44th St., Suite #400,
New York, NY 10036
Stewart F. Lane
www.mrbroadway.com
    Stellar Productions.

**Susan Gallin Productions Inc.**
180 W. 58 St. #4B, New York, NY 10019
Susan Gallin
Tel: (212) 840-1725
sgallin@aol.com
    Spamalot, Woman Before a Glass, The Retreat From Moscow, Man of La Mancha, Hedda Gabler, The Shape of Things, Fully Committed, Burn This, The Rothschilds, Cowgirls, Other People's Money, From the Mississippi Delta, Angels in America, Stomp, The Cryptogram (London). **Application.** What to Submit: full script. Material must be: unoptioned, unproduced. How to Submit: agent.

**Arielle Tepper Productions**
1501 Broadway, #1301,
New York, NY 10036

---

# PUBLISHERS

**Alaska Quarterly Review (AQR)**
3211 Providence Dr.,
Anchorage, AK 99508
Ronald Spatz
Tel: (907) 786-6916; Fax: (907) 786-6916
www.uaa.alaska.edu/aqr
    Est. 1982. Fiction, short plays, poetry and literary nonfiction in traditional and experimental styles. Semiannual. Response Time: 6 mos. Style: open to all styles. **Application.** What to Submit: application, full script. Opportunity/Award: 1 contributors copy and a 1-year subscription.

**Anchorage Press Plays Inc.**
617 Baxter Ave.,
Louisville, KY 40204-1105
Marilee Hebert Miller
Tel: (502) 583-2288; Fax: (502) 583-2288
applays@bellsouth.net
www.applays.com
    Est. 1935. Performances licensed. Educational, professional and amateur venues. Response Time:

6 -9 mos. Style: Various - original, adaptation, musical, translation. **Application.** What to Submit: full play script following criteria in submission guidelines from website. (No screenplays.). Material Must Be: For child, youth, teen, or young adult audience. Opportunity/Award: royalty. How to Submit: See submission guidelines on website.

**Arte Publico Press**
452 Cullen Performance Hall,
Houston, TX 77204
Nicolas Kanellos
Tel: (713) 743-2845; Fax: (713) 743-3080
appinfo@mail.uh.edu
www.arte.uh.edu
    Est. 1979. Contemporary and recovered lit by US Hispanic authors. Response Time: 6 mos. **Application.** What to Submit: full script, SASE. Material Must Be: unpublished, in English or Spanish. Opportunity/ Award: royalty, copies.

**Asian American Writers Workshop**
16 W. 32nd St. #10-A,
New York, NY 10001
Nina Sharma
Tel: (212) 494-0061; Fax: (212) 494-0062
desk@aaww.org
www.aaww.org
> Est. 1992. Semiannual paperback incl
> short fiction, poems, essays, stage
> scripts, translations and artwork.
> semiannual. Response Time: 8 mos.
> **Application.** What to Submit: full
> script (4 copies). Opportunity/Award:
> 2 copies.

**Asian Theatre Journal**
2840 Kolowalu St., Honolulu, HI 96822
Tel: (888) 847-7377 ext. 8833
Fax: (800) 650-7811
uhpjourn@hawaii.edu
www.uhpress.hawaii.edu/journals
> Dedicated to performing arts of Asia,
> traditional and modern, incl. original
> and translated plays. **Application.**
> What to Submit: query, submissions
> not returned.

**Audience**
303 Park Ave. S., #1440,
New York, NY 10010
M. Stefan Strozier
Tel: (646) 620-7406; Fax: (646) 620-7406
submissions@worldaudience.org
www.worldaudience.org
> Quarterly literary journal of short
> stories, poetry, plays, interviews,
> essays, and more. Response Time: 2-4
> wks. Style: all styles. **Application.**
> What to Submit: query, synopsis,
> 10-page sample. Opportunity/Award:
> royalties. How to Submit: unsolicited,
> professional recommendation, agent.

**Baker's Plays**
45 W. 25th St., New York, NY 10010
Roxane Heinze-Bradshaw
Tel: (212) 255-8085; Fax: (212) 627-7753
publications@bakersplays.com
www.bakersplays.com
> Response Time: 8 mos. What to
> Submit: full script, audio, resume,
> SASE. Material Must Be: produced.
> Opportunity/Award: royalty. How to
> Submit: web submissions.

**Big Dog Publishing**
P.O. Box 1400, Tallevast, FL 34270
Dawn Remsing
Fax: (941) 358-7606
info@bigdogplays.com
www.bigdogplays.com
> Est. 2005. Plays for family and school
> audiences (K-12). Publishes 25-40
> plays/year. Response Time: 2-3 mos.
> **Application.** What to Submit: entire
> script, synopsis, cast breakdown,
> cover letter, production history, music,
> SASE, no email submissions accepted.
> Material Must Be: unpublished,
> prefers produced works. Opportunity/
> Award: 50% royalty, 10% book,
> complimentary copies (50% discount
> on additional copies).

**Broadway Play Publishing Inc. (BPPI)**
56 E. 81st St., New York, NY 10028
Christopher Gould
Tel: (212) 772-8334; Fax: (212) 772-8358
sara@broadwayplaypubl.com
www.broadwayplaypubl.com
> Est. 1982. Response Time: 2 mos
> query, 4 mos script. Style: comedy,
> drama. **Application.** What to Submit:
> query. Material Must Be: produced,
> original. Opportunity/Award: 10%
> book, 80% amateur, 90% stock
> royalty; 10 complimentary copies.

**Brooklyn Publishers**
1841 Cord St., Odessa, TX 79762
David LeMaster
Tel: (432) 550-5532; Fax: (432) 368-0340
info@brookpub.com
www.brookpub.com
> Est. 1996.: performers grades 6-12.
> Response Time: 2 mos. Style: comedy,
> drama, mystery, parody, adaptation.
> **Application.** What to Submit: full
> script with short play synopsis and
> author bio. Opportunity/Award:
> royalty, 8 copies.

**Callaloo**
4212 TAMU, Texas A&M University,
College Station, TX 77843-4212
Charles H. Rowell
Tel: (979) 458-3108; Fax: (979) 458-3275
callaloo@tamu.edu
www.callaloo.tamu.edu

Quarterly journal devoted to creative work by and critical studies of the work of African-Americans and peoples of African descent throughout the African Diaspora. Original, unpublished essays, interviews, short fiction, poetry, drama, and visual art, as well as studies of life and culture in the Black world and wide-ranging cultural criticism. Response Time: 6 mos. Style: Literature, art. **Application.** What to Submit: query, full script (3 copies mailed), SASE. Material Must Be: Max 10,000 words (approx. 25 single-spaced pages, 12 point font). Opportunity/Award: complimentary copies. How to Submit: Mailed copies.

### Capilano Review TCR
2055 Purcell Way, N.
Vancouver, BC Canada
Tamara Lee
Tel: (604) 984-1712
contact@thecapilanoreview.ca
www.thecapilanoreview.ca
>Est. 1972. Response Time: 4 mos. Style: Poetry, drama, visual arts. What to Submit: SASE (Canadian postage). Material Must Be: unpublished. Opportunity/Award: publication, pay. **Application.** How to Submit: See website for guidelines.

### Contemporary Drama Service
885 Elkton Dr.,
Colorado Springs, CO 80907
Arthur Zapel
Fax: (719) 594-9916
editor@meriwether.com
www.contemporarydrama.com
>Est. 1970. School, college, church and amateur venues. age 12-30, cast limit 20. Response Time: 1 mo. Style: no translation. **Application.** What to Submit: query, SASE. Author Must Be: age 16 or older, resident or citizen of US. Material Must Be: unoptioned, unpublished, unproduced. Opportunity/Award: 10% royalty.

### Drama Source
1588 E. 361 North, St. Anthony, ID 83445
Daris Howard
Tel: (208) 624-4726; Fax: (208) 496-5402
info@dramasource.com
www.dramasource.com
>Est. 1997. Response Time: 3-6 mos. Style: G rated, family friendly. **Application.** What to Submit: query, synopsis, audio (sample of music). Opportunity/Award: 70% royalty, 10% sales, 50% video, short scripts/plays no royalty. How to Submit: Regular mail, script. Deadline. September.

### Dramatic Publishing Company
311 Washington St., Woodstock, IL 60098
Linda Habjan
Tel: (800) 448-7469; Fax: (800) 334-5302
plays@dramaticpublishing.com
www.dramaticpublishing.com
>Est. 1885. Performances licensed, all venues but 1st Class. Response Time: 8 mos. **Application.** What to Submit: full script, SASE.

### Dramatics Magazine
2343 Auburn Ave., Cincinnati, OH 45219
Don Corathers
Tel: (513) 421-3900; Fax: (513) 421-7077
dcorathers@edta.org
www.edta.org/publications/dramatics.asp
>Est. 1929. Natl. monthly magazine for HS theater students & teachers, printing 7 one-acts and full-lengths/ yr. Response Time: 5 mos. Style: comedy, drama. **Application.** What to Submit: full script. Material Must Be: unpublished. Opportunity/Award: $100-$500 honorarium, 5 copies. How to Submit: email or hard copy.

### Dramatists Play Service, Inc.
440 Park Ave. S., New York, NY 10016
Michael Q. Fellmeth
Tel: (212) 683-8960; Fax: (212) 213-1539
fellmeth@dramatists.com
www.dramatists.com
>Performances licensed. All venues except commercial. Response Time: 6 mos. Style: comedy, drama, musical. **Application.** What to Submit: query,

synopsis. Opportunity/Award: 10%
book, 80% amateur, 90% stock; 10
copies.

**Eldridge Publishing Company Inc.**
Box 14367, Tallahassee, FL 32317
Nancy S. Vorhis
Tel: (850) 385-2463; Fax: (850) 385-2463
editorial@histage.com
www.histage.com
Est. 1906. Performances licensed,
all venues. Response Time: 2 mos.
**Application.** What to Submit: query,
full script, audio, SASE. How to
Submit: email (MS Word, PDF) to
newworks@histage.com. Opportunity/
Award: 10% book, 50% amateur/
educational.

**Empire Publishing Service**
Box 1344, Studio City, CA 91614
Joseph W. Hill
Tel: (818) 784-8918
empirepubsvc@att.net
www.ppeps.com
Est. 1960. Publishes performing arts
books, incl. sheet music. Distributes
for Players Press, Java Publications,
Arte Publico Press, D-Books Intl., and
others. Also distributes performing
arts cassettes through direct mail and
trade sales. Response Time: from 3
to 365 days. **Application.** What to
Submit: query, SASE. Material Must
Be: produced. Opportunity/Award:
royalty.

**Green Integer**
6022 Wilshire Blvd., #202C,
Los Angeles, CA 90036
Per Bregne
Tel: (323) 857-1115
info@greeninteger.com
www.greeninteger.com
Works published to date incl. essays,
interviews, poems, plays, speeches
and novels. Response Time: 1 mo.
Style: comedy, drama, translation.
**Application.** What to Submit: query.
Material Must Be: unpublished.
Opportunity/Award: royalty, 10 copies.

**Gumbo Media**
Box 480443, Denver, CO 80248
A. Doyle
Fax: (305) 575-1187
mail@contentprovidermedia.com
www.gumbomedia.com
Markets comedy scripts, e-books,
stories, lyrics, film, etc. Licenses
lyrics, scripts, music, content, stories,
educational products, etc.

**HaveScripts.com**
204 Oakengate Turn,
Virginia Beach, VA 23462
Jean Klein
inbasket@havescripts.com
www.havescripts.com
Est. 2003. Online catalog of new plays.
Response Time: 1 mo. **Application.**
What to Submit: query, submissions
not returned. Material Must Be:
unpublished.

**Lazy Bee Scripts**
2 Wood Rd., Ashurst,
Southhampton, England, UK
Stuart Ardern
Response Time: query response within
7 days. More information at www.
lazybeescripts.co.uk/Publishing.
Style: all styles. **Application.** What
to Submit: query by e-mail or SASE
overseas postage. Material Must Be:
unpublished. Opportunity/Award:
royalties. How to Submit: unsolicited
query.

**Lillenas Publishing Company**
Box 419527, Kansas City, MO 64141
Kimberly R. Messer
Tel: (816) 931-1900; Fax: (816) 412-8390
drama@lillenas.com
www.lillenasdrama.com
Perfs licensed (school, church, dinner
& community). Response Time: 4 mos.
Style: comedy, drama. **Application.**
What to Submit: full script, SASE.
Material Must Be: unpublished,
produced. Opportunity/Award:
outright purchase or royalty.

**Limelight Scripts**
152 Southey Hill, Sheffield, UK S5 8BN
Dewey Willis, Jacqueline Willis
info@limelightscripts.com
www.limelightscripts.co.uk
  Est. 2005. Response Time: 24 hours.
  Style: comedy, drama. **Application.**
  What to Submit: query, synopsis,
  SASE. Author Must Be: over 18.
  How to Submit: invitation only, make
  inquiry.

**Meriwether Publishing Ltd.**
885 Elkton Dr.,
Colorado Springs, CO 80907
Arthur L. Zapel
Tel: (719) 594-4422; Fax: (888) 594-4436
editor@meriwether.com
www.meriwetherpublishing.com
  Style: Plays and Books. **Application.**
  What to Submit: theatre arts books
  written by drama educators and
  professionals, plus DVDs, CDs, and
  videos for classroom use. Material
  Must Be: In type space 1 1/2. How to
  Submit: Mail with SASE.

**Moose Hide Books**
684 Walls Rd., Sault Ste. Marie,
Ontario P6A-5K6 Canada
Richard Mousseau
Tel: (705) 779-3331; Fax: (707) 779-3331
rmousseau@moosehidebooks.com
www.moosehidebooks.com
  Time: 1 month. What to Submit:
  query, SASE. How to Submit:
  unsolicited.

**Music Theatre International (MTI)**
421 W. 54th St., New York, NY 10019
Russell Ochocki
Tel: (212) 541-4684; Fax: (212) 397-4684
www.mtishows.com
  Est. 1952. Performances licensed, all
  venues. MTI is a secondary licensing
  agency and prefers musicals that
  have been produced. Style: musical.
  **Application.** What to Submit: query.
  Material Must Be: produced.

**Norman Maine Publishing**
Box 1400, Tallevast, FL 34270
Dawn Remsing
info@normanmaineplays.com
www.normanmaineplays.com
  Est. 2005. Plays for community,
  professsional, and university theatre.
  Response Time: 2-3 mos. **Application.**
  What to Submit: Send entire script,
  synopsis, cast breakdown, cover letter,
  production history, music, SASE,
  no email submissions accepted.
  Material Must Be: unpublished, prefers
  produced and/or award-winning works.
  Opportunity/Award: 50% royalty, 10%
  book, complimentary copies (50%
  discount on additional copies).

**Original Works Publishing**
4611½ Ambrose Ave.,
Los Angeles, CA 90027
Jason Aaron Goldberg
info@originalworksonline.com
www.originalworksonline.com
  Deadline: ongoing. Est. 2000. Fees:
  never. Response Time: 1-2 months.
  Style: comedy, drama, musical, truly
  original works. No adaptations,
  translations or works for younger
  audiences. **Application.** What to
  Submit: Full length, one act, ten
  minute collections, monologues/
  one-person shows, musicals. Author
  Must Be: over 18. Material Must
  Be: produced. Opportunity/Award:
  80% production royalty, 15% sales; 2
  copies, wholesale discounts. How to
  Submit: email play as PDF or word
  doc w/synopsis, history, accolades,
  resume. See website for full detals.

**PAJ: A Journal of Performance and
Art**
Box 532, Village Sta.,
New York, NY 10014
Bonnie Marranca
Tel: (212) 243-3885; Fax: (212) 243-2885
pajpub@mac.com
www.mitpress.mit.edu/paj
  Est. 1976. Response Time: 2 mos
  query, 2 mos script. Style: plays by
  American authors; plays in translation.

**Application.** What to Submit: query, synopsis - see website.

**Playscripts, Inc.**
450 Seventh Ave., Suite 809,
New York, NY 10123
Mark Armstrong
Tel: (866) 639-7529
submissions@playscripts.com
www.playscripts.com
Est. 1998. Acting editions sold and performances licensed to amateur/ professional venues worldwide. Style: Full-length plays, one-act plays, very short plays. Material Must Be: unpublished by another exclusive publisher. **Application.** How to Submit: see website for latest submission preferences and guidelines; electronic submissions preferred.

**Players Press Inc.**
Box 1132, Studio City, CA 91614
Robert W. Gordon
Tel: (818) 789-4980
Est. 1960. Response Time: 2 wks query, 6 mos script. Style: all styles. **Application.** What to Submit: query, SASE. Material Must Be: unpublished, produced. Opportunity/Award: royalties.

**Poems & Plays**
MTSU English Dept.,
Murfreesboro, TN 37132
Gaylord Brewer
Tel: (615) 898-2712
gbrewer@mtsu.edu
www.mtsu.edu/english/poemsandplays/
Est. 1993. annual. Response Time: 3 mos. **Application.** What to Submit: full script, SASE. Material Must Be: unpublished. Opportunity/Award: 1 copy. Deadline: Nov. 30, 2010.

**Popular Play Service**
Box 3365, Bluffton, SC 29910
Tel: (843) 705-7981
popplays@hargray.com
www.popplays.com
Performances licensed. All venues, particularly community. Not

accepting submissions at this time. Style: comedy, farce. **Application.** What to Submit: query letter (note theme addressed), synopsis, cast 26 scene list, SASE. Material Must Be: unoptioned, unpublished, unproduced, still in development. Opportunity/ Award: feedback. How to Submit: professional recommendation.

**Prism International**
Buchanan E462, 1866 Main Mall,
Vancouver, BC V6T-1Z1 Canada
Elizabeth Ross
Tel: (604) 822-2514; Fax: (604) 822-3616
prismpoetry@gmail.com
www.prism.arts.ubc.ca
Est. 1959. quarterly. Response Time: 6 mos. What to Submit: query, full script, resume, SASE (Canadian). Material Must Be: unpublished. Opportunity/Award: $20/printed pg. **Application.** How to Submit: no email submissions.

**Samuel French Inc.**
45 W. 25th St., New York, NY 10010
Roxane Heinze-Bradshaw
Tel: (212) 206-8990; Fax: (212) 206-1429
publications@samuelfrench.com
www.samuelfrench.com
Est. 1830. Performances licensed for amateur, stock, professional and foreign venues in all media. Response Time: 2 mos. **Application.** What to Submit: Query Letter & 10 page sample, SASE. Opportunity/Award: 10% sales, performance royalty. How to Submit: Submit Query via online form or mail.

**Smith and Kraus**
Box 127, Lyme, NH 03768
Marisa Smith
Tel: (603) 643-6431; Fax: (603) 643-1831
editor@smithkraus.com
www.smithkraus.com
Time: 3 wks query; 4 mos script. Style: no musical. **Application.** What to Submit: query, synopsis. Opportunity/ Award: payment or royalty.

**Speert Publishing**
New York, NY
Eleanore Speert
Tel: (212) 979-7656
espeert@speertpublishing.com
www.speertpublishing.com
Self-publishing services for acting
editions of original plays. Response
Time: 1 wk. Style: no musical.
**Application.** What to Submit: query.
How to Submit: email.

**Tams-Witmark Music Library Inc.**
560 Lexington Ave.,
New York, NY 10022
Tel: (212) 688-2525; Fax: (212) 688-3232
info@tamswitmark.com
www.tams-witmark.com
Classic broadway musicals for stage
performance around the world.

**Theatre Communications Group (TCG)**
520 8th Ave., Fl. 24, New York, NY 10018
Terence Nemeth
Tel: (212) 609-5900 ext. 239
Fax: (212) 609-5901
tnemeth@tcg.org
www.tcg.org
Opportunity/Award: 7%-10% royalty.

**Theater Magazine**
Box 208244, New Haven, CT 6520
Tom Sellar
www.theatermagazine.org
Est. 1968. Tri-quarterly journal
of criticism, reports, interviews
and plays. Response Time: 6 mos.
**Application.** What to Submit: query.
Material Must Be: unpublished.

**Theatrefolk**
P.O. Box 1064, Crystal Beach,
Ontario L0S-1B0 Canada
Craig Mason
Tel: (866) 245-9138; Fax: (877) 245-9138
tfolk@theatrefolk.com
www.theatrefolk.com
We publish plays specifically for
student performers: simple. Response
Time: 6-8 wks. Style: all styles.
**Application.** What to Submit: full
script. Material Must Be: suitable
for high school or middle school

performers. Opportunity/Award:
royalties. How to Submit: unsolicited.
Deadline: Year round.

**TheatreForum**
9500 Gilman Dr., 0344,
La Jolla, CA 92093
Adele Edling Shank
Fax: (858) 534-1080
ashank@ucsd.edu
www.theatreforum.org
Editors: Jim Carmody, John Rouse,
Adele Edling Shank, Theodore Shank.
Plays must have been professionally
produced. Style: adventuresome.
**Application.** What to Submit: query
with professional recommendation,
submissions not returned. Material
Must Be: produced professionally.
Opportunity/Award: $200, 10 copies.
How to Submit: electronically.

**Theatrical Rights Worldwide**
1359 Broadway, #914,
New York, NY 10018
Steve Spiegel
Tel: (866) 378-9758; Fax: (212) 643-1322
licensing@theatricalrights.com
www.theatricalrights.com
Est. 2006. Staff: Steve Spiegel (Pres/
CEO). Response Time: 3-6 mos. Style:
musical. **Application.** What to Submit:
query, full script, audio. Material Must
Be: unpublished. Opportunity/Award:
royalties. How to Submit: professional
recommendation, agent.

**Univ. of Virginia Dept. of Theater**
Box 5103, Charlottesville, VA 22905
Jeanmarie Williams

**Zoetrope: All-Story**
916 Kearny St., San Francisco, CA 94133
www.all-story.com
First serial rights are required.:
quarterly. Response Time: five months.
Style: comedy, drama. **Application.**
What to Submit: full script (1 entry
at a time), submissions returned with
SASE. Material Must Be: unpublished.
Opportunity/Award: publication,
$1000. How to Submit: unsolicited,
agent submission.

# Career Development Opportunities

---

## COLONIES AND RESIDENCIES

**Altos de Chavon**
66 5th Ave., #604-A,
New York, NY 10011
Carmen Lorente
Tel: (212) 229-5370; Fax: (212) 229-8988
altos@earthlink.net
www.altosdechavon.com
> Est. 1981. 3-mo residencies in
> La Romana, Dominican Rep, for
> visual artists, writers, musicians,
> and architects. Material Must Be:
> Summary of manuscript or writing,
> critiques of previously written and
> published work. **Submission.** Via
> postal mail. Deadline: Aug. 15, 2010.

**Atlantic Center for the Arts**
1414 Art Center Ave.,
New Smyrna Beach, FL 32168
James Frost
Tel: (386) 427-6975; Fax: (386) 427-5669
program@atlanticcenterforthearts.org
www.atlanticcenterforthearts.org
> Est. 1982. Residencies of 3 wks with
> master artists on FL's east coast.
> Workspace incl black box theater,
> music/recording studio, dance studio,
> art & sculpture studios, digital lab,
> and resource library. $25 application,
> $850 program: $800 limit room/
> board. **Submission.** Application
> (view online), SASE, Submission/
> Application Fee: $25.00.

**Bellagio Center Creative Arts
Residencies**
Villa Serbelloni, Via Roma 1,
Bellagio, CO 22021
> How To Submit: online.

**Blue Mountain Center**
Box 109, Blue Mt. Lake, NY 12812
Ben Strader
Tel: (518) 352-7391
bmc@bluemountaincenter.org
www.bluemountaincenter.org
> Residencies of 4 wks (Jun-Oct) in
> Adirondack Mts. Workspace incl
> music studio. Cell phones are not
> allowed on the property. **Submission.**
> Query, application, 30-pg sample, bio,
> Submission/Application Fee. $20.00.
> Deadline: Feb. 1, 2010.

**Byrdcliffe Arts Colony Artist-in-
Residence (AIR)**
34 Tinker St., Woodstock, NY 12498
Katherine Burger
Tel: (845) 679-2079; Fax: (845) 679-4529
wguild@ulster.net
www.woodstockguild.org
> Colony establish 1980. Located in
> the Catskill Mountains, Woodstock,
> NY. Some use of historic Byrdcliffe
> Theater possible. There are four,
> 4-week sessions per season. Cost $300.
> Residents provide own food. Phone
> number May-Sept. ONLY: 845-679-
> 8540. Style: Playscript. Opportunity/
> Award: The Handel Fellowship,
> awarded to one playwright per year.
> A free residency plus a $1000 stipend.
> **Submission.** Application, SASE. How
> To Submit: Download an application
> from our website. Work sample,
> work plan, CV, fee, and names of
> two recommendors. Submission/
> Application Fee: $35.00. Deadline:
> Mar. 1, 2010.

**Camargo Foundation**
1 ave Jermini, Cassis, 13260 France
Leon Selig
Tel: (113)-344-2011; Fax: (113)-344-2013
apply@camargofoundation.org
www.camargofoundation.org

   The interdisciplinary residency
   program is intended to give fellows
   the time and space they need to realise
   their projects. The Foundation's
   hillside campus overlooks the
   Mediterranean Sea in Cassis,
   France; it includes thirteen furnished
   apartments, a reference library, and
   three art/music studios. Fellows
   are provided with accommodation
   on campus. Residencies are one
   semester (either early-September to
   mid-December or mid-January to the
   end of May). **Submission.** Online
   application form, resume, 3 references,
   a 1000 word project description, up
   to 3 work samples, totalling no more
   than 30 pages. Times New Roman,
   12-point font. Work sample from
   proposed work preferred. Material
   Must Be: specific creative project.
   How To Submit: online. Deadline: Jan.
   12, 2010.

**Centrum Artistic Residencies Program**
Box 1158, Port Townsend, WA 98368
Lisa Werner
Tel: (360) 385-3102 ext. 128
lisa@centrum.org
www.centrum.org/residencies

   Est. 1980. Awarded in one week
   blocks, residencies may be of any
   duration, time and space permitting.
   2009 fee of $275/week includes private
   housing with full kitchen in a coastal
   state park. Fee is expected to increase
   in 2010. Successful applicants submit
   20% deposit to confirm residency
   dates. Style: New work by individuals
   or collaborative groups. **Submission.**
   Proposal of the new work you will be
   focused on, resume/curriculum vita,
   work sample. How To Submit: Hard
   copy or by email.

**Djerassi Resident Artists Program**
2325 Bear Gulch Rd.,
Woodside, CA 94062
Judy Freeland
Tel: (650) 747-1250
drap@djerassi.org
www.djerassi.org

   Est. 1979. 4-5 wk residence (Mar.-
   Nov.) for writers and artists on
   580-acre ranch near San Francisco.
   Living space, studio space and meals
   provided. **Submission.** Application,
   full script, submissions not returned,
   Submission/Application Fee: $35.00.
   Deadline: Feb. 15, 2010.

**Edward Albee Foundation**
14 Harrison St., New York, NY 10013
Jakob Holder
Tel: (212) 226-2020; Fax: (212) 226-5551
info@albeefoundation.org
www.albeefoundation.org

   Est. 1966. Residencies of 1 mo. (June-
   Sept.) in Montauk, NY, for writers
   and composers. Annual. **Submission.**
   Application, full script, SASE.
   Deadline: Mar. 1, 2010.

**Envision Retreat**
Voice And Vision, 520 8th Ave., #316,
New York, NY 10018
Jean Wagner
Tel: (212) 268-3717
vandv@vandv.org
www.vandv.org

   Projects initiated by women in
   summer workshop development on
   Bard College campus. Style: Works by
   women artists. **Submission.** 2 copies
   of full script or description of project,
   resumes of all collaborators. Core
   artist must be a woman. Fee: $15.00.
   Deadline: Feb. 1, 2010.

**Feminist Women's Writing Workshops
Inc. (FW3)**
Box 6583, Ithaca, NY 14850
Kit Wainer
pipkit@aol.com

   Residencies of 8 days in July.
   Residents are housed in private
   rooms in a house on campus of

Hobart and William Smith Coll. in Geneva, NY. $560 program fee: scholarships available. Style: all styles. **Submission.** Application. Author Must Be: female. How To Submit: send SASE in fall for application.

**The Field Artward Bound Residency Program**
161 6th Ave., Fl. 14, New York, NY 10013
Patricia Burgess
Tel: (212) 691-6969 ext. 14
Fax: (212) 255-2053
patricia@thefield.org
www.thefield.org
   Residencies of 10-14 days (Jun-Sep) at rural facilities outside NYC.: free ($100 refundable deposit): room/ board, travel. Response Time: 1 mo. posted at www.thefield.org 2-3 months prior to deadline. Style: performing, text-based performance. **Submission.** Application. Author Must Be: depends on residency opportunity of NYC area, 3-yr professional.

**Gell Center of the Finger Lakes**
740 University Ave., Rochester, NY 14607
Kathy Pottetti
Tel: (585) 473-2590 ext. 103
Fax: (585) 442-9333
Kathyp@wab.org
www.wab.org
   Fees: $50/night. **Submission.** Sample.

**Hambidge Center**
Box 339, Rabun Gap, GA 30568
Debra Sanders
Tel: (706) 746-5718; Fax: (706) 746-9933
center@hambidge.org
www.hambidge.org
   Residencies of 2-8 wks (Feb.-Dec.) on 600 acres in Blue Ridge Mts. Residents housed in private cottage-studios for emerging, mid-career or established writers, performers, visual artists and other disciplines. Fees: $30 application, $150/wk: annual. **Submission.** Application (pdf on web), 30-pg sample (3 copies), audio, resume, SASE, Submission/ Application Fee: $30.00. Deadlines:

Jan. 15, 2010 for May-Aug. 2010, April 15 for Sept.-Dec. 2010, Sept. 15 for March 2011.

**Hawthornden Retreat for Writers**
Hawthornden Castle, Lasswade, Scotland
Tel: 44-131-440 -2180
Fax: 44-131-440-1989
S.M. Gaskell
office@hawthornden.com
   Est. 1982. Residencies of 4 wks (Feb.-July, Sept.-Dec.) in 17th-century castle, 40-min. bus to Edinburgh. Residents housed in study bedrooms. room/board: annual. **Submission.** Application, 10-15 pg. sample. Author Must Be: produced or published. How To Submit: by application form. Deadline: June 30, 2010.

**Hedgebrook**
2197 Millman Rd., Langley, WA 98260
Amy Wheeler
Tel: (360) 321-4786; Fax: (360) 321-2171
connect@hedgebrook.org
www.hedgebrook.org
   Est. 1988. Residencies of 2-6 wks in 48-acre retreat on Whidbey Island. Residents housed in private cottages with electricity and wood stoves. 1 bathhouse serves all 6 cottages. Writers eat in farmhouse each night; meals by staff chef using local organic food. "No cost writing retreat". **Submission.** Application. Author Must Be: female. Opportunity/Award: no cost writing retreat, Submission/ Application Fee: $25.00. Deadline: Sept. 24, 2010.

**Helene Wurlitzer Foundation of New Mexico**
P.O. Box 1891, Taos, NM 87571
Michael Knight
Tel: (505) 758-2413; Fax: (505) 758-2559
HWF@taosnet.com
www.wurlitzerfoundation.org
   Est. 1956. Residences of 3 mos (Jan.-Nov.) for visual artists, writers and composers. Individual single-floor dwellings accessible for walkers but not wheel chairs; composer studios

each have a grand piano. Artists must provide for their own meals and materials. Style: Artist Residency Program. **Submission.** Application and materials. Material Must Be: as requested on application. No exceptions. Opportunity/Award: Three month residency, rent and utility free. How To Submit: Send SASE, request application via email or download from website. Deadline: Jan. 18, 2010 for residency in 2011.

**Institute of Gunnar Gunnarsson - Klaustrid**
Skriduklaustur, 701 Egilsstadir, Egilsstadir, Iceland
Halladora Tomasdohir
Tel: (354)-471-2990; Fax: (354)-471-2991
klaustur@skriduklaustur.is
www.skriduklaustur.is
> Est. 1989. room / board. Response Time: 2-3 mos. Style: all styles. **Submission.** Application. Deadline: Jun. 15, 2010.

**International Writing Program (IWP)**
430 N. Clinton St., Iowa City, IA 52242
Christopher Merrill
Tel: (319) 335-0128; Fax: (319) 335-3843
iwp@uiowa.edu
www.iwp.uiowa.edu
> Est. 1967. For writers of fiction, poetry, drama, or screenplays who are not US residents. 3 mo. residency (Aug. - Nov.) Author Must Be: published author, proficient in English.

**Isle Royale National Park Artist-in-Residence**
800 E. Lakeshore Dr.,
Houghton, MI 49931
Greg Blust
Tel: (906) 482-0984; Fax: (906) 482-8753
greg_blust@nps.gov
www.nps.gov/isro
> Est. 1991. 2-3 wk residency (June-Sept.) in primitive cabin supplied with propane light, stove, fridge, and canoe. Artist conducts 1 program/wk and donates a finished piece after a year of residency. Style: Open to all

art forms. **Submission.** application, sample, audio, SASE. Author Must Be: 18 years or older. How To Submit: Contact the park for application. Deadline: Feb. 16, 2010.

**The John Steinbeck Writer's Room**
Long Island Univ.-Southampton Campu,
Southampton, NY 11968
Robert Gerbereux
Tel: (631) 287-8382; Fax: (631) 287-4049
library@southampton.liu.edu

**Kalani Oceanside Retreat Village**
RR2, Box 4500, 12-6860 Kalapana
Kapoho Beach Road, Pahoa, HI 96778
Richard Koob
Tel: (808) 965-7828; Fax: (808) 965-0527
artists@kalani.com
www.kalani.com
> Artist residencies of 2 wks to 3 mos in 4 lodges and 22 cottage rooms on 120 acres of secluded coast forest. Fee incl. meals and use of facilities. Work space limited to shared multipurpose studios in lodges. Fees: $590-1690 /wk: stipend (May-October). **Submission.** Application. How To Submit: email.

**Kimmel Harding Nelson (KHN) Center for the Arts**
801 3rd Corso, Nebraska City, NE 68410
Denise Brady
Tel: (402) 874-9600; Fax: (402) 874-9600
info@khncenterforthearts.org
www.khncenterforthearts.org
> 2-8 week residencies for visual artists, writers, music composers. $25 application fee: $100/wk, housing and studiowebsite for description of program and application guidelines. Response Time: approx. 2 mos. Opportunity/Award: Residency with weekly stipend. **Submission.** See guidelines on website. How To Submit: see guidelines on website, Submission/Application Fee: $25.00. Deadline: Two deadlines each year: Mar. 1 and Sept. 1.

**La MaMa Playwright Retreat**
74-A E. 4th St., New York, NY 10003
Est. 2007.

**Lanesboro Residency Program Fellowships**
103 Parkway Ave. N., Box 152,
Lanesboro, MN 55949
Sara Decker
Tel: (507) 467-2446; Fax: (507) 467-4446
Info@lanesboroarts.org
www.lanesboroarts.org
> Assistance: Residency award $625/wk;
> Artists' retreat space also available for
> rent. **Submission.** Application. How
> To Submit: Download application
> from website: www.lanesboroarts.org.
> Deadline: June 30, 2010.

**Ledig House Writers Residency Program**
55 5th Ave., Fl. 15, New York, NY 10003
DW Gibson
Tel: (212) 206-6060; Fax: (212) 206-6114
writers@artomi.org
www.artomi.org
> Est. 1992. Residencies of 1 wk-2 mos
> (Mar-Jun, Sep-Nov) in Catskill Mts.
> Residents provided with separate or
> combined work/bedroom areas. All
> meals included. Twice a year (spring/
> fall). **Submission.** Query, 10-pg
> sample, bio, SASE. Deadline: Nov. 20,
> 2010.

**Leighton Artists' Colony for Independent Residencies**
Box 1020 Station 28, 107 Tunnel
Mountain Rd, Banff, Al T1L-1H5 Canada
Tel: (800) 565-9989; Fax: (403) 762-6345
arts_info@banffcentre.ca
www.banffcentre.ca
> Applications accepted year round.
> for writers, composers and visual
> artists housed in private rooms w/bath,
> phone, and cleaning service. Studios
> incl washroom, phone, CD/tape player,
> piano (3 of 8 studios), with computer
> (Mac or PC), printer and wireless
> access. **Submission.** See website.
> Author Must Be: professional level.
> How To Submit: mail, fax or email,

> Submission/Application Fee: various,
> see website.

**MacDowell Colony**
100 High St., Peterborough, NH 3458
Courtney Bethel
Tel: (603) 924-3886 ext. 113
Fax: (603) 924-9142
admissions@macdowellcolony.org
www.macdowellcolony.org
> Est. 1907. Residencies up to 8 wks
> (Jun-Sep, Oct-Jan, Feb-May) for
> uninterrupted time and seclusion
> to work and enjoy a community of
> creative artists. Workspace incl.
> studios.: $1,000 stipend limit,
> travel: triannual. Response Time:
> 10 weeks. **Submission.** Project
> proposal, application, synopsis, full
> script (3 copies of complete script).
> Opportunity/Award: travel and
> financial assistance available, based
> on need - aid applications mailed upon
> acceptance. How To Submit: send
> application and materials by deadline,
> Submission/Application Fee: $20.00.
> Deadlines: Jan 15, April 15, and Sept.
> 15, 2010.

**Millay Colony for the Arts**
454 East Hill Rd, Box 3,
Austerlitz, NY 12017
Calliope Nicholas
Tel: (518) 392-3103; Fax: (518) 392-4944
apply@millaycolony.org; http://www.
millaycolony.org
> Est. 1973 on former estate of Edna
> St. Vincent Millay. Month-long
> residencies (Apr-Nov) for writers,
> visual artists and composers accepted
> by jury process, emerging writers
> as well as established, no cost for
> residency, travel expenses only. $35
> application, outside US $65: room/
> board/chef at no cost, travel expenses
> only. Annual. Response Time: by
> 2/1/2011. **Submission.** Application
> plus three sample copies up to 30
> pages in standard industry form.
> Include bio and artist statement. How
> To Submit: download application on
> website. Deadline: Oct. 1, 2010.

**Montana Artists Residency**
Box 8, Basin, MT 59631
Debbie Sheehan
Tel: (406) 225-3500
mar@mt.net
www.montanarefuge.org
> Est. 1993. Residencies of 1-9 mos in
> Nov-Jul (6/15 deadline). Fully funded
> residencies for Writers in Oct (5/15
> deadline) and American Indian Artists
> in Sep (4/15 deadline). Facilities incl.
> 2 apts. w/large studios, 1 soundproof
> apt., and 1 small studio apt.; all incl.
> kitchen, double bed, private phone,
> and wireless internet. $300-550/
> mo. **Submission.** Application, 15-
> pg sample (3 copies), audio, resume.
> Deadline: Apr. 15, May 15, and June
> 15, 2010.

**New York Mills Arts Retreat**
24 N. Main Ave., Box 246,
New York Mills, MN 56567
Tel: (218) 385-3339
info@kulcher.org
www.kulcher.org
> **Submission.** Query, synopsis,
> 12-pg sample, resume, letters of
> recommendation, SASE.

**Ragdale Foundation**
1260 N. Green Bay Rd.,
Lake Forest, IL 60045
Regin Igloria
Tel: (847) 234-1063 ext. 206
Fax: (847) 234-1063
admissions@ragdale.org
www.ragdale.org
> Est. 1976. Residencies of 2 wks-2 mos
> (Jun-Dec, Jan-Apr) for composers,
> artists, and writers in private rooms
> with meals included. Workspace incl.
> 1 composing studio, 3 visual arts
> studios, and 8 writing rooms. Public
> workshops also offered. $25/day:
> financial aid w/demonstrated need.
> Response Time: 3 mos. **Submission.**
> Query, application, synopsis, sample,
> SASE. How To Submit: Apply
> online: www.ragdale.org/residency/
> app, Submission/Application Fee:
> $30. Deadline: January 15, May 15,
> September 15 annually.

**Rocky Mountain National Park Artist-in-Residence Program**
1000 Hwy. 36, Estes Park, CO 80517
Tel: (970) 586-1206
www.nps.gov/romo
> **Submission.** query, application, 6-pg
> sample (writers), audio (composers),
> resume (6 copies of all above),
> submissions not returned, Submission/
> Application Fee: $35.00. Deadline:
> Dec. 1, 2010.

**Studio for Creative Inquiry**
College of Fine Arts, #111,
Pittsburgh, PA 15213
Marge Myers
Tel: (412) 268-3454; Fax: (412) 268-2829
mmbm@andrew.cmu.edu
www.cmu.edu/studio
> Est. 1989. Currently accepting
> proposals for experimental and
> interdisciplinary arts projects that
> don't require full funding by CMU.
> Proposals should be submitted at
> least 6 mos in advance of the desired
> residency. **Submission.** Query, sample,
> resume.

**Sundance Institute Playwrights Retreat**
8530 Wilshire Blvd., Fl. 3,
Beverly Hills, CA 90211
Ignacia Delgado
Tel: (310) 360-1981, Fax: (310) 360-1969
theatre@sundance.org
www.sundance.org
> Est. 2001. 18-day retreat for 5
> playwrights and 1 theater composer
> at Ucross Foundation, Clearmont,
> WY. $500 stipend, room/board,
> travel. Annual. Material Must Be:
> unproduced. **Submission.** Invite.

**U.S./Japan Creative Artists' Program**
1201 15th St. NW, #330,
Washington, DC 20005
Margaret P. Mihori
Tel: (202) 653-9800; Fax: (202) 418-9802
jusfc@jusfc.gov
www.jusfc.gov
> Est. 1979. 5-mo residency in Japan
> for produced professional US artists.
> up to $6,000 stipend, room/board,
> travel, language training and storage,

400,000 yen/mo stipend, 100,000 yen/mo housing supplement, 100,000 yen for professional services: annual. **Submission.** Application on line. Author Must Be: citizen or resident of US. How To Submit: online. Deadline: Feb. 1, 2010.

**Ucross Foundation Residency Program**
30 Big Red Ln., Clearmont, WY 82835
Sharon Dynak
Tel: (307) 737-2291; Fax: (307) 737-2322
rsalvatore@ucross.org
www.ucrossfoundation.org
   Est. 1981. Residencies of 2 weeks to 6 weels (Feb-Jun, Jul-Nov) near Big Horn Mts. Residents are provided living & studio space plus meals. Semiannual (March 1 and October 1). **Submission.** Application, SASE, Submission/Application Fee: $40.00. Deadline: Mar. 1, 2010.

**Virginia Center for the Creative Arts (VCCA)**
154 San Angelo Dr., Amherst, VA 24521
Sheila Pleasants
Tel: (434) 946-7236; Fax: (434) 946-7239
vcca@vcca.com
www.vcca.com
   Est. 1971. Residencies of 2 wks-2 mos on 12-acre hilltop in foothills of Blue Ridge Mts near Sweet Briar College. Daily contribution: $30-$60/day: room/board/studio. Response Time: 2 mos. **Submission.** Application, full script, submissions not returned. Material Must Be: VCCA does not accept scholarly projects, Submission/Application Fee: $25.00. Deadline: Jan. 15, May 15, Sep. 15, 2010.

**Women's Work Lab**
456 W. 37th St., New York, NY 10018
Melody Brooks
Tel: (212) 630-9945
contact@nptnyc.org
www.nptnyc.org
   Monthy meetings for Development.: annual. Style: All styles. **Submission.** Check website for application and deadline. Author Must Be: female,

women of color encouraged. Material Must Be: unoptioned, unpublished, unproduced. Opportunity/Award: reading; workshop production. Deadline: Jan. 1, 2010.

**William Inge Center for the Arts**
Box 708, 1057 W. College Ave.,
Independence, KS 67301
Peter Ellenstein
Tel: (620) 332-5490
info@ingecenter.org
www.ingecenter.org
   Est. 2002. 2 playwrights in 9-wk residency at Inge home (Sep-Nov or Mar-May), with 1-wk Actors' Equity Reading workshop of new play, and some teaching. $4,000 stipend, room, travel: semiannual. Response Time: 6 mos. **Submission.** query, script (best work), resume, bio and references, description of project, SASE. Author Must Be: produced with three Equity productions. Material Must Be: unproduced. Opportunity/Award: AEA Workshop Reading of unproduced play. How To Submit: Attach to email or by post. Deadline: rolling.

**Yaddo**
Box 395, Saratoga Springs, NY 12866
Candace Wait
Tel: (518) 584-0746; Fax: (518) 584-1312
chwait@yaddo.org
www.yaddo.org
   Est. 1900. Residencies of 2 wks-2 mos on 400-acre turn-of-century estate in Saratoga Springs, NY. Room/board, and private studio space free of charge.: room/board, travel (limited): semiannual. Style: Fiction, nonfiction, drama, poetry, libretto, translation. **Submission.** The original and two copies of the application form; three copies of a professional resume of no more than two pages; the nonrefundable application fee; SASE; three copies of a work sample (as described in the instructions); two letters of recommendation (sent separately by the writers of the letters). Yaddo

does not accept applications or letters of recommendation electronically or by fax - all application materials must be assembled according to the instructions and physically mailed to Yaddo. Letters of recommendation are to be submitted separately by the person writing the letter and must be mailed, not faxed or submitted electronically. Author Must Be: Writing at a professional level. Opportunity/Award: Residency. Submission/Application Fee: $30. Deadline: Jan. 1 and Aug. 1, 2010.

## CONFERENCES AND FESTIVALS

**6 Women Playwriting Festival**
Box 1073, Colorado Springs, CO 80901
Donna Guthrie
www.sixwomenplayfestival.com
> Est. 2007. Frequency: annual. Production: age 16 and older, cast of 2-4. Response Time: 2 mos. Style: 10 minute plays. **Application.** What To Submit: full script, SASE, 3 copies, title sheet. Author Must Be: age 16 or older, female. Material Must Be: unproduced. Opportunity/Award: $100 plus travel. Deadline: Oct. 31, 2010.

**Actors Theatre of Louisville, Humana Festival [KY]**
316 W. Main St., Louisville, KY 40202
Amy Wegener
Tel: (502) 584-1265;  Fax: (502) 561-3300
awegener@actorstheatre.org
www.actorstheatre.org/humana_
submission.htm
> Est. 1976. Festival of 10-15 produced plays in Mar-Apr, incl. premieres and second productions. Assistance: room/ board, travel, per diem. Frequency: annual. **Application.** What to Submit: Agent submission only for full scripts; or synopsis and 10-pg sample. No electronic queries. Opportunity/ Award: Full-length, unproduced (or not reviewed). How To Submit: agent.

**Annual Black Theatre Festival**
5919 Hamilton Ave, Cincinnati, OH 45224
Don Sherman
Tel: (513) 241-6060; Fax: (513) 241-6671
www.cincyblacktheatre.com

**Application.** How To Submit: unsolicited, year-round open submissions.

**Appalachian Festival of Plays and Playwrights**
PO Box 867, Abingdon, VA 24212
Nicholas Piper
Tel: (276) 619-3316; Fax: (276) 619-3335
apfestival@bartertheatre.com
www.bartertheatre.com/festival
> Est. 2001. Plays must be written by Appalachian playwright or must contain Appalachian settings & themes. Stagings of 2 plays from previous AFPP, and readings of 6 new scripts in 2-wk fest, judged by panel. Staff: Richard Rose (Artistic Dir), Nicholas Piper (Festival Director). **Application.** What to Submit: full script, SASE. Author Must Be: Appalachian. Material Must Be: unoptioned, unpublished, unproduced. Opportunity/Award: $250-$500, 5% royalty. How To Submit: Please submit unbound manuscript, mail. Deadline: Mar. 31, 2010.

**Attic Theatre One-Act Marathon**
5429 W. Washington Blvd.,
Los Angeles, CA 90016
Jaime Gray
Tel: (323) 525-0600; Fax: (323) 525-0661
litmanager@attictheatre.org
www.attictheatre.org
> Entries read by ensemble, finalists read by staff, with 3-10 selected for production or reading in marathon. Panel from L.A. theater community chooses 2 winners. Frequency: annual

Production: cast limit 8, no orchestra, unit set. Response Time: 4 mos. Style: comedy, drama. **Application.** What To Submit: query, application, synopsis, full script (2 copies), character breakdown, bio, SASE. Material Must Be: unproduced. Opportunity/Award: $300 1st, $150 2nd, publication. Deadline: Feb. 28, 2010.

**Baldwin New Play Festival**
9500 Gilman Dr., MC0509,
La Jolla, CA 92093
Allan Havis
Tel: (858) 534-3791; Fax: (858) 534-8931
ahavis@ucsd.edu
www.theatre.ucsd.edu
Est. 2006. Assistance: room/board, travel Frequency: annual. Response Time: by 4/1/10. Style: comedy, drama. **Application.** What To Submit: application, synopsis, full script, SASE. Author Must Be: college undergrad. Material Must Be: unpublished, unproduced. Opportunity/Award: $1,000, reading. How To Submit: electronic and US postal. Deadline: Mar. 19, 2010.

**Barnstormers Theatre**
Box 434, Tamworth, NH 3886
Clayton Phillips
Tel: (603) 323-8500; Fax: (603) 323-8982
office@barnstormerstheatre.org
www.barnstormerstheatre.org
Evening of original one-acts in Oct. Frequency: annual. Production: cast limit 6. **Application.** What to Submit: full script. Material Must Be: unoptioned, unpublished, unproduced. Opportunity/Award: $100 honorarium. Deadline: Mar. 15, 2010.

**Bay Bilingual Foundation of the Arts (BFA)**
421 N. Ave. 19, Los Angeles, CA 90031
Margarita Galban
Tel: (323) 225-4044; Fax: (323) 225-1250
bfamanagement@sbcglobal.net
www.bfatheatre.org
Est. 1973. Summer reading fest of new works. Assistance: TBA. Frequency: annual. Production: cast limit 10,

simple set. Response Time: 6 mos-1 yr. Style: All styles. **Application.** What To Submit: query, full script, SASE. Opportunity/Award: TBA. How To Submit: unsolicited.

**Black Playwrights Festival**
4520 N. Beacon, Chicago, IL 60640
Jackie Taylor
Tel: (773) 769-4451; Fax: (773) 769-4533
blackensemble@aol.com
www.blackensemble.org
Year-round open submissions. Clearly note script is for festival. See website for details.

**Blank Theatre Company Young Playwrights Festival**
P.O. Box 38756, Hollywood, CA 90038
Stacy Reed
Tel: (323) 871-8018; Fax: (323) 661-3903
reed@theblank.com
www.youngplaywrights.com
Est. 1990. Winning plays assigned mentors and given professional workshop. Frequency: annual. Response Time: by mid-May. **Application.** What to Submit: query, full script, submissions not returned. Author Must Be: age 19 or younger. Material Must Be: unoptioned, unpublished. Deadline: Mid March.

**Boomerang Theatre Company**
P.O. Box 237166, Ansonia Station,
New York, NY 10023
Tim Errickson
Tel: (212) 501-4069
info@boomerangtheatre.org
www.boomerangtheatre.org
Est. 1999. Annual reading series of new plays. Style: no musical. **Application.** What To Submit: query, synopsis, 10-pg sample, resume, SASE if necessary. Material Must Be: unproduced. Deadline: Sept. 30, 2010.

**Boston Theater Marathon**
949 Commonwealth Ave.,
Boston, MA 2215
Kate Snodgrass
Tel: (617) 353-5443
newplays@bu.edu

www.bu.edu/btm

Est. 1999. 50 10-min plays by New England playwrights by 50 New England theaters over 10 hrs in 1 day. Frequency: annual. Production: small orchestra, minimal set. Response Time: 4 mos. Alternate website: www.bostonplaywright.org. Style: comedy, drama, musical. **Application.** What To Submit: full script, SASE, 10 minutes. Author Must Be: resident of New England. Opportunity/Award: production. How To Submit: mail. Deadline: Nov. 15, 2010.

**Boulder International Fringe Festival**
1020½ Portland St., Boulder, CO 80302

**Centre Stage South Carolina New Play Festival**
Box 8451, Greenville, SC 29604
Brian Haimbach
Tel: (864) 233-6733; Fax: (864) 313-9026
haimbach@hotmail.com
www.centrestage.org

Est. 2002. 4 finalists receive readings in 1-week fest. Audience selects winner for full production next season. Finalists receive response session and development assistance from professional playwright in residence (past residents include Lee Blessing, Arlene Hutton, Jeffrey Sweet). Frequency: annual. Production: age 12 or older, cast limit 6, minimal set. Response Time: by 8/1/10. Style: adaptation, comedy, drama. **Application.** What To Submit: synopsis, full script, scripts will not be returned. Material Must Be: unpublished, unproduced. Opportunity/Award: Full Production. How To Submit: Postal Mail to address above. Deadline: Feb. 1, 2010.

**Children's Festival at the Annenberg Ctr for the Performing Arts**
3680 Walnut St., Philadelphia, PA 19104

**Cleveland Public Theatre New Plays Festival**
6415 Detroit Ave., Cleveland, OH 44102
Tel: (216) 631-2727; Fax: (216) 631-2575

www.cptonline.org

Biennial four-week festival of staged readings. Assistance: room/board, travel, per diem. Frequency: biennial. Production: cast of up to 10, simple set. Style: all styles. **Application.** What To Submit: synopsis, sample, SASE. Material Must Be: unoptioned, unproduced. Opportunity/Award: $1,000 and $250 awards, reading. How To Submit: unsolicited.

**Coe College Playwriting Festival & Symposia**
1220 1st Ave. NE,
Cedar Rapids, IA 52402
Susan Wolverton
Tel: (319) 399-8624; Fax: (319) 399-8557
swolvert@coe.edu
www.public.coe.edu/departments/theatre

Est. 1993. Biennial spring fest. Winner of New Works for the Stage Competition receives weeklong residency, workshop with students, and staged reading. Assistance: room/board, travel. Frequency: biennial Production: age 16-50, cast of 3-8 Response Time: 8 wks. Style: comedy, drama. **Application.** What To Submit: 1-pg synopsis, full script, SASE. Author Must Be: citizen of US. Material Must Be: unpublished, unproduced, in development stage. Opportunity/Award: $500, reading. How To Submit: unsolicited. Deadline: Nov. 1, 2010.

**Cultural Conversations**
116 Arts Bldg., Penn State U. School of Theatre, University Park, PA 16802
Susan Russell
sbr13@psu.edu
www.culturalconversations.psu.edu

2010 festival is devoted to new works that explore disability of any kinds. Est. 2007. Readings of 3 new plays addressing themes of local and global diversity. One week rehearsal, Two week festival. Playwright funded residency 2-3 days. Frequency: annual. Response Time: by 1/15 each year. Style: comedy, drama. **Application.** What To Submit: full

script, SASE. Material Must Be:
unoptioned, unpublished, unproduced.
Opportunity/Award: reading. How To
Submit: unsolicited. Deadline: Oct.
31, 2010.

**Firehouse Theatre Project's Festival of
New American Plays**
1609 W. Broad St., Richmond, VA 23220
Carol Piersol
Tel: (804) 355-2001; Fax: (804) 355-0999
info@firehousetheatre.org
www.firehousetheatre.org
Est. 2003. Frequency: annual.
Response Time: 7 mos. Style: comedy,
drama, musical, no translation.
**Application.** What To Submit: full
script (playwright's information on
removable cover page ONLY) and
letter of professional recommendation,
submissions not returned. Author
Must Be: resident or citizen of USA.
Material Must Be: unproduced,
previous reading OK if no admission
charged. Opportunity/Award: $1,000
1st prize, $500 2nd prize, staged
reading for both 1st and 2nd place
plays. How To Submit: mail only,
no electronic submissions accepted.
Deadline: June 30, 2010.

**Florida Studio Theatre's Richard &
Betty Burdick New Play Reading Series**
1241 N. Palm Ave., Sarasota, FL 34236
Cristin Kelly
Tel: (941) 366-9017; Fax: (941) 955-4137
ckelly@floridastudiotheatre.org
www.floridastudiotheatre.org
May workshop readings of 3 new
full-length plays or musicals by
contemporary US writers. Assistance:
stipend, room/board, travel.
Frequency: annual. **Application.** What
to Submit: query, synopsis, sample,
SASE, CD if musical. How To Submit:
E-mail or mail. Full guidelines at
http://www.floridastudiotheatre.
org/new_plays.php, Unsolicited
from Florida residents, Agent or
professional recommendation
otherwise.

**Fresh Fruit Festival**
145 E. 27th St., #1-A,
New York, NY 10016
Carol Polcovar
artisticdirector@freshfruitfestival.com
www.freshfruitfestival.com
Est. 2003. Frequency: annual.
Response Time: 2 mos. Style:
Related to the interests of the LGBT
Community. **Application.** What To
Submit: Application and work (www.
freshfruitfestival.com). Author Must
Be: Open, women and minority groups
encouraged to apply. Material Must
Be: unoptioned, not performed in
NYC, related in some way to LGBT
culture. Opportunity/Award: Selected
productions get a percentage of the
door and a minimun guarantee.
Fresh Fruit Awards of Distinction are
rewarded to outstanding festival work.
How To Submit: application posted
online. www.freshfruitfestival.com.
Deadline: Feb. 15, 2010.

**Fringe of Toronto Theatre Festival**
344 Bloor St., #208,
Toronto, Ontario M5S-3A7 Canada
Tel: (416) 966-1062; Fax: (416) 966-5072
general@fringetoronto.com
www.fringetoronto.com
How To Submit: See website.

**FusionFest**
8500 Euclid Ave., Cleveland, OH 44106
Seth Gordon
Tel: (216) 795-7000; Fax: (216) 795-7007
sgordon@clevelandplayhouse.com
www.clevelandplayhouse.com
Est. 1995. Reading series of new plays.
Assistance: $1,000 stipend, room/
board, travel. Response Time: 6 mos.
**Application.** What to Submit: query,
synopsis, 10-pg sample, SASE. Author
Must Be: a resident of Ohio. Material
Must Be: unoptioned, unproduced.
How To Submit: agent.

**FutureFest**
1301 E. Siebenthaler Ave.,
Dayton, OH 45414
Fran Pesch

Tel: (937) 424-8477 ext. 101
dp_futurefest@yahoo.com
/www.daytonplayhouse.org
> Est. 1990. Adjudicated July festival of
> new work with 3 full productions and
> 3 staged readings. Frequency: annual.
> Deadline from August 1st to October
> 31st, 2010. Please see website for more
> details. Style: no musical, no childrens
> theater. **Application.** What To Submit:
> synopsis, full script, submissions
> not returned. Material Must Be:
> unoptioned, unpublished, unproduced,
> longer than 75 minutes. Opportunity/
> Award: $1, 000, production, reading.
> Deadline: Oct. 31, 2010.

**Genesis Festival**
P.O. Box 238, 7 Livingston Ave.,
New Brunswick, NJ 8901
Marshall Jones
Tel: (732) 545-8100; Fax: (732) 907-1864
info@crossroadstheatrecompany.org
www.crossroadstheatrecompany.org
> Frequency: annual. **Application.** What
> to Submit: query letter (note theme
> addressed), synopsis, 30-pg writing
> sample, bio. Opportunity/Award:
> reading. How To Submit: unsolicited.
> Deadline: Dec. 31, 2010.

**Gettysburg College One-Act Festival**
300 N. Washington St., Box 428,
Gettysburg, PA 17325
Chris Kauffman
www.gettysburg.edu
> Assistance: room, travel. Frequency:
> annual. Opportunity/Award:
> production. **Application.** How To
> Submit: email. Deadline: Sept. 1, 2010.

**Golden Thread Festival**
131 10th St., San Francisco, CA 94103
Torange Yeghiazarian
Tel: (415) 626-4061; Fax: (415) 626-1138
www.goldenthread.org
> Est. 1996. Assistance: $100 stipend.
> Frequency: annual. Length: 10-
> 40 minutes. **Application.** What to
> Submit: full script, submissions not
> returned. Deadline: Mar. 1, 2010.

**Inspirato Festival**
124 Broadway Ave., Ste. 112,
Toronto, Ontario M4P-1V8 Canada
Dominik Loncar
Tel: (416) 832-222
inspirato@ca.inter.net
www.inspiratofestival.ca
> What to Submit: Ten-minute plays
> based on a theme (see website). Author
> Must Be: Any nationality - submitted
> in English only. Material Must
> Be: Emailed. Opportunity/Award:
> Production. **Application.** How To
> Submit: as per instructions on website.
> Deadline: Dec. 31, 2010.

**International Mystery Writers' Festival**
101 Daviess St., Owensboro, KY 42303
Kimberly Johnson
Tel: (270) 687-2770
kjohnson@riverparkcenter.org
www.newmysteries.org
> Est. 2007. Accepts Plays, Teleplays
> or Short Screenplays of Mystery/
> Thriller genre. Assistance: Travel
> assistance varies. Frequency: annual.
> Response Time: 3 months. Style:
> Mysteries/Thrillers only. Adaptation,
> drama. **Application.** What To Submit:
> full script, submission not returned.
> Material Must Be: unproduced.
> Opportunity/Award: $1,000-$10,000.
> How To Submit: unsolicited. Deadline:
> Nov. 30, 2010.

**Irish Arts Festival**
1061 N. Broadway, Yonkers, NY 10701
Louisa Burns-Bisogno
Tel: (914) 964-8272
taracircle@aol.com
www.taracircle.org
> Festival of readings in Sept.
> **Application.** What to Submit: full
> script, submissions returned with
> SASE. Material Must Be: unoptioned,
> unpublished, unproduced. How To
> Submit: unsolicited.

**Jewish Ensemble Theater Festival of
New Plays**
6600 W. Maple Rd.,
West Bloomfield, MI 48322

Christopher Bremer
Tel: (248) 788-2900; Fax: (248) 788-5160
c.bremer@jettheatre.org
www.jettheatre.org
> Est. 1989. Chris Bremer (Managing
> Dir). Style: English only - all styles.
> **Application.** What To Submit: full
> script, SASE. Material Must Be: Cast
> limited to 8. Opportunity/Award: $100,
> reading if selected. How To Submit:
> hard copy by mail. Deadline: Aug. 1st
> each year.

**The Jungle Theater**
2951 Lyndale Ave. S.,
Minneapolis, MN 55408
Buffy Sedlachek
Tel: (612) 822-4002
buffy@jungletheater.com
www.jungletheater.com
> Frequency: annual. Response Time: 8
> mos. Style: no musical. **Application.**
> What To Submit: synopsis, sample.
> Author Must Be: age 21 or older.

**Kitchen Dog Theater (KDT) New Works Festival**
3120 McKinney Ave., Dallas, TX 75204
Tina Parker
Tel: (214) 953-2258; Fax: (214) 953-1873
tina@kitchendogtheater.org
www.kitchendogtheater.org
> Est. 1990. Winner receives production,
> travel stipend, and royalty; 7 finalists
> receive reading. Please visit KDT
> website and read mission statement
> under FAQ's section to see what
> types of material would be of
> particular interest. Other artistis staff:
> Christopher Carlos (Co-Artistic Dir).
> Frequency: annual. Response Time:
> 8 mos. **Application.** What to Submit:
> full script, submissions not returned.
> How To Submit: full scripts by mail
> only - no copies or partial scripts
> accepted. Deadline: Jan. 1, 2010.

**Lark Play Development Center: Playwrights' Week**
939 8th Ave., #301, New York, NY 10019
Andrea Hiebler
Tel: (212) 246-2676 ext. 37

andreah@larktheatre.org
www.larktheatre.org
> The first step in development at the
> Lark is Playwrights' Week, a Sep fest
> of public readings with script in-hand.
> Frequency: annual. Response Time:
> 9 mos. **Application.** What to Submit:
> application, full script (1 entry/author).
> Author Must Be: age 18 or older.
> How to Submit: application online.
> Deadline: Nov. 15, 2010.

**Last Frontier Theatre Conference**
Box 97, Valdez, AK 99686
Dawson Moore
Tel: (907) 834-1614; Fax: (907) 834-1611
dmoore@pwscc.edu
www.pwscc.edu/conference
> Est. 1993. Application free. See
> website for conference fees. Response
> Time: by 3/15/2010. Style: comedy,
> drama. **Application.** What To Submit:
> synopsis, full script. Material Must
> Be: unproduced. Opportunity/Award:
> reading. How To Submit: unsolicited.
> Deadline: Jan. 15, 2010.

**Lavender Footlights Festival**
P.O. Box 942107, Miami, FL 33194
Ryan Capiro
Tel: (305) 433-8111; Fax: (305) 672-7818
Ryan@Lavenderfootlights.org
www.lavenderfootlights.org
> Est. 2000. Fest of readings with
> gay and lesbian themes. Frequency:
> annual. See website for details. Style:
> comedy, drama, musical. **Application.**
> What To Submit: synopsis, full script,
> SASE. Material Must Be: unproduced
> in FL. Opportunity/Award: reading.
> How To Submit: Online, mail.
> Deadline: Dec. 1, 2010.

**Little Festival of the Unexpected**
Box 1458, Portland, ME 4104
Daniel Burson
Tel: (207) 774-1043; Fax: (207) 774-0576
dburson@portlandstage.com
www.portlandstage.com
> Est. 1989. 1-wk fest of new plays with
> writers developing work thru staged
> readings. Assistance: $300 stipend.

Frequency: annual. Production: cast limit 8. Style: adaptation, comedy, drama. **Application.** What To Submit: query, synopsis, 10-pg sample. Material Must Be: unoptioned, unpublished, unproduced. How To Submit: mail hardcopy of 10-pg sample. Deadline: Dec. 31, 2010.

**Marathon of One-Act Plays**
549 W. 52nd St., New York, NY 10019
Tel: (212) 247-4982
rowan@ensemblestudiotheatre.org
www.ensemblestudiotheatre.org
Est. 1977. Annual fest in May-June. Production: cast of up to 6, simple. Response Time: 6-9 months. Style: comedy, drama. **Application.** What To Submit: full script, SASE. Material Must Be: unoptioned, unpublished, professionally unproduced in NYC. Opportunity/Award: publication, reading. How To Submit: unsolicited. Deadline: Dec. 1, 2010.

**National Asian American Theatre Festival (NAATF)**
520 8th Ave., #309, New York, NY 10018
Est. 2007. Two weeks of Asian American theaters and performers in venues around NYC.

**National Black Theatre Festival**
610 Coliseum Dr.,
Winston-Salem, NC 27106
Larry Leon Hamlin
nbtf@bellsouth.net
www.nbtf.org
Est. 1989. Biennial (odd years) fest in Aug of productions about the Black experience. **Application.** What to Submit: full script (2 copies, 3-hole punched), cast and scene breakdown.

**New Jersey Playwrights Festival of New Plays**
Box 1663, Bloomfield, NJ 07003
Lenny Bart
Tel: (973) 259-9187; Fax: (973) 259-9188
info@12mileswest.org
www.12mileswest.org

Annual fest of plays by NJ playwrights. Production: cast of 2-7, unit set. Response Time: 1 yr. **Application.** What to Submit: synopsis, full script (3 copies), cast breakdown, SASE. Author Must Be: resident of NJ.

**New Professional Theatre Writers Festival**
229 W. 42nd St., #501,
New York, NY 10036
Mark D. Wood
Tel: (212) 398-2666; Fax: (212) 398-2924
newprof@aol.com
www.newprofessionaltheatre.com
Est. 1991. Annual fest of work by African-Americans, Asians, and Latinos. Also business seminars, mentoring, and 2-wk residencies. Assistance: $1,000. **Application.** What to Submit: full script, musical w/audio, submissions not returned. Material Must Be: unoptioned, unpublished, unproduced, original. How To Submit: see website. Deadline: June 1, 2010.

**New South Play Festival**
Box 5376, Atlanta, GA 31107
J. Caleb Boyd
Tel: (404) 523-1477 ext. 113
literary@horizontheatre.com
www.horizontheatre.com
Est. 1997. Summer fest of developmental workshops, readings and productions, showcasing contemporary southern writers, settings and themes. Frequency: annual. Production: cast limit 8. Response Time: 6 mos. **Application.** What to Submit: query, 10 page sample, SASE. Opportunity/Award: production, reading.

**New Women Playwright's Festival**
Box 518, Tampa, FL 33601
Karla Hartley
www.tampacenter.com

**New York City 15-Minute Play Fest**
145 W. 46th St., Fl. 3,
New York, NY 10036

Elizabeth Keefe
Tel: (212) 869-9809
liz@americanglobe.org
www.americanglobe.org
> Est. 1993. 2-wk fest in May of 4-5
> new plays each night under Equity
> Showcase. Frequency: annual.
> Production: cast of 2-10, no set.
> Response Time: 2 mos. **Application.**
> What to Submit: full script, SASE.
> Material Must Be: unpublished.
> Opportunity/Award: $100 award, $25
> royalty. Deadline: Dec. 15, 2010.

**New York Television Festival**
22 W. 19th St. Suite 5K,
New York, NY 10011
Ned Canty
Tel: (212) 675-5840
scriptcontest@nytvf.com
www.nytvf.com
> See website for full details. Style:
> Comedy. What To Submit: Full
> Script. Author Must Be: 18. Material
> Must Be: not optioned, not produced,
> not published. Opportunity/Award:
> Development deal with Fox. Deadline:
> check website.

**Pegasus Players Young Playwrights Festival**
1145 W. Wilson Ave., Chicago, IL 60640
Christopher Schram
Tel: (773) 878-9761; Fax: (773) 271-8057
info@pegasusplayers.org
www.pegasusplayers.org
> Frequency: annual. Style: musical.
> **Application.** What To Submit:
> query letter (note theme addressed),
> submissions returned with SASE.
> Author Must Be: age 11-19, resident
> of Chicago. Opportunity/Award: $250
> 1st prize, $50 to runners-up, possible
> future production, reading. How To
> Submit: unsolicited.

**Penn State New Musical Theatre Festival**
PSU School of Theatre, 103 Arts Bldg.,
University Park, PA 16801
Raymond Sage
Tel: (814) 863-5999

www.psunewmusicals.org
> Est. 2006. Two week festival, 2 or
> more musicals in 29 hour equity
> format. Production: ages 18-25.
> Style: musical. **Application.** What
> To Submit: script, recording, or any
> pertinent materials. Opportunity/
> Award: cash honorarium. How To
> Submit: mail.

**Penobscot Theatre**
131 Main Street, Bangor, ME 04401
Scott RC Levy
Tel: (207) 947-6618
info@penobscottheatre.org
www.penobscottheatre.org
> 2 wk. New Play Fest. featuring
> readings & workshops. Response
> Time: works selected notified by
> 5/1/09. **Application.** What to Submit:
> cover letter stating how this festival
> will help in the development of the
> piece; 10-minutes, one-acts, and/or
> full-length plays and musicals with
> cover letter stating how this festival
> will help in the development of the
> piece. Material Must Be: unpublished,
> unproduced. Deadline: Feb. 14, 2010.

**Pick of the Vine**
2449 N. Park Blvd., Santa Ana, CA 92706
Mark Piatelli
mark@littlefish.org
www.littlefishtheatre.org
> Fest of one-acts and shorts in Jan-Feb.
> Production: cast limit 6, minimal set.
> Response Time: 1 mo. **Application.**
> How To Submit: unsolicited, email.
> Deadline: Aug. 15, 2010.

**Playfest - Harriett Lake Festival of New Plays**
812 E. Rollins St., #100, Orlando, FL 32803
Patrick Flick
Fax: (407) 447-1701
patrickf@orlandoshakes.org
www.orlandoshakes.org
> Est. 1989. 10 new plays receive
> readings, 2-3 developmental in Festival
> of new plays. Assistance: stipend,
> room/board, travel, actors, directors,
> rehearsal time, access to copiers, email,

etc., while on site. **Application.** What to Submit: 1-pg synopsis (no longer than 200 words), 10-pg sample, bio of writer, casting including doubling, name, address, email on the cover page of the submission. Please see website for exact or add'l submission reqs. Material Must Be: unpublished, suitable to our mission. Please see website. Deadline: Aug. 1, 2010.

### Political Theatre Festival
209 W. Page St., #208, St. Paul, MN 55107
Christina Akers
Tel: (651) 224-8806
info@teatrodelpueblo.org
www.teatrodelpueblo.org
Est. 2001. One-acts about political issues of Latino identity. Assistance: stipend. Production: cast limit 3, up to 3 set pieces. Style: interactive encouraged. **Application.** What To Submit: synopsis, full script, resume/bio, submissions not returned. Material Must Be: in English or Spanish. Opportunity/Award: production, reading. Deadline: Aug. 1, 2010.

### Premiere Stages Play Festival
Hutchinson Hall, 1000 Morris Ave., Union, NJ 07083
John Wooten
www.kean.edu/premierestages
Est. 2004. Annual fest for playwrights born or living in NJ, CT, NY, PA. Three public readings in Apr, full Equity production of winner in July. Production: cast limit 8. Style: comedy, drama. **Application.** What To Submit: synopsis, 8-pg sample, cast list, production history, bio. Full script through agent only. Author Must Be: resident of NY, NJ, CT, or PA. Material Must Be: unoptioned, unpublished, unproduced. Opportunity/Award: $2,000 1st, $750 2nd, $500 3rd, reading. Deadline: Jan. 15. 2010.

### Samuel French, Inc. Off-Off-Broadway Short-Play Festival
45 W. 25 St., New York, NY 10010
Kenneth Dingledine
Tel: (212) 206-8990; Fax: (202) 206-1429
oobfestival@samuelfrench.com
www.samuelfrench.com
Est. 1976. Summer 1-wk fest in NYC. 40 shows. 6 finalists chosen for publication and representation by Samuel French. Frequency: annual. **Application.** What to Submit: application, script. Material Must Be: unpublished. Opportunity/Award: publication. How To Submit: thru producing sponsor.

### San Francisco Fringe Festival (SFFF)
156 Eddy St., San Francisco, CA 94102
Christina Augello

### Scratch Pad Festival
2911 Centenary Blvd.,
Shreveport, LA 71134
Don Hooper
Tel: (318) 869-5074; Fax: (318) 869-5760
dhooper@centenary.edu
www.centenary.edu/theatre
Est. 2006. Frequency: annual. Production: age 12-40, cast of 2-20 Response Time: by early fall. **Application.** What to Submit: synopsis, 10-pg sample, submissions not returned. Material Must Be: unoptioned, unproduced. Opportunity/Award: Production and/or reading.

### Short Attention Span PlayFEST
5261 Whitsett Ave. #20,
Valley Village, CA 91607
Kimberly Davis Basso
Tel: (978) 667-0550
kdb@atlantisplaymakers.com
www.atlantisplaymakers.com
Est. 1998. Frequency: annual. See website for complete submission guidelines. Style: comedy, drama. What To Submit: full script, submissions not returned. Material Must Be: unpublished, unproduced. Opportunity/Award: honorarium, audience award. How To Submit: mail, email. Deadline: Mar. 15, 2010.

**Southern Appalachian Playwrights'
Conference**
Box 1720, Mars Hill, NC 28754
Rob Miller
Tel: (828) 689-1384; Fax: (828) 689-1272
sart@mhc.edu
www.sartplays.org
> Est. 1981. Readings & critique of
> 5-6 plays in 3-day conference at
> Mars Hill Coll. Assistance: N/C.
> Frequency: Annually, one-time
> award. Production: cast, orchestra,
> full. Response Time: Aug/Sept
> announcement. Style: Comedy,
> Drama, Musical, no translation, no
> adaptations. **Application.** What To
> Submit: 2 copies of full script; specific
> guidelines by request or on sartplays.
> org/guidelines.htm. Material Must
> Be: Not Published, unproduced,
> amatuer produced scripts are eligible.
> Opportunity/Award: $1,000 award,
> possible future production. How To
> Submit: unsolicited, professional
> recommendation, agent. Deadline:
> Oct. 31, 2010.

**Summer Play Festival (SPF)**
Box 778, New York, NY 10108
Sarah Bagley
Tel: (212) 279-4040; Fax: (212) 297-4041
info@spfnyc.com
www.spfnyc.com
> Est. 2003. Production: cast
> limit 10. Style: no translation or
> adaptation. **Application.** What
> To Submit: application, full script
> (w/ pg numbers). Author Must Be:
> unproduced by NYC over 99 seats.
> How To Submit: email (pdf, doc, rtf).
> Deadline: Nov. 1, 2010.

**Summer Playwrights Festival**
762 Fulton St., San Francisco, CA 94102
RH Johnson
joesdreamseries@yahoo.com
Alabama Shakespeare Festival
1 Festival Dr., Montgomery, AL 36117
Nancy Rominger
Tel: (334) 271-5300; Fax: (334) 271-5348
www.asf.net
> Est. 1972. Souther Writers' Project
> develops new plays with Southern

or African-American themes by
Southern or African-American
writers. **Application.** How To Submit:
unsolicited for Southern Writers
Project only, all else agent.

**Summer Shorts**
444 Brickell Ave., #229, Miami, FL 33131
Tel: (305) 755-9401; Fax: (305) 755-9404
www.citytheatre.com
> Est. 1996. Fest of shorts in Jun-
> Jul, incl. up to 20 productions on
> Mainstage and 10-20 for Festival
> Series readings. Scripts also
> considered for Shorts Cuts school
> tours. Production: age 20-70, cast of
> 8-10, no orchestra, unit set. What to
> Submit: full script, audio. Opportunity/
> Award: royalty. **Application.** How
> To Submit: thru Actors Theater of
> Louisville 10-Min Fest. Deadline:
> Nov. 1, 2010.

**Theatre Building Chicago**
1225 W. Belmont Ave., Chicago, IL 60657
Allan Chambers
Tel: (773) 929-7367 ext. 222
Fax: (773) 327-1404
jsparks@theatrebuildingchicago.org
www.theatrebuildingchicago.org
> Est. 1984. 2-day Aug fest with Equity
> and non-Equity actors in readings of 8
> full-length musicals. Works not ready
> for fest are considered for development
> series. Theatre for Young Audiences
> programming must be 1-hour
> maximum, 5 actors maximum; age
> appropriate for ages 3-7. Frequency:
> annual. Production: cast limit 16,
> piano only, no set. Response Time:
> 3 mos. Style: musical. **Application.**
> What To Submit: application,
> submissions not returned. Material
> Must Be: considered work-in-progress.
> Opportunity/Award: reading. How To
> Submit: professional recommendation.
> Deadline: Oct. 1, 2010.

**Theatre Three [NY] One-Act Play
Festival**
Box 512, 412 Main St.,
Port Jefferson, NY 11777
Jeffrey Sanzel

Tel: (631) 928-9202; Fax: (631) 928-9120
www.theatrethree.com
Est. 1969. Annual festival of one-act plays in March. Production: 2-8, minimal set. Response Time: 8 mos. Style: comedy, drama, experimental. **Application.** What To Submit: full script, visit website for detailed guidelines, SASE. Material Must Be: unproduced. Opportunity/Award: $70. Deadline: Sept. 30, 2010.

## Vital Signs

2162 Broadway, Fl. 4, New York, New York 10024
scripts@vitaltheatre.org; http://www.vitaltheatre.org
Festival of new short plays.

## Women-at-Arms Festival

138 S. Oxford St., #5-C,
Brooklyn, NY 11217
Carrie Brewer
Tel: (718) 857-2751
info@ladycavaliers.org
www.ladycavaliers.org
10 plays given public readings in fall, 5 given full production in spring. Production: cast limit 5, minimal set. Material Must Be: unpublished, unproduced professionally. Opportunity/Award: 1st $500, production (5 finalists), reading.

## Womenkind Festival

Box 2668, Times Sq. Sta.,
New York, NY 10108
Emma Palzere-Rae
Tel: (212) 875-7079
lovearmd@aol.com
www.nyct.net/cosmicleopard
Festival of self-produced, self contained one-woman shows celebrating women's history month. Frequency: biennial. Production: cast of 1 woman. Response Time: 5/15/04. Style: all styles. **Application.** What To Submit: query letter (note theme addressed). How To Submit: unsolicited.

## Woodstock Fringe

Box 157, Lake Hill, NY 12448
Wallace Norman
Tel: (845) 810-0123; Fax: (212) 602-0061
wnorman@woodstockfringe.org
www.woodstockfringe.org
Est. 2003. Monthlong fest of theater and song at Byrdcliffe Arts Colony. Assistance: $250 stipend, travel. Frequency: annual. Production: cast of 2-6. Response Time: 6 mos. **Application.** What to Submit: query, synopsis, 15-pg sample, SASE. Opportunity/Award: 6% royalty, $300 minimum for full-length works. How To Submit: See http://www.woodstockfringe.org/participate.htm for submission guidelines.

## Year-End Series (YES) New Play Festival

NKU, FA228,
Highland Heights, KY 41099
Sandra Forman
Tel: (859) 572-6303; Fax: (859) 572-6057
forman@nku.edu
www.nku.edu/~theatre
Est. 1983. Biennial (odd yrs) fest in April of 3 new works receive full productions. Playwrights flown in for final week of rehearsals and opening night. Style: comedy, drama, musical. **Application.** What To Submit: full script, SASE. Material Must Be: unpublished, unproduced. Opportunity/Award: $500, production. Deadline: Nov. 1, 2010.

## CONFERENCES AND FESTIVALS (*FEE CHARGED*)

**Actors' Playhouse National Children's Theatre Festival**
280 Miracle Mile, Coral Gables, FL 33134
Earl Maulding
Tel: (305) 444-9293 ext. 615
Fax: (305) 444-4181
maulding@actorsplayhouse.org
www.actorsplayhouse.org
> Est. 1994. Annual 4-day fest. Winning show runs 4-6 wks. Non-Equity. Assistance: possible travel. Production: cast limit 8, touring set. Style: musical. **Application.** What To Submit: $500, production. Material Must Be: unpublished, Opportunity/Award: $500, production. How To Submit: See Call to Competition on website. Submission/Application Fee: $10. Deadline: Apr. 1, 2010.

**American College Theater Festival (ACTF)**
Kennedy Center, Washington, DC 20566
Susan Shaffer
kcactf@kennedy-center.org
www.KC/ACTF.org
> Est. 1969. National fest of student productions, selected from regional college fests. Regional deadlines vary. Michael Kanin (1910-93) arranged for awards for the national fest (see website). What to Submit: application, 1-pg synopsis, full script. Author Must Be: college student. Material Must Be: original. Submission/Application Fee: $350. Deadline: Dec. 1, 2010.

**Ashland New Plays Festival**
Box 453, Ashland, OR
Dolores Marx
Tel: (541) 488-7995
info@AshlandNewPlays.org
www.ashlandnewplays.org
> Est. 1992. Fest in Oct. with 12 hrs rehearsal for 2 unstaged readings with professional director and actors (often from Oregon Shakespeare Fest). Playwrights may live outside the USA, but scripts must speak to a US-based audience. Workshops offered during fest. Assistance: $500 stipend, room (1 wk). Frequency: annual. Production: cast limit 8. Response Time: by 8/2010. Style: comedy, drama, mystery, suspense. **Application.** What To Submit: query, application, synopsis, full script, bio, casting list. Material Must Be: unpublished, unproduced, Opportunity/Award: reading, $500. Submission/Application Fee: $15. Deadline: Jan. 15, 2010.

**Baltimore Playwrights Festival**
Box 38537, Baltimore, MD 21231
Miriam Bazensky
chairman@baltimoreplaywrightsfestival.org
www.baltimoreplaywrightsfestival.com
> Est. 1981. Plays chosen by 1 of 6 companies for 3-wk summer production. Selected public readings given thru year. Frequency: annual. Style: Full length/one acts. **Application.** What To Submit: synopsis, full script (3 copies). Author Must Be: current or former resident or employee in MD. Material Must Be: unpublished, unproduced, Opportunity/Award: up to $250, honoraria up to $100. How To Submit: email. see website for details. Submission/Application Fee: $10. Deadline: April 1st and September 30th, 2010.

**Bay Area Playwrights Festival (BAPF)**
1616 16th Street, Suite 350,
San Francisco, CA 94103
Jonathan Spector
Tel: (415) 626-2176
literary@playwrightsfoundation.org
www.playwrightsfoundation.org
> Est. 1976. BAPF is 2-wk Jul fest of 5-6 full-length plays by US writers, given rehearsal and 2 readings (1 wk apart for rewrites) before production. Assistance: stipend, room/board, travel. Frequency: annual. Response Time: 4 mos. Style: comedy, drama.

**Application.** What To Submit: query, full script, submissions not returned. Author Must Be: US resident. Material Must Be: unproduced, original, in English, Opportunity/Award: workshopped readings. How To Submit: mail. Submission/Application Fee: $20. Deadline: Nov. 30, 2010.

**Black Box New Play Festival**
199 14th St., Brooklyn, NY 11215
Heather S. Curran
info@galleryplayers.com
www.galleryplayers.com
Est. 1996. AEA/Non-AEA showcase. 3 week run of show plus workshop. Style: comedy, drama, no musical, no translation. **Application.** What To Submit: synopsis, full script, resume, submissions not returned. Author Must Be: resident of CT, NJ, NY. Material Must Be: unproduced, readings ok, Opportunity/Award: production. How To Submit: unsolicited. Submission/Application Fee: $10. Deadline: Nov. 1, 2010.

**Cincinnati Fringe Festival**
1120 Jackson St., Cincinnati, OH 45202
Eric Vosmeier
Tel: (513) 421-3235
fringesubmissions@knowtheatre.com
www.knowtheatre.com
www.cincyfringe.com
Est. 2003. Fringe Festival occurs annually late May/early June. See applications online at cincyfringe.com for specifics. Frequency: annual. Response Time: 3 mos. Style: all styles. **Application.** What To Submit: application, materials will not be returned. Material Must Be: 90 minutes or less, Opportunity/Award: split box offc. How To Submit: unsolicited. Submission/Application Fee: $35. Deadline: Dec. 17, 2010.

**Collaboraction: Sketchbook Festival**
437 N. Wolcott, #201, Chicago, IL 60622
Anthony Moseley
www.collaboraction.typepad.com
Annual festival of short plays. Check website for details. Style: audience

participation. **Application.** What To Submit: application, full script. Material Must Be: unproduced. How To Submit: email (rtf or doc only). Submission/Application Fee: $10. Deadline: Dec. 15, 2010.

**Edinburgh Festival Fringe**
180 High St., Edinburgh, Scotland
Paul Gudgin
Tel: 44-131-226-0026
admin@edfringe.com
/www.edfringe.com
Est. 1947. To participate, you need to organize every aspect of bringing your production to Edinburgh. Fees: £10 info sub., £352.50/entry office fee.

**Fire Rose Prods. 10-Min. Play Festival**
11240 Magnolia Blvd. #204, North Hollywood, CA 91601
Kaz Matamura
Tel: (818) 760-4155
info@fireroseproductions.com
www.fireroseproductions.com
Est. 2000. Equity 99-seat. Frequency: annual. Response Time: 3 mos. **Application.** What to Submit: full script, submissions not returned. Submission/Application Fee: $5.00. Deadline: Mar. 31 and Sept. 30, 2010.

**GAYFEST NYC**
1 River Pl., #917, New York, NY 10036
Bruce Robert Harris
Tel: (212) 868-5570; Fax: (212) 868-3196
www.gayfestnyc.com
Monthlong fest (May-June) of new works by gay authors or with gay-friendly subjects, incl. three productions (2 plays, 1 musical) and reading series of works-in-progress, from hard-hitting dramas to jewel-box musicals. Production: cast limit 10, up to 3 settings. Response Time: 4 mos. Style: drama, musical theatre. **Application.** What To Submit: synopsis, full script (2 copies), audio, bio, character breakdown, SASE. Material Must Be: unoptioned, unpublished, unproduced, original, Opportunity/Award: $100 stipend. How To Submit: unsolicited.

Submission/Application Fee: $20.
Deadline: Oct. 31, 2010.

**Juneteenth Legacy Theatre**
3723 Bashford Ave., Louisville, KY 40218
Kristi Papailler
juneteenthlegacy@aol.com
www.juneteenthlegacytheatre.com
    Est. 1999. Staged readings on African-
    American experience in 19th-20th
    centuries, incl. Harlem Renaissance,
    Caribbean/Native American
    influences, contemporary youth, and
    new images of women. Send 3 copies
    of submissions to KY address above,
    send 1 copy w/entry fee to JLT, 605
    Water St., #21-B, New York, NY
    10002. Style: adaptation, comedy,
    drama. **Application.** What To Submit:
    query, full script (4 copies: send 3 to
    KY, 1 to NY), SASE, Opportunity/
    Award: reading. Submission/
    Application Fee: $15. Deadline: Mar.
    15, 2010.

**Long Beach Playhouse New Works
Festival**
5021 East Anaheim St.,
Long Beach, CA 90804
Jo Black-Jacob
Tel: (562) 494-1014 ext. 507
Fax: (562) 961-8616
joblack@dslextreme.com
www.lbph.com
    Est. 1989. Fest of 4 new plays in
    staged readings (Spring) plus possible
    consideration of a world premiere
    prod. of previous year's winner.
    Staff: Joan VanHooten, Executive
    Director LBPH x 503. Frequency:
    annual. Production: cast limit 10,
    limited set. Response Time: 3 mos
    after festival concludes. Style: no
    musical. **Application.** What To
    Submit: application, synopsis, full
    script, cast list, SASE. Material Must
    Be: unproduced, Opportunity/Award:
    $100 reading $300 full production.
    Submission/Application Fee: $10.
    Deadline: scripts accepted all year
    round; plays received by September

30th will be considered for the
following Spring Festival.

**Lorna Littleway's Juneteenth Jamboree
of New Plays**
605 Water St. #21B, New York, NY 10002
Lorna Littleway
juneteenthlegacy@aol.com
www.juneteethlegacytheater.com
    Est. 1990 Juneteeth Jamboree, Hosted
    by Actors Theatre, presents readings
    for one preformance of plays about
    African-American experience and its
    legacy during first three weekends in
    June. Assistance: $75 travel. Response
    Time: 3-6 months. Style: adaptation,
    comedy, drama. **Application.** What
    To Submit: submissions returned with
    SASE, Opportunity/Award: reading.
    How To Submit: unsolicited, 4 copies.
    Fees: $15 application.

**National Music Theater Conference
(OMTC)**
305 Great Neck Rd., Waterford, CT 06385
Paulette Haupt
Tel: (860) 443-5378 ext. 301
litoffice@theoneill.org
www.theoneill.org
    Est. 1978. Artistic Director, Paulette
    Haupt. 2-3 wk residency (Jul-Aug),
    with rehearsal and in-hand public
    readings. Assistance: stipend.
    Frequency: annual. Production: no
    orchestra, no set. Style: musical.
    **Application.** What To Submit:
    application, see website. Material
    Must Be: unproduced, Opportunity/
    Award: professional workshop, public
    reading. How To Submit: application
    guidelines available at www. theoneill.
    org. Submission/Application Fee: $35.
    Deadline: Dec. 1, 2010.

**National Playwrights Conference
(OPC)**
The O'Neill, 305 Great Neck Rd.,
Waterford, CT 06385
Martin Kettling
Tel: (860) 443-5378 ext. 227
litoffice@theoneill.org
www.oneill.org

Est. 1964. Artistic Director, Wendy C. Goldberg. Month residency (Jun-Jul), incl. 4-day workshop and 2 in-hand readings with professional actors and directors. Assistance: $1,000 stipend, room/board, travel. Frequency: annual. **Application.** What to Submit: application, full script (3 copies). Material Must Be: unproduced, Opportunity/Award: Professional Workshop, Public Reading. How To Submit: application @ www.theoneill.org. Submission/Application Fee: $35. Deadline: Oct. 2010.

**Old Opera House Theatre Company**
**New Voice Play Festival**
204 N. George St.,
Charles Town, WV 25414
Tel: (304) 752-4420
ooh@oldoperahouse.org
www.oldoperahouse.org
Est. 2001. Call or email for application and deadlines. One act play festival-plays 10 to 40 minutes in length. Opportunity/Award: $250 plus performance for first place, $100 plus performance for second place and $50 plus staged reading for third place. Submission/Application Fee: $10 per playwright. Deadline: Mar. 1, 2010.

**Perishable Theatre Women's**
**Playwriting Festival**
Box 23132, Providence, RI 02903
Tel: (401) 331-2695; Fax: (401) 331-7811
wpf@perishable.org
www.perishable.org
Fall festival. Up to 3 winners produced in mainstage season. Publication in anthology. Assistance: travel, accommodation. Frequency: biennial. Style: all styles. **Application.** What To Submit: full script (up to 2 entries), cast and scene breakdown, submissions returned with SASE. Author Must Be: female. Material Must Be: unoptioned, unproduced, Opportunity/Award: $500 award, possible future production, publication. How To Submit:

unsolicited. Submission/Application Fee: $10. Deadline: Jan. 15, 2010.

**Pittsburgh New Works Festival**
**(PNWF)**
Box 42419, Pittsburgh, PA 15203
Lora Oxenreiter
Tel: (412) 881-6888
info@pittsburghnewworks.org
www.pittsburghnewworks.org
Est. 1991. Non-Equity 6-wk fest mid-August thru September, 6 staged readings, 12 staged productions, 18 production companies under fest umbrella. Frequency: annual. Production: age 12 and up, cast limit 8, simple set, 40 minute limit. Style: Novel, contemporary one acts, no musical. **Application.** What To Submit: synopsis, 1 hard copy, electronic submission to email address, SASE, cover letter with bio and contact information. Material Must Be: unproduced, Opportunity/Award: $500 to (voted) best play, $50 to playwrights of produced scripts. Submission/Application Fee: $15. Deadline: Apr. 1, 2010.

**Raymond J. Flores Short Play Festival**
5 E. 22nd St., #9-K, New York, NY 10010
Carlos Jerome
Tel: (212) 673-9187
info@aroundtheblock.org
www.aroundtheblock.org
Est. 2004. Part of annual Urban Arts Fest is its Raymond J. Flores Short Play Competition & Reading Series. Staff: Gloria Zelaya, Louis Vuolo (Co-dir, Theater Arts).Theme: Life and aspirations in New York City. For Spanish and Chinese plays, we would appreciate your including a one-paragraph synopsis in English, otherwise we shall assign one of our judges to write such a synopsis. Frequency: annual. Style: no musical. **Application.** What To Submit: application, full script (2 copies, unless e-mailed), 1-paragraph bio. Author Must Be: owner of all production and publishing rights. Material Must

Be: in English, Spanish or Chinese, Opportunity/Award: $50, reading. How To Submit: Email, postal mail or hand delivery. Submission/Application Fee: $5. Deadline: Nov. 30, 2010.

**Seven Devils Playwrights Conference**
343 E. 30th St., #19-J,
New York, NY 10016
Jeni Mahoney
jeni@idtheater.org
www.idtheater.org
Est. 2001. Equity 2-wk play development conference in McCall, ID, ending w/fully staged readings of new plays. **Application.** What to Submit: please see website. Material Must Be: unproduced. How To Submit: please see website. Submission/Application Fee: $5. Deadline: Dec. 31, 2010.

**ShowOff! Playwriting Festival**
31776 El Camino Real,
San Juan Capistrano, CA 92675
Tom Scott
Tel: (949) 248-0808
box_office@sbcglobal.net
www.caminorealplayhouse.org
Est. 1993. Frequency: annual. Response Time: 3 mos. Show in January. Style: No musicals or children's plays. **Application.** What To Submit: full script, submissions not returned. See website for submission details. Material Must Be: unpublished. Submission/Application Fee: $10. Deadline: Oct. 15, 2010.

**Tennessee Williams/New Orleans Literary Festival**
938 Lafayette St., #514,
New Orleans, LA 70113
Laura Miller
Tel: (504) 581-1144; Fax: (504) 581-3270
info@tennesseewilliams.net
www.tennesseewilliams.net
Frequency: annual. Production: small, minimal. Opportunity/Award: $1,500, reading followed by production. **Application.** How To Submit: www. tennesseewilliams.net/contest.

Submission/Application Fee: $25. Deadline: Nov. 1, 2010.

**Theater Resources Unlimited (TRU)/ TRU Voices**
Players Theater, 115 MacDougal St.,
New York, NY 10012
Bob Ost
Tel: (212) 714-7628; Fax: (212) 864-6301
trunltd@aol.com
www.truonline.org
Winter musical series (est. 1999) and spring play series (est. 1997) of 3-4 readings each. Prefer submissions from producers, but writers may submit and TRU will try to find a sponsoring producer. Frequency: annual. Production: cast limit 12 (with doubling). Response Time: 3 to 6 months. Style: Open to a range of work, from mainstream commercial to non-traditional. What To Submit: Application, plus 2 each: synopsis, letter of intention, full script, audio (CD preferred). No SASE (we do not return scripts unless requested). Material Must Be: No performances before a paying audience in the New York area. Opportunity/Award: TRU Voices New Plays and New Musicals Reading Series - AEA developmental staged readings with invited industry panel. How To Submit: Download application and guidelines from www.truonline.org or send an SASE to Theater Resources Unlimited/TRU Voices, 309 W. 104th Street, 1D, NYC NY 10025 (note: this is a different address than the one for script submissions). Submission/Application Fee: $25. Deadlines: Jan. 1, 2010 for plays, Aug. 31, 2010 for musicals (deadlines extended a week for submissions that have a producer attached).

**Trustus Playwrights' Festival**
Box 11721, Columbia, SC 29211
Sarah Hammond
Tel: (803) 254-9732; Fax: (803) 771-9153
trustus@trustus.org
www.trustus.org

Est. 1984. Staged reading in Aug.,
followed by 1-yr. development,
culminating in mainstage production.
Frequency: annual. Production: ages
15-55, cast limit 8, unit set. Response
Time: 3 mos. Style: comedy, drama.

**Application.** What To Submit:
application, synopsis, SASE. Material
Must Be: unproduced. Opportunity/
Award: $750, production, reading.
Submission/Application Fee: $15.
Deadline: Dec. 1, 2009 - Feb. 1, 2010.

# CONTESTS

**Anna Zornio Memorial Children's
Theatre Playwriting Award**
UNH Theatre/Dance Dept., PCAC,
30 Academic Way, Durham, NH 3824
Michael Wood
Tel: (603) 862-3038; Fax: (603) 862-0298
mike.wood@unh.edu
www.unh.edu/theatre-dance/zornio
Est. 1979. Quadrennial award for
original children's script, selected by
UNH Youth Drama Program. Students
and faculty produce premiere.
**Application.** What to Submit:
application, full script, audio, cast/tech
list, SASE. Author Must Be: resident
of US or Canada. Material Must Be:
unoptioned, unpublished, unproduced,
original. How To Submit: email.
Deadline: Mar. 2, 2012.

**Arena Stage Student Ten-Minute Play
Competition**
1101 6th St., SW, Washington, DC 20024

**Arthur W. Stone New Play Award**
Box 8608, Ruston, LA 71272
Louisiana Tech University
Tel: (318) 257-2711; Fax: (318) 257-4571
stoneplaywritingaward@yahoo.com
www.performingarts.latech.edu
Est. 2006. Assistance: room/board,
travel. Frequency: biennial. Opens for
submissions: Oct. 1, 2010. Production:
college age. Response Time: May
30, 2011. What to Submit: Text, bio,
synopsis, production history. Material
Must Be: full script, bio, synopsis,
production history. Opportunity/
Award: $500, plus production. How
To Submit: email (DOC, FDR, RTF).
Deadline: Mar. 1, 2011.

**Aurora Theatre Company: Global Age
Project**
2081 Addison St., Berkeley, CA 94704
Matthew Graham Smith
Tel: (510) 843-4042; Fax: (510) 843-4826
literary@auroratheatre.org
www.auroratheatre.org
Annual festival celebrating fresh
forward-looking visions of global
significance. Response time: 5 months.
**Application.** What to Submit: Full
script. Material Must Be: Unproduced.
Award/Grant/Stipend: $1,000 for 1st
place, reading (finalists). Deadline:
Aug. 1, 2010.

**Award Blue**
Box 445, Buckley, IL 60918
Steven Packard
Tel: (217) 394-2772
buntville@yahoo.fr
Est. 1999. Frequency: annual.
**Application.** What to Submit: full
script, bio. Author Must Be: IL high
school student. Opportunity/Award:
$200. Deadline: May 31, 2010.

**Babes With Blades - Joining Sword and
Pen**
3605 Clarence Ave., Berwyn, IL 60402
Amy E. Harmon
newplays@BabesWithBlades.org
www.babeswithblades.org
See website for updated info and
deadline. Contest est. 2005; company
est. 1997. Joining Sword & Pen:
bi-annual playwriting competition.
New Plays Development Program:
3-reading workshop cycle. 2 scripts
accepted per year. **Application.**
Material Must Be: Must include

fighting roles for women! Opportunity/
Award: $1,000 cash prize. How To
Submit: via mail or email - see website
for details.

**Baker's Plays High School Playwriting
Contest**
45 W. 25th Street #9,
New York, NY 10010
Roxane Heinze-Bradshaw
Tel: (212) 255-8085; Fax: (212) 627-7753
www.bakersplays.com
Est. 1989. For student plays, preferably
about HS experience. Plays must be
accompanied by complete application
form. Submissions accepted after
November 1, 2009. Notification of
awards in May 2010. **Application.**
What to Submit: full script, SASE,
application form. Author Must Be:
HS student. Material Must Be:
produced. Opportunity/Award: $500
1st, $250 2nd, $100 3rd, publication,
royalty. How To Submit: see website.
Deadline: Jan. 30, 2010.

**Beverly Hills Theatre Guild Julie
Harris Playwright Awards**
Box 148, Beverly Hills, CA 90213
Candace Coster
Tel: (310) 273-3390
www.beverlyhillstheatreguild.org
Frequency: annual. Style: comedy,
drama. **Application.** What To Submit:
query, application, full script. Author
Must Be: citizen or resident of US.
Material Must Be: unoptioned,
unpublished, unproduced, original, in
English. Opportunity/Award: $3,500
1st, $2,500 2nd, $1,500 3rd. Deadline:
Nov. 1, 2010.

**Beverly Hills California Musical
Theatre Award**
Box 148, Beverly Hills, California 90213
Patricia Mock
Tel: (310) 273-3390
www.beverlyhillstheatreguild.org
Style: musical. **Application.** What
To Submit: query, application, full
script, audio. Author Must Be: resident
of CA, citizen of US. Material Must

Be: unproduced, original, in English.
Opportunity/Award: $4,000. Deadline:
Nov. 15, 2010.

**Beverly Hills Theatre Guild Youth
Theatre Marilyn Hall Awards**
Box 148, Beverly Hills, CA 90213
Candace Coster
Tel: (310) 273-3390
www.beverlyhillstheatreguild.org
Frequency: annual. **Application.**
What to Submit: query, application,
full script. Author Must Be: citizen
or resident of US. Material Must Be:
unoptioned, unpublished, unproduced,
in English. Opportunity/Award: $700
1st, $300 2nd. Deadline: Feb. 28, 2010.

**Brevard Little Theatre New-Play
Competition**
P.O. Box 426, Brevard, NC 28712
Gene O'Hare
Tel: (828) 883-2751
Acara@citcom.net
www.brevardlittletheatre.com
No limit on submissions by one author.
Production: cast limit: 10 simple set.
**Application.** What to Submit: query,
full script, SASE. Material Must
Be: unproduced, original (staged
readings allowed). Opportunity/
Award: public production, personal
plaque, accommodations for two at
attendance. Deadline: July 31, 2010.

**Chicano/Latino Literary Prize in
Drama**
322 Humanities Hall, Irvine, CA 92697
Evelyn Flores
Tel: (949) 824-5443; Fax: (949) 824-4762
cllp@uci.edu
www.hnet.uci.edu
Est. 1974. The yearly call for entries is
genre specific, rotating through drama
(2010), novel (2011), short story (2012),
and poetry (2013). Assistance: travel.
Frequency: quadrennial. Style: all
styles. **Application.** What To Submit:
full script (3 copies). Author Must Be:
citizen or resident of US. Material
Must Be: unpublished, in Spanish or
English. Opportunity/Award: $1,000

1st prize; $500 2nd prize; $250 3rd prize, publication. How To Submit: unsolicited. Deadline: Jun. 1, 2010.

**California Young Playwrights Contest**
Playwrights Project, 2356 Moore St., #204, San Diego, CA 92110
Deborah Salzer
Tel: (619) 239-8222; Fax: (619) 239-8225
write@playwrightsproject.com
www.playwrightsproject.com
Est. 1984. All entrants receive evaluation. Winners work with a dramaturg and receive 4 performances at a professional theatre in San Diego. Assistance: room/board, travel. Frequency: annual. Style: comedy, drama. **Application.** What To Submit: query, full script (2 copies). Author Must Be: age 18 or younger, resident of CA. Material Must Be: unoptioned, unpublished, original. Opportunity/Award: $100, production. Deadline: June 1, 2010.

**Canadian Jewish Playwriting Competition**
Jewish Theater, 750 Spadina Ave., Fl. 2, Toronto, Ontario M5R-3B2 Canada
Esther Arbeid
Tel: (416) 924-6211 ext. 606
esthera@mnjcc.org
www.mnjcc.org
Frequency: annual. Response Time: no reponse unless play is chosen as winner, no feedback from jury. Author Must Be: Canada or strong Canadian ties. Material Must Be: unpublished, unproduced. Opportunity/Award: 4 hour workshop with public reading, professional artists only. Deadline: June 30, 2010.

**Central Missouri State University Competition**
Theater Dept., Martin 113, Warrensburg, MO 64093
Richard Herman
Tel: (660) 543-4020
tilden@ucmo.edu
www.cmsu.edu

Est. 2001. CMSU Theater Dept. has produced children's plays for over 25 years in its academic season and with Central Missouri Rep. It is now focusing on world-premiere originals, through its national competition. Top prize is $400 and a 5-show run on the CMSU mainstage.

**Charles M. Getchell Award, SETC**
P.O.Box 9868, Greensboro, NC 27429
Chris Hardin
Tel: (864) 656-5415; Fax: (864) 656-1013
hardin@apsu.edu
www.setc.org
**Application.** What To Submit: application, full script sent electronically. Author Must Be: resident or student in AL, FL, GA, KY, MS, NC, SC, TN, VA or WV. Material Must Be: unpublished, unproduced. Opportunity/Award: $1,000. How To Submit: On line application only. Deadline: June 1, 2010.

**Christopher Brian Wolk Award**
312 W. 36th St., 6th floor, New York, NY 10018
Kim T. Sharp
Tel: (212) 868-2055; Fax: (212) 868-2056
ksharp@abingdontheatre.org
www.abingdontheatre.org
Est. 2001. Frequency: annual. Production: cast limit 8. Response Time: 3-6 mos. Style: comedy, drama. **Application.** What To Submit: Mail printed and bound copy of entire script, character breakdown, synopsis, production history, bio; see website for updates. Author Must Be: citizen of US. Material Must Be: unoptioned, unproduced in NYC. Opportunity/Award: $1,000 and staged reading. How To Submit: regular mail. Deadline: June 1, 2010.

**Cincinnati Playhouse in the Park Mickey Kaplan New American Play Prize**
Box 6537, Cincinnati, OH 45206
Tel: (513) 345-2242; Fax: (513) 345-2254
www.cincyplay.com

Est. 2004. Frequency: annual. Style: drama, comedy, musical, adaptation; no translation; full-length only. **Application.** What To Submit: Agent submission of full script. Non-agent: synopsis, 10 pages dialog, character breakdown, playwright bio, production history. Include audio tape or CD of selections from score for musicals. SASE. Author Must Be: citizen of US. Material Must Be: unoptioned, unpublished, unproduced. Opportunity/Award: $15,000 production. Deadline: Dec. 31, 2010.

**Dale Wasserman Drama Award**
UWM English Dept.,
3243 N. Downer Ave., Madison, WI 53201
Marilyn L. Taylor
Est. 1964. Frequency: annual.

**David Calicchio Emerging American Playwright Prize**
397 Miller Ave., Mill Valley, CA 94941
Est. 2007. **Application.** How To Submit: see website for submission guidelines.

**Deep South Writers Conference Contest**
Box 44691, Lafayette, LA 70504
Willard Fox

**Dorothy Silver Playwriting Competition**
26001 S. Woodland Ave.,
Beachwood, OH 44122
Deborah Bobrow
Tel: (216) 831-0700 ext. 1378
Fax: (216) 831-7796
dbobrow@clevejcc.org
www.clevejcc.org
Award for original works of significant, fresh perspective on Jewish experience. Frequency: annual. Response Time: 4 mos. **Application.** What to Submit: full script, audio, SASE if playwright would like materials returned. Material Must Be: unoptioned, unpublished, unproduced. Opportunity/Award: $1,000, reading, ad in American Theatre Magazine. How To Submit: Send materials (email submissions not accepted). Deadline: Dec. 31, 2010.

**Dr. Floyd Gaffney Playwriting Award on the African-American Experience**
9500 Gilman Drive, MC 0344,
La Jolla, CA 92093
Allan Havis
Tel: (858) 534-4004; Fax: (858) 534-8931
www.theatre.ucsd.edu/playwritingcontest
Est. 2007. Contest seeking scripts highlighting the African-American experience in contemporary or historical terms. No adaptations. **Application.** What to Submit: application, full script. Author Must Be: undergraduate, enrolled student. Material Must Be: See applications for guidelines. Opportunity/Award: $1,000. How To Submit: unsolicited.

**Edgar Allan Poe Award for Best Play**
1140 Broadway, St. 1507,
New York, NY 10001
Margery Flax
Tel: (212) 888-8171
mwa@mysterywriters.org
/www.mysterywriters.org
Est. 1945. Frequency: annual. Style: comedy, drama, musical. **Application.** What To Submit: application, full script (5 copies), and Playbill, submissions not returned. Material Must Be: produced. Deadline: Nov. 30, 2010.

**Emerging Playwright Award**
17 E 47th St., New York, NY 10017
Frances Hill
Tel: (212) 421-1380; Fax: (212) 421-1387
urbanstage@aol.com
www.urbanstages.org

**Essential Theatre Playwriting Award**
1414 Foxhall Lane #10, Atlanta, GA 30316
Peter Hardy
Tel: (404) 212-0815
pmhardy@aol.com
www.essentialtheatre.com
Style: Any style. **Application.** What To Submit: full script. Please put contact info on front page; number pages. Author Must Be: resident of GA. Material Must Be: unproduced. Opportunity/Award: $600, production.

How To Submit: email or regular mail.
Deadline: Apr. 23, 2010.

**Firehouse Center for the Arts**
Market Square, Newburyport, MA 01950
Firehouse Arts Center
Tel: (978) 462-7336
kimm@firehouse.org
www.firehouse.org
Deadline: August each year. Style:
New Work. **Application.** What
To Submit: 4 Copies. Author Must
Be: New England Resident. How
To Submit: Guidelines on website.
Deadline: Aug. 8, 2010.

**Fort Wayne Civic Theatre-Northeast
Indiana Playwright Contest**
303 E. Main St., Fort Wayne, IN 46802
Phillip H. Colglazier
Tel: (260) 422-8641; Fax: (260) 422-6900
pcolglazier@fwcivic.org
www.fwcivic.org
**Application.** Submit an entry form,
play synopsis (1 page), 10 pp of script,
and playwright's bio. Additional
Guidelines: Consult website for
submission guidelines. Entry form
available on-line at www.fwcivic.org.
**Application.** Author Must Be: 19 or
older. Current or former resident of
Northeast Indiana within a 90 mile
radius of Fort Wayne, IN. Opportunity/
Award: Reading, Production,
1st Place-$750, 2nd Place-$500,
3rd Place-$250. How To Submit:
Unsolicited. Deadline: Sept. 1, 2010.

**Fred Ebb Award**
231 W. 39th St., #1200,
New York, NY 10018
info@fredebbfoundation.org
/www.fredebbfoundation.org
Est. 2005. Named for lyricist Fred
Ebb (1928-2004), award recognizes
excellence by a songwriter or
songwriting team that hasn't yet
achieved significant commercial
success. Frequency: annual.
Response Time: by Nov. 31, 2010.
Style: musical. **Application.** What
To Submit: application, audio (up
to 4 songs), lyrics and context for
songs. Author Must Be: produced,
published, or professional workshop
member. Opportunity/Award: $50,000.
Deadline: See website for deadline.

**Goshen College Peace Playwriting
Contest**
1700 S. Main St., Goshen, IN 46526
Douglas Caskey
Tel: (574) 535-7393; Fax: (574) 535-7660
douglc@goshen.edu
www.goshen.edu
Renumeration: 1st Place: $500,
production, room and board to attend
rehearsals and/or production. 2nd
Place: $100, possible production.
Frequency: biennial. Notification
May 31st, 2012. Style: One Act
play. **Application.** What To Submit:
1-paragraph synopsis, full script,
resume. Material Must Be: unproduced,
15-20 minute in length. Opportunity/
Award: $500 1st; $100 2nd, production.
Deadline: Dec. 31, 2011.

**Harold Morton Landon Translation
Award**
584 Broadway, #604,
New York, NY 10012
Alex Dimethroph
Tel: (212) 274-0343 ext. 17
Fax: (212) 274-9427
academy@poets.org
www.poets.org
Est. 1976. Recognizes translation
of poetry (incl. verse drama) from
any language into English. A noted
translator chooses the winning book
published that year. Frequency:
annual. Style: translation of poetry.
**Application.** What To Submit: full
script (1 copy). Author Must Be: citizen
of US. Material Must Be: plays in verse;
translation of poetry. Opportunity/
Award: $1,000. How To Submit:
unsolicited. Deadline: see website.

**Hawai'i Prize**
46 Merchant St., Honolulu, HI 96813
Harry Wong III
Tel: (808) 536-4222; Fax: (808) 536-4226
kumukahuatheatre@hawaiiantel.net
www.kumukahua.org

Frequency: annual - first Tuesday of January. See website for full submission policy. **Application.** What to Submit: full script (3 copies). Opportunity/Award: $600. Deadline: Jan. 4, 2010.

**Intersection for the Arts James D. Phelan Literary Award**
446 Valencia St.,
San Francisco, CA 94103
Chida Chaemchaeng Kevin Chen
Tel: (415) 626-2787
chida@theintersection.org
www.theintersection.org
Est. 1937. Named for James Duval Phelan (1861-1930). Frequency: annual. **Application.** What to Submit: application, full script (3 copies). Author Must Be: age 20-35 on 3/31. must have been born in CA. Material Must Be: unpublished. Opportunity/ Award: $2,000. Deadline: Mar. 31, 2010.

**Jane Chambers Playwriting Award**
Dept. of Perf. Arts, Georgetown U.,
108 Davis Center, Box 571063,
Washington, DC 20057
Maya Roth
mer46@georgetown.edu
www.athe.org/wtp/html/chambers.html
Award for plays and performance texts by females that reflect a feminist perspective and contain a majority of opportunities for women performers. Named in honor of lesbian playwright Jane Chambers, and administered by the Women and Theatre Program of ATHE. Style: Feminist plays and performance texts written by women with a majority of roles for female performers. We welcome experimentations in style and form, and understand feminism varies in relation to experiences of race, sexuality, class, geography, ability and identity. **Application.** What To Submit: Application, synopsis, full script (3 copies), resume. Submissions are not returned. Author Must Be: female. Material Must Be: Material

must be original work, and not yet published. Opportunity/Award: $500 and a public reading at the annual ATHE Conference. How To Submit: Consult the website each December for current guidelines, as organizers/ submission addresses rotate. Deadline: Feb. 15, 2010.

**Jane Chambers Student Playwriting Award**
230 W. 56th St., #65-A,
New York, NY 10019
Jen-Scott Mobley
jen-scottm@nyc.rr.com
www.athe.org/wtp/html/chambers.html
Award for plays and texts by female students that reflect a feminist perspective and contain a majority of opportunities for women performers. Frequency: annual. Check website for deatails. **Application.** What to Submit: application, synopsis, full script (2 copies), resume, submissions not returned. Author Must Be: female student. Material Must Be: original. Opportunity/Award: $150, reading. How To Submit: Consult website each December for current guidelines, as organizers/submission addresses rotate. Deadline: Feb. 15, 2010.

**Kansas Playwright Contest**
400 W. 11th St., Coffeyville, KS 67337
Mark Frank
Tel: (620) 251-7700; Fax: (620) 251-7098
markf@coffeyville.edu
www.ccc.cc.ks.us

**L. Arnold Weissberger Award**
Box 428, Williamstown, MA 01267
Justin Waldman
Tel: (413) 458-3200; Fax: (413) 458-3147
ssanders@wtfestival.org
www.wtfestival.org
Est. 1988. Honors theater attorney and supporter L. Arnold Weissberger (1907-81). Frequency: annual. Style: drama, no musical, no screenplay. **Application.** What To Submit: query, SASE. Material Must Be: unpublished, professionally unproduced.

Opportunity/Award: $10,000, publication. How To Submit: invite. Deadline: June 15, 2010.

## Laity Theatre Company
343 E. Palmdale Blvd, Ste. 8,
Palmdale, CA 93551
James Goins
Tel: (661) 223-5585 Fax: (661) 430-5423
contact@laityarts.org
www.laityarts.org
Submit Query, Synopsis or Treatment, 15 page sample. Subject: Women, Theatre for young adults, writers of color, disabilities. Style: Comedy, Variety, Drama, Musical, Translation. **Application.** What To Submit: Full-Length Plays, Full-Length Musicals, One-Act Plays, One-Act Musicals. Material Must Be: not produced, not published. Opportunity/Award: Reading, Workshop. How To Submit: Unsolicited. Deadline: Mar. 15, 2010.

## Latino Playwriting Award
Kennedy Center, Education Div.,
Washington, DC 20566
Susan Shaffer
Tel: (202) 416-8857
skshaffer@kennedy-center.org
The award will be presented to the author of the best student-written play by a Latino student playwright participating in KC/ACTF. Opportunity/Award: $2,500.

## Lewis Galantiere Award
225 Reinekers Ln., #590,
Alexandria, VA 22314
Tel: (703) 683-6100; Fax: (703) 683-6122
ata@atanet.org
www.atanet.org
Est. 1982. Biennial award (even yrs) for outstanding published translation from language other than German into English. Assistance: $500 travel. Frequency: biennial (even yrs). Style: translation. **Application.** What To Submit: query, 10-pg sample of original and translation (2 copies), full script of translation (2 copies), bio. Material Must Be: published,

from language other than German. Opportunity/Award: $1,000. Deadline: May 1, 2010.

## LiveWire Chicago Theatre
P.O. Box 11226, Chicago, IL 60611
Josh Weinstein
Tel: (312) 533-4666
livewirechicago@gmail.com
www.livewirechicago.com/vision
LiveWire presents VisionFest, an annual short play festival surrounding a central theme. See website for theme guidelines, submission criteria and more info. Style: Adaptation, comedy or variety, drama. **Application.** What To Submit: full script. Opportunity/Award: reading. How To Submit: unsolicited. Deadline: May 1, 2010.

## Lorraine Hansberry Playwriting Award
Kennedy Center, Education Div.,
Washington, DC 20566
Susan Shaffer
Tel: (202) 416-8857; Fax: (202) 416-8802
skshaffer@kennedy-center.org
www.kennedy-center.org/education/actf
Award for a student-written play on the African-American experience. Plays accepted only from college/univ. participating in KC/ACTF program. **Application.** How To Submit: Play must be entered by a college or university participating in the KC/ACTF program. A registration fee of $200 (associate level) or $250 (participating) must be paid to qualify.

## Mark Twain Playwriting Award
American Coll. Theater Festival,
Education Ofc., Kennedy Center,
Arlington, VA 22210
Susan Shaffer
Tel: (202) 416-8857; Fax: (202) 416-8802
skshaffer@kennedy-center.org
www.kennedy-center.org/education/actf
Plays accepted only from college/univ. participating in KC/ACTF program. Style: comedy. Opportunity/Award: $2,500 26 fellowship opportunity(1st); $1,500 (2nd), publication (1st place

only). **Application.** How To Submit: Play must be entered by a college or university participating in the KC/ACTF program. A registration fee of $200 (associate level) or $250 (participating) must be paid to qualify.

**Met Life Nuestras Voces Playwriting Competition**
138 E. 27th St., New York, NY 10016
Allison Astor-Vargas
Tel: (212) 225-9950
aav@repertorio.org
www.repertorio.org
 Est. 1999. Frequency: annual. Response Time: 6 mos. Style: comedy, drama. **Application.** What To Submit: application, full script, submissions not returned. Author Must Be: age 18 or older, resident or citizen of US. Material Must Be: unpublished. Opportunity/Award: production, reading. Deadline: June 1.

**Mildred & Albert Panowski Playwriting Award**
Northern Michigan University, 1401 Presque Isle, Marquette, MI 49855
Stefan Mittelbrunn
Tel: (906) 227-2559; Fax: (906) 227-2567
www.nmu.edu/theatre
 Est. 1977. Winning playwright expected to participate in script development workshop during summer. Assistance: room/board, travel. Frequency: annual. Style: comedy, drama. **Application.** What To Submit: 1-pg synopsis, full script, SASE. Material Must Be: unoptioned, unpublished, unproduced. Opportunity/Award: $2,000, production. Deadline: Oct. 31, 2010.

**Morton R. Sarett National Playwriting Competition**
4505 Maryland Pkwy., Box 455036, Las Vegas, NV 89154
Stacey Jansen
Tel: (702) 895-3663
www.unlv.edu/programs/nct
 A memorial to Morton R. Sarett, the award is funded by Gwynneth

and Robert C. Weiss. Assistance: room, travel. Frequency: biennial (odd numbered years). **Application.** What to Submit: application, 50-word synopsis, full script (2 copies), audio. Material Must Be: unpublished, unproduced, original, in English. Opportunity/Award: $3,000, production. Deadline: Feb. 1, 2011.

**Mountain Playhouse Playwriting Contest**
7713 Somerset Pike, Box 205, Jennerstown, PA 15547
Erica Poslonski
Tel: (814) 629-9201 ext. 118
Fax: (814) 629-9201
erica@mountainplayhouse.com
www.mountainplayhouse.org
 Frequency: annual. Production: cast limit 8. Style: comedy. **Application.** What To Submit: full script. Material Must Be: unproduced, not previously submitted for this award unless revised 70% or more. How To Submit: www.mountainhouse.org/playhouse/contest.php, Opportunity/Award: $3,000, reading. Deadline: Dec. 31, 2010.

**Naples Players ETC**
701 5th Ave. S., Naples, FL 34102-6662
Joe Moran
Tel: (239) 434-7340
www.naplesplayers.com
 Author Must Be: must reside in Collier, Lee, Charlotte, Glades or Hendry county in Florida and may not be a member of the anonymous judging panel. Style: Comedy or Variety, Drama. 10 - 30 minutes in length. **Application.** Material Must Be: Not Produced, Not published. Opportunity/Award: Reading. Deadline: May 31, 2010.

**Nathan Miller History Play Contest**
1614 20th St. NW, Washington, DC 20009
Laura VanDruff
Tel: (202) 518-5357 ext. 2
lvandruff@spreng-erandlang.com
 Frequency: annual. Material Must Be: unproduced. Opportunity/Award:

$2,000. **Application.** How To Submit: Contact Sprenger Land Foundation for sumbission guidelines. Deadline: Dec. 31, 2010.

**National Latino Playwriting Award**
343 S. Scott Avenue, Tucson, AZ 85701
Elaine Romero
Renumeration: $1,000. What to Submit: full-length (over 90 minutes), mid-length (30-60 minutes). Author Must be resident of US, or Mexico; Latino. Deadline: Dec. 31, 2010.

**National Playwriting Competition**
Dept. WEB, 306 W. 39th St., Suite 3, New York, NY
Tel: (212) 307-1140; Fax: (212) 307-1454
writeaplay@aol.com
www.youngplaywrights.org
Every play submitted receives a response. Frequency: annual. Style: no adaptation, musical. **Application.** What To Submit: full script, submissions returned with SASE. Author Must Be: age 18 or younger, resident of US. Opportunity/Award: possible future production, reading. How To Submit: unsolicited.

**National Student Playwriting Award**
John F. Kennedy Center for the Performing Arts, Washington, DC 20566
Susan Shaffer
Tel: (202) 416-8857; Fax: (202) 416-8802
skshaffer@kennedy-center.org
www.kennedy-center.org/education/actf
Plays accepted only from college/univ. participating in KC/ACTF program. **Application.** How To Submit: Play must be entered by a college or university participating in the KC/ACTF program. A registration fee of $200 (associate level) or $250 (participating) must be paid to qualify.

**National Ten-Minute Play Contest**
316 W. Main St., Louisville, KY 40202
Amy Wegener
Tel: (502) 584-1265; Fax: (502) 561-3300
awegener@actorstheatre.org
www.actorstheatre.org

Est. 1989. Frequency: annual.
**Application.** What to Submit: full script (1 entry/author), SASE. Author Must Be: citizen or resident of US. Material Must Be: full script (1 entry/author). Opportunity/Award: $1,000, production consideration. How To Submit: unsolicited. Deadline: Nov. 1, 2010.

**North Carolina New Play Project (NCNPP)**
Greensboro Playwright's Forum,
Greensboro Cultural Center,
Greensboro, NC 27401
Stephen Hyers
Tel: (336) 335-6426; Fax: (336) 373-2659
drama@greensboro-nc.gov
www.playwrightsforum.org
Frequency: annual. Production: small cast, simple set. Response Time: 6 mos. **Application.** What to Submit: 10 pages. Author Must Be: resident of NC. Material Must Be: unpublished, unproduced professionally, original. Opportunity/Award: $500. How To Submit: email (DOC, PDF, RTF). Deadline: Aug. 15, 2010.

**Ohioana Career Award**
274 E. 1st Ave., #300, Columbus, OH 43201
Linda Hengst
Tel: (614) 466-3831; Fax: (614) 728-6974
ohioana@ohioana.org
www.ohioana.org
Est. 1943. Award to native Ohioan for outstanding professional accomplishments in arts and humanities. Recipient is honored guest at Ohioana Day and must be present to receive award. Assistance: room/board. Frequency: annual. **Application.** What to Submit: query, application, 10-pg sample, 2-pg resume, submissions not returned. Author Must Be: native of OH. Deadline: Dec. 31st of each year.

**Ohioana Citations**
274 E. 1st Ave., #300, Columbus, OH 43201
Linda Hengst
Tel: (614) 466-3831; Fax: (614) 728-6974

ohioana@ohioana.org
www.ohioana.org
Est. 1945. Award for outstanding
contributions and accomplishments in
specific area of arts and humanities.
Four citations may be given each year.
Assistance: room/board. Frequency:
annual. **Application.** What to Submit:
query, application, 10-pg sample, 2-pg
resume, submissions not returned.
Author Must Be: native or 5-yr resident
of OH. How To Submit: professional
recommendation. Deadline: Dec. 31st
of each year.

**Ohioana Pegasus Award**
274 E. 1st Ave., #300, Columbus, OH 43201
Linda Hengst
Tel: (614) 466-3831; Fax: (614) 728-6974
ohioana@ohioana.org
www.ohioana.org
Est. 1964. Award for unique or
outstanding contributions or
achievements in arts and humanities,
given at discretion of trustees.
Assistance: room/board. Frequency:
annual. Response Time: by May 31,
2010. **Application.** What to Submit:
query, application, 10-pg sample, 2-pg
resume, submissions not returned.
Author Must Be: native or 5-yr resident
of OH. How To Submit: professional
recommendation. Deadline: Dec. 31st
of each year.

**One-Act Playwriting Competition**
900 N. Benton Ave.,
Springfield, MO 65802
Dr. Mick Sokol
Tel: (417) 873-6821
msokol@drury.edu
www.drury.edu
Est. 1984. Frequency: biennial.
Accepting submissions between May
1 and Dec 1, 2010. Response Time:
by April 1, 2011. **Application.** What
to Submit: full script, SASE. Material
Must Be: unpublished, unproduced.
Opportunity/Award: $300 1st, $150
2nd, $150 3rd. Deadline: Dec. 1, 2010.

**The Open Book Playwriting
Competition**
525 West End Ave., #12-E,
New York, NY 10024
Marvin Kaye
theopenbook@juno.com
Est. 1994. Equity Showcase,
readers theater. Frequency: annual.
Production: cast limit 7, minimal set.
Style: adaptation, comedy, drama.
**Application.** What To Submit: full
script, SASE. Author Must Be:
resident or citizen of US. Material
Must Be: unoptioned, unproduced.
Opportunity/Award: 10% box office.
Fees: $15

**Pacific Rim Prize**
46 Merchant St., Honolulu, HI 96813
Harry Wong III
Tel: (808) 536-4222; Fax: (808) 536-4226
kumukahuatheatre@hawaiiantel.net
www.kumukahua.org
Frequency: annual. Plays preferred
on Hawaii-experience/culture.
**Application.** What to Submit: full
script (3 copies). Opportunity/Award:
$450. Deadline: Jan. 4, 2010.

**Palindromic Play Challenge**
Box 22420, Denver, CO 80222
Steve Hunter
Contest for scripts that honor the
concept of palindromes in a creative
fashion and have dramatic potential.
Frequency: palindromic years (next in
2112). Response Time: May 15. What
to Submit: full script, submissions
returned with SASE. Material Must
Be: unpublished, unproduced, still
in development. Opportunity/Award:
reading. How To Submit: unsolicited.

**Paula Vogel Award for Playwriting**
John F. Kennedy Center for the
Performing Arts, Washington, DC 20566
Susan Shaffer
Tel: (202) 416-8857; Fax: (202) 416-8802
skshaffer@kennedy-center.org
www.kennedy-center.org/education/actf
Est. 2003. Award for a student-written
play that celebrates diversity and

encourages tolerance while exploring issues of disempowered voices not traditionally considered mainstream. Plays accepted only from college/univ. participating in KC/ACTF program.

**PEN/Laura Pels Foundation Awards for Drama**
588 Broadway, #303, New York, NY 10012
Nick Burd
Tel: (212) 334-1660 ext. 108
nick@pen.org
www.pen.org
> Est. 1998. Award to US playwright in mid-career writing in English with professional productions of at least 2 full-lengths (excl. musicals, translations) in theaters of at least 299 seats. Playwrights don't apply on their behalf but are nominated by peers. Frequency: annual. Opportunity/Award: $7,500. How To Submit: professional recommendation. Deadline: Jan. 16, 2010.

**Playwrights First Award**
15 Gramercy Park S.,
New York, NY 10003
Emily Andrew
Tel: (212) 744-1312
> Est. 1993. Frequency: annual. Production: in English. Response Time: by May 1, 2011. Style: comedy, drama. **Application.** What To Submit: full script, resume, submissions not returned. Material Must Be: unproduced, in English, by 1 author. Opportunity/Award: $1,000 award, reading. Deadline: Oct. 15, 2010.

**Promising Playwright Contest**
Box 2167, Annapolis, MD 21404
Tel: (410) 268-7373
www.cplayers.com
> Est. 1973. Winning playwright urged to attend rehearsals. Frequency: annual. Production: cast of up to 10, up to 2 sets, suitable for arena production. Style: no adaptation, musical. **Application.** What To Submit: full script, submissions returned with SASE. Author Must Be:

resident of original 13 colonies, WV or DC. Material Must Be: unproduced. Opportunity/Award: $750 award, possible future production. How To Submit: unsolicited, send SASE in fall for application.

**Regent University Theatre One-Act Play Competition**
1000 Regent University Dr.,
Virginia Beach, VA 23464
Gillette Elvgren
Tel: (757) 226-4223; Fax: (757) 226-4279
theatre@regent.edu
www.regent.edu/theatre

**Resident Prize**
46 Merchant St., Honolulu, HI 96813
Harry Wong III
Tel: (808) 536-4222; Fax: (808) 536-4226
kumukahuatheatre@hawaiiantel.net
www.kumukahua.org
> Frequency: annual. Check website for full submission details. What to Submit: full script (3 copies). Author Must Be: resident of HI. Opportunity/Award: $250. Deadline: Jan. 4, 2010.

**Richard Rodgers Awards for Musical Theater**
633 W. 155th St., New York, NY 10032
Jane E. Bolster
Tel: (212) 368-5900; Fax: (212) 491-4615
academy@rtsandletters.org
www.artsandletters.org
> Est. 1978. Awards for musicals by writers and composers not already established in this field. Staff: Virginia Dajani (Exec. Dir.), J.D. McClatchy (Pres.). Frequency: annual. Response Time: March 1, 2011. Style: musical. **Application.** What To Submit: application, synopsis, full script, CD, SASE. Author Must Be: citizen or resident of US. Deadline: Nov. 2, 2010.

**Robert Bone Memorial Playwriting Award**
Sammons Ctr., 3630 Harry Hines Blvd,
Dallas, TX 75219
Raphael Perry

**Robert Chesley Award**
828 N. Laurel Ave.,
Los Angeles, CA 90046
Victor Bumbalo
Tel: (323) 658-5981
VictorTom@aol.com
> Est. 1991. In honor of Robert Chesley
> (1943-90) to recognize gay and
> lesbian themed work. Nominations
> open in early fall. Frequency: annual.
> **Application.** What to Submit: full
> script, SASE. Material Must Be:
> gay themed. Opportunity/Award: a
> residency and stipend at the Wurlitzer
> Foundation in Taos, New Mexico.

**Robert J. Pickering Award for
Playwriting Excellence**
89 Division St., Coldwater, MI 49036
J. Richard Colbeck
Tel: (517) 279-7963
J7eden@aol.com
> Est. 1984. Award for unproduced plays
> and musicals. Frequency: annual.
> **Application.** What to Submit: full
> script, SASE. Material Must Be:
> unproduced. Opportunity/Award: $200
> 1st, $50 2nd, $25 3rd. Deadline: Dec.
> 31, 2010.

**Ruby Lloyd Apsey Award**
ASC 255, 1530 3rd Ave. S.,
Birmingham, AL 35294
Lee Shackleford
Tel: (205) 975-8755; Fax: (205) 934-8076
leeshack@uab.edu
www.theatre.hum.uab.edu
> In even-number years, UAB seeks
> new, original full-lengths on racial or
> ethnic issues, with ethnically diverse
> casting. Production: college age. Style:
> comedy, drama. **Application.** What
> To Submit: full script. Opportunity/
> Award: $1000, reading. How To
> Submit: Electronic OK but prefer
> recyclable hard copy. Winner
> announced on web site at www.theatre.
> hum.uab.edu/apsey.htm. Deadline:
> Dec. 3, 2010.

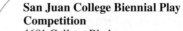

**San Juan College Biennial Play
Competition**
4601 College Blvd.,
Farmington, NM 87402
Theresa A. Carson

**Scholastic Art & Writing Awards**
557 Broadway, New York, NY 10012
Bryan Doerries
info@artandwriting.org
www.artandwriting.org
> Est. 1923. National awards in 2
> categories (grades 7-8; grades 9-12),
> selected from regional contests.
> Regional deadlines vary. Regional
> Gold Key works are considered for
> national awards. Style: comedy,
> drama. **Application.** What To Submit:
> application (2 copies), full script.
> Author Must Be: student (grades
> 7-12) in US or Canada. Material Must
> Be: by 1 author, 5 to 50 pages. How
> To Submit: see website for details.
> Deadline: By region.

**Sky Cooper New American Play Prize**
397 Miller Ave., Mill Valley, CA 94941
> Est. 2007. How To Submit: see website
> submission guidelines.

**Southern Playwrights Competition**
700 Pelham Rd. N,
Jacksonville, AL 36265
Joy Maloney
Tel: (256) 782-5469
jmaloney@jsu.edu
www.jsu.edu/depart/english/southpla.htm
> Est. 1991. Frequency: annual. Style:
> no musical. **Application.** What To
> Submit: application, synopsis, full
> script, SASE. Author Must Be: native
> or resident of South. Material Must Be:
> unoptioned, unproduced professionally.
> Opportunity/Award: $1,000,
> production. Deadline: Jan. 15, 2010.

**Summerfield G. Roberts Award**
1717 8th St., Bay City, TX 77414
Janet Hickl
Tel: (979) 245-6644; Fax: (979) 244-3819
srttexas@srttexas.org
www.srttexas.org

Award for creative writing about the Republic of Texas, to encourage literature & research about the events and personalities of 1836-46. Frequency: annual. **Application.** What to Submit: full script (5 copies), SASE. Opportunity/Award: $2,500. Deadline: Jan. 15, 2010.

## Susan Smith Blackburn Prize
3239 Avalon Pl., Houston, TX 77019
Emilie Kilgore
www.blackburnprize.org

Est. 1978. Plays accepted only from specified source theaters in US, UK and Ireland. Writers should bring their work to the attention of the theatre companies listed on website. Frequency: annual. Style: comedy, drama, musical. **Application.** What To Submit: full script (2 copies), SASE. Author Must Be: female. Material Must Be: unproduced or produced within a year of deadling submission, in English. Opportunity/Award: $20,000 winner; $5,000 special commendation; $1,000 finalists. Deadline: Sept. 15, 2010.

## TeCo Theatrical Productions New Play Competition
215 S. Tyler St., Dallas, TX 75208
Teresa Coleman Walsh
Tel: (214) 948-0716; Fax: (214) 948-3706
teresa@tecotheater.org
www.tecotheater.org

Est. 1993. Multicultural theater promoting quality theatre through dramatic artistic expression. Assistance: travel. Frequency: annual. Production: cast limit 4, minimal set and costume changes. Response Time: 2 mos. Style: Comedy. **Application.** What To Submit: One-act play. Author Must Be: Resident of metro Dallas area. Material Must Be: Unoptioned, unproduced, unsolicited. Opportunity/ Award: $1,000. How To Submit: Must be postmarked by deadline; no emails.

## The Ten Minute Musicals Project
Box 461194, West Hollywood, CA 90046
Michael Koppy
info@TenMinuteMusicals.org
www.TenMinuteMusicals.org

Est. 1989. Frequency: annual. Production: cast limit 10. Style: musicals. **Application.** What To Submit: full script, audio, lead sheets/ score, SASE. Opportunity/Award: $250. How To Submit: by mail. Deadline: Aug. 31, 2010.

## Ten-Minute Play Festival
Kennedy Center for the Performing Arts, Washington, DC 20566
Susan Shaffer
Tel: (202) 416-8857; Fax: (202) 416-8802
skshaffer@kennedy-center.org
www.kennedy-center.org/education/actf

Plays accepted only from college/ univ. participating in KC/ACTF program. Frequency: annual. Style: no translation. **Application.** What To Submit: application, synopsis, full script. Author Must Be: resident of US, college student. Opportunity/ Award: $1,000 award, possible future production, feedback. How To Submit: college recommendation. Play must be entered by a college or university participating in the KC/ACTF program. A registration fee of $200 (associate level) or $250 (participating) must be paid to qualify. Fees: $15 aplication fee. Deadline: Nov. 1, 2010.

## Tennessee Williams/New Orleans Literary Festival One-Act Play Competition
938 Lafayette St., #328,
New Orleans, LA 70113
Tel: (504) 581-1144; Fax: (504) 529-2430
info@tenneseewilliams.net
www.tennesseewilliams.net

## Theater for Youth Playwriting Award
Kennedy Center for the Performing Arts, Washington, DC 20566
Susan Shaffer
Tel: (202) 416-8857; Fax: (202) 416-8802
skshaffer@kennedy-center.org

www.kennedy-center.org/education/actf
Award for student-written play
appealing to young people in grades
K-12. Plays accepted only from
college/univ. participating in KC/
ACTF program. **Application.** How
To Submit: Play must be entered by a
college or university participating in
the KC/ACTF program. A registration
fee of $200 (associate level) or $250
(participating) must be paid to qualify.

**Theodore Ward Prize**
72 E. 11th St., #413, Chicago, IL 60605
Andrea Dymond
Tel: (312) 344-6340
www.colum.edu/undergraduate/theater/
workshops.php
   Frequency: annual. What to Submit:
   full script, SASE. Author Must Be:
   resident of US, African-American.
   Material Must Be: unproduced.
   Opportunity/Award: $2,000 1st, $500
   2nd, production. Deadline: July 1,
   2010.

**Three Genres Drama Contest**
2225 Mount Vernon Ave.,
Riverside, CA 92507
Stephen Minot
s.minot@juno.com
www.creativewriting.ucr.edu
   Frequency: quadrennial.

**Towngate Theatre Playwriting Contest**
Stifel FAC, 1330 National Rd.,
Wheeling, WV 26003
Kate H. Crosbie
Tel: (304) 242-7700; Fax: (304) 242-7747
kcrosbie@oionline.com
www.oionline.com
   Est. 1976. check website for programs
   and contest details.Assistance: $500
   room/board limit, travel. Frequency:
   annual. Response Time: by 5/15. Style:
   comedy, drama. **Application.** What
   To Submit: full script, SASE. Material
   Must Be: unpublished, unproduced.
   Opportunity/Award: $300, production.
   Deadline: Jan. 1 annually.

**Towson University Prize for Literature**
8000 York Rd., Towson, MD 21252
Edwin Duncan
Tel: (410) 704-2871; Fax: (410) 704-3999
drjohnson@towson.edu
www.towson.edu/english
   Est. 1979. Frequency: annual.
   **Application.** What to Submit:
   application, full script (3 copies).
   Letter of acceptance from publisher.
   Author Must Be: resident of MD.
   Material Must Be: published.
   Opportunity/Award: $1,000. How To
   Submit: On-line website. Deadline:
   June 15, 2010.

**Ungar German Translation Award**
225 Reinekers Ln., #590,
Alexandria, VA 22314
Lois Feverle
Tel: (703) 683-6100; Fax: (703) 683-6122
ata@atanet.org
www.atanet.org
   Biennial award (odd yrs) for
   outstanding published translation from
   German into English. Assistance:
   $500 travel. Frequency: biennial (odd
   years). Style: translation. **Application.**
   What To Submit: query, 10-pg sample
   of original and translation (2 copies),
   full script of translation (2 copies), bio.
   Material Must Be: published, from
   German original. Opportunity/Award:
   $1,000, certificate of recognition, $100
   towards annual conference. How To
   Submit: regular mail. Deadline: June
   1, 2011.

**Vermont Playwrights Award**
Valley Players, P.O. Box 441,
Waitsfield, VT 05673
Sharon Kellermann
Tel: (802) 583-2774
valleyplayers@madriver.com
www.valleyplayers.com
   Est. 1982. Frequency: annual. Style:
   full-length non-musical, comedy,
   dramacomedy, drama. **Application.**
   What To Submit: application, full
   script, SASE. Author Must Be:
   resident of ME, NH, VT. Material
   Must Be: unoptioned, unpublished,

unproduced. Opportunity/Award:
$1,000, production or reading. How
To Submit: Call or go online for forms
and instructions. Deadline: Feb. 1,
2010.

## VSA arts Playwright Discovery Program

818 Connecticut Ave. NW, #600,
Washington, DC 20006
Elena Widder
Tel: (202) 628-2800
hwww.vsarts.org
Est. 1984. Annual contest for one-
acts by students grades 6-12 on how
disability affects a person's life.
Response Time: 2 mos. **Application.**
What to Submit: application, full
script. Author Must Be: Resident or
Citizen of US, grades 6-12. Material
Must Be: unoptioned, unpublished,
unproduced. Opportunity/Award:
$2000, production, trip to Washington
DC for production of play. How To
Submit: online. Deadline: Apr. 15,
2010.

## Wichita State University (WSU) New Play Competition

1845 Fairmount, Campus Box 153,
Wichita, KS 67260
Steve Peters
Tel: (316) 978-3360; Fax: (316) 978-3202
www.finearts.wichita.edu/performing
Contest for original plays of at least
90 min. by undergrad or graduate
students enrolled in any US college.
ACTF production of new, unproduced
script. Frequency: annual. Response
Time: by March 15. Style: comedy,
drama. **Application.** What To Submit:
query, full script, SASE. Author Must
Be: US college student. Material Must
Be: unpublished, unproduced, original.
Deadline: Jan. 15, 2010.

## Write a Play! NYC Contest

Young Playwrights Inc, PO Box 5134,
New York, NY 10185
Tel: (212) 594-5440
admin@youngplaywrights.org
www.youngplaywrights.org

Open to all NYC students in 3
categories: elementary, middle, and
high school. All receive certificate
of merit, written evaluation, and
invitation to awards ceremony.
Frequency: annual. Style: All
except musicals and adaptations.
**Application.** What To Submit: full
script, submissions not returned.
Author Must Be: resident of NYC,
student in elementary, middle or high
school. Material Must Be: original.
Opportunity/Award: Cash prize
awarded to winners in each division.
All playwrights receive an evaluation
of their play. How To Submit: Visit
www.youngplaywrights.org for
submission instructions. Deadline:
Mar. 1, 2010.

## Young Playwrights Inc. National Playwriting Competition

Box 5134, New York, NY 10185
Tel: (212) 594-5440; Fax: (212) 684-4902
admin@youngplaywrights.org
www.youngplaywrights.org
Est. 1981 by Stephen Sondheim and
Dramatists Guild members. Young
Playwrights Inc. identifies and
develops young US playwrights by
involving them as active participants
in the highest quality professional
productions of their plays. Style: All
except musicals and adaptations.
**Application.** What To Submit: full
script. Author Must Be: age 18 or
younger. Material Must Be: Original.
Opportunity/Award: Winning
playwrights receive a trip to New
York City to participate in the Young
Playwrights Conference and an off-
Broadway staged reading of their
work. Deadline: Jan. 2, 2010.

## CONTESTS (*FEE CHARGED*)

**Arts & Letters Prize in Drama**
GCSU Campus Box 89,
Milledgeville, GA 31061
David Muschell
Tel: (478) 445-1289; Fax: (478) 445-5961
al@gcsu.edu
www.al.gcsu.edu/
Est. 1999. Response Time: 3 mos.
**Application.** What to Submit:
query, full script. Material Must
Be: unpublished, original, in
English, Opportunity/Award:
$1,000, production, publication,
1-yr subscription (2 issues). How To
Submit: separate cover sheet with
playwright information. Submission/
Application Fee: $15. Deadline: Mar.
15, 2010.

**Aurand Harris Memorial Playwriting Award**
NETC, 215 Knob Hill Dr.,
Hamden, CT 6518
Joseph Juliano
Tel: (617) 851-8535
mail@netconline.org
www.netconline.org
Est. 1997. Honors Aurand Harris
for his lifetime dedication to all
aspects of professional theater for
young audiences. Frequency: annual.
Response Time: by Nov. 1, 2010.
Style: comedy, drama. **Application.**
What To Submit: application, full
script. Material Must Be: unpublished,
unproduced, Opportunity/Award:
$1, 000 1st, $500 2nd. Submission/
Application Fee: $10. Deadline: May
1, 2010.

**Community Theatre Association of Michigan**
4026 Lester, Oscoda, MI 48750
Vincent Weiler
vweiler@ioscoresa.net
www.communitytheatre.org
Frequency: annual. Style: comedy,
drama. **Application.** What To
Submit: full script, SASE. Author

Must Be: resident of Michigan.
Material Must Be: Full evening's
entertainment; several one-acts will
meet requirement. Opportunity/Award:
$500. How To Submit: U. S. Mail;
check website for details. Submission/
Application Fee: $20. Deadline: May
15, 2010.

**Das Goldkiel**
Box 445, Buckley, IL 60918
Steven Packard
buntville@yahoo.fr
Est. 1999. Frequency: annual.
**Application.** What to Submit: full
script, resume. Material Must Be:
unpublished, unproduced, original;
in English, French, German, Italian,
Portuguese or Spanish. Opportunity/
Award: $250. Submission/Application
Fee: $8. Deadline: May 31. 2010.

**David C. Horn Prize**
Box 209040, New Haven, CT 6520
Keith Condon
www.dchornfoundation.org
Est. 2006. Style: no musical. What
To Submit: full script (unbound),
cover pg (w/title, contact info, pg
count), cast/scene list, submissions
not returned. Author Must Be: citizen
of US, Canada, UK or Ireland, not
published in full-length. Material
Must Be: unpublished, unproduced
professionally, original, in English.
Opportunity/Award: $10,000,
publication by Yale Press, staged
reading at Yale Rep. Submission/
Application Fee: $25. Deadline: Aug.
15, 2010.

**David Mark Cohen Playwriting Award**
Kennedy Center, Education Div.,
Washington, DC 20566
Susan Shaffer
Tel: (202) 416-8857; Fax: (202) 416-8802
skshaffer@kennedy-center.org
www.kennedy-center.org/education/actf

Plays accepted only from college/univ. participating in KC/ACTF program. Assistance: travel. Frequency: annual. Style: no translation. What To Submit: application, synopsis, full script. Author Must Be: resident of US, college student. Opportunity/Award: $1,000 award, publication by Dramatic Publishing, reading. **Application.** How To Submit: college recommendation, Play must be entered by a college or university participating in the KC/ACTF program. A registration fee of $200 (associate level) or $250 (participating) must be paid to qualify. Fees: $15 application fee. Deadline: Nov. 1, 2010.

**Dubuque Fine Arts Players One Act Play Contest**
1686 Lawndale St., Dubuque, IA 52001
Gary Arms
gary.arms@clarke.edu
Est. 1977. Frequency: annual. Production: cast of 2-5, unit set. Response Time: 6 mos. **Application.** What to Submit: application, full script (2 copies), SASE. Material Must Be: unpublished, unproduced. Opportunity/Award: $600 1st, $300 2nd, $200 3rd. Submission/Application Fee: $10. Deadline: Jan. 31, 2010.

**FirstStage One-Act Play Contest**
Box 38280, Los Angeles, CA 90038
Dennis Safren
Tel: (323) 350-6271
firststagela@aol.com
www.firststagela.org
Est. 1983. Staged readings of 3 finalists. Frequency: annual. Response Time: 3 wks. **Application.** What to Submit: full script, submissions not returned. Material Must Be: unproduced. Opportunity/Award: $300 1st, $100 2nd/3rd, reading. Submission/Application Fee: $10. Deadline: Nov. 25, 2010.

**Francesca Primus Prize**
American Theater Critics,
773 Nebraska Ave. W., St. Paul, MN 55117
Katie Burger

Tel: (602) 956-2310
atc_admin@msn.com
www.americantheatrecritics.org
In memory of Francesca Primus (d.1992). Frequency: annual. Style: comedy, drama. **Application.** What To Submit: query, full script (6 copies), portfolio. Author Must Be: female. Material Must Be: professionally produced in previous yr. Opportunity/Award: $10,000. How To Submit: professional recommendation. Submission/Application Fee: $25. Deadline: Feb. 28, 2010.

**George R. Kernodle Playwriting Contest**
619 Kimpel Hall, Fayetteville, AR 72701
Roger Gross
Tel: (479) 575-2953; Fax: (479) 575-7602
rdgross@uark.edu
www.uark.edu
Frequency: annual since 1985. Style: all styles. **Application.** What To Submit: full script (up to 3 entries accepted), cover letter verifying no publ., no production. Material Must Be: unpublished, unproduced, Opportunity/Award: $300 1st, $200 2nd, $100 3rd. Fees: $3/script (paid to first reader).

**Georgia College and State University**
Porter Hall CBX 066,
Milledgeville, GA 31061
Karen Berman
Tel: (478) 445-1980; Fax: (478) 445-1633
kbermanth@aol.com
www.gcsu.edu/musicandtheatre
Please submit cover letter and biography of two pages or less. Style: comedy or variety, drama. **Application.** What To Submit: full script. Author Must Be: available for short residency. Material Must Be: not optioned, not published, not produced. Opportunity/Award: Production/$2000. How To Submit: separate cover sheet with author's name and address. Submission/Award/Grant/Stipend: $2,000. Application Fee: $20. Deadline: Dec. 1, 2010.

**ool New Play Award**
Pkwy. N., Marietta, GA 30062
Todd Ristau
Tel: (540) 362-6386
tristau@studioroanoke.org
www.setc.org/scholarship
> **Application.** What to Submit: full
> script, SASE. Author Must Be:
> student in AL, FL, GA, KY, MS,
> NC, SC, TN, VA or WV. Material
> Must Be: unpublished, unproduced.
> Opportunity/Award: $250, reading.
> Submission/Application Fee: $10.
> Deadline: Dec. 1, 2010.

**Irish American Theatre Co.**
PO Box 1647, New York, NY 10028
Thomas Henry
Tel: (917) 929-0169
iatc@excite.com
> Please provide a brief bio. Style:
> comedy or variety, drama, translation.
> **Application.** What To Submit: query,
> synopsis or treatment, 10 page sample.
> Author Must Be: 18 or older. Material
> Must Be: Not optioned, not produced,
> not published. Opportunity/Award:
> reading, workshop. How To Submit:
> Unsolicited. Submission/Application
> Fee: $10. Deadline: Oct. 31, 2010.

**Jackie White Memorial National
Children's Play Writing Contest**
309 Parkade Blvd., Columbia, MO 65202
Betsy Phillips
Tel: (573) 874-5628
bybetsy@yahoo.com
www.cectheatre.org
> Est. 1988. In memory of Jackie Pettit
> White (1947-91). All scripts read by
> at least 3, finalists by at least 9. All
> receive written evaluation. Frequency:
> annual. Production: at least 7 speaking
> roles, sets appropriate for community
> theaters. Response Time: by Aug. 31,
> 2010. **Application.** What to Submit:
> application, full script, SASE. Material
> Must Be: unpublished. Opportunity/
> Award: $500. Submission/Application
> Fee: $25 entry. Deadline: June 1, 2010.

**Jean Kennedy Smith Playwriting
Award**
Kennedy Center, Education Div.,
Washington, DC 20566
Susan Shaffer
Tel: (202) 416-8857; Fax: (202) 416-8802
skshaffer@kennedy-center.org
www.kennedy-center.org/education/actf
> Award for a student-written play on
> disability. Plays accepted only from
> college/univ. participating in KC/
> ACTF program. Frequency: annual.
> Style: no translation. **Application.**
> What To Submit: application, synopsis,
> full script. Author Must Be: resident
> of US, college student. Opportunity/
> Award: $2,500 award, publication by
> Dramatic Publishing, feedback. How
> To Submit: college recommendation,
> Play must be entered by a college or
> university participating in the KC/
> ACTF program. A registration fee
> of $200 (associate level) or $250
> (participating) must be paid to qualify.
> Fees: $15 aplication fee. Deadline:
> Dec. 1, 2010.

**Jewel Box Theatre Playwriting
Competition**
3700 N. Walker Ave.,
Oklahoma City, OK 73118
Chuck Tweed
Tel: (405) 521-1786
www.jewelboxtheatre.org
> Est. 1986. Frequency: annual.
> Submissions sent between Oct–Jan.
> Response Time: by May 30,
> 2011. Style: adaptation, comedy,
> drama. **Application.** What To
> Submit: application, full script,
> SASE, online. Material Must Be:
> unoptioned, unpublished, unproduced.
> Opportunity/Award: $500.
> Submission/Application Fee: $15.
> Deadline: Jan. 19, 2011.

**John Gassner Memorial Playwriting
Award**
NETC, 215 Knob Hill Dr.,
Hamden, CT 06518
Joseph Juliano
Tel: (617) 851-8535

mail@NETConline.org
www.NETConline.org
Est. 1967. Honors theater historian
John Gassner for his lifetime
dedication to all aspects of
professional and academic theater.
Frequency: annual. Response Time:
by Nov. 1, 2010. Style: comedy,
drama. **Application.** What To Submit:
application, full script. Material
Must Be: unpublished, unproduced.
Opportunity/Award: $1,000 1st, $500
2nd. How To Submit: submissions not
returned. Submission/Application Fee:
$10. Deadline: Apr. 15, 2010.

## John Cauble Short Play Awards Program

Kennedy Center, Education Div.,
Washington, DC 20566
Susan Shaffer
Tel: (202) 416-8857; Fax: (202) 416-8802
skshaffer@kennedy-center.org
www.kennedy-center.org/education/actf
Plays accepted only from college/
univ. participating in KC/ACTF
program. Frequency: annual. Style:
no translation. **Application.** What
To Submit: application, synopsis,
full script. Author Must Be: resident
of US, college student. Opportunity/
Award: $1,000 award, publication by
Samuel French, feedback. How To
Submit: college recommendation,
Play must be entered by a college or
university participating in the KC/
ACTF program. A registration fee
of $200 (associate level) or $250
(participating) must be paid to qualify.
Fee: $15 application fee. Deadline:
Nov. 1, 2010.

## Lionheart Theatre's Make the House Roar Prize

Prize Coordinator, Lionheart Theatre's
Make the House Roar Prize,
Norcross, GA 30091
Daphne Mintz
Tel: (770) 885-0425
admin@afterdinnertheatre.org
www.afterdinnertheatre.org

Style: comedy. What T
script, synopsis, chara(
Material Must Be: unp
Opportunity/Award: $2
production. Submissio
$10. Deadline: Jan. 31

## Maxim Mazumdar New Play Competition

1 Curtain Up Alley, Buffalo, NY 14202
Joyce Stilson
Tel: (716) 852-2600; Fax: (716) 852-2266
newplays@alleyway.com
www.alleyway.com
Est. 1990. Named for Maxim
Mazumdar (1953-87). Winning full-
length receives premiere production
in mainstage season. Winning one-act
receives premiere in Buffalo Quickies
fest. Frequency: annual. Response
Time: Oct. 1, Nov. 1. **Application.**
What to Submit: full script, SASE.
Material Must Be: unoptioned,
unproduced. Opportunity/Award:
$400 (full-length), $100 (one-act).
Submission/Application Fee: $25.
Deadline: July 1 annually.

## McLaren Memorial Comedy Playwriting Competition

2000 W. Wadley Ave., Midland, TX 79705
Andy Salcedo
Tel: (432) 682-2544
mclaren1@mctmidland.org
www.mctmidland.org
Est. 1989. Staff: Marla Cooper,
Brenda Tumlin. Frequency: annual.
Style: comedy. **Application.** What To
Submit: full script, SASE. Material
Must Be: unoptioned, unpublished,
unproduced. Opportunity/Award:
$400 (full-length), $200 (one-act).
Submission/Application Fee: $15.
Deadline: Feb. 28, 2010.

## Mississippi Theatre Association

1297 Bardwell Rd., Starkville, MS 39759
Kris Lee
Tel: (812) 320-3534
tklee1976@gmail.com
www.mta-online.org

This competition is designed to recognize and promote the works of Mississippi playwrights and is open to all Mississippi writers either in state or abroad. Style: Comedy or Variety, Drama. **Application.** What To Submit: Application, Synopsis or Treatment, Full script. Author Must Be: 18 or older. Material Must Be: Not produced, not published, not optioned. How To Submit: Unsolicited. Award/Grant/Stipend: $500, reading. Submission/Application Fee: $10. Deadline: Sept. 1, 2010.

## Moving Arts Premiere One-Act Competition

Box 481145, Los Angeles, CA 90048
Trey Nichols
Tel: (323) 666-3259; Fax: (323) 666-2841
www.movingarts.org

Frequency: annual. Production: cast limit 8, unit set. Style: comedy, drama. **Application.** What To Submit: query, full script, SASE. Material Must Be: unproduced in L.A. Opportunity/ Award: $200, production. Submission/ Application Fee: $10. Deadline: Feb. 1, 2010.

## Musical Theater Award

Kennedy Center, Education Div., Washington, DC 20566
Susan Shaffer
Tel: (202) 416-8857; Fax: (202) 416-8802
skshaffer@kennedy-center.org
www.kennedy-center.org/education/actf

Plays accepted only from college/univ. participating in KC/ACTF program. Frequency: annual. Style: musical, no translation. **Application.** What To Submit: application, synopsis, full script. Author Must Be: resident of US, college student. Opportunity/ Award: $1,000 for music; $1,000 for book; $1,000 for lyrics, feedback. How To Submit: college recommendation, Play must be entered by a college or university participating in the KC/ ACTF program. A registration fee of $200 (associate level) or $250 (participating) must be paid to qualify.

Fees: $15 aplication fee. Deadline: Nov. 1, 2010.

## National Children's Theatre Festival

280 Miracle Mile, Coral Gables, FL 33134
Earl Maulding
Tel: (305) 444-9293 ext. 615
www.actorsplayhouse.org

Response Time: Oct. 1, 2010. Submission/Application Fee: $10. Deadline: Apr. 1, 2010.

## National New Play Network

c/o Woolly Mammoth Theatre Company, 641 D Street NW, Washington, DC 20004
Jason Loewith
Tel: (202) 312-5270; Fax: (202) 289-2446
jason@nnpn.org
www.nnpn.org

Check website for 2011 deadlines. Style: Politically-themed, non musical, full length. **Application.** What To Submit: See www.nnpn. org/prog_smith.php. Material Must Be: Unproduced in New York City. Opportunity/Award: $2,500, production. How To Submit: Unsolicited. Submission/Application Fee: $10. Deadline: check website for 2011 deadlines.

## New Rocky Mountain Voices

Box 790, Westcliffe, CO 81252
Dick Senff
wcpa@ris.net
www.westcliffecenter.org

Est. 1999. Winning plays staged at Jones Theater in Westcliffe, CO. Authors asked to speak afterward. Frequency: annual. Production: cast of 4-8, unit set. Response Time: 2 mos. Style: comedy, drama. **Application.** What To Submit: query, synopsis, full script, no author on title page. On letter only. SASE. Author Must Be: resident of Rocky Mts (AZ, CO, ID, MT, NM, UT). Material Must Be: unproduced professionally. Opportunity/Award: $200, production. Submission/Application Fee: $10. Deadline: Apr. 1, 2010.

**Next Generation Playwriting Contest**
c/o Brooklyn Creative League,
540 President Street, Brooklyn, NY 11215
Kimberly Wadsworth
Tel: (212) 244-7803; Fax: (212) 244-7813
info@ReverieProductions.org
www.ReverieProductions.org
Est. 2004. New work from established
& emerging writers on socio-
political issues in highly theatrical
contexts. Finalists recieve public
staged reading; grand prize receives
workshop production and possible
full production in NYC. Staff: Colin
D. Young (Artistic Dir). Frequency:
annual. Style: comedy, drama, radio.
**Application.** What To Submit:
application, full script, SASE. Material
Must Be: unpublished, not produced
in NY, NJ or CT. Opportunity/Award:
$500 (full-length at least 60 minutes
long) - no one acts! How To Submit:
Please follow guidelines on website.
Submission/Application Fee: $18.
Deadline: Dec. 15, 2010.

**Northeastern Original One-Act**
Playwriting Competition
23 Norden St., New Britain, CT 6051
Jerilyn Nagel
Tel: (860) 223-3147
nbrep@nbrep.org
www.nbrep.org
Staged readings of 4-6 plays in June
festival. Frequency: annual. Response
Time: 5/15/04. Style: comedy,
drama, mystery. **Application.** What
To Submit: synopsis, submissions
returned with SASE. Material Must
Be: unpublished. Opportunity/Award:
$150 1st prize, $100 2nd prize, $50
3rd prize. How To Submit: send
SASE in fall for application. Fees: $15
application fee.

**PEN Center USA Literary Awards**
P.O. Box 637, Culver City, CA 90212
Tamara Crater
Tel: (310) 862-1555 ext. 361
Fax: (310) 862-1556
awards@penusa.org
www.penusa.org

Est. 1982. Prizes for
and screenplays. Fre
**Application.** What
application, full scr
submissions not returned. Au...
Must Be: author must reside west of
the Mississippi River, or in the states
of Minnesota or Louisiana. Material
Must Be: Originally published or
produced in 2009. Opportunity/
Award: $1,000. How To Submit: Mail
the submission form, payment, and
script copies to the address listed.
Submission/Application Fee: $35.
Deadline: Jan. 31, 2010.

**PEN Translation Prize**
588 Broadway, #303, New York, NY 10012
Nick Burd
Tel: (212) 334-1660 ext. 108
nick@pen.org
www.pen.org
Est. 1963. Please visit website
for more info. Style: translation.
**Application.** What To Submit: full
script (3 copies), submissions not
returned. Material Must Be: published
in US. Opportunity/Award: $3, 000.
Submission/Application Fee: $50 or
waived. Deadline: Dec. 15, 2010.

**Prix Hors Pair**
Box 445, Buckley, IL 60918
Steven Packard
buntville@yahoo.fr
Est. 1999. Frequency: annual.
**Application.** What to Submit:
full script, resume. Material Must
Be: original; in English, French,
German, Italian, Portuguese or
Spanish. Opportunity/Award: $200.
Submission/Application Fee: $8.
Deadline: May 31, 2010.

**Public Access Television Corp. (PATC)**
1111 Marcus Ave., #LL27,
Lake Success, NY 11042
Shirley Bruno
Tel: (516) 629-3710; Fax: (516) 629-3704
pachannel@aol.com
www.patv.org

One-act
. annual.
..lts, unit set.
*86* .ths. Style: comedy,
..l. What To Submit:
..ssions returned with
..rial Must Be: unpublished,
..ed. How To Submit: Unsolicited.
..5. Deadline: July 15, 2010.

**Reva Shiner Full-Length Play Contest**
107 W. 9th St., Bloomington, IN 47404
Sonja Johnson
Tel: (812) 334-1188
www.newplays.org
BPP is a development group. Winning
writers are expected to be part of
development process. Frequency:
annual. **Application.** What to Submit:
query, full script, audio. Material
Must Be: unpublished, unproduced.
Opportunity/Award: $500, production.
How To Submit: unsolicited.
Submission/Application Fee: $10.
Deadline: Oct. 31, 2010.

**Reverie Productions**
520 Eighth Ave., #317,
New York, NY 10018
Kimberly Wadsworth
Tel: (212) 244-7803; Fax: (212) 244-7813
kimberly@reverieproductions.org
www.reverieproductions.org
Est. 2002. Check website for
guidelines. Frequency: annual.
Response Time: April. Style: comedy,
drama. **Application.** What To Submit:
application, full script, SASE. Material
Must Be: unoptioned, unpublished,
unproduced. Opportunity/Award: $500
and at least a workshop production.
Submission/Application Fee: $18.
Deadline: Dec. 15, 2010.

**Stanley Drama Award**
Wagner College, One Campus Road,
Staten Island, NY 10301
Todd Alan Price
todd.price@wagner.edu
www.wagner.edu/stanleydrama/
Est. 1957. Frequency: annual.
Response Time: 6 mos. What to

Submit: full script (1 entry/author),
audio, SASE. Material Must Be:
unoptioned, unpublished, unproduced.
Opportunity/Award: $2,000. Fee: $20
application. Deadline: Oct. 31, 2010.

**Theatre in the Raw Play Writing
Contest**
3521 Marshall St., Vancouver, BC Canada
Jay Hamburger
Tel: (604) 708-5448; Fax: (604) 708-1454
theatreintheraw@telus.net
www.theatreintheraw.ca
Est. 1994. Frequency: 6th Biennial
One-Act Play Writing Contest; every
two years.Production: cast limit 6, set
limit 2 (scene limit 3). Style: comedy,
drama, radio, plays/broadcast.
**Application.** What To Submit:
full script, SASE, standard 8.5x11
form; no published copies. Material
Must Be: unoptioned, unpublished,
unproduced. Opportunity/Award:
CA$150 1st, CA$75 2nd, CA$50 3rd.
Submission/Application Fee: $25 US/
Can. Deadline: Dec. 31, 2011.

**Theatre Oxford 10-Minute Play Contest**
PO Box 1321, Oxford, MS 38655
Dinah Swan
theatreoxford@yahoo.com
www.10minuteplays.com
Est. 1998. Frequency: annual.
Production: casts 2-4, minimal
set, props. Only winners and
finalists will be contacted. Style:
no musical. **Application.** What To
Submit: full script, submissions
not returned. Material Must Be:
unoptioned, unpublished, unproduced.
Opportunity/Award: $1,000,
production. Submission/Application
Fee: $10. Deadline: Feb. 16, 2010.

**Urban Stages Emerging Playwright
Award**
555 8th Ave., Suite #1800,
New York, NY 10018
Frances Hill
urbanstage@aol.com
www.urbanstages.org

Est. 1986. Frequency: annual.
Production: cast limit 7. Response
Time: 3 mos. Style: comedy, drama.
**Application.** What To Submit: full
script, SASE. Material Must Be:
unoptioned, unpublished, unproduced.
Opportunity/Award: $500 (in lieu
of royalty), production. Submission/
Application Fee: $10.

**W. Keith Hedrick Playwriting Contest**
Box 940, Hudson, NY 12534
Jan M. Grice
Tel: (518) 851-7244
jangrice2002@yahoo.com
/www.hrc-showcasetheatre.org
  Est. 1993. 1 winner and 4 finalists
  receive public staged reading by
  professional actors. Frequency: annual.
  Production: cast limit 8. Response
  Time: 3 mos. **Application.** What to
  Submit: full script, SASE. Author
  Must Be: resident of Northeast.

Material Must Be: unpublished.
Opportunity/Award: $500 1st,
$100 finalist, reading. Submission/
Application Fee: $5. Deadline: May
1, 2010.

**Writer's Digest Writing Competition**
700 East State Street, Iola, WI 54990
Tel: (715) 445-4612 ext. 13430
Fax: (715) 445-4087
writing-competition@fwpubs.com
www.writersdigest.com
  Est. 1931. Assistance: travel.
  Frequency: annual. Style: All.
  **Application.** What To Submit:
  application, 1-pg synopsis,
  15-pg sample. Material Must
  Be: unpublished, unproduced.
  Opportunity/Award: $3,000 1st.
  Submission/Application Fee: $15.
  Deadline: May 15, 2010; June 1, 2010
  late entry w/fee.

# GRANTS AND FELLOWSHIPS

**Alabama State Council on the Arts**
201 Monroe St., Montgomery, AL 36130
Randy Shoults
Tel: (334) 242-4076 ext. 224
Fax: (334) 240-3269
randy.shoults@arts.alabama.gov
www.arts.state.al.us
  Opportunities incl. Artist Fellowships
  and Artist in Education Residency
  in performing artists (music, dance,
  theater), literature (fiction, creative
  nonfiction, poetry, screenwriting,
  playwriting), and visual artists.
  Author Must Be: 2-yr resident of AL.
  Deadline: Mar. 1, 2010.

**Alaska State Council on the Arts
(ASCA)**
411 W. 4th Ave., #1-E,
Anchorage, AK 99501
Tel: (888) 278-7424; Fax: (907) 269-6601
www.eed.state.ak.us/aksca
  Est. 1966. Opportunities incl.
  quarterly Career Opportunity Grants

and biennial Connie Boochever Artist
Fellowships (Aug 31 deadline, odd
yrs). **Submission.** 10-pg sample,
audio. Author Must Be: age 18 or
older, resident of AK. Deadline: See
website for various deadlines.

**Allen Lee Hughes Fellowship Program**
1101 6th St. SW, Washington, DC 20024
Stacey Stewart
Tel: (202) 554-9066; Fax: (202) 488-4056
fellows@arenastage.org

**American Antiquarian Society
Fellowships**
185 Salisbury St., Worcester, MA 01609
Cheryl McRell
Tel: (508) 471-2149; Fax: (508) 754-9069
cmcrell@mwa.org
www.americanantiquarian.org
  Up to 4 fellowships to creative and
  performing artists and writers for 4-wk
  residency to research works about pre-
  20th century US history. Assistance:

$1,200/mo, travel. Response Time: by 12/5/10. **Submission.** See directions on website. Deadline: Oct. 5, 2010.

**American-Scandinavian Foundation (ASF)**
58 Park Ave., New York, NY 10016
Tel: (212) 879-9779; Fax: (212) 249-3444
grants@amscan.org
www.amscan.org
Grants for short visits and fellowships for full year of study or research in Denmark, Finland, Iceland, Norway or Sweden. $20 application: annual. **Submission.** $23,000 fellowship limit; $5, 000 grant limit. Author Must Be: citizen or resident of US, college graduate, proficient in host language preferred. Opportunity/Award: $20,000 fellowship limit; $4,000 grant limit. How To Submit: online, Submission/Application Fee: $2.00. Deadline: Nov. 2, 2010.

**America's Media Makers**
1100 Pennsylvania Ave. NW, Washington, DC 20506
Margaret Scrymser
Tel: (202) 606-8269; Fax: (202) 606-8557
publicpgms@neh.gov
www.neh.gov
Development and production grants for humanities projects of broad appeal.: $30,000-$500,000 grant: January and August each year. Response Time: 6 mos. Style: documentary. **Submission.** Application, submissions not returned. How To Submit: online. Deadline: Jan. 13 and Aug. 18, 2010.

**Arizona Commission on the Arts (ACA)**
417 W. Roosevelt St., Phoenix, AZ 85003
Jennifer Tsukayama
Tel: (602) 771-6501; Fax: (602) 256-0282
www.azarts.gov
Est. 1966. Artist Career Advancement Grants (ACAG) and Artist Project Grants. Check website for deadlines. Author Must Be: age 18 or older, resident of AZ, not a student. **Submission.** Online.

**Artist Trust**
1835 12th Ave., Seattle, WA 98122
Monica Miller
Tel: (206) 467-8734 ext. 10
Fax: (206) 467-9633
info@artisttrust.org
www.artisttrust.org
Grants for Artist Projects (GAP) program. $1,500 stipend: annual. Response Time: 4 mos. **Submission.** Application, 12-pg sample, audio. Author Must Be: age 18 or older, resident of WA, not a student. Deadline: Feb. 19, 2010.

**Artists' Fellowships**
New York Foundation for the Arts, 20 Jay St,, suite 740, Brooklyn, NY 11201
Margie Lempert
Tel: (212) 366-6900; Fax: (212) 366-1778
fellowships@nyfa.org
www.nyfa.org
Est. 1984. Artists' Fellowships are intended to fund an artist's vision or voice, regardless of the level of her or his artistic development. Grants of $7000 are given to individual originating artists living in New York State. **Submission.** Application. Author Must Be: age 18 or older, resident of NYS, not a student. Deadline: Oct. 15, 2010.

**Asian Cultural Council**
6 West 48th St., 12th Fl, New York, NY 10036
Cecily D. Cook
Tel: (212) 843-0403; Fax: (212) 843-0343
acc@accny.org
www.asianculturalcouncil.org
Est. 1963. Support for cultural exchange in performing/visual arts between US and Asia, primarily fellowships for artists from Asia to pursue projects in US, but some support for Americans for research and creative work in Asia. Annual. **Submission.** Inquiry form on website. Author Must Be: citizen of US or Asian country. Opportunity/Award: individual fellowship. How To Submit: Submit inquiry form by Oct. 15 and application postmarked by Nov. 15.

**Aurand Harris Fellowship**
617 Baxter Ave., Louisville, KY 40204
Marilee Miller
info@childrenstheatrefoundation.org
www.childrenstheatrefoundation.org
Est. 1958. For individuals with specific
projects or with specific plans for
developing excellence in children's
theater. Annual 4/1. **Submission.**
Application, info on websites,
submissions not returned. Author Must
Be: age 18 or older, resident or citizen
of US. Material Must Be: unoptioned.
Opportunity/Award: $5,000 max.
Deadline: Apr. 1, 2010.

**Brooklyn Arts Council (BAC)**
55 Washington St., Suite 218,
Brooklyn, NY 11201
Tel: (718) 625-0080; Fax: (718) 625-3294
bac@brooklynartscouncil.org
www.brooklynartscouncil.org
Formerly BACA (Brooklyn Arts &
Culture Assoc.).

**Bush Artist Fellows Program**
332 Minnesota St., #E-900,
St. Paul, MN 55101
Julie Dalgleish
Tel: (651) 227-5222; Fax: (612) 297-6485
www.bushfoundation.org
Est. 1976. Fellowships of 1-2 years
in literature, script works, and film/
video. $44,000 grant: biennial. Style:
all styles. **Submission.** Application.
Author Must Be: age 25 or older,
resident of MN, ND, SD, or northwest
WI, produced or workshopped, not a
student.

**California Arts Council**
1300 I St., #930, Sacramento, CA 95814
Barry Hessenius
Tel: (916) 322-6555; Fax: (916) 322-6575
cac@cwo.com
www.cac.ca.gov

**CEC ArtsLink**
435 Hudson St, Fl. 8,
New York, NY 10014
Chelsey Morell
Tel: (212) 643-1985 ext. 22

Fax: (212) 643-1996
al@cecartslink.org
www.cecartslink.org
Est. 1992. Grants for collaborative
projects with colleagues in Central
and Eastern Europe, Russia, Central
Asia and the Caucasus alternating
between visual/media arts (2011) and
performing arts or literature (2010).
Grants up to $10,000. **Submission.**
Application. How To Submit:
Application available on-line. Mail
application. Deadline: Jan. 15, 2010.

**Colorado Council on the Arts**
1625 Broadway, #2700,
Denver, CO 80202
Jeanette Albert
Tel: (303) 892-3802; Fax: (303) 892-3848
coloarts@state.co.us
www.coloarts.org
Grants only. We do not offer
fellowships. **Submission.** Online only.
Deadline: Mar. 11, 2010.

**Connecticut Commission on Culture &
Tourism (CCT)**
One Constitution Plaza, 2nd Fl.,
Hartford, CT 06103
Tamara Dimitri
Tel: (860) 256-2720
tamara.dimitri@ct.gov
www.cultureandtourism.org
Artistic fellowships alternating
between visual art (odd yrs) and
choreography, fiction, music
composition and film/video,
playwriting, and poetry (even yrs).
Author Must Be: Author must have
lived and worked in CT for one year
minimum, current full time residents
of CT. Deadline: Sep. 1, 2010.

**Delaware Division of the Arts**
820 N. French St., Wilmington, DE 19801
Kristin Pleasanton
Tel: (302) 577-8278; Fax: (302) 577-6561
kristin.pleasanton@state.de.us
www.artsdel.org
Invidual artists fellowships. Annual.
**Submission.** Application, 15-20 pg
sample, SASE. Author Must Be: age

18 or older, resident of DE, not a student. Deadline: Aug. 2, 2010.

**Don and Gee Nicholl Fellowships**
1313 Vine St., Hollywood, CA 90028
Greg Beal
Tel: (310) 247-3010; Fax: (310) 247-3794
nicholl@oscars.org
www.oscars.org/nicholl
　　Est. 1986. Film competition for screenwriters who haven't earned more than $5K in film or TV. Up to five $30K fellowships each year. Staff: Shawn Guthrie (Asst.). $30. Annual. Style: no adaptation, no translation. **Submission.** Application, full script. Opportunity/Award: $30,000. How To Submit: unsolicited. Deadline: May 1. 2010.

**Emerging Artists of Color Fellowships**
New York Theatre Workshop ATTN: Fel, 83 East 4th Street, 2nd Floor,
New York, NY 10003
Gita Reddy and Jen Zoble
　　Est. 1995. Four fellowships total for playwrights, directors, and/or designers of color. Fellows are given access to rehearal space, office facilities and equipment, casting assitance, mentoring, and other forms of support as determined on an individual basis. $4000 stipend to all fellows including theatergoing opportunities.

**Fiscal Sponsorship**
20 Jay St., Suite 740, Brooklyn, NY 11201
Mary Six Rupert
Tel: (212) 366-6900 ext. 223
Fax: (212) 366-1778
msrupert@nyfa.org
www.nyfa.org/fs
　　Est. 1971. Allows artists to apply for funds usually available only to nonprofits. Fees: $100 contract fee (if accepted), 8% admin fee. Frequency: semiannual. Response Time: 10 Weeks. **Submission.** Application, SASE. Author Must Be: not a student. Deadline: First Friday of May and November.

**Fulbright Program for US Scholars**
3007 Tilden St. NW, Suite 5L,
Washington, DC 20008
Anne Clift Boris
scholar@cies.iie.org
www.cies.org/us_scholars
　　Est. 1947. Grants for US faculty or professionals to research or lecture abroad for 2-12 mos. in 140 countries. Grant/stipend varies, room/board varies, travel varies: annual. **Submission.** Application, SASE. Author Must Be: citizen of US. Opportunity/Award: award varies. Deadline: see website.

**George Bennett Fellowship**
20 Main St., Exeter, NH 3833
Ralph Sneeden
english@exeter.edu
www.exeter.edu
　　Est. 1968. Fellowship for academic year to early-career writer, who will live in Exeter and be available to students but not be on faculty nor be required to teach. $13,000 stipend, room/board: annual. **Submission.** Application, 30 pages from novel, 2 stories. Author Must Be: writing a work in process, Submission/Application Fee: $5.00. Deadline: December 1st, 2010.

**Hodder Fellowship**
Lewis Center for the Arts, Princeton Univ.
185 Nassau St., Princeton, NJ 08544
Janine Braude
Tel: (609) 258-4096; Fax: (609) 258-2230
jbraude@princeton.edu
www.princeton.edu/arts/lewis_center/society_of_fellows/
　　1-yr fellowship for Academic Year 2011-12 for individuals outside academia to pursue independent projects. Candidates for the PhD program are not eligible. Princeton University is an equal opportunity employer and complies with applicable EEO and affirmative action regulations. For general application and information see www.princeton.edu/dof/ApplicantsInfo.htm. It is

strongly recommended that all interested candidates use the online application process. **Submission.** Project proposal, 10-pg sample, resume. Author Must Be: poets, playwrights, novelists, creative nonfiction writers and translators who have published one highly acclaimed book and are undertaking significant new work. Material Must Be: sent to the above postal address. Opportunity/Award: $63,900 stipend. How To Submit: Apply online at http://jobs.princeton.edu and send materials to above address. Deadline: Nov. 1, 2010.

**Indiana Arts Commission (IAC)**
100 North Senate Avenue, Room N505,
Indianapolis, IN 46204
Bobbie Garver
Tel: (317) 232-1268
IndianaArtsCommission@iac.in.gov
www.in.gov/arts
Est. 1969. Individual Artist Program (IAP). See website for deadlines. $2,000 grant limit. **Submission.** Application, 10-pg sample (10 copies). Author Must Be: age 18 or older, resident of IN, not a student. Deadline: Feb. 1, 2011.

**Institute of Puerto Rican Culture**
Box 9024184, San Juan, Puerto Rico 902
Teresa Tio
Tel: (787) 724-0700; Fax: (787) 724-8393
www@icp.gobierno.pr

**Iowa Arts Council**
600 E. Locust, Des Moines, IA 50319
Linda Lee
Tel: (515) 242-6194
Linda.lee@iowa.gov
www.iowaartscouncil.org
Time: Appx. 4-6 wks. Author Must Be: age 18 or older, resident of IA, not a student. Opportunity/Award: Project Grants: Major Grant up to $10, 000; Mini Grant up to $1, 500. **Submission.** See information on web site. Deadlines: Major Grants: April 1, 2010. Mini Grants: 1st business day of

each month: check website from year to year.

**The Japan Foundation**
152 W. 57th St., Fl. 17,
New York, NY 10019
Yukihiro Ohira
Tel: (212) 489-0299; Fax: (212) 489-0409
info@jfny.org
www.jfny.org
Touring Grants help U.S. nonprofit organizations present Japanese performing arts in the U.S. and Canada. Collaboration Grants help American and Japanesse artists develop new works, which will further an appreciation of Japanese culture when presented to American audiences. **Submission.** Application. How To Submit: unsolicited.

**Jerome Playwright-in-Residence Fellowships**
2301 Franklin Ave. E.,
Minneapolis, MN 55406
Kevin McLaughlin
Tel: (612) 332-7481; Fax: (612) 332-6037
info@pwcenter.org
www.pwcenter.org
Fellowships to emerging playwrights for 1-yr residency (Jul-Jun) in MN using Center services. $10,000 fellowship + $1,000 in development support: annual. **Submission.** Application. Author Must Be: citizen or resident of US, not produced professionally more than twice. How To Submit: online. Deadline: Refer to website.

**John Simon Guggenheim Memorial Foundation**
90 Park Ave., New York, NY 10016
Keith B. Lewis
Tel: (212) 687-4470; Fax: (212) 697-3248
fellowships@gf.org
www.gf.org
Est. 1925. Fellowship to scholars and artists for research or creation. **Submission.** Query, application, sample. Deadline: Sep. 15, 2010.

**Jonathan Larson Performing Arts Foundation**
Box 672, Prince St. Sta.,
New York, NY 10012
Nancy Diekmann
Tel: (212) 529-0814; Fax: (212) 253-7604
jlpaf@aol.com
www.jlpaf.org
Est. 1996. Annual grants to theater composers, lyricists, book writers and to theaters developing new musicals by former Larson award recipients. annual. Response Time: 4 mos. Style: musical. **Submission.** Application, SASE. Opportunity/Award: $2,500-$15,000. Deadline: Aug. 29, 2010.

**Kentucky Arts Council**
500 Mero St., Fl. 21, Frankfort, KY 40601
Amber Luallen
Tel: 888/833-2787, ext. 479
Amber.Luallen@ky.gov
www.artscouncil.ky.gov
Annual fellowships alternating between visual artists and media artists (2007) and writers, composers, choreographers, and interdisciplinary artists (2008). Deadline: Feb. 1, 2010.

**Kleban Award**
424 W. 44th St., New York, NY 10036
Tel: (212) 757-6960; Fax: (212) 265-4738
newdramatists@newdramatists.org
www.newdramatists.org/kleban_award.htm
Deadline: September 15 for the following year, to lyricists and librettists working in the American musical theater. Annual. Style: musical. **Submission.** See application for guidelines. Author Must Be: produced or member of a professional musical theater workshop. Opportunity/Award: $100,000 each to a lyricist and a librettist. How To Submit: See application for guidelines. Deadline: Sep. 15, 2010.

**Literature Fellowships: Translation Projects**
1100 Pennsylvania Ave. NW,
Washington, DC 20506
Tel: (202) 682-5400; Fax: (202) 682-5666
litfellowships@arts.gov
www.arts.gov

**Louisiana Division of the Arts**
Box 44247, Baton Rouge, LA 70804
Danny Belanger
Tel: (225) 342-8180; Fax: (225) 342-8173
dbelanger@crt.state.la.us
www.crt.state.la.us/arts
Deadline: First Monday in March.

**Ludwig Vogelstein Foundation, Inc.**
4001 Inglewood Ave., Suite 101-309,
Redondo Beach, CA 90278
Diana Braunschweig
lvf@earthlink.net
Grants to individuals working in playwriting, fiction/non-fiction, and the visual arts (painting, sculpture, printmaking, etc. No film/video/ photography), and to unaffiliated scholars/historians, based on artistic merit and financial need. Opportunity/ Award: $1,000-$3,000. **Submission.** Email inquiries.

**Maine Arts Commission**
25 State House Station, Augusta, ME 4333
Donna McNeil
Tel: (207) 287-2724; Fax: (207) 287-2725
donna.mcneil@maine.gov
mainearts.maine.gov
See website for 2010 deadline. Author Must Be: age 18 or older, resident of ME, not a student. Submission/ Application Fee: $0.

**Many Voices Playwriting Residency Awards**
2301 Franklin Ave. E.,
Minneapolis, MN 55406
Kevin McLaughlin
Tel: (612) 332-7481; Fax: (612) 332-6037
info@pwcenter.org
www.pwcenter.org
Grants, education, and development opportunities to writers of color living in MN. Two beginning playwrights receive a $1,000 stipend and $250 in development funds. Three emerging playwrights receive a $3,500 stipend and $1,000 in development funds.

Annual. **Submission.** Application. Author Must Be: resident of MN. How To Submit: online. Deadline: Refer to website.

**Maryland State Arts Council**
175 W. Ostend St., Ste. E,
Baltimore, MD 21230
Sharon Blake
Tel: (410) 767-6536
sblake@msac.org
www.msac.org
Grants alternating between dance, music, playwriting, poetry, crafts, photography, and sculpture (2006) and fiction, media, performance, paper, painting, installation and computer art (2007).

**Massachusetts Cultural Council (MCC)**
10 St. James Ave., Fl. 3,
Boston, MA 02116
Dan Blask
Tel: (617) 727-3668 ext. 329
Fax: (617) 727-0044
dan.blask@art.state.ma.us
www.massculturalcouncil.org
Grants alternating between dance, drawing, prose, painting, poetry, traditional arts (2010) and crafts, film/video, music, photography, playwriting, sculpture (2011).
check Web site for award amount.
**Submission.** Application. Author Must Be: age 18 or older, resident of MA. How To Submit: online.

**McKnight Advancement Grants**
2301 Franklin Ave. E.,
Minneapolis, MN 55406
Kevin McLaughlin
Tel: (612) 332-7481; Fax: (612) 332-6037
info@pwcenter.org
www.pwcenter.org
Grants to advance a writer's art and career. $25,000 grant: annual. **Submission.** Application. Author Must Be: 2-yr resident of MN, professionally produced, not recipient of this grant in past 3 yrs. How To Submit: online. Deadline: Refer to website.

**McKnight National Playwriting Residency and Commission**
2301 Franklin Ave. E.,
Minneapolis, MN 55406
Kevin McLaughlin
Tel: (612) 332-7481; Fax: (612) 332-6037
info@pwcenter.org
www.pwcenter.org
Commissioning and production of new works from nationally recognized playwrights. Recipient in residence at Center while play is in development. $12,500 grant: annual. **Submission.** Application. Author Must Be: nationally recognized playwright with 2 full professional productions. (must not be Minnesota resident). How To Submit: agent. Deadline: Refer to website.

**McKnight Theater Artist Fellowship**
2301 Franklin Ave. E.,
Minneapolis, MN 55406
Steve Moulds
Tel: (612) 332-7481; Fax: (612) 332-6037
info@pwcenter.org
www.pwcenter.org
Fellowships to theater artists other than writers whose work demonstrates exceptional artistic merit and potential. $25,000 grant: annual. **Submission.** Application. Author Must Be: resident of MN. How To Submit: online. Deadline: Apr. 10, 2010.

**Meet the Composer Grant Programs**
90 John Street, Suite 312,
New York, NY 10038
Dereck Geary
Tel: (212) 645-6949; Fax: (212) 645-9669
mtc@meetthecomposer.org
www.meetthecomposer.org
Est. 1974. Response Time: Varies, consult guidelines. Various programs. Style: all styles. **Submission.** Application, audio. Author Must Be: U.S. citizen or permanent resident. How To Submit: unsolicited. Deadline: consult website.

**Michener Center for Writers**
702 E. Dean Keeton St., Austin, TX 78705
Graduate Coordinator
Tel: (512) 471-1601; Fax: (512) 471-9997
mcw@www.utexas.edu
www.utexas.edu/academic/mcw
Est. 1993. Financial assistance for full-time students in MFA program. $25,000 stipend, free tuition: annual. **Submission.** Playwrights submit a full-length play or two one-act plays. Author Must Be: holder of a BA degree. How To Submit: Mail hard copy to Michener Center, Submission/Application Fee: Must submit an on-line application to the UT Graduate Admissions Office along with an application fee. Deadline: Dec. 15.

**Nebraska Arts Council**
1004 Farnam St., Plaza Level,
Omaha, NE 68102
J.D. Hutton
Tel: (402) 595-2122; Fax: (402) 595-2334
www.nebraskaartscouncil.org
Individual Artist Fellowship (IAF): annual. **Submission.** Application, SASE. Author Must Be: resident of NE. Deadline: Nov. 15, 2010.

**New Generations Program: Future Collaborations**
520 8th Ave., Fl. 24, New York, NY 10018
David Nugent
Tel: (212) 609-5900; Fax: (212) 609-5901
grants@tcg.com
www.tcg.org
International travel grant. See website for more opportunities. Deadline: See website.

**New Hampshire State Council on the Arts**
2½ Beacon St., Suite 225,
Concord, NH 03301-4447
Jane Eklund
Tel: (603) 271-0791
jane.eklund@dcr.nh.gov
www.nh.gov/nharts
$5,000 Fellowships awarded to 6 individual artists annually. Criteria are: Artistic excellence based on work sample, and professional commitment based on resume. **Submission.** Application, 20-pg sample (6 copies). Author Must Be: age 18 or older, resident of NH, not a fulltime student. Opportunity/Award: Artist Fellowship Grant. How To Submit: See web page for application. Deadline: Early April 2010, see website.

**New Jersey State Council on the Arts**
Box 306, Trenton, NJ 8625
Don Ehman
Tel: (609) 984-7023; Fax: (609) 989-1440
don@arts.sos.state.nj.us
www.njartscouncil.org
Artists fellowships in 14 disciplines, 7/yr (playwrights in even yrs, composers in odd yrs) thru Mid-Atlantic Arts Foundation (midatlanticarts.org). See website for details. Author Must Be: age 18 or older, resident of NJ, not a student. Deadline: Jul. 15, 2010.

**New York Coalition of Professional Women in the Arts & Media**
Box 2537, Times Sq. Sta.,
New York, NY 10108
collaboration@nycwam.org
www.nycwam.org
Est. 1990. NYCWAM Collaboration Award is to encourage professional women in the arts and media to work collaboratively with other women on the creation of new works.

**New York State Council on the Arts (NYSCA)**
175 Varick St., Fl. 3, New York, NY 10014
Heather Hitchens
Tel: (212) 627-4455; Fax: (212) 620-5911
http://www.nysca.org

**New York Theatre Workshop (NYTW) Playwriting Fellowship**
83 E. 4th St., New York, NY 10003
Geoffrey Scott
Tel: (212) 780-9037; Fax: (212) 460-8996
www.nytw.org
Visit Website for list of Fellowships and opportunities.

**North Dakota Council on the Arts**
1600 E. Century Ave., #6,
Bismarck, ND 58503
Jan Webb
Tel: (701) 328-7590; Fax: (701) 328-7595
comserv@nd.gov
www.nd.gov/arts
 Est. 1984. Individual Artist
 Fellowship. Rotates thru literary and
 musical arts (2010), traditional, dance,
 and theater arts (2011), visual arts/
 crafts and media arts (2012). $2,500
 grant: triennial. Response Time: 3
 mos. **Submission.** Application, SASE.
 Author Must Be: age 18 or older,
 resident of ND. Material Must Be:
 unpublished, new work. Deadline: Feb.
 15, 2010.

**Ohio Arts Council**
727 E. Main St., Columbus, OH 43205
Ken Emerick
Tel: (614) 728-4421; Fax: (614) 466-4494
www.oac.state.oh.us
 Individual Excellence Awards in
 choreography, fiction/nonfiction,
 poetry, play/screen writing, criticism
 and music composition. $5,000-
 $10,000 grants: annual. **Submission.**
 Application, full script (4 copies),
 audio. Author Must Be: 1-yr resident
 of OH, not a student. Deadline: Sept.
 1, 2010.

**Oklahoma Arts Council**
Box 52001-2001,
Oklahoma City, OK 73152
Suzanne Tate
Tel: (405) 521-2931; Fax: (405) 521-6418
okarts@arts.ok.gov
www.arts.ok.gov

**Page 73 Productions**
138 S. Oxford St. #5C,
Brooklyn, NY 11217
Liz Jones
Tel: (718) 598-2099; Fax: (718) 398-2794
info@p73.org
www.p73.org
 Est. 1997. Committed to developing
 and producing the work of emerging
 playwrights. Fellowship program

applicants considered for future
projects, incl. writing group, summer
residency, and mainstage production.
$2,000 stipend; annual. **Submission.**
Specific application form and list
of materials available at www.p73.
org in the months prior to the May 1
deadline. Author Must Be: resident of
US, have 2 full-lengths or 3 one-acts,
never had production in NYC larger
than an AEA showcase production,
not a student. Opportunity/Award: The
P73 Playwriting Fellowship is a yearlong program providing development
and career support and a $5,000 cash
stipend. Applicants to the program
are also considered for Page 73's other
development programs (a writing
group and a summer residency). How
To Submit: see specific guidelines and
materials on our website. Deadline:
May 1 annually.

**Pennsylvania Council on the Arts**
Finance Bldg, #216, Harrisburg, PA 17120
Jamie Dollish
Tel: (717) 525-5542; Fax: (717) 783-2538
www.pacouncilonthearts.org
 Est. 1966. Annual. Response Time: 8
 mos. **Submission.** Application. Author
 Must Be: resident of PA. Deadline:
 Aug. 1, 2010.

**Pew Fellowships in the Arts (PFA)**
Philadelphia Center for Arts,
1608 Walnut St., 18th Floor,
Philadelphia, PA 19103
Melissa Franklin
Tel: (267) 350-4920; Fax: (267) 350-4997
pfa@pcah.us
www.pewarts.org
 Est. 1991. Awards rotate in 4-yr cycle
 (3 disciplines chosen each Aug), incl.
 choreography, crafts, fiction/creative
 nonfiction, folk/traditional arts, media
 arts, music composition, painting,
 performance art, poetry, sculpture/
 installation, stage/screen scripts,
 and works on paper. $5,000 grant.
 **Submission.** Application. Author Must
 Be: age 25 or older, 2-year resident of
 eastern PA (Bucks, Chester, Delaware,

Montgomery, Philadelphia cos.), not a student. Opportunity/Award: $60,000. How To Submit: on-line application at www.pewarts.org.

**Pilgrim Project**
35 E. 21st St., Floor 6,
New York, NY 10010
Davida Goldman
Tel: (212) 627-2288; Fax: (212) 627-2184
davida@firstthings.com
Est. 1987. Small grants for a reading, workshop or full production of plays that deal with questions of moral significance. Grants are for production of plays and not administrative costs.: $1,000-$7,000 grant. Response Time: 5 mos. **Submission.** Full script, SASE.

**Princess Grace Foundation USA Playwriting Fellowship**
150 E. 58th St., Fl. 25,
New York, NY 10155
Jelena Tadic
Tel: (212) 317-1470; Fax: (212) 317-1473
grants@pgfusa.org
www.pgfusa.org
Est. 1982. 10-wk residency with New Dramatists; $7,500 stipend; and publication/representation by Samuel French for 1 winning playwright. $7,500 grant: annual. Response Time: by 9/30/10. Style: comedy, drama. **Submission.** Application, full script. Author Must Be: resident or citizen of US. Material Must Be: unpublished, unproduced, original. Opportunity/Award: publication, residency. How To Submit: Application online. Deadline: Mar. 31, 2010.

**The Public Theater/Emerging Writers Group**
425 Lafayette St., New York, NY 10003
Seeks to target playwrights at the earliest stages in their careers. The Public hopes to create an artistic home for a diverse and exceptionally talented group of up-and-coming writers. $3,000 grant. See website for further details.

**Radcliffe Institute Fellowships**
8 Garden Street, Cambridge, MA 02138
Application Office
Tel: (617) 496-1324; Fax: (617) 495-8136
fellowships@radcliffe.edu
www.radcliffe.edu/fellowships
To support scholars, scientists, artists, and writers of exceptional promise and demonstrated accomplishments to pursue work in academic and professional fields and in the creative arts. Deadline: Oct. 1, 2010.

**Rhode Island State Council on the Arts**
1 Capitol Hill, Fl. 3, Providence, RI 2908
Cristina DiChiera
Tel: (401) 222-3880; Fax: (401) 422-3018
cristina@arts.ri.gov
www.arts.ri.gov
Fellowships in: film/video, play/screenwriting (April 1st); choreography and music composition (October 1st). Assistance: $5,000 and $1,000 Fellowship. $500-$10,000 Project Grant. Frequency: annual. **Submission.** Application. Author Must Be: age 18 or older, resident of RI, not a student. Material Must Be: completed within the past 3 years. How To Submit: Go to http://www. art.ri.gov/grants/guidelines. Deadline: April 1 and Oct. 1 every year.

**Rome Prize**
7 E. 60th St., New York, NY 10022
Tel: (212) 751-7200
info@aarome.org
www.aarome.org
Est. 1894. Annual yearlong fellowships to 15 emerging artists (literature, music, etc.) and 15 scholars (Italian studies). Literature candidates must be nominated through the American Academy of Arts and Letters. Music candidates may apply themselves. **Submission.** Application, 2-3 orchestral scores, CDs of included scores, resume, 1-pg proposal, 3 reference letters. Author Must Be: recipient of BA in music. Deadline: Nov. 30, 2010.

**South Carolina Arts Commission**
1800 Gervais St., Columbia, SC 29201
Jeanette Guinn
Tel: (803) 734-8677
jguinn@arts.us.gov
www.southcarolinaarts.com
Fellowships in three categories each yr, rotating between prose/poetry (odd yrs) and visual arts/crafts (even yrs), with third changing category, music, dance, theater. $5,000 grant. **Submission.** Application, support materials, SASE. Author Must Be: age 18 or older, 2-yr resident of SC, not a student. Deadline: Oct. 1, 2010.

**South Dakota Arts Council**
711 E. Wells Ave., Pierre, SD 57501
Michael Pangburn
Tel: (605) 773-3301; Fax: (605) 773-5657
sdac@state.sd.us
www.artscouncil.sd.gov
Est. 1966. $3,000 grant: annual. Response Time: 3 mos. **Submission.** Application, 30-pg sample, SASE. Author Must Be: resident of SD. Deadline: Mar. 1, 2010.

**TCG/ITI Travel Grants**
520 8th Ave., Fl. 24, New York, NY 10018
Mohammad Shatara
Tel: (212) 609-5900; Fax: (212) 609-5901
mshatara@tcg.org
www.tcg.org
Travel grants in fall/winter and spring/summer for travel to Russia and Eastern and Central Europe, to foster cultural exchange and artistic partnerships. $3,000 grant: semiannual. Response Time: 2 months. **Submission.** See website for details. Author Must Be: US Citizen, affiliated with a U.S. theatre company.

**Theatre Communications Group**
520 Eighth Ave. Fl. 24, New York, NY
David Nugent
www.tcg.org
Grants to professional nonprofit theaters for playwright residencies of at least 6 months. Playwrights create new work in residence at a host theatre. Individuals apply in collaboration with a host theater.. Response Time: 7 months. Style: adaptation, comedy, drama. **Submission.** Application. Author Must Be: resident of US. Opportunity/Award: $25000 award, program. How To Submit: with host theater.

**Travel & Study Grant Program**
400 Sibley St., #125, St. Paul, MN 55101
Cynthia Gehrig
Tel: (651) 224-9431; Fax: (651) 224-3439
www.jeromefdn.org
Author Must Be: resident of MN or NYC, emerging artist. Deadline: Feb. 15, 2011.

**U.S. Dept. of State Fulbright Program for US Students**
809 United Nations Plaza,
New York, NY 10017
Walter Jackson
Tel: (212) 984-5330
www.us.fulbrightonline.org
Est. 1946. Funds for graduate study, research, or teaching. Students in US colleges must apply thru campus Fulbright Advisers. Those not enrolled in US may apply directly to IIE. Annual. **Submission.** Application. Deadline: Oct 1 2010.

**United States/Japan Creative Artists' Fellowship**
1201 15th St. NW, Ste. 330,
Washington, DC 20005
Ms. Margaret Miltor
Tel: (202) 653-9800; Fax: (202) 653-9802
artist@jusfc.gov
www.jusfc.gov
6 month residency in Japan: up to $600,000 per month; up to $6000 per-departure costs. Annual. **Submission.** Application, submissions retured with SASE. Author Must Be: resident of US. How To Submit: unsolicited.

**Utah Arts Council**
617 E. South Temple,
Salt Lake City, UT 84102
Margaret Hunt

Tel: (801) 236-7555; Fax: (801) 236-7556
www.arts.utah.gov
Doesn't accept theatre scripts.

**Van Lier Fellowship**
424 W. 44th St., New York, NY 10036
2-yr program to help young,
economically disadvantaged
playwrights in NYC who are Asian-
American, African-American, Native
American or Latino.

**Vermont Arts Council**
136 State St., Drawer 33,
Montpelier, VT 5633
Sonia Rae
Tel: (802) 828-3293; Fax: (802) 828-3363
srae@vermontartscouncil.org
www.vermontartscouncil.org
Est. 1994. Opportunity Grants for
programs (organizations) creation, and
for artist development. Assistance:
$250–$5,000 grant. Annual.
Response Time: 2 mos. **Submission.**
Application, synopsis, 10-pg sample,
SASE. Author Must Be: age 18 or
older, resident of VT, not a student.
How To Submit: online. Deadline:
Various, see website.

**Virginia Commission for the Arts**
223 Governor St., Fl. 2,
Richmond, VA 23219
Peggy J. Baggett
Tel: (804) 225-3132; Fax: (804) 225-4327
arts@arts.virginia.gov
www.arts.virginia.gov
Artists Fellowships in rotating disciplines
announced each June. Annual.
**Submission.** Application. Author Must
Be: age 18 or older, resident of VA.
Opportunity/Award: $5,000. Deadline:
Aug. 1, 2010.

**Walt Disney Studios/ABC
Entertainment Writing Fellowship
Program**
500 S. Buena Vista St.,
Burbank, CA 91521
Tel: (818) 560-6894
abc.fellowship@abc.vom
www.abctalentdevelopment.com

Est. 1990. Fellowship for 1 year
in Disney's film or TV division in
Los Angeles. Disney retains right
of first refusal on work done during
fellowship. room/board, travel: annual.
**Submission.** Application, sample, cast
and scene breakdown, SASE. Material
Must Be: unpublished, unproduced.
How To Submit: unsolicited. Deadline:
Jun. 31, 2010.

**Wisconsin Arts Board**
101 E. Wilson St., Fl. 1,
Madison, WI 53702
Mark Fraire
Tel: (608) 264-8191; Fax: (608) 267-9629
mark.fraire@wisconsin.gov
www.arts.state.wi.us/static
Artist Fellowship Awards of
unrestricted funds to professional WI
artists. Rotating between Lit Arts,
Music Composition, Choreography/
Performance Art (even yrs), and
Visual/Media Arts (odd yrs). $8,000
grant: biennial. **Submission.** Online
application, 2-pg statement, 25-pg
sample, 3-track audio (composers
only), 3-pg resume, SASE. Author
Must Be: 1-yr resident of WI, not a fine
arts student. Deadline: Sep. 17, 2010.

**WordBRIDGE Playwrights Laboratory**
221 Brooks Center, Dept. of Performing
Arts, Clemson, SC 29634
Mark Charney, David White
Tel: (864) 656-5415; Fax: (864) 656-1013
cmark@clemson.edu
www.wordbridge.org
Submissions open in late fall 2010.
**Submission.** Application, full script
sent electronically. Author Must Be:
Student or graduate student. Material
Must Be: unpublished, unproduced.
Opportunity/Award: Two weeks at
WordBRIDGE in Clemson, S.C. How
To Submit: On line application only.
Deadline: Jan. 15, 2010.

**Wyoming Arts Council**
2320 Capitol Ave., Cheyenne, WY 82002
Rita Basom
Tel: (307) 777-7742; Fax: (307) 777-5499

ebratt@state.wy.us
www.wyoarts.state.wy.us
Performing Arts Fellowships are
awarded annually, in a 4-yr rotation.
In 2009, fellowships are for musical
performance. In 2010, fellowships are
for theater direction, choreography,
and stage design.

# THEATERS

**12 Miles West Theatre Company**
Box 1663, Bloomfield, NJ 7003
Lenny Bart
Tel: (973) 259-9187; Fax: (973) 259-9187
info@12mileswest.org
www.12mileswest.org
Est. 1992. Equity SPT-1. Production:
cast of 2-7, simple set. Response Time:
1 yr. What to Submit: query, synopsis,
full script, SASE, Opportunity/Award:
$500 or 5% royalty.

**16th St. Theater**
6420 16th. St., Berwyn, IL 60402
Ann Filmer
Tel: (708) 795-6704
info@16thstreettheater.org
www.16thstreettheater.org
We give preference to writers residing
in Illinois who are able to commit
to being a "playwright-in-residence"
for the season. We happily welcome
"second productions." No musicals
please. We are an Equity CAT Tier
N 49-seat new theater 10 miles west
of downtown Chicago dedicated to
writers. See web site for production
history. Style: Adaptation, Comedy
or Variety, Drama. Material Must Be:
Strong preference for IL. residents.

**1812 Productions**
421 N. 7th St., #218,
Philadelphia, PA 19123
Jennifer Childs
Tel: (215) 592-9560; Fax: (215) 592-9580
jen@1812productions.org
www.1812productions.org

Est. 1997. Response Time: 6 mos.
Style: comedy, musical comedy.
What To Submit: synopsis, character
breakdown, 10-page excerpt, musicals
please include cd.

**5th Avenue Theatre**
1308 5th Ave., Seattle, WA 98101
Bill Berry
Tel: (206) 625-1418; Fax: (206) 292-9610
info@5thavenue.org
www.5thavenue.org
Est. 1980. Production: cast of 8 or
more. Response Time: 6 mos. Style:
musical. What To Submit: full script,
audio. Material Must Be: unproduced.
How To Submit: agent.

**A Noise Within (ANW)**
234 S. Brand Blvd., Glendale, CA 91204
Geoff Elliot
Tel: (818) 240-0910; Fax: (818) 240-0826
boxoffice@anoisewithin.org
www.anoisewithin.org
Est. 1991. Equity Special Agreement.
Response Time: 8 mos. Style:
adaptation, translation of classical
work. What To Submit: full script.

**A. D. Players**
2710 W. Alabama St., Houston, TX 77098
Lee Walker
Tel: (713) 526-2721; Fax: (713) 521-1475
lee@adplayers.org
www.adplayers.org
Est. 1967. Production: cast limit 10
(mainstage)/8 (children's), piano
only, limited sets. Response Time:
3-6 mos. What to Submit: query,

synopsis, 10-pg sample. Material Must
Be: query, synopsis, 10-pg sample.
How To Submit: email professional
recommendation.

## Abingdon Theatre Company
312 W. 36th St., Fl. 6,
New York, NY 10018
Kim T. Sharp
Tel: (212) 868-2055; Fax: (212) 868-2056
ksharp@abingdontheatre.org
www.abingdontheatre.org
No musicals. Est. 1993. Equity
readings and full productions.
Production: cast limit 8. Response
Time: 3 - 6 mos. Deadline is ongoing.
Style: comedy, drama. What To
Submit: Mail printed and bound copy
of entire script, character breakdown,
synopsis, production history, bio, see
website for updates. Author Must
Be: US citizen. Material Must Be:
unoptioned, unproduced in NYC,
Opportunity/Award: All submission
considered for Christopher Brian Wolk
Award (see listing). How To Submit:
Regular mail.

## About Face Theatre (AFT)
1222 W. Wilson Ave., Fl. 2,
Chicago, IL 60640
Bonnie Metzgar, Art. Dir.
Rick Dildine, Mgr. Dir.
Tel: (773) 784-8565; Fax: (773) 784-8557
rick@aboutfacetheatre.com
www.aboutfacetheatre.com
Est. 1995. New plays exploring gender
and sexuality. Opportunities incl.
production and workshop/reading.
Production: no fly space. Style: all
styles, performance art considered.
What To Submit: Please check website
for guidelines.

## Absinthe-Minded Theatre Company
1484 Stadium Ave., Bronx, NY 10465
Ralph Scarpato
Tel: (212) 714-4696
rscarp@aol.com

## Act II Playhouse
56 E. Butler Pike, Ambler, PA 19002
Bud Martin
bud@act2.org
www.act2.org
Est. 1998. 130-seat SPT. Staff: Bud
Martin (Producing Artistic Director),
Harriet Power (Associate Artistic
Director). Style: comedy, drama,
musical. What To Submit: synopsis,
full script, SASE. Material Must Be:
unproduced.

## ACT Theater (A Contemporary Theatre)
700 Union St., Seattle, WA 98101
Anita Montgomery
Tel: (206) 292-7660; Fax: (206) 292-7670
act@acttheatre.org
www.acttheatre.org
Est. 1965. Equity LORT C. Special
programs incl. new play award and
new play development workshops.
Response Time: 6 mos. How To
Submit: agent, playwrights in WA,
OR, AK, ID, MT can submit synopsis
and 10 page sample.

## Acting Company
Box 898, Times Sq. Sta.,
New York, NY 10108
Margot Harley
Tel: (212) 258-3111; Fax: (212) 258-3299
mail@theactingcompany.org
www.theactingcompany.org
Est. 1972. Prefer solo one-acts on US
historical figures for HS tours and full-
length adaptations of classic novels.
Production: cast limit 13, touring
theater. How To Submit: agent.

## Actors Art Theatre (AAT)
6128 Wilshire Blvd., #110,
Los Angeles, CA 90048
Jolene Adams
actorsart@actorsart.com
www.actorsart.com
Est. 1994. 32-seat theater developing
plays thru workshops and labs.
Produces 1 original play each year,
plus one-acts and solos under Equity
99-seat. Production: no orchestra.

Response Time: 1 yr. Style: no
musical. What To Submit: query,
synopsis, 10-pg sample, submissions
not returned. Material Must Be:
unoptioned, unproduced on West
Coast, Opportunity/Award: 6% royalty.
How To Submit: email.

**Actors Collective**
447 W. 48th St., Ste. 1W,
New York, NY 10036
Catherine Russell
Tel: (212) 445-1016; Fax: (212) 445-1015
postarvis@aol.com
www.perfect-crime.com
     Est. 1981. Equity Off-Broadway.
     Production: cast limit 8. Response
     Time: 1 mo. What to Submit: query,
     SASE. How To Submit: brief synopsis,
     SASE.

**Actor's Express**
887 W. Marietta St. NW, #J-107,
Atlanta, GA 30318
Freddie Ashley
Tel: (404) 875-1606; Fax: (404) 875-2791
freddie@actorsexpress.com
www.actors-express.com
     Est. 1988. AEA Guest Artist Contract.
     Opportunities incl. readings,
     workshops, production. Assistance:
     room/board, travel. Response Time:
     6 mos. Style: no adaptation. What
     To Submit: full script, Opportunity/
     Award: 6%-8% royalty. How To
     Submit: agent.

**Actors Theatre of Louisville [KY]**
316 W. Main St., Louisville, KY 40202
Amy Wegener
Tel: (502) 584-1265; Fax: (502) 561-3300
awegener@actorstheatre.org
www.actorstheatre.org
     Reading cycle April-Oct; best time
     to submit: April-August. Est. 1964.
     Equity LORT B, C and D. 1980
     Regional Theater Tony winner.
     Response Time: 9 mos. What to
     Submit: query, synopsis, 10-pg sample.
     Material Must Be: unproduced. How
     To Submit: agent.

**Actors Theatre of Phoenix**
P.O. Box 1924, Phoenix, AZ 85001
Matthew Wiener
Tel: (602) 253-6701; Fax: (602) 254-9577
info@actorstheatrePHX.org
www.actorstheatrephx.org
     Est. 1985. Production: cast limit
     8. Response Time: 10 mos. Style:
     contemporary, political, comedy,
     drama. How To Submit: professional
     recommendation.

**Adirondack Theatre Festival**
Box 3203, Glens Falls, NY 12801
Mark Fleischer
Tel: (518) 798-7479; Fax: (518) 793-1334
atf@ATFestival.org
www.atfestival.org
     Est. 1995. Production: cast limit 10,
     no fly space. Response Time: 6 mos
     query, 6 mos script. How To Submit:
     synopsis, 10 sample pages and
     professional recommendation.

**Adventure Stage Chicago (ASC)**
1012 N. Noble St., Chicago, IL 60641
Tom Arvetis
Tel: (773) 342-4141; Fax: (773) 278-2621
email@adventurestage.org
www.adventurestage.org
     Est. 1998. Annual TYA season.
     Production: ages 18 and older, cast
     limit 10. Response Time: 1 mo. What
     to Submit: synopsis, 10-pg sample,
     character breakdown, Opportunity/
     Award: 6% royalty. How To Submit:
     By mail.

**African Continuum Theatre Co.
(ACTCo)**
3523 12th St. NE, Fl. 2,
Washington, DC 20017
JoAnn M. Williams
Tel: (202) 529-5763; Fax: (202) 529-5764
jmwilliams@africancontinuumtheatre.com
www.africancontinuumtheatre.com
     Est. 1996. Fresh Flavas Reading
     Series: staged readings of three-works-
     in-progress per year. Production: small
     cast, unit set.

**AfroSolo Theatre Company**
762 Fulton St. #307,
San Francisco, CA 94102
Thomas Robert Simpson
Tel: (415) 771-2376; Fax: (415) 771-2312
info@afrosolo.org
www.afrosolo.org
　　Solo work only, usually to be
　　performed by writer. Send up to 10pg
　　synosis, bio, photo. Deadline: ongoing.
　　Style: Written by African Americas or
　　African American diaspora. How To
　　Submit: email, mail.

**Alabama Shakespeare Festival**
1 Festival Dr., Montgomery, AL 36117
Bruce Sevy
Tel: (334) 271-5300; Fax: (334) 271-5348
www.asf.net

**All Arts Matter**
Box 513, Greenville, NY 10283
Tony DeVito
Tel: (518) 966-4038
allartsmatter@juno.com
www.allartsmatter.org
　　Est. 2000. Producing unit of
　　diversified arts organization.
　　Reading series and play productions.
　　Assistance: Royalty and/or room/
　　board, travel. Response Time: 6 wks.
　　What to Submit: full script, SASE.
　　How To Submit: agent.

**Allenberry Playhouse**
Box 7, Boiling Springs, PA 17007
Claude Giroux
Tel: (717) 960-3211; Fax: (717) 960-5280
Aberry@allenberry.com
www.allenberry.com
　　Production: age 20-60, cast of
　　6-10, orchestra limit 5. Style:
　　adaptation, comedy, musical, farce.
　　What To Submit: query, 20-pg
　　sample, submissions not returned,
　　Opportunity/Award: royalty.

**Alley Theatre**
615 Texas Ave., Houston, TX 77002
Mark Bly
Tel: (713) 228-9341 ext. 369
Fax: (713) 222-6542
webmaster@alleytheatre.org

www.alleytheatre.org
　　Est. 1947. 1996 Regional Theater Tony
　　winner. Response Time: 3 months.
　　Style: Open. No restrictions. How To
　　Submit: Professional recommendation
　　or inquiry letter.

**Alliance Theatre**
1280 Peachtree St. NE,
Atlanta, GA 30309
Celise Kalke
Tel: (404) 733-4650; Fax: (404) 733-4625
allianceinfo@woodruffcenter.org
www.alliancetheatre.org
　　Est. 1968. Equity LORT B and D,
　　TYA. 2007 Regional Theater Tony
　　winner. 11 shows in 2 spaces: 800-
　　seat proscenium, 200-seat black box.
　　Response Time: 1 yr. What to Submit:
　　query, 10-pg sample, full script,
　　SASE. How To Submit: agent.

**Allied Theater Group/Stage West**
821 West Vickery Blvd.,
Fort Worth, TX 76107
Jim Covault
Tel: (817) 784-9378; Fax: (817) 348-8392
boxoffice@stagewest.org
www.stagewest.org
　　Equity SPT. Formerly Stage West
　　& Fort Worth Shakespeare Festival.
　　Production: cast limit 9. Response
　　Time: 1 mo query, 3 mos script. Style:
　　adaptation, comedy, drama, musical,
　　translation. What To Submit: query,
　　synopsis.

**Altarena Playhouse / Alameda Little
Theater**
1409 High St., Alameda, CA 94501
Susan Dunn
Tel: (510) 764-9718
www.altarena.org
　　Est. 1938. Non-Equity volunteer
　　community theater offering readings,
　　new works by local playwrights.
　　Production: cast limit 16, orchestra
　　limit 10, minimal set, in the round.
　　Response Time: 6 mos. Style: comedy,
　　drama, musical, solo. What To Submit:
　　query, full script. Author Must Be:
　　resident of Bay Area. How To Submit:
　　professional recommendation.

**Amas Musical Theatre**
115 MacDougal St., #2-B,
New York, NY 10012
Donna Trinkoff
Tel: (212) 563-2565; Fax: (212) 239-8332
amas@amasmusical.org
www.amasmusical.org
> Est. 1968. Most productions begin in
> Six O'Clock Musical Theater Lab,
> featuring staged readings of new
> musicals (at least 3 in spring, 3 in fall).
> Production: small cast (multi-ethnic
> encouraged). Response Time: at least 6
> mos. Style: musical. What To Submit:
> synopsis, full script, audio, scene list,
> SASE.

**American Folklore Theatre (AFT)**
Box 273, Fish Creek, WI 54212
Jeffrey Herbst
Tel: (920) 854-6117; Fax: (920) 854-9106
aft@folkloretheatre.com
www.folkloretheatre.com
> Est. 1990. Equity LOA, LORT D.
> Original musical works for families.
> Production: cast of 3-10. Style:
> musical. What To Submit: email
> synopsis, cast breakdown, script
> sample, regular mail include SASE,
> Opportunity/Award: commission and
> royalty. How To Submit: professional
> recommendation.

**American Music Theater Festival/
Prince Music Theater**
100 S. Broad St., #650,
Philadelphia, PA 19110
Tel: (215) 972-1000; Fax: (215) 972-1020
www.princemusictheater.org

**American Theater Company**
1909 W. Byron St., Chicago, IL 60613
Tel: (773) 929-5009; Fax: (773) 929-5171
info@atcweb.org
www.atcweb.org
> Est. 1985. Style: musical or, play.
> What To Submit: Please see website
> for submission opportunities. Material
> Must Be: Address the mission
> statement: "What does it mean to be
> an American?"

**American Theatre of Harlem**
138 S. Oxford St., Brooklyn, NY 11217
Keith Johnston
Tel: (718) 857-2783; Fax: (718) 398-2794
info@americantheatreofharlem.org
www.americantheatreofharlem.org

**American Theatre of Actors, Inc. (ATA)**
314 W. 54th St., New York, NY 10019
James Jennings
Tel: (212) 581-3044
americantheatreofactors@gmail.com
www.americantheatreofactors.org
> Est. 1976. New plays by new writers
> for 1-4 wks, both Equity and non-
> Equity. Plays rehearse 3-4 wks.
> Production: age 20-80, cast of 3-6, set
> limit 2. Response Time: 3 wks. Style:
> comedy, drama. What To Submit: full
> script, SASE. Author Must Be: age
> 20 or older, resident of US. Material
> Must Be: unoptioned, unpublished,
> unproduced.

**Amphibian Productions**
1300 Gendy Street, Fort Worth, TX 76107
Kathleen Culebro
Tel: (817) 923-3012
info@amphibianproductions.org
www.amphibianproductions.org
> Est. 2000. Produces plays and
> readings in Ft. Worth and New
> York City. Production: cast limit 6,
> set limit 2. Response Time: 8 mos.
> Style: no musical. What To Submit:
> query, SASE, Opportunity/Award:
> production, reading. How To Submit:
> professional recommendation via
> regular mail, do not email.

**Animated Theaterworks Inc.**
240 Central Park S., #13-B,
New York, NY 10019
Elysabeth Kleinhans
info@animatedtheaterworks.org
www.animatedtheaterworks.org
> Est. 1999. Readings and showcase
> productions of new and developing
> works. Production: cast limit 6,
> unit set. Response Time: 6 mos.
> Style: comedy, drama. What To
> Submit: query, synopsis, 10-15 pg

sample, SASE for return of materials if desired. Material Must Be: unpublished, unproduced. How To Submit: Hard copy only by mail.

**Arden Theatre Company**
40 N. 2nd St., Philadelphia, PA 19106
Dennis Smeal
dsmeal@ardentheatre.org
www.ardentheater.org
Est. 1988. Equity LORT D, TYA. 7 shows/yr in 360-seat and 175-seat house. Response Time: 10 wks. Style: adaptation, drama, musical. What To Submit: synopsis, 10-pg sample, submissions not returned. Agent - full script. How To Submit: Email. See website for submission detail.

**Arena Players Repertory Theatre**
296 Rte. 109, E. Farmingdale, NY 11735
Fred De Feis
Tel: (516) 293-0674; Fax: (516) 858-0292
arena109@aol.com
www.arenaplayers.org
Est. 1950. Production: cast of 2-10. Response Time: 6 mos. What to Submit: query, synopsis, full script, SASE. Material Must Be: unoptioned, unpublished, unproduced, Opportunity/Award: $600.

**Arena Stage**
1101 6th St. SW, Washington, DC 20024
Janine Sobeck
Tel: (202) 554-9066; Fax: (202) 488-4056
www.arenastage.org
Est. 1950. Equity LORT B+, B and D. 1976 Regional Theater Tony winner. Response Time: 3 mos. Opportunity/ Award: How To Submit: professional recommendation. Agent only, no unsolicited.

**Arizona Theatre Company**
Box 1631, Tucson, AZ 85702
Jennifer Bazzell
Tel: (520) 884-8210 ext. 8510
jbazzell@arizonatheatre.org
www.arizonatheatre.org
Est. 1966. Equity LORT B. Response Time: 6 mos. What to Submit: query,

synopsis, 10-pg sample, SASE. How To Submit: Out-of-state writers must submit query packet before sending entire script; does not accept material via email.

**Arkansas Repertory Theatre**
Box 110, Little Rock, AR 72201
Robert Hupp
Tel: (866) 6TH-EREP; Fax: (501) 378-0012
www.therep.org
Production: small cast. Response Time: 3 mos query, 6 mos script. What to Submit: query, synopsis.

**Ars Nova**
511 W. 54th St., New York, NY 10019
Jason Eagan
Tel: (212) 489-9800; Fax: (212) 489-1908
www.arsnovanyc.com
Ars Nova is committed to developing and producing eclectic theater, comedy and music to feed today's popular culture. To that end, Ars Nova strives to meld disciplines and give clear voice to a new generation of artists. Ars Nova was founded in memory of Gabe Weiner. Opportunity/ Award: music series, comedy series, and a playwrights group. "out loud" play reading series.

**ART Station**
Box 1998, Stone Mountain, GA 30086
Jon Goldstein
Tel: (770) 469-1105; Fax: (770) 469-0355
jon@artstation.org
www.artstation.org
Est. 1986. Equity SPT. Works representing Southern experience. Production: cast limit 6. Response Time: 1 yr. Style: comedy, musical. What To Submit: synopsis, 10-pg sample, SASE, Opportunity/Award: 7% royalty. How To Submit: through regular mail, no emails please.

**Art Within**
1080 Holcomb Bridge Rd., Bldg. 200, , Roswell, GA 30076
Bryan Coley
artwithin@artwithin.org

/www.artwithin.org
    Est. 1995. Commission 5 full-lengths
    each year for workshop and showcase.
    Response Time: 6 months. Style:
    all styles. What To Submit: Query,
    synopsis, full script, submissions
    returned with SASE. Material Must
    Be: Not Optional, Not Published,
    Not Produced, Opportunity/Award:
    $2,000. How To Submit: unsolicited.

**Artists Repertory Theatre**
1516 SW Alder St., Portland, OR 97205
Stephanie Mulligan
Tel: (503) 241-9807 ext. 110
Fax: (503) 241-8268
www.artistsrep.org
    Est. 1981. Equity SPT-8, with 7
    shows per season on 2 stages, plus
    staged readings. Response Time:
    2 mos query, 6 mos script. Style:
    Contemporary; fresh adaptation of
    classics, small cast musicals. What To
    Submit: query, synopsis, SASE.

**ArtsPower National Touring Theatre**
271 Grove Ave. Bldg. A, Velena, NJ
07044
Gary Blackman
gblackman@artspower.org
www.artspower.org
    Tourable theater presenting one-act
    plays and musicals for young and
    family audiences. Production: cast
    limit 4. Style: adaptation, drama,
    musical. What To Submit: synopsis,
    audio, SASE. Material Must Be:
    unpublished.

**Arvada Center for the Arts and
Humanities**
6901 Wadsworth Blvd., Arvada, CO 80003
Kathy Kuehn
Tel: (720) 898-7285; Fax: (720) 898-7217
www.arvadacenter.org
    Est. 1976. Production: cast of 6-9,
    minimal set. Response Time: 5 mos
    query, 8 mos script. What to Submit:
    query, synopsis. Not currently
    accepting submissions.

**Asian American Theater Company**
690 Fifth St., #211,
San Francisco, CA 94107
Pearl Wong
Tel: (415) 543-5738
www.asianamericantheater.org
    Est. 1973. What to Submit: synopsis,
    30-pg sample, submissions not
    returned. How To Submit: mail, email
    preferred.

**Asolo Repertory Theatre**
5555 N. Tamiami Tr., Sarasota, FL 34243
Sasso Lauryn
Tel: (941) 351-9010; Fax: (941) 351-5796
lit_intern@asolo.org
www.asolo.org
    Est. 1960. What to Submit: Letter of
    Inquiry, 10 page sample, electronic
    submission, email. How To Submit:
    invite, email preferred.

**Asylum Theatre**
4441 Rockaway Beach St.,
Las Vegas, NV 89129
Sarah O'Connell
Tel: (702) 604-3417; Fax: (702) 650-0242
sarah@asylumtheatre.org
www.asylumtheatre.org
    Est. 1997. Assistance: 100-200.
    Style: all styles. What To Submit:
    Full script, One-Acts, Short Script,
    SASE optional. Material Must Be:
    unoptioned, prefer non-produced but
    not required. How To Submit: email.

**Atlantic Theater Company**
76 9th Ave., #537, New York, NY 10011
Christian Parker
Tel: (212) 691-5919; Fax: (212) 645-8755
literary@atlantictheater.org
www.atlantictheater.org
    Est. 1985. Off-Broadway, LOA.
    4-show mainstage season, 2-show
    second stage season. Staff: Neil Pepe
    (Artistic Dir). Response Time: 6 mos.
    Style: all styles. What To Submit:
    query, synopsis, 20 pg sample, full
    script, audio, SASE. How To Submit:
    professional recommendation, agent,
    inquiry.

**Attic Ensemble**
83 Wayne St., Jersey City, NJ 07302
Mary Anne Murphy
Tel: (201) 413-9200
info@atticensemble.org
www.atticensemble.org
> Est. 1970. Production: cast 4-8,
> character ages 15-65, unit set or
> conceptual. Style: comedy, drama, no
> musical. What To Submit: full script,
> submissions returned with SASE.
> Author Must Be: ages 15-65. How To
> Submit: unsolicited.

**Aurora Theatre, Inc. [GA]**
128 E Pike St., Lawrenceville, GA 30045
Anthony Rodriguez
Tel: (678) 226-6222
info@auroratheatre.com
www.auroratheatre.com
> Established in 1996, Aurora Theatre
> has a 100-seat studio and 248 Main
> Stage. Style: Musicals, Plays that help
> create a new generation of theatre
> goers. What To Submit: full script,
> audio, bio. How To Submit: Send an
> inquiry email to info@auroratheatre.
> com.

**b current**
Artscape Wychwood Barns,
601 Christie St., Studio 251,
Toronto, Ontario M6F-4C7 Canada
Kayla McGee
Tel: (416) 533-1500; Fax: (416) 533-1560
office@bcurrent.ca
www.bcurrent.ca
> Toronto-based arts company that
> presents and supports performance
> works emerging from the Canadian
> and International Black Diaspora. b
> current hosts annual themed festival.
> See website for details. Style: cultural,
> contemporary. What To Submit: Plays
> or other performance creations. How
> To Submit: By mail, or email. See
> website for deadline.

**B Street Theatre**
2711 B St., Sacramento, CA 95816
Buck Busfield
Tel: (916) 443-5391 ext. 107

Fax: (916) 443-0874
www.bstreettheatre.org
> Est. 1991. Equity SPT & TYA. 220
> seat thrust. Production: cast limit 6,
> no fly. Style: comedy, drama. How To
> Submit: agent.

**Bailiwick Repertory Theatre**
3023 N. Clark, #327, Chicago, IL 60657
Kevin Mays
Tel: (773) 883-1090
Bailiwick@Bailiwick.org
www.bailiwick.org
> Est. 1982. Mainstage Series; Deaf
> Bailiwick Artists; The Lesbian
> Initiative; College/University
> Playwriting Festival. How To Submit:
> online.

**Barksdale Theatre**
114 W. Broad St., Richmond, VA 23220
Janine Serresseque
Tel: (804) 783-1688; Fax: (804) 288-6470
TheatreIVandBarksdale@gmail.com
www.barksdalerichmond.org
> Est. 1953. Production: small cast, no
> fly or wing space. Response Time:
> 6 mos query, 1 yr script. What to
> Submit: query, synopsis, full script.
> How To Submit: email j.serresseque@
> theatreirichmond.org, or regular mail.

**Barrington Stage Company**
30 Union Street, Pittsfield, MA 01201
Tel: (413) 499-5446; Fax: (413) 499-5447
info@berkshire.net
www.barringtonstageco.org
> Est. 1995. Production: cast of 4-8
> (plays) or 10-12 (musicals), modest set.
> Response Time: 1 mo query, 6 mos
> script. What to Submit: query, 1-pg
> synopsis, 10-pg sample, audio.

**Barrow Group**
312 W. 36th St., #4-W,
New York, NY 10018
Literary Dept.
Tel: (212) 760-2615
development@barrowgroup.org
www.barrowgroup.org
> Est. 1986. Equity Nonprofit Tier 2.
> Offers 1-2 mainstage shows/yr, plus

readings and workshops. Response Time: 1 mo query, 4 mos script. What to Submit: no unsolicited. agents only.

**Barter Theatre**
PO Box 867, Abingdon, VA 24212
Richard Rose
Tel: (276) 628-3991; Fax: (276) 619-3335
barterinfo@bartertheatre.com
www.bartertheatre.com
  Best to submit June through December. Est. 1933. Equity LORT D. 1948 Regional Theater Tony winner. Response Time: 6-8 months. Style: all styles. What To Submit: query, synopsis, 10-pg. sample, audio, submission returned with SASE, Opportunity/Award: reading, royalties. How To Submit: professional recommendation, agent, invite.

**Bay Street Theatre**
Box 810, Sag Harbor, NY 11963
Sybil Christopher
Tel: (631) 725-0818; Fax: (631) 725-0906
www.baystreet.org
  Est. 1991. Equity LORT C. Opportunities incl. mainstage season and play reading series. Production: cast limit 9, unit set, no fly or wing space. Response Time: 6 mos. How To Submit: agent.

**Belmont Italian American Playhouse**
2385 Arthur Ave., Bronx, NY 10458
Dante Albertie
Tel: (718) 364-4348; Fax: (718) 563-5053
thebelmont@hotmail.com
  Production: cast of up to 6. Response Time: 5/15/04. Style: musical, no translation. What To Submit: synopsis, full script, submissions returned with SASE. Material Must Be: unpublished, unproduced. How To Submit: unsolicited.

**Berkeley Repertory Theatre**
2025 Addison St., Berkeley, CA 94702
Madeleine Oldham
Tel: (510) 647-2900; Fax: (510) 647-2976
info@berkeleyrep.org
www.berkeleyrep.org

Est. 1968. 1997 Regional Theater Tony winner. Response Time: 8 mos. What to Submit: full script, SASE. Author Must Be: Bay Area Resident. How To Submit: mail.

**Berkshire Public Theater**
Box 860, 30 Union St.,
Pittsfield, MA 01202
Frank Bessell

**Berkshire Theatre Festival**
P.O. Box 797, Stockbridge, MA 01262
Kate Maguire
Tel: (413) 298-5536 ext. 18
Fax: (413) 298-3368
www.berkshiretheatre.org
  Est. 1928. Equity. Opportunities incl. new works, small musicals. Production: cast of up to 8. Response Time: only if interested. What to Submit: submissions not returned. How To Submit: agent.

**Black Dahlia Theatre**
5453 W. Pico Blvd.,
Los Angeles, CA 90019
Tel: (323) 525-0085
info@thedahlia.com
www.thedahlia.com

**Black Ensemble Theater**
4520 North Beacon, Chicago, IL 60640
Jackie Taylor
BlackEnsemble@aol.com
www.blackensembletheater.org
  Est. 1976. Style: musicals only, except for Black Playwrights Fest and drama.

**Black Rep**
1717 Olive St., Fl. 4, St. Louis, MO 63103
Ron Himes
Tel: (314) 534-3807; Fax: (314) 534-4035
ameerch@theblackrep.org
www.theblackrep.org
  Est. 1976. What to Submit: query, synopsis, 3-5 pg. sample, resume to Ameer Harper, Assistant to Executive Director, at ameerh@theblackrep.org.

**Black Spectrum Theatre**
119-07 Merrick Boulevard,
Jamaica, NY 11434
Literary Manager
Tel: (718) 723-1800; Fax: (718) 723-1806
info@blackspectrum.com
www.blackspectrum.com
> How To Submit: Mail full script and
> contact information.

**Black Swan Theater**
825-C Merrimon Ave., #318,
Asheville, NC 28804
David B. Hopes
Fax: (828) 251-6603
swanthtre@aol.com
www.blackswan.org
> Est. 1988. Non-Equity theater
> specializing in developing new scripts
> or revisiting classics. Production:
> modest cast, simple set. Response
> Time: 3 mos. What to Submit: full
> script. Material Must Be: unpublished.

**Blinn College Theatre Arts Program**
902 College Ave., Brenham, TX 77833
Bradley Nies
Tel: (979) 830-4269; Fax: (979) 830-4860
bnies@blinn.edu
www.blinn.edu/finearts/theatre.html

**Bloomsburg Theatre Ensemble (BTE)**
226 Center St., Bloomsburg, PA 17815
Gerard P. Stropnicky
Tel: (570) 784-5530; Fax: (570) 784-4912
www.bte.org
> Est. 1978. Production: small to mid-
> sized cast, unit set. Response Time:
> 3 mos query, 6 mos script. Style:
> adaptation, translation. What To
> Submit: query, synopsis, sample.
> How To Submit: professional
> recommendation.

**BoarsHead Theatre**
425 S. Grand Ave., Lansing, MI 48933
Molly Keenan
Tel: (517) 484-7800; Fax: (517) 484-2564
www.boarshead.org
> Est. 1966. Equity SPT-6, 250 seat
> house. John Dale Smith (Executive
> Director). Response Time: 6 mos.

> What to Submit: query, synopsis,
> SASE, Opportunity/Award: royalty.

**Bond Street Theatre**
2 Bond St., New York, NY 10012
Joanna Sherman
Tel: (212) 254-4614; Fax: (212) 460-9378
info@bondst.org
www.bondst.org
> Response Time: 1 mo. Style: nonverbal
> scripts (dance, masks, music, circus
> arts, gestural arts). What To Submit:
> query, synopsis, SASE.

**Borderlands Theater**
Box 2791, Tucson, AZ 85702
Toni Press-Coffman
Tel: (520) 882-8607; Fax: (520) 884-4264
tpplay@cox.net
www.borderlandstheater.org
> Est. 1986. Production: cast limit 12,
> minimal set. Response Time: 1 mo
> query, 6 mos script. Style: adaptation,
> translation. What To Submit: query,
> synopsis.

**Boston Playwrights' Theatre**
949 Commonwealth Ave.,
Boston, MA 02215
Michael Duncan Smith
Tel: (617) 353-5443; Fax: (617) 353-6196
newplays@bu.edu
www.bu.edu/bpt
> Est. 1981. Equity SPT. Opportunities
> incl. production and workshop.
> Production: cast limit 8, black
> box set. Response Time: 6 mos.
> What to Submit: query, SASE.
> Author Must Be: student or alum
> of Boston Univ. Material Must Be:
> unoptioned, unpublished, unproduced,
> Opportunity/Award: $500 honorarium.
> How To Submit: unsolicited.

**Brat Productions**
56 S. 2nd St., Philadelphia, PA 19106
Tel: (215) 627-2577; Fax: (215) 627-4304
brat@bratproductions.org
www.bratproductions.org
> Est. 1996. Production: cast limit 7,
> unit set. Response Time: 1 mo query,
> 6 mos script. What to Submit: query,
> synopsis, sample.

**Brava! for Women in the Arts**
2781 24th St., San Francisco, CA 94110
Hetal Patel
Tel: (415) 641-7657; Fax: (415) 641-7684
info@brava.org
www.brava.org
    Est. 1986. Response Time: 6 mos
    query, 8 mos script. What to Submit:
    query, synopsis, sample. Author Must
    Be: woman, woman of color, LGBTQ
    issues. How To Submit: email.

**Break A Leg Productions**
Box 20503, Hammarskjold Ctr.,
New York, NY 10017
Elisa London
breakalegproductionsnyc@yahoo.com
www.breakalegproductions.com
    Est. 1995. Equity Showcase. Staff: Teri
    Black (Artistic Dir.). Production: age
    20-60, cast of 8-10, unit set. Response
    Time: 9 mos. Style: comedy. What To
    Submit: full script, SASE.

**Bristol Riverside Theatre [PA]**
Box 1250, Bristol, PA 19007
Keith Baker
Tel: (215) 785-6664; Fax: (215) 785-2762
Keith@brtstage.org
www.brtstage.org
    Est. 1986. Production: cast limit 10
    (plays) or 18 (musicals), orchestra limit
    9. Response Time: 18 mos. What to
    Submit: full script.

**Broken Watch Theatre Company**
6495 Broadway, Unit 2M,
New York, NY 10471
Drew DeCorleto
Tel: (212) 397-2935; Fax: (775) 263-6024
contact@brokenwatch.org
www.brokenwatch.org
    Est. 2001. Equity Showcase. Style:
    comedy, drama. What To Submit:
    synopsis, SASE. Author Must Be:
    resident or citizen of US. Material
    Must Be: unoptioned, unpublished,
    unproduced. How To Submit:
    professional recommendation.

**Buntville Crew**
118 North Railroad, Buckley, IL 60918
Steven Packard
buntville@yahoo.fr
    Est. 1999. What to Submit: full
    script. Material Must Be: unoptioned,
    unpublished. How To Submit:
    unsolicited.

**Burning Coal Theatre Company**
Box 90904, Raleigh, NC 27675
Jerome Davis
Tel: (919) 834-4001; Fax: (919) 834-4002
burning_coal@ipass.net
www.burningcoal.org
    Est. 1995. 4 staged readings/yr.
    Response Time: 6 mos. What to
    Submit: full script, SASE. Author
    Must Be: resident of, or connected to
    NC. Material Must Be: unpublished,
    unproduced, Opportunity/Award:
    reading. Deadline: Dec. 16, 2010.

**Caffeine Theatre**
PO Box 1904, Chicago, IL 60690
Jennifer Shook
Tel: (312) 409-4778
info@caffeinetheatre.com
www.caffeinetheatre.com
    Please see mission and recent
    programming at www.caffeinetheatre.
    com: plays in conversation with the
    poetic tradition. Style: Adaptation,
    Comedy or Variety, Drama, Musical,
    Translation. What To Submit: Not
    currently accepting unsolicited
    work, Opportunity/Award: Reading,
    Workshop, Production, Royalties.
    How To Submit: Professional
    recommendation, agent.

**Caldwell Theatre Company**
7901 N. Federal Hwy.,
Boca Raton, FL 33487
Patricia Burdett
Tel: (561) 241-7380; Fax: (561) 997-6917
patricia@caldwelltheatre.com
www.caldwelltheatre.com
    Est. 1975. Equity LOA. Playsearch
    series reads 4 plays annually with 500-
    600 people in audience. Production:
    cast of up to 8. Response Time:

varies. Style: all styles. What To
Submit: synopsis, # of characters, set
requirements, character description,
production history, resume.

**California Theatre Center**
Box 2007, Sunnyvale, CA 94087
Will Huddleston
Tel: (408) 245-2979; Fax: (408) 245-0235
resdir@ctcinc.org
www.ctcinc.org
   Est. 1976. Nonprofit for youth. Theatre
   for young audiences- non- equity. Two
   types of scripts sought: Cast of 4-8 one
   hour plays performed by ADULTS for
   children. Cast of 15-30 one-hour plays
   performed by children. Production:
   cast limit 6, touring set. Response
   Time: 4 mos. What to Submit: query,
   synopsis, SASE, Opportunity/Award:
   neg. fee. How To Submit: unsolicited.

**Capital Repertory Theatre**
111 N. Pearl St., Albany, NY 12207
Maggie Mancinelli-Cahill
Tel: (518) 462-4531; Fax: (518) 465-0213
info@capitalrep.org
www.capitalrep.org
   Est. 1981. LORT D.

**Casa Manana Inc.**
930 W. 1st St., #200, Ft. Worth, TX 76102
Wally Jones
Tel: (817)-321-5012; Fax: (817)-332-5711
wally.jones@casamanana.org
www.casamanana.org

**Celebration Theatre**
7985 Santa Monica Blvd., #109-1,
Los Angeles, CA 90046
Zina Camblin
Tel: (323) 957-1884; Fax: (323) 957-1826
admin@celebrationtheatre.com
www.celebrationtheatre.com
   Deadline rolling. Est. 1982. Equity
   99-seat. Accepting scripts for
   Celebrating New Works, a workshop
   series for unproduced works. Work
   must fall within Celebration Theatre's
   Mission Statement. Production: cast
   limit 12. Response Time: none unless
   interested. What to Submit: 1-pg

synopsis, full script, bio. Material
Must Be: original, unproduced. How
To Submit: hard copy via mail.

**Celtic Arts Center (An Claidheamh Soluis)**
4843 Laurel Canyon Blvd.,
Studio City, CA 91607
Tel: (818) 760-8322
celt@celticartscenter.com
www.celticartscenter.com
   99-seat. Style: all styles. What To
   Submit: query, synopsis, SASE. How
   To Submit: unsolicited.

**Center Stage [MD]**
700 N. Calvert St., Baltimore, MD 21202
Drew Lichtenberg
Tel: (410) 986-4042
dlichtenberg@centerstage.org
www.centerstage.org
   Est. 1963. Equity LORT B, C. What
   to Submit: query, synopsis, 10-pg
   sample, audio, SASE. Material Must
   Be: unproduced.

**Center Stage Community Playhouse**
Box 138, Westchester Square Station,
Bronx, NY 10461
John Liszewski
Tel: (212) 823-6434
info@centerstageplayhouse.org
www.centerstageplayhouse.org
   Est. 1969. Nonprofit community
   theater. Response Time: 2 mos. Style:
   adaptation, comedy, drama. What
   To Submit: query, SASE. Material
   Must Be: unoptioned, unpublished,
   unproduced. How To Submit: invite.

**Center Theater Company**
1010 N. W. C. Macinnes Pl.,
Tampa, FL 33602
Karla Hartley
Tel: (813) 222-100;0 Fax: (813) 222-1057
www.tbpac.org
   Est. 1987. Formerly Tampa Bay PAC.
   Production: small cast, unit set.
   Response Time: 2 months. Style:
   comedy, drama. What To Submit: full
   script. Author Must Be: woman. How
   To Submit: unsolicited.

**Center Theatre Group (CTG)**
601 W. Temple St.,
Los Angeles, CA 90012
Mike Sablone
Tel: (213) 972-8033
scriptsi@ctgla.org
www.centertheatregroup.org
Est. 1967. Incl. Ahmanson Theatre and
Mark Taper Forum (1977 Regional
Theater Tony winner) at Music Center
in L.A. and Kirk Douglas Theatre in
Culver City. Response Time: 6 wks.
What to Submit: query, synopsis, 5-10
pg sample, SASE. How To Submit:
mail, email.

**Chameleon Theatre Company Ltd.**
25-26 42nd St., #3-B, Astoria, NY 11103
Robert D. Carver
robertcarver@yahoo.com
chameleonthatrecompanyltd.org
Est. 1987. Dedicated to developing
new plays and musicals, primarily
originated in-house or recommended
by professional associates. Staff: Cash
Tilton (Co-Artistic Dir). Response
Time: 2 mos. What to Submit: query,
SASE. Material Must Be: unoptioned,
unpublished, unproduced. How To
Submit: professional recommendation.

**Charleston Stage**
Box 356, Charleston, SC 29402
Julian Wiles
Tel: (843) 577-5967; Fax: (843) 577-5422
www.charlestonstage.com
Est. 1977. In residence at the Historic
Dock Street Theater. Production: small
cast. Response Time: 2 mos. How To
Submit: professional recommendation.

**Charter Theatre**
Box 3505, Reston, VA 20195

**Cherry Lane Theatre**
38 Commerce St., New York, NY 10014
Dave Batan
Tel: (212) 989-2020; Fax: (212) 989-2867
company@cherrylanetheatre.org
www.cherrylanetheatre.org

**Chicago Theater Company**
500 E. 67th St., Chicago, IL 60637
Tel: (773) 493-5360; Fax: (773) 493-0360
www.chicagotheatrecompany.com

**Court Theatre**
5535 S. Ellis Ave., Chicago, IL 60637
Jeff Tamburri
Tel: (773) 702-7005; Fax: (773) 834-1897
info@courttheatre.org
www.courttheatre.org
Est. 1955. Equity LORT D. In
residence at Univ. of Chicago. New
adaptations and translations of
classical material or new work that
corresponds to a classical-based
repertory. Production: cast of 8-10,
thrust stage, limited fly. Style:
adaptation, translation. What To
Submit: query, synopsis, 10-pg sample.
How To Submit: invite.

**Children's Theatre Company (CTC)
[MN]**
2400 3rd Ave. S., Minneapolis, MN 55404
Elissa Adams
Tel: (612) 874-0500; Fax: (612) 874-8119
eadams@childrenstheatre.org
www.childrenstheatre.org
Est. 1965. 2003 Regional Theater Tony
winner. How To Submit: agent.

**Children's Theatre of Cincinnati [OH]**
2106 Florence Ave., Cincinnati, OH 45206
Jack Louiso
Tel: (513) 569-8080
www.thechildrenstheatre.com

**Childsplay**
900 S. Mitchell Dr., Tempe, AZ 85281
David Saar
Tel: (480) 350-8101; Fax: (480) 921-5777
info@childsplayaz.org
www.childsplayaz.org
Est. 1977. Non-Equity TYA. 6
mainstage and 3 touring productions/
yr. Opportunities incl Whiteman New
Plays Program. Production: cast of
2-12. What to Submit: synopsis, 10 pg
sample, SASE.

**Cider Mill Playhouse**
2 S. Nanticoke Ave., Endicott, NY 13760
Tel: (607) 748-7363
www.cidermillplayhouse.com
  Est. 1976. Production: small cast, unit
  set, no fly space. Response Time: 6
  months. Style: adaptation, comedy,
  drama, translation. How To Submit:
  agent submission.

**Cincinnati Black Theatre Company**
5919 Hamilton Ave., Cincinnati, OH 45224
Don Sherman
Tel: (513) 241-6060; Fax: (513) 241-6671
www.cincyblacktheatre.com

**Cincinnati Playhouse in the Park**
Box 6537, Cincinnati, OH 45206
Attn: Literary
Tel: (513) 345-2242; Fax: (513) 345-2254
www.cincyplay.com
  Est. 1960. Equity LORT B+ and D.
  2004 Regional Theater Tony winner.
  Response Time: 8 mos. Style: All
  genres, full-length. How To Submit:
  Agent submission of full script. Non-
  agent: synopsis, 10 pages dialog,
  character breakdown, playwright bio,
  production history. Include audio tape
  or CD of selections from score for
  musicals. SASE.

**Cincinnati Shakespeare Festival**
719 Race St., Cincinnati, OH 45202
Brian Isaac Phillips
Tel: (513) 381-2289; Fax: (513) 381-2298
csfed@cincyshakes.com
www.cincyshakes.com
  Est. 1993. Style: adaptation,
  translation, solo pieces. What To
  Submit: query, synopsis, 20 pg sample.

**Cinnabar Theater**
3333 Petaluma Blvd. N.,
Petaluma, CA 94952
Elly Lichenstein
Tel: (707) 763-8920 ext. 104
Fax: (707) 763-8929
elly@cinnabartheater.org
www.cinnabartheater.org
  Est. 1970. Equity MBATT. Will
  consider operas. What to Submit: no
  unsolicited submissions.

**City Theatre [FL]**
444 Brickell Ave., #229, Miami, FL 33131
Stephanie Norman
Tel: (305) 755-9401; Fax: (305) 755-9404
summershorts@citytheatre.com
www.citytheatre.com
  Est. 1996. Opportunities incl. Summer
  Shorts fests (thru Actors Theater of
  Louisville), as well as Short Cuts
  educational tours, Festival Reading
  Series, and Kid Shorts Project.
  Summer Shorts also incl. City
  Dialogues guest artist residency. What
  to Submit: full script, submissions not
  returned. Material Must Be: bilingual
  encouraged. Opportunity/Award:
  royalty.

**City Theatre Company [PA]**
1300 Bingham St., Pittsburgh, PA 15203
Carlyn Aquiline
Tel: (412) 431-4400; Fax: (412) 431-5535
caquiline@citytheatrecompany.org
www.citytheatrecompany.org
  Est. 1974. Produces contemporary and
  new work. Prefer plays of substance
  and ideas; fresh use of language or
  form; plays by under-represented
  voices. Production: cast limit 8, prefers
  6, 5 or fewer. Style: Full-length plays,
  musicals, translations, adaptations,
  solo pieces. What To Submit: Query
  including the name and contact info
  for a professional reference, synopsis,
  10 pg sample, audio, cast list, resume,
  development/production history,
  SASE. How To Submit: Query by mail.

**Clarence Brown Theatre (CBT)**
206 McClung Tower, Knoxville, TN 37996
Calvin MacLean
Tel: (865) 974-6011; Fax: (865) 974-4867
cbt@utk.edu
www.clarencebrowntheatre.org
  Est. 1974. Response Time: 1 mo. Style:
  comedy, drama. What To Submit:
  query, synopsis, 1-2 pg sample.

**Classical Theatre of Harlem**
520 Eighth Ave., #313,
New York, NY 10018
Tel: (212) 564-9983; Fax: (212) 564-9109
info@classicaltheatreofharlem.org

www.classicaltheatreofharlem.com
Opportunity/Award: workshops and
free public reading.

**Cleveland Play House**
8500 Euclid Ave., Cleveland, OH 44106
Seth Gordon
Tel: (216) 795-7000; Fax: (216) 795-7005
sgordon@clevelandplayhouse.com
www.clevelandplayhouse.com
Est. 1916. Response Time: 2 mos
query, 6 mos script. What to Submit:
query, synopsis, 10 pg sample, resume,
SASE.

**Cleveland Public Theatre**
6415 Detroit Ave., Cleveland, OH 44102
Raymond Bobgan
Tel: (216) 631-2727; Fax: (216) 631-2575
rbobgan@cptonline.org
www.cptonline.org
Est. 1983. Response Time: 9-12
mos. Style: experimental, poetic;
politically, intellectually, or spiritually
challenging. What To Submit: query,
1-pg synopsis, 10 pg sample, SASE,
Opportunity/Award: production.

**Clubbed Thumb**
141 E. 3rd Street, #11H,
New York, NY 10009
Tel: (212) 802-8007; Fax: (212) 228-0153
info@clubbedthumb.org
www.clubbedthumb.org
See website for details.

**Colleagues Theater Company**
321 W. 76th St., #2-B,
New York, NY 10023
Len Stanger
Est. 1996.

**Colony Theatre Company**
555 N. Third St., Burbank, CA 91502
Michael David Wadler
Tel: (818) 558-7000; Fax: (818) 558-7110
michaelwadler@colonytheatre.org
www.colonytheatre.org
Est. 1975. Equity LOA. Production:
cast limit 4. What to Submit: query,
synopsis, first 10 pages, breakdown,

resume. How To Submit: regular mail
only.

**Columbus Children's Theatre (CCT)**
177 E. Naghten St., Columbus, OH 43215
William Goldsmith
Tel: (614) 224-6673 ext. 25
Fax: (614) 224-8844
BGShows@aol.com
www.colschildrenstheatre.org
Est. 1963. Production: Prefer shows
with both adults and young people.
Response Time: 4 mos. What to
Submit: 45-55 min script. Material
Must Be: appropriate for K - 5. How
To Submit: by email or regular mail.

**Commonweal Theatre Company**
Box 15, Lanesboro, MN 55949
Hal Cropp
hal@commonwealtheatre.org
www.commonwealtheatre.org
Est. 1989. Non-Equity company
producing at least 1 new work/season.
Production: cast of 3-10. Response
Time: 6 mos. Style: adaptation,
comedy, drama. What To Submit:
query, synopsis, 10-pg sample, SASE.
Material Must Be: unproduced,
Opportunity/Award: 8% royalty.

**Conejo Players Theatre**
351 S. Moorpark Rd.,
Thousand Oaks, CA 91361
Shawn Lanz
Tel: (805) 495-3715; Fax: (805) 435-8100
www.conejoplayers.org
Est. 1958. Mainstage productions
run 5 wks; Afternoon series, 4 wks;
Children's series, 2 wks. Response
Time: 3 mos. Style: comedy, drama,
musical. What To Submit: full script,
SASE, Opportunity/Award: royalty.

**Coney Island, USA**
1208 Surf Ave., Brooklyn, NY 11224
Dick D. Zigun
Tel: (718) 372-5159; Fax: (718) 372-5101
dzigun@coneyisland.com
www.coneyisland.com
Est. 1980. Response Time: 1 mo
query, 6 mos script. Style: vaudeville,

Americana sideshow. What To Submit: query, synopsis, resume, reviews.

**Congo Square Theatre Company**
2936 N. Southport #210,
Chicago, IL 60657
Derrick Sanders
Tel: (773) 296-0968
www.congosquaretheatre.org

**Contemporary Arts Center**
900 Camp St., New Orleans, LA 70130
Jeff Zielinski
Tel: (504) 528-3805
www.cacno.org

**Cornerstone Theater Company**
708 Traction Ave.,
Los Angeles, CA 90013
Laurie Woolery
Tel: (213) 613-1700 ext. 16
Fax: (213) 613-1714
lwoolery@cornerstonetheater.org
www.cornerstonetheater.org
    Est. 1986. Primaily interested in collaborating with playwrights to develop new work. Response Time: 6 mos. Style: Please see website. What To Submit: query letter, 5 pgs of script.

**Coterie Theatre**
2450 Grand Blvd., #144,
Kansas City, MO 64108
Jeff Church
Fax: (816) 474-7112
www.coterietheatre.org
    Est. 1979. Equity TYA.Production: cast limit 10, orchestra limit 3, no fly or wing space. Response Time: 1 mo query. Style: adaptation, drama, musical. What To Submit: query, synopsis, 1-scene sample, audio, SASE. How To Submit: prefer email unless a musical.

**Country Playhouse Houston**
12802 Queensbury, Houston, TX 77024
    Est. 1956.

**Creative Evolution**
21-70 Crescent St., #A-1,
Astoria, NY 11105

Michelle Colletti
Tel: (718) 821-2682
cevolution@mindspring.com
www.creative-evolution.org
    Est. 2000. Nonprofit for women to present work in development. Staff: Lisa Haas (Treasurer). What to Submit: query, 1-pg proposal, sample, resume. How To Submit: email.

**Crossroads Theatre Company [NJ]**
P.O. Box 238, 7 Livingston Ave.,
New Brunswick, NJ 08901
Marshall Jones
Tel: (732) 545-8100; Fax: (322) 907-1864
www.crossroadstheatrecompany.org
    Est. 1978. How To Submit: no unsolicited scripts.

**Cumberland County Playhouse**
Box 484, Crossville, TN 38557
Jim Crabtree
Tel: (931) 484-4324; Fax: (931) 484-6299
jcrabtree@ccplayhouse.com
www.ccplayhouse.com
    Est. 1965. Response Time: 2 wks query, 1 yr script. What to Submit: query, synopsis.

**Curan Repertory Company**
561 Hudson St., #88,
New York, NY 10014
Ken Terrell
Tel: (212) 479-0821
kenatcuran@hotmail.com
www.curan.org
    Est. 1990. Non-Equity. 5 original full-length plays and one-act fest each season. Production: cast of 2-15, small set. Response Time: 4 mos. Style: adaptation, comedy, drama, translation. What To Submit: query, 10-pg sample, SASE. How To Submit: unsolicited, agent.

**Dad's Garage Theatre Co.**
280 Elizabeth St., #C-101,
Atlanta, GA 30307
Scott Warren
scott@dadsgarage.com
www.dadsgarage.com

Est. 1995. Style: adaptation, comedy, musical. What To Submit: query, synopsis, sample, Opportunity/Award: royalty. How To Submit: professional recommendation.

**Dallas Children's Theater**
5938 Skillman St., Dallas, TX 75231
Artie Olaisen
artie.olaisen@dct.org
www.dct.org
Est. 1984. Professional family theater. Style: Children's plays, musicals, young persons. What To Submit: query, synopsis, cast/scene list, cover letter. How To Submit: mail or email. Deadline: rolling.

**Dallas Theater Center**
3636 Turtle Creek Blvd., Dallas, TX 75219
Kevin Moriarty
Tel: (214) 526-8210; Fax: (214) 521-7666
www.dallastheatercenter.org
Est. 1959. Response Time: 1 yr. What to Submit: synopsis, 10-pg sample. How To Submit: professional recommendation.

**Danisarte**
PO Box 286146, 1617 Third Ave., New York, NY 10128
Alicia Kaplan
Tel: (212) 561-0191
Danisarte@aol.com
www.danisarte.org
Est. 1992. Production: cast limit 6. What to Submit: query, SASE. Material Must Be: unpublished, unproduced. How To Submit: invite.

**Deaf West Theatre (DWT)**
5114 Lankershim Blvd., North Hollywood, CA 91601
Ed Waterstreet
Est. 1991.

**Delaware Theatre Company**
200 Water St., Wilmington, DE 19801
Anne Marie Cammarato
Tel: (302) 594-1104; Fax: (302) 594-1107
literary@delawaretheatre.org
www.delawaretheatre.org

Est. 1978. Equity LORT D. Opportunities incl. reading and production. Season is usually 5-6 productions. Production: cast limit 10, small orchestra, unit set. Response Time: 6 mos. How To Submit: agent submission only.

**Denver Center for the Performing Arts (DCPA)**
1101 13th St., Denver, CO 80204
Douglas Langworthy
www.dcpa.org
Est. 1972. Home of Denver Center Theatre Company. Opportunity/Award: reading.

**Detroit Repertory Theatre**
13103 Woodrow Wilson St., Detroit, MI 48238
Tel: (313) 868-1347; Fax: (313) 868-1705
detrepth@aol.com
www.detroitreptheatre.com
Est. 1957. Equity SPT-3. Production: age 18-65, cast of 5-7, non-traditional casting. Response Time: 6 mos. What to Submit: full script, SASE. Material Must Be: unproduced, Opportunity/Award: 8% royalty. How To Submit: no online submissions.

**Directors Company**
311 W. 43rd St., #307, New York, NY 10036
Tel: (212) 246-5877
directorscompany@aol.com

**Discovery Theater**
Box 23293, Washington, DC 20026
Roberta Gasbarre
Tel: (202) 633-8700; Fax: (202) 343-1073
info@discoverytheater.org
www.discoverytheater.org
Heritage, science, cultural themes. Style: Museum theatre, cultural and educational performances. What To Submit: Synopsis, program information. Material Must Be: See website. How To Submit: unsolicited.

**District of Columbia Arts Center
(DCAC)**
2438 18th St., NW,
Washington, DC 20009
Tel: (202) 462-7833
info@dcartscenter.org
www.dcartscenter.org
    Est. 1989. Nonprofit in Adams Morgan
neighborhood that supports emerging
artists trying to get a foothold in
the public arena. What to Submit:
Proposals for performances in the
theater space. How To Submit: http://
www.dcartscenter.org/submit_theater.
htm. Rolling deadline.

**Diversionary Theatre**
4545 Park Blvd., #101,
San Diego, CA 92116
Dan Kirsch
Tel: (619) 220-0097; Fax: (619) 220-0148
boxoffice@diversionary.org
www.diversionary.org
    Est. 1986. 3rd oldest LGBT theater
in US. 6-show season and new-work
readings in 106-seat space. Staff: Bret
Young (Managing Dir). Response
Time: 6 mos. What to Submit:
application, synopsis, 15-pg sample,
Opportunity/Award: royalty. How To
Submit: online.

**Dixon Place**
161A Christie St., New York, NY 10002
Ellie Covan
Tel: (212) 219-0736; Fax: (212) 219-0761
contact@dixonplace.org
www.dixonplace.org
    Est. 1986. Nonprofit laboratoty theater
for NY- based performing and literary
artists to create and develop new
works in front of a live audience.

**Dobama Theatre**
2340 Lee Rd.,
Cleveland Heights, OH 44118
Marge Boduszek
Tel: (216) 932-6838; Fax: (216) 932-3259
dobama@dobama.org
www.dobama.org
    Est. 1959. Production: cast limit 9, no
fly. What to Submit: query, synopsis,

sample. Author Must Be: resident of
Ohio.

**Doorway Arts Ensemble**
5904 Beech Ave., Bethesda, MD 20817
Claire Myles
Tel: (301) 530-4349; Fax: (301) 530-4349
info@doorwayarts.org
www.DoorwayArts.org
    See website for details. Style:
no children's plays. What To
Submit: Strongest 10 page sample.
Opportunity/Award: Staged readings,
possible production. How To Submit:
email. Deadline: Year round.

**Dorset Theatre Festival**
Box 510, Dorset, VT 5251
Carl Forsman
Tel: (802) 867-2223; Fax: (802) 867-0144
theatre@sover.net
www.dorsettheatrefestival.org
    Dorset only accepts scripts of writers
in residence or by invitation.

**Double Edge Theatre**
948 Conway Rd., Ashfield, MA 01330
Mathew Glassman
Tel: (413) 628-0277; Fax: (203) 886-3293
office@doubleedgetheatre.org
www.doubleedgetheatre.org
    Est. 1982. Opportunities incl.
Individual Artist Retreats. Response
Time: 6 mos. Style: original ensemble
performance, physical theatre. What
To Submit: video. How To Submit:
email/regular mail.

**Directors Project/The Drama League**
520 Eighth Ave, #320,
New York, NY 10018
Roger T. Danforth
Tel: (212) 244-9494; Fax: (212) 244-9191
www.dramaleague.org

**Dream Theatre**
484 W. 43rd St., #14-Q,
New York, NY 10036
Andrea Leigh
Tel: (212) 564-2628
andrealeigh88@hotmail.com

Est. 2001. New works, esp. by/for women, that have not been optioned or produced in NYC. Application. Best Way: e-mail. Response Time: 6 mos. Style: drama, comedy, adaptation. What To Submit: synopsis, full script, submissions not returned. How To Submit: e-mail, regular mail. Deadline: ongoing.

**John Drew Theater at Guild Hall**
158 Main St., East Hampton, NY 11937
Josh Gladstone
Est. 1931. Equity LOA summer season. Staff: James Lawson (Assoc Artistic Dir). What to Submit: query, synopsis, audio, submissions not returned. How To Submit: professional recommendation.

**Duo Theater**
PO Box 1200, Cooper Station,
New York, NY 10276
Tel: (212) 598-4320
duotheater@msn.com
www.duotheater.org

**East West Players**
120 N. Judge John Aiso St.,
Los Angeles, CA 90012
Jeff Liu
Tel: (213) 625-7000 ext. 27
Fax: (213) 625-7111
jliu@eastwestplayers.org
www.eastwestplayers.org
Est. 1965. 4 mainstage productions/ season in addition to readings. Especially interested in work by Asian-Americans. Response Time: 9 mos. What to Submit: no query required; send synopsis, full script, resume, SASE. How To Submit: by regular mail only; no e-submissions.

**Echo Theatre**
PO Box 820698, Dallas, TX 75382
Tel: (214) 904-0500
www.echotheatre.org

**El Centro Su Teatro**
4725 High St., Denver, CO 80216
Tony Garcia

Tel: (303) 296-0219; Fax: (303) 296-4614
john@suteatro.org
www.suteatro.org
Est. 1971. Production: cast of 4 +. Response Time: 6 mos. Style: What To Submit: full script. Material Must Be: Related to Latino experience, bilingual encouraged.

**Electric Theatre Company**
Literary Manager, PO Box 854,
Scranton, PA 18501
John Beck
Tel: (570) 558-1520
jbeck@electrictheatre.org
www.electrictheatre.org
Est. 1992. Production: cast limit 6. Response Time: 3 mos. Style: comedy, drama. What To Submit: 10 page dialogue sample, short synopsis. Material Must Be: unproduced. How To Submit: mail or email. Deadline: ongoing.

**Emerging Artists Theatre (EAT)**
15 West 28th St., 3rd Floor,
New York, NY 10001
Paul Adams
Tel: (212) 247-2429
eattheatre@gmail.com
www.eatheatre.org
Est. 1993. Develop and produce new work from shorts to full-lengths. Production: 20-70, cast 2-10. Response Time: 3-6 mos. Style: comedy, drama, musical. What To Submit: query, synopsis (full-lengths), by email, SASE. Material Must Be: unproduced. How To Submit: call for scripts thru DG and InsightforPlaywrights.com. Deadline: For Illuminating Artists New Works Series - Nov 15th, Fall Eatfest - April 1st, Spring Eatfest - July 1st.

**Encompass New Opera Theatre**
138 S. Oxford St., #1-A,
Brooklyn, NY 11217
Roger Cunningham
Tel: (718) 398-4675; Fax: (718) 398-4684
encompassopera@yahoo.com
www.encompassopera.org

Est. 1975. Contemporary opera
and music theater. Staff: Roger Jeff
Cunningham. Style: musical. What
To Submit: query, synopsis, audio,
SASE. How To Submit: professional
recommendation.

**Encore Theatre**
2016 Main St., #1615, Houston, TX 77002
Harold Haines

**Enrichment Works**
5605 Woodman Ave., # 207,
Valley Glen, CA 91401
Abraham Tetenbaum
Tel: (818) 780-1400; Fax: (818) 780-0300
atetenbaum@enrichmentworks.org
www.enrichmentworks.org
    Est. 1999. Nonprofit presenting
    tours in L.A. schools, libraries and
    museums and community venues of
    works to inspire learning. Also accepts
    musical plays. Production: cast limit
    3, touring set. Response Time: 6
    mos. Style: comedy, drama, musical.
    What To Submit: full script, SASE,
    Opportunity/Award: 10% royalty.

**Ensemble Studio Theatre (EST)**
549 W. 52nd St., New York, NY 10019
Tel: (212) 247-4982; Fax: (212) 664-0041
est@ensemblestudiotheatre.org
www.ensemblestudiotheatre.org
    Est. 1972. Staff: William Carden
    (Producing Dir), Paul Slee (Exec Dir).

**The Ensemble Theatre [TX]**
3535 Main St., Houston, TX 77002
Eileen J. Morris
Tel: (713) 520-0055; Fax: (713) 520-1269
ejmorris@ensemblehouston.com
www.ensemblehouston.com
    Est. 1976. The Ensemble Theatre
    produces contemporary and classical
    works devoted to the portrayal of
    the African-American experience.
    Production: cast limit 5, touring
    set. Response Time: 3 mos. What
    to Submit: query, synopsis, sample,
    audio, resume, SASE, Opportunity/
    Award: work that has been produced;

one-act plays. How To Submit:
between March and August.

**Ensemble Theater [Cleveland, OH]**
Box 181309, Cleveland Heights, OH 44118
Martin Cosentino
Tel: (216) 321-2930
ensemble-theater@sbcglobal.net
www.ensemble-theater.com
    Style: American. What To Submit:
    One act + synopsis/abstract,
    Opportunity/Award: residency,
    productions. How To Submit: mail.

**Ensemble Theatre of Cincinnati [OH]**
1127 Vine St., Cincinnati, OH 45202
D. Lynn Meyers
Tel: (513) 421-3555; Fax: (513) 562-4104
administration@cincyetc.com
www.cincyetc.com
    Est. 1986. Production: cast limit 10,
    simple set. What to Submit: Query
    letter, synopsis, sample, resume, &
    SASE. Material Must Be: A world or
    regional premiere. How To Submit:
    Please inquire ahead of sending as
    to whether or not ETC is currently
    accepting new scripts.

**Express Children's Theatre**
446 Northwest Mall, Houston, TX 77092
Pat Silver
Tel: (713) 682-5044; Fax: (713) 682-5033
expresstheatre@sbcglobal.net
www.expresstheatre.com
    Est. 1991. In residence at Houston
    Community Coll. Central Fine Arts
    Dept. Production: cast of 3-4, touring
    set. Response Time: 2 wks query, 8
    wks script. After school programs,
    summer camps, Saturday workshops.
    Style: multi-ethnic. What To Submit:
    query, synopsis. Material Must Be:
    bilingual encouraged.

**First Stage Children's Theater [WI]**
325 W. Walnut St., Milwaukee, WI 53212
Jeff Frank
Tel: (414) 267-2929; Fax: (414) 267-2930
jfrank@firststage.org
www.firststage.org

Est. 1987. Response Time: 3 mo
query, 9 mos script. Style: adaptation,
musical, translation. What To Submit:
query, synopsis, resume.

**Flat Rock Playhouse**
Box 310, Flat Rock, NC 28731
Scott Treadway
Tel: (828) 693-0403 ext. 204
Fax: (828) 693-6795
frp@flatrockplayhouse.org
www.flatrockplayhouse.com
How To Submit: hard copy by mail.

**Florida Repertory Theatre**
2267 1st St., Fort Myers, FL 33901
Jason Parrish
Tel: (239) 332-4665 ext. 35
Fax: (239) 332-1808
jason.parrish@floridarep.org
www.floridarep.org
Est. 1989. Equity LORT D. 8
mainstage plays Sep-Jun. Staff: Robert
Cacioppo (Producing Artistic Dir).
Production: cast limit 10, orchestra
of 4-5, sets limit 2. Response Time: 1
yr. Style: all styles. What To Submit:
synopsis, full script, SASE. How To
Submit: agent.

**Florida Stage**
262 S. Ocean Blvd.,
Manasquan, NJ 33462
Jonathan Wemette
Tel: (561) 585-3404 ext. 116
Fax: (561) 588-4708
jon@floridastage.org
www.floridastage.org
New work. Est. 1987. Equity LORT
C. Thought-provoking, issue-oriented
material. Opportunities incl New
Works Fest. Production: cast of 2-6,
unit set. Response Time: 4 mos.
Style: comedy, drama, musical,
political. What To Submit: Complete
script, playwright bio, production
history. Material Must Be: agent only
submissions. How To Submit: email.

**Florida Studio Theatre**
1241 N. Palm Ave., Sarasota, FL 34236
Cristin Kelly

Tel: (941) 366-9017; Fax: (941) 955-4137
ckelly@floridastudiotheatre.org
www.floridastudiotheatre.org
Response Time: 2 months query, 6
mos script. What to Submit: query,
synopsis, 5-pg sample, SASE, CD if
musical. How To Submit: email (Word
or PDF) or mail, unsolicited from
Florida residents, agent submission
otherwise.

**Folger Theatre**
201 E. Capitol St., SE,
Washington, DC 20003
Est. 1986.

**Ford's Theatre Society**
511 10th St., NW, Washington, DC 20004
Paul Tetreault
Tel: (202) 638-2941; Fax: (202) 638-6269
www.fordstheatre.org
Est. 1968. Equity LORT. 4-5 shows/
yr, incl. perhaps 1 original play or
musical. Staff: Mark Ramont (Assoc
Prod/Artistic Dir). Production:
orchestra limit 7. Response Time: 1 yr.
What to Submit: query, synopsis, 10-
pg sample, SASE, Opportunity/Award:
royalty. How To Submit: professional
recommendation.

**Fountain Theatre**
5060 Fountain Ave.,
Los Angeles, CA 90029
Simon Levy
Tel: (323) 663-2235; Fax: (323) 663-1629
fountaintheatre1@aol.com
www.fountaintheatre.com
Equity 99-seat. Production: cast limit
12, unit set, no fly. Response Time: 3
mos. Style: no translation. What To
Submit: query, synopsis, Opportunity/
Award: 6% royalty. How To Submit:
professional recommendation.

**Freed-Hardeman University**
Theater Dept., 158 E. Main St.,
Henderson, TN 38340
Cliff Thompson
Tel: (731) 989-6780
cthompson@fhu.edu

Style: all styles. What To Submit: synopsis, 30-pg writing sample, submissions returned with SASE. How To Submit: unsolicited.

**Freedom Repertory Theatre**
1346 N. Broad St., Philadelphia, PA 19121
Patricia Hobbs
Tel: (215) 765-2793; Fax: (215) 765-4191
www.freedomtheatre.org
   Est. 1966. Response Time: 3 mos.
   How To Submit: professional
   recommendation.

**GableStage**
1200 Anastasia Ave.,
Coral Gables, FL 33134
Joseph Adler
Tel: (305) 446-1116 Fax: (305) 445-8645
jadler@gablestage.org
www.gablestage.org
   Est. 1979. Equity SPT-5. 6
   productions/yr. What to Submit: query.

**Gas & Electric Arts**
Box 38524, Philadelphia, PA 19104
Lisa Jo Epstein

**Geffen Playhouse**
10886 LeConte Ave.,
Los Angeles, CA 90024
Amy Levinson Millan
Tel: (310) 208-6500; Fax: (310) 208-0341
www.geffenplayhouse.com
Est. 1995. Response Time: 6 mos. How To
Submit: agent.

**George Street Playhouse**
9 Livingston Ave.,
New Brunswick, NJ 8901
Jeremy Stoller
Tel: (732) 846-2895; Fax: (732) 247-9151
www.georgestplayhouse.org
   Est. 1974. Equity LORT C.
   Productions, readings, tours of issue-
   oriented 40-min one-acts for schools,
   and Next Stage Fest workshops.
   Prefer fresh perspectives on society,
   compelling personal and human
   stories that entertain, challenge, and
   stretch the imagination. Production:
   cast limit 7. Response Time: 10 mos.

Style: no translation. What To Submit: query, synopsis, 10-pg sample, cast/ scene list, tech needs. How To Submit: professional recommendation.

**Georgia Shakespeare**
4484 Peachtree Rd. NE,
Atlanta, GA 30319
Richard Garner
Tel: (404) 264-0020; Fax: (404) 504-3414
richard@gashakespeare.org
www.gashakespeare.org/
   Est. 1985. How To Submit: see
   website.

**Germinal Stage Denver**
2450 W. 44th Ave., Denver, CO 80211
Ed Baierlein
Tel: (303) 455-7108
gsden@privatei.com
www.germinalstage.com
   Est. 1974. Production: cast limit
   10. Response Time: 2 wks query, 6
   mos script. What to Submit: query,
   synopsis, 5-pg sample.

**Geva Theatre Center**
75 Woodbury Blvd., Rochester, NY 14607
Marge Betley
Tel: (585) 232-1366; Fax: (585) 232-4031
www.gevatheatre.org
   Est. 1972. Equity LORT B and D.
   Produces classics to musicals to new
   works, incl. readings and workshops.
   Staff: Jean Gordon Ryon (New Plays
   Coord.). Assistance: stipend, room/
   board, travel. Response Time: 3 mos
   query; 6 mos script. What to Submit:
   query, synopsis, 10-pg sample,
   SASE. How To Submit: professional
   recommendation.

**Golden Fleece Ltd.**
70-A Greenwhich Ave., #256,
New York, NY 10011
Lou Rodgers
Tel: (212) 691-6105
info@goldenfleeceltd.org
www.goldenfleeceltd.org
   Est. 1974. Golden Fleece Ltd. nurtures,
   develops and produces new works by
   emerging American composers as well

as playwrights, lyricists and librettists. The Composers Chamber Theatre; annual commissioned opera/music theater production; Square One Series of works by composers, lyricists and librettists in progress; Argonaut Series of new works by poets and playwrights in progress. Production: all ages, cast limit of 8, orchestra of 4, set varies. Response Time: varies. Style: all styles. What To Submit: synopsis or treatment, resume, submission returned if SASE provided. Material Must Be: unpublished, unproduced. How To Submit: unsolicited, professional recommendation.

**Goodman Theatre**
170 N. Dearborn St., Chicago, IL 60601
Tanya Palmer
Tel: (312) 443-3811
info@goodman-theatre.org
www.goodmantheatre.org
Est. 1925. Equity LORT B+ and C. 1992 Regional Theater Tony winner. Staff: Robert Falls (Artistic Dir.), Roche Schulfer (Exec. Dir.). Response Time: 6 - 8 wks. What to Submit: 10 pg sample, resume, synopsis, SASE. How To Submit: agent, professional recommendation.

**Goodspeed Musicals**
6 Main St, P.O. Box A,
East Haddam, CT 06423-0281
Donna Lynn Cooper Hilton
Tel: (860) 873-8664; Fax: (860) 873-2329
info@goodspeed.org
www.goodspeed.org
Est. 1959. 1995 Regional Theater Tony winner. Style: musical. What To Submit: submit a synopsis, demo and bios of the authors. Materials will not be returned. Please allow 6 months for response to materials. How To Submit: agent.

**Great Lakes Theater Festival**
1501 Euclid Ave., # 300,
Cleveland, OH 44115
Charles Fee
Tel: (216) 241-5490; Fax: (216) 241-6315
mail@greatlakestheater.org
www.greatlakestheater.org
Est. 1961. Response Time: 3 mos. Style: adaptation, translation, relevant to classical repertoire. How To Submit: professional recommendation.

**Green Light Productions**
459 Columbus Ave., #192,
New York, NY 10024
Armen Pandola

**Greenbrier Valley Theatre**
113 E. Washington St., Lewisburg, WV 24901
Cathey Sawyer
Tel: (304) 645-3838; Fax: (304) 645-3818
www.gvtheatre.org
Est. 1967. Equity LOA. Production: age 7 and older, cast of 6-10, orchestra of 1-4, set limit 1. Response Time: 6 mos. Style: adaptation, comedy or variety, drama, musical. What To Submit: synopsis, 5-pg sample, submissions not returned. Author Must Be: resident of US. Material Must Be: unoptioned, unproduced. How To Submit: professional recommendation, agent.

**Gretna Theatre**
Box 578, Mt. Gretna, PA 17064
Larry Frenock
Tel: (717) 964-3322
www.gretnatheatre.com
Est. 1927. Equity Guest Artists LOA.

**Growing Stage - The Children's Theatre of New Jersey**
P.O. Box 36, Netcong, NJ 7857
Stephen L. Fredericks
Tel: (973) 347-4946; Fax: (973) 691-7069
info@growingstage.com
www.growingstage.com
Est. 1982. We review submissions May–August only. Response Time: 4 mos. What to Submit: Synopsis, character breakdown, sample scene; SASE. Material Must Be: for young audiences.

**Guthrie Theater**
818 S. 2nd St., Minneapolis, MN 55415
Jo Holcomb
Tel: (612) 225-6000; Fax: (612) 225-6004
www.guthrietheater.org
    Est. 1963. Equity LORT A, B, D. 1982
    Regional Theater Tony winner. New
    3-theater complex opened 2006, incl.
    1100-seat thrust, 700-seat proscenium,
    and 199-seat studio. Response Time:
    varies. What to Submit: full script.
    Material Must Be: requested by
    the Guthrie - no unsolicited scipt
    submissions accepted.

**Hadley Players**
204 W. 134th St., New York, NY 10030
Tel: (212) 368-9314
hadleyplayers@yahoo.com
    What to Submit: 10 pg. sample, SASE.

**Halcyon Theatre**
3334 W. Wilson #1, Chicago, IL 60625
Tony Adams
Tel: (312) 458-9170
submissions@halcyontheatre.org
www.halcyontheatre.org
    For submissions policies go to
    halcyontheatre.org/submissions.
    Style: All. What To Submit: Full
    script, Opportunity/Award: Reading,
    Workshop, Production. How To
    Submit: Unsolicited, Professional
    recommendation, Agent. Deadline:
    rolling.

**Hangar Theatre KIDDSTUFF**
Box 205, Ithaca, NY 14851
Tel: (607) 273-8588
literary@hangartheatre.org
www.hangartheatre.org
    Response Time: 6 mos. Accepting
    scripts all year round. What to Submit:
    full script, SASE, Opportunity/Award:
    royalty. How To Submit: by mail;
    ATT: Literary Assistant.

**Harlequin Productions of Cayuga
Community College**
197 Franklin St., Auburn, NY 13021
Robert Frame
framer@cayuga-cc.edu

www.cayuga-cc.edu
    Est. 1958. 6 perfs over 2 weekends
    (fall and spring) with college students
    in high-quality extracurricular
    program. Production: age 16-35,
    cast of 7-14. Response Time: 1 yr.
    Style: adaptation, comedy, drama.
    What To Submit: full script, SASE,
    Opportunity/Award: flat fee.

**Hartford Stage**
50 Church St., Hartford, CT 6103
Jeremy B. Cohen
Tel: (860) 525-5601; Fax: (860) 224-0183
litman@hartfordstage.org
www.hartfordstage.org
    Est. 1963. Equity LORT B. 1989
    Regional Theater Tony winner. What
    to Submit: full script. How To Submit:
    agent, unsolicited (CT residents only),
    professional recommendation.

**Harwich Junior Theatre (HJT)**
Box 168, 105 Division St.,
West Harwich, MA 02671
Nina Schuessler
Tel: (508) 432-2002; Fax: (508) 432-0726
hjt@capecod.net
www.hjtcapecod.org
    Est. 1951 New plays for
    intergenerational casts and audiences.
    Production: intergenerational, no fly.
    Response time: 6 months. What to
    Submit: synopsis, SASE, Opportunity/
    Award: royalty.

**Hedgerow Theatre**
64 Rose Valley Rd., Media, PA 19063
Penelope Reed
Tel: (610) 565-4211 ext. 101
preed@hedgerowtheatre.org
www.hedgerowtheatre.org
    Est. 1923. Readings of new plays by
    Delaware Valley writers in readings
    and workshops. Production: cast of
    2-8. Response Time: 2 mos query, 4
    mos script. Style: comedy, mystery,
    everything. What To Submit: query,
    synopsis. Author Must Be: Material
    Must Be: unpublished, unproduced.

**Hip Pocket Theatre**
Box 136758, Ft. Worth, TX 76136
Diane Simons
Tel: (817) 246-9775; Fax: (817) 246-5651
hpt@hippocket.org
www.hippocket.org
    Est. 1977. Production: simple set,
    outdoor amphitheater. Response Time:
    2 mos. What to Submit: synopsis,
    sample, audio.

**Hippodrome State Theatre**
25 SE 2nd Pl., Gainesville, FL 32601
Tamerin Dygert
Tel: (352) 373-5968
dramturg@thehipp.org
www.thehipp.org
    Est. 1973. Equity SPT. Production:
    cast limit 6, unit set. Response Time: 5
    mos. How To Submit: agent.

**Honolulu Theatre for Youth**
229 Queen Emma Sq.,
Honolulu, HI 96813
Eric Johnson
Tel: (808) 839-9885; Fax: (808) 839-7018
htyeric@gmail.com
www.htyweb.org
    Est. 1955. Producing and
    commissioning new plays, Sep-
    May. Production: cast limit 5. What
    to Submit: query, submissions not
    returned.

**Horizon Theatre Rep [NY]**
41 E. 67th St., New York, NY 10021
Rafael De Mussa
Tel: (212) 737-3357; Fax: (212) 737-5103
info@htronline.org
www.htronline.org
    Est. 2000. Equity Showcase.
    Production: ages 16-75, cast size
    4-15. Response Time: 1 mo. Style: no
    musical. What To Submit: synopsis,
    submissions not returned. Material
    Must Be: unoptioned, unproduced.

**Horse Trade Theater Group**
85 E. 4th St., New York, NY 10003
Erez Ziv
Tel: (212) 777-6088; Fax: (212) 777-6120
office@horsetrade.info

www.horsetrade.info
    Horse Trade is a self-sustaining
    theater development group; with a
    focus on new work. It is the home of
    FRIGID New York - the first and only
    festival of its kind in New York City.
    What to Submit: full script, query,
    sample, SASE. How To Submit: See
    instructions on website, professional
    recommendation.

**Hubris Productions**
724 W. Roscoe Street, #3S,
Chicago, IL 60657
Jacob Green
Tel: (773) 398-3273
jacob@hubrisproductions.com
hubrisproductions.com
    We accept plays during the month
    of September every year. Style: all.
    What To Submit: query. 10 pg sample.
    Material Must Be: not optioned. not
    produced. not published.

**Hudson Theatres**
6539 Santa Monica Blvd.,
Los Angeles, CA 90038
Elizabeth Reilly
Tel: (323) 856-4252; Fax: (323) 856-4316
ereilly@hudsontheatre.com
www.hudsontheatre.com
    Est. 1991. Primarily rental house
    Equity 99-seat. Hollywood Theatre
    Row complex incl. Mainstage, and
    Backstage (Comedy Central in
    residence); 43-seat Guild; and Caffe
    Bacio. Response Time: 6 mos query, 1
    yr script. Style: no musical! What To
    Submit: query, synopsis, 10 pg sample.
    How To Submit: mail, email.

**The Human Race Theatre Company**
126 N. Main St., #300, The Loft Theatre,
Dayton, OH 45402
Kevin Moore
contact@humanracetheatre.org
www.humanracetheatre.org
    Est. 1986. Opportunities incl. Loft
    Season: 6 shows/small to medium
    size casts; Educational touring;
    Musical workshops and Residencies.
    Response time: 6 mos. Style:

Regional Theatre mix: Contemporary, Classics, Original. What To Submit: For Musicals: Refer to Submission guideline on our Website For Plays: Letter of Introduction with synopsis & history. Author Must Be: How To Submit: By regular mail or email.

**Huntington Theatre Company**
264 Huntington Ave., Boston, MA 02115
Charles Haugland
Tel: (617) 273-1503; Fax: (617) 353-8300
chaugland@huntingtontheatre.bu.edu
www.huntingtontheatre.org
Est. 1981. Equity LORT B+ and C. Response Time: 1 year. Style: What To Submit: full script, SASE (for return). How To Submit: unsolicited (MA, RI writers only), agent (US Canada, UK).

**Hyde Park Theatre**
511 W. 43rd St., Austin, TX 78751
Peck Phillips
Tel: (512) 479-7530
hydeparktheatre@gmail.com
www.hydeparktheatre.org
Est. 1992. Southwest, U.S. and world premieres of alternative and classic works that challenge modern audiences. Also Frontera Fest, 5-wk unjuried fringe fest. Play Development Reading Series. Response Time: 3 mos query, 6 mos script. Style: no musical. What To Submit: query, synopsis, SASE.

**Hypothetical Theatre Company**
344 E. 14th St., New York, NY 10003
Amy Feinberg
Tel: (212) 780-0800 ext. 254
htc@hypotheticaltheatre.org
www.hypotheticaltheatre.org
Est. 1986. Response Time: 6 mos. Style: adaptation, comedy, drama. What To Submit: full script, SASE. Material Must Be: unproduced in NYC. How To Submit: agent.

**Idaho Repertory Theatre (IRT)**
University of Idaho - Box 442008, Moscow, ID 83844
Dean Panttaja

theatre@uidaho.edu
www.idahorep.org
Production: ages 13-35, cast of 2-10. Response Time: 4 mos. What to Submit: query. Author Must Be: new/ emerging writer. Material Must Be: unpublished, Opportunity/Award: royalty. How To Submit: email.

**Illinois Theatre Center**
Box 397, Park Forest, IL 60466
Etel Billig
Tel: (708) 481-3510; Fax: (708) 481-3693
www.ilthctr.org
Est. 1976. Production: cast limit 9 (play) or 14 (musical). Response Time: 1 mo query, 2 mos script. Best submission time: Nov-Jan. What to Submit: query, synopsis, SASE.

**Illusion Theater**
528 Hennepin Ave., #704, Minneapolis, MN 55403
Michael Robins
Fax: (612) 337-8042
info@illusiontheater.org
www.illusiontheater.org
Est. 1974. Response Time: 1 yr. Style: any. How To Submit: professional recommendation, email.

**Imagination Stage**
4908 Auburn Ave., Bethesda, MD 20814
Janet Stanford
Tel: (301) 961-6060; Fax: (301) 718-9526
kbryere@imaginationstage.org
www.imaginationstage.org
Est. 1979. Production: cast of 4-10. Style: drama, musical. What To Submit: query, sample, 10 page, outline. Material Must Be: no longer than 75 minutes, Opportunity/Award: internships. How To Submit: regular mail, email.

**Impact Theatre [CA]**
Box 12666, Berkeley, CA 94712
Melissa Hillman
melissa@impacttheatre.com
www.impacttheatre.com
Est. 1996. Response Time: varies. Seeking all types of full-length plays except theatre for young

audiences. Style: all styles. What To Submit: full script via email. Material Must Be: unoptioned. How To Submit: unsolicited, professional recommendation, agent.

**Indiana Repertory Theatre**
140 W. Washington St.,
Indianapolis, IN 46204
Richard J. Roberts
Tel: (317) 635-5277; Fax: (317) 236-0767
rroberts@irtlive.com
www.irtlive.com
Est. 1972. Equity LORT, 6-show Signature Series (Sep-May) in 600-seat proscenium mainstage, 2-show Discovery Series for family/ youth in 300-seat thrust upperstage. Production: cast limit 10. Response Time: 6 mos. Style: original, adaptation, translation, solo; no musical. What To Submit: query, synopsis, resume; all via email. Material Must Be: Midwest voice (we are especially interested in Midwest voices, but not exclusively). How To Submit: email.

**INTAR (International Arts Relations) Theatre**
Box 756, New York, NY 10108
Megan Smith
Tel: (212) 695-6134
intar@intartheatre.org
www.intartheatre.org
Est. 1966. Equity LOA. Opportunities incl. workshops, productions of works in progress, and mainstage productions. Response Time: 3 mos. Style: comedy, drama. What To Submit: full script. Author Must Be: Latino. Material Must Be: unproduced.

**InterAct Theatre Company [PA]**
2030 Sansom St., Philadelphia, PA 19103
Rebecca Wright
Tel: (215) 568-8077; Fax: (215) 568-8095
bwright@interacttheatre.org
www.interacttheatre.org
Est. 1988. Resident company at Adrienne Theatre. Production: 1-8. Response Time: 6-12 months. What to Submit: query, synopsis, writing

sample, bio, SASE. How To Submit: unsolicited.

**Interborough Repertory Theater Inc. (IRT)**
154 Christopher St., #3-B,
New York, NY 10014
Kori Rushton
Tel: (212) 206-6875; Fax: (212) 206-7037
krushton@irttheater.org
www.irt.dreamhost.com
Est. 1986. Equity Showcase. Provides accessible theater to schools and families of diverse cultural backgrounds in an atmosphere where theater professionals can grow and develop. What to Submit: query, SASE.

**International City Theatre**
1 World Trade Center, #300,
Long Beach, CA 90831
Shashin Desai
Tel: (562) 495-4595; Fax: (562) 436-7895
shashinict@earthlink.net
www.ictlongbeach.org
Est. 1985. Equity SPT, Long Beach PAC resident company, 349-seat venue. Staff: Caryn Desai (Gen Mgr). Production: cast limit 9, orchestra limit 6. Response Time: 6 mos. What to Submit: synopsis, sample, full script, SASE, Opportunity/Award: 7% royalty. How To Submit: professional recommendation.

**Irish Arts Center**
553 W. 51st St., New York, NY 10019
Pauline Turley
Tel: (212) 757-3318; Fax: (212) 247-0930
info@irishartscenter.org
www.irishartscenter.org
Est. 1972.

**Irish Repertory Theatre**
132 W. 22nd St., New York, NY 10011
Kara Manning
Tel: (212) 255-0270; Fax: (212) 255-0281
kara@irishrep.org
www.irishrep.org
Ongoing new works reading series reflecting the Irish and Irish American experience. Female playwrights and

writers of color encouraged. What to Submit: Unsolicited: 20 page sample, synopsis, cover letter, audio if musical, SASE, Agent or solicited submissions: entire script, cast breakdown, cover letter. No email submissions unless solicited as such. Material Must Be: unpublished, not produced in the U.S. (Ireland/UK productions permissible).

**Irondale Ensemble Project**
85 S. Oxford St., Brooklyn, NY 11217
Jim Niesen
Tel: (718) 488-9233; Fax: (718) 788-0607
irondalert@aol.com
www.irondale.org
Est. 1983. Equity LOA. Classic work in unorthodox production and original work combining new and classic styles of performance, music, dance and design. For playwrights looking for permanent ensemble. Production: cast limit 9. Response Time: 10 wks. What to Submit: query.

**Jewish Theater of New York**
Box 845, Times Sq. Sta.,
New York, NY 10108
Liz Lauren
Tel: (212) 494-0050
thejtny@aol.com
www.jewishtheater.org
Est. 1994. Response Time: 3 mos. Style: comedy, drama, musical. What To Submit: synopsis, submissions not returned. Material Must Be: unoptioned, unpublished, unproduced. How To Submit: invite.

**Judith Shakespeare Company NYC**
367 Windsor Hwy., #409,
New Windsor, NY 12553
Joanne Zipay
Tel: (212) 592-1885
judithshakes@gmail.com
www.judithshakespeare.org
Est. 1995. Offers RESURGENCE concert reading series and full productions of new plays with heightened language and significant roles for women. Style: Classical with emphasis on roles for women. What To Submit: plays. Material Must Be:

Heightened language with significant roles for women, Opportunity/Award: Reading/Possible production. How To Submit: regular mail.

**Kairos Italy Theater (KIT)**
50 E. 8th Street, #12B,
New York, NY 10003
Laura Caparrotti
Fax: (801) 749-6727
info@kitheater.com
www.kitheater.com
Est. 2002. KIT's mission is to produce plays by and about Italian authors and Italian themes. Production: 5. Style: all styles. What To Submit: send email with synopsis, sample pages. How To Submit: send email with synopsis, sample pages.

**Kansas City Repertory Theatre**
4949 Cherry St., Kansas City, MO 64110
Eric Rosen
Tel: (816) 235-2727; Fax: (816) 235-5367
www.kcrep.org
Est. 1964. Formerly Missouri Repertory Theatre. Equity LORT B. How To Submit: invite.

**Karamu House Inc.**
2355 E. 89th St., Cleveland, OH 44106
Terrence Spivey
Tel: (216) 795-7070
espivey@karamu.com
www.karamu.com
Nonprofit community-based arts and educational organization to encourage and support the preservation, celebration and evolution of African-American culture and provide a vehicle for social, economic and educational development.

**Kavinoky Theatre**
320 Porter Ave., Buffalo, NY 14221
David Lamb
Tel: (716) 829-7668
www.kavinokytheatre.com
Est. 1981. Production: cast limited 7, no fly, limited wing. Response Time: 1 mo. How To Submit: professional recommendation.

**Kentucky Repertory Theatre at Horse Cave**
Box 215, 101 E. Main St.,
Horse Cave, KY 42749
Robert Brock
Tel: (270) 786-1200; Fax: (270) 786-5298
rbrock@kentuckyrep.org
www.kentuckyrep.org
> Est. 1977. Equity LOA. Formerly Horse Cave Theater. Production: cast limit 10, unit set. What to Submit: query. Author Must Be: resident of KY. Material Must Be: unproduced. How To Submit: professional recommendation.

**Kidworks Touring Theatre Co.**
3524 N. Leavitt Ave. 2nd Floor,
Chicago, IL 60618
Andrea Salloum
Tel: (773) 972-7112
kidworkstheatre@aol.com
www.kidworkstheatre.org
> Est. 1987.

**The Killing Kompany**
21 Turn Ln., Levittown, NY 11756
Jon Avner
Tel: (212) 772-2590; Fax: (212) 202-6495
killingkompany@killingkompany.com
www.killingkompany.com
> Interactive shows for dinner theater.

**Kumu Kahua Theatre**
46 Merchant St., Honolulu, HI 96813
Harry Wong III
Tel: (808) 536-4222; Fax: (808) 536-4226
kumukahuatheatre@hawaiiantel.net
ww.kumukahua.org
> Est. 1971. Response Time: 4 mos. Style: adaptation, comedy, drama. What To Submit: full script, SASE. How To Submit: mail.

**Kuntu Repertory Theatre**
Dept. of Africana Studies,
4140 Wesley W. Posvar Hall,
Pittsburgh, PA 15260
Dr. Vernall A. Lillie
Tel: (412) 624-7298
info@kuntu.org
www.kuntu.org

Est. 1974. What to Submit: full script.

**L.A. Theatre Works (LATW)**
681 Venice Blvd., Venice, CA 90291
Vicki Pearlson
Tel: (310) 827-0808; Fax: (310) 827-4949
latw@latw.org
www.latw.org
> Est. 1974. Live performances and studio recordings for broadcast over public radio. Some published as Plays on Tape, for which authors receive a percentage of gross sales. Response Time: 6 mos. Style: adaptation, comedy, drama. How To Submit: agent, no unsolicited.

**La Jolla Playhouse**
Box 12039, La Jolla, CA 92039
Gabriel Greene
Tel: (858) 550-1070; Fax: (858) 550-1075
www.lajollaplayhouse.org
> Est. 1947. LORT B, C. 1993 Regional Theater Tony winner. Commissions playwrights and provides developmental support thru Page to Stage readings (est. 2001). Response Time: 2 mos query, 1 yr script. What to Submit: 10-page sample accepted from Southern California- based playwrights. Include SASE. How To Submit: full script from agent only.

**La MaMa Experimental Theater Club**
74-A E. 4th St., New York, NY 10003
Ellen Stewart
Tel: (212) 254-6468
web@lamama.org
www.lamama.org
> Est. 1961. Response Time: 6 mos. How To Submit: professional recommendation.

**Labyrinth Theater Company**
16 W. 32nd St. #101, New York, NY 10001
Philip S. Hoffman
Tel: (212) 513-1080; Fax: (212) 513-1123
lab@labtheater.org
www.labtheater.org

**Laguna Playhouse**
Box 1747, Laguna Beach, CA 92652
Donna Inglima
www.lagunaplayhouse.com
     Est. 1920. Staff: Andrew Barnicle
     (Artistic Dir). How To Submit: invite.

**The Lark Theatre Company**
939 8th Ave., #301, New York, NY 10019
Miles Lott
Tel: (212) 246-2676; Fax: (212) 246-2609
submissions@larktheatre.org
www.larktheatre.org

**Latino Theater Company**
514 S. Spring St., Los Angeles, CA 90013
Lori Zimmerman
     Est. 1985. Committed to creating and
     producing passionate, truthful, and
     world-class theater with artists of all
     culture.

**Lifeline Theatre**
6912 N. Glenwood Ave.,
Chicago, IL 60626
Dorothy Milne
Tel: (773) 761-4477; Fax: (773) 761-4582
info@lifelinetheatre.com
www.lifelinetheatre.com
     Est. 1982. Production: cast limit 9.
     Style: adaptation. What To Submit:
     query, synopsis, SASE. Author Must
     Be: resident of Chicago. How To
     Submit: invite.

**Lightning Strikes Theatre Company**
Box 7329, New York, NY 10116
Talia Rubel
Tel: (212) 713-5334
lstc@lightningstrikes.org
www.lightningstrikes.org

**Lincoln Center Theater**
150 W. 65th St., New York, NY 10023
Anne Cattaneo
Tel: (212) 362-7600
info@lct.org
www.lct.org
     Est. 1966. Equity LORT A & B.
     Response Time: 2 mos. How To
     Submit: agent.

**Little Fish Theatre (LFT)**
397 W 11th St, San Pedro, CA 90731
Melanie Jones
Tel: (310) 512-6030
melanie@littlefishtheatre.org
www.littlefishtheatre.org
     Est. 2002. Equity 99-seat. Offers
     full-length plays that are innovative
     and thought-provoking, socially
     and culturally relevant, challenging
     and entertaining. Staff: Lisa Coffi
     (Producing Artistic Director) Melanie
     Jones (Artistic Dir). No longer
     accepting full length plays, see website
     for annual Pick of the Vine short
     play festival and more details. Style:
     one act, short play. What To Submit:
     script. How To Submit: see website for
     details.

**Lodestone Theatre Ensemble**
Box 1072, Studio City, CA 91614
     Est. 1999. Asian-American nonprofit
     to develop, create, promote and present
     edgy, compelling and impassioned
     works that bridge communities
     through truthful and entertaining
     artistry.

**Lookingglass Theatre [IL]**
2936 N. Southport Ave., Fl. 3,
Chicago, IL 60657
Margot Bordelon
info@lookingglasstheatre.org
www.lookingglasstheatre.org
     Ensemble-based theater producing
     primarily company-developed
     projects. Shows are highly physical
     with strong narrative, no kitchen
     sink or talking heads. Response
     Time: May 15. Style: adaptation,
     drama, translation. What To Submit:
     query letter (note theme addressed),
     synopsis, submissions returned with
     SASE. Material Must Be: unoptioned.
     How To Submit: professional
     recommendation, agent submission.

**Looking Glass Theatre [NY]**
422 W. 57th St., New York, NY 10019
Erica Nilson
Tel: (212) 307-9467

lgtlit@yahoo.com
www.lookingglasstheatrenyc.com
Est. 1993. Off-Off Broadway
Showcase Theatre. Production:
minimal. Response Time: 6 mos-1 yr.
Style: all styles. What To Submit: full
script. How To Submit: unsolicited.
Deadline: ongoing.

**Lorraine Hansberry Theater**
777 Jones St., San Francisco, CA 94109
Stanley Williams
Tel: (415) 345-3980; Fax: (415) 345-3983
theatre@lhtsf.org
www.lhtsf.org
Style: all styles. What To Submit:
synopsis, full script, submissions
returned with SASE. Author Must Be:
Any. Material Must Be: Any. How To
Submit: unsolicited.

**Lost Nation Theater**
39 Main St., City Hall,
Montpelier, VT 5602
Mr. Kim Bent
Tel: (802) 229-0492
info@lostnationtheater.org
www.lostnationtheater.org
Est. 1977.Production: cast limit 8,
unit set, no fly. Response Time: 2 mo
query, 4 mos script. What to Submit:
query, synopsis, sample, resume in
November.

**Lyric Stage Company of Boston**
140 Clarendon St., Boston, MA 02116
Spiro Veloudos
spiro-veloudos@lyricstage.com
www.lyricstage.com
Est. 1974. Opportunities incl. Growing
Voices new work development
program. Production: cast limit 6
(plays) or 12 (musicals), modest
orchestra, unit set. Response Time:
2 mos query, 6 mos script. Style:
comedy, musical. What To Submit:
query, 1-pg synopsis, 15-pg sample,
audio, cast list, SASE. Author Must
Be: resident of MA, women and
minorities encouraged.

**Magic Theatre**
Ft. Mason Ctr., Bldg. D,
San Francisco, CA 94123
Erin Gilley
Tel: (415) 441-8001; Fax: (415) 771-5505
www.magictheatre.org
Production: cast limit 8. Response
Time: 8 mos script. Style: comedy,
drama. What To Submit: script
and cover letter. Author Must Be:
Represented by Agent or a Bay Area
Local. Material Must Be: unproduced.
Rolling deadline.

**Main Street Theater**
2540 Times Blvd., Houston, TX 77005
Rebecca Greene Udden
Tel: (713) 524-3622; Fax: (713) 524-3977
rudden@mainstreettheater.com
www.mainstreettheater.com
Est. 1975. Production: cast limit 9.
What to Submit: query, synopsis,
20 pg sample, Opportunity/Award:
royalty.

**Marin Theater Company (MTC)**
397 Miller Ave., Mill Valley, CA 94941
Margot Melcon
Tel: (415) 388-5200 ext. x3303
Fax: (415) 388-1217
margot@marintheatre.org
www.marintheatre.org
Est. 1966, Jasson Minadakis
(Artistic Director) Ryan Rilette
(Managing Director). Response
Time: 6 - 9 months. What to Submit:
general submissions, full script via
agent; 2 play prize competitions;
open submission (see website for
competition guidelines), Opportunity/
Award: awards for competition: $2500,
$10,000. How To Submit: agent.

**Ma-Yi Theatre Company**
520 8th Ave, #309, New York, NY 10018
Ralph B. Pena
Tel: (212) 971-4862
info@ma-yitheatre.org
www.ma-yitheatre.org
Est. 1989. Style: original new plays.
What To Submit: query, 1 pg synopsis,
bio. submissions not returned. Material

Must Be: unoptioned, unpublished, unproduced.

## MCC Theater
311 W. 43rd St., #302,
New York, NY 10036
Stephen Willems
Tel: (212) 727-7722; Fax: (212) 727-7780
literary@mcctheater.org
www.mcctheater.org
   Est. 1986. Equity ANTC. Production: cast limit 10. Response Time: 2 mos. What to Submit: query, synopsis, 10-pg sample, SASE. Material Must Be: unoptioned, unproduced in NYC.

## McCarter Theater Center
91 University Pl., Princeton, NJ 08540
Carrie Hughes
Tel: (609) 258-6500; Fax: (609) 497-0369
literary@mccarter.org
www.mccarter.org
   Equity LORT B+, C, and D. 1994 Regional Theater Tony winner. Response Time: 6 mos. What to Submit: full script, SASE. How To Submit: agent.

## Meadow Brook Theatre
207 Wilson Hall, Oakland Univ.,
Rochester, MI 48309
David L. Regal
Tel: (248) 370-3322
kgentile@mbtheatre.com
www.mbtheatre.com
   Est. 1967. Equity LORT C. 600-seat venue. Production: no fly. What to Submit: synopsis, SASE.

## Merrimack Repertory Theatre
132 Warren St., Lowell, MA 01852
Literary Department
Tel: (978) 654-7563; Fax: (978) 654-7575
info@merrimackrep.org
www.merrimackrep.org
   Est. 1979. Equity LORT D. Production: cast limit 8. Prefer digital scripts. Response Time: 12 mos. Style: no musical. What To Submit: full script, SASE. Author Must Be: represented by a recognized literary agent. How To Submit: agent only.

## Merry-Go-Round Playhouse
17 Williams St., Fl. 2, Auburn, NY 13021
Carole Estabrook
Tel: (315) 255-1305; Fax: (315) 252-3815
youthinfo@merry-go-round.com
www.merry-go-round.com
   Est. 1958. Production: cast of 2-4, unit set. What to Submit: synopsis, full script, submissions not returned, Opportunity/Award: royalty.

## MetroStage
1201 N. Royal St., Alexandria, VA 22314
Carolyn Griffin
Tel: (703) 548-9044; Fax: (703) 548-9089
info@metrostage.org
www.metrostage.org
   Est. 1984. Equity SPT. Production: cast limit 6 - 8, orchestra limit 5, unit set. Style: drama, musical. What To Submit: synopsis, 10-pg sample, SASE. Author Must Be: represented by an agent or theatre. Material Must Be: already workshopped, musicals must have a demo, Opportunity/ Award: royalty. How To Submit: agent or theatre.

## Metro Theater Company
8308 Olive Blvd., St. Louis, MO 63132
Carol North
Tel: (314) 997-6777 ext. 101
Fax: (314) 997-1811
carol@metrotheatercompany.org
www.metrotheatercompany.org
   Est. 1973. Mainstage shows, tours and commissions of theater for children and family audiences. Production: cast limit 10. Response Time: 3 mos. What to Submit: synopsis, sample, SASE, Opportunity/Award: 6% royalty. How To Submit: professional recommendation.

## Milk Can Theatre Company
260 West 52nd St., No. 23A,
New York, NY 10019
Julie Fei Fan Balzer
info@milkcantheatre.org
www.milkcantheatre.org
   Est. 2003. Staff: Julie Fei-Fan Balzer (Artistic Dir.). What to Submit: full length by invitation only.

**Milwaukee Chamber Theatre**
Broadway Theatre Center, 158 N.
Broadway, Milwaukee, WI 53202
Jacque Troy
Tel: (414) 276-8842 ext. 118
Fax: (414) 277-4477
jacque@chamber-theatre.com
www.milwaukeechambertheatre.com
    Est. 1975. Equity SPT. Production:
    small cast, unit set. Response Time:
    6 mos. Style: All. What To Submit:
    query, synopsis, 10-pg sample, SASE.
    Author Must Be: From Wisconsin
    or writing about Wisconsin themes
    (this material will be given first
    consideration). Material Must Be:
    Small cast pieces - full length -
    will accept Chamber musicals,
    Opportunity/Award: New works
    usually featured in our Montgomery
    Davis Play Development Series as
    a public reading before considering
    production. How To Submit:
    professional recommendation.
    Deadline: Accepting all year round.

**Milwaukee Repertory Theater**
108 E. Wells St., Milwaukee, WI 53202
Literary Director
Tel: (414) 224-1761; Fax: (414) 224-9097
www.milwaukeerep.com
    Est. 1954. Response Time: 4 mos.
    Style: no musical. How To Submit:
    professional recommendation.

**Miracle Theatre Group**
425 SE 6th Ave., Portland, OR 97214
Olga Sanchez
Tel: (503) 236-7253
olga@milagro.org
www.milagro.org
    Est. 1985. Production: cast limit 10, no
    fly. Response Time: 5 mos. Style: no
    musical. What To Submit: full script.
    Author Must Be: Hispanic.

**Missouri Repertory Theatre**
4949 Cherry St., Kansas City, MO 64110
Peter Altman
Tel: (816) 235-2727; Fax: (816) 235-6562
theatre@umkc.edu

www.missourireptheatre.org
    Est. 1964. Equity LORT B. Style:
    adaptation, comedy, drama,
    translation. How To Submit: agent
    submission.

**Mixed Blood Theatre Company**
1501 S. 4th St., Minneapolis, MN 55454
Aditi Kapil
Tel: (612) 338-0937
literary@mixedblood.com
www.mixedblood.com
    Est. 1976. Response Time: 4 mos.
    What to Submit: query, synopsis, 10-
    pg sample, SASE.

**Montana Repertory Theater**
Dept. of Theater & Dance, The University
of Montana, Missoula, MT 59812
Salina Chatlain
Tel: (406) 243-6809; Fax: (406) 243-5726
salina.chatlain@mso.umt.edu
www.montanarep.org
    Est. 1967. Production: touring set.
    Response Time: 3 mos query, 6
    mos script. What to Submit: query,
    synopsis, resume.

**Moving Arts**
Box 481145, Los Angeles, CA 90048
Trey Nichols
Tel: (323) 666-3259
info@movingarts.org
www.movingarts.org
    Est. 1992. 99-seat. Response Time:
    3 mos query, 5 mos script. Style: no
    musical. What To Submit: query,
    synopsis, 20-pg sample, resume,
    SASE. Material Must Be: unproduced
    in L.A.

**Mu Performing Arts**
355 Wabasha St. N, #140,
St. Paul, MN 55102
Rick Shiomi
Tel: (651) 789-1012; Fax: (651) 789-1015
info@muperformingarts.org
www.muperformingarts.org
    Est. 1992. Formerly Theater Mu.
    Equity and non-Equity. Production:
    cast limit 15, simple set. Response
    Time: 2 mos query, 3 mos script. Style:
    What To Submit: query, full script.

Material Must Be: relating to Asian American themes. How To Submit: Contact Artistic Director Rick Shiomi at ricks@muperformingarts.org.

**Music Theatre of Connecticut**
Box 344, Westport, CT 6880
Kevin Connors

**Music Theater of Santa Barbara**
1216 State St., #200,
Santa Barbara, CA 93101
Elise Unruh
Tel: (805) 962-1922; Fax: (805) 963-3510
www.sbclo.com
Formerly Santa Barbara CLO. Style: musical. What To Submit: full script, submissions returned with SASE. How To Submit: unsolicited.

**Musical Theatre Works**
27 W. 20th St., #706,
New York, NY 10011
Thomas Cott
Tel: (212) 677-0040
www.mtwnyc.org
Est. 1983. MTW is the only not-for-profit theater in New York devoted solely to the development of new musicals. Some commissions available. Response Time: May 15. Style: musical. What To Submit: synopsis, submissions returned with SASE. Author Must Be: older than 18. Material Must Be: unoptioned, unpublished, unproduced, Opportunity/Award: reading. How To Submit: professional recommendation.

**The National Theatre**
1321 Pennsylvania Ave., NW,
Washington, DC 20004
Est. 1835.

**National Theatre of the Deaf**
139 N. Main St., West Hartford, CT 06107
Aaron M. Kubey
Tel: (860) 236-4193 or (860) 607-1334
Fax: (860) 236-4163
akubey@ntd.org
www.ntd.org
Est. 1967. Production: cast limit 10, touring set. Response Time: 1 mo

query, 6 mos script. Style: adaptation, comedy, drama. What To Submit: query, synopsis, sample, SASE. Material Must Be: unproduced professionally.

**National Yiddish Theater – Folksbiene**
45 E. 33rd St., New York, NY 10016
Zalmen Mlotek
Tel: (212) 213-2120; Fax: (212) 213-2186
info@folksbiene.org
www.folksbiene.org
Formerly Folksbiene Yiddish Theatre.

**New Conservatory Theatre Center**
25 Van Ness Ave., Lower Lobby,
San Francisco, CA 94102
Ed Decker
Tel: (415) 861-4914; Fax: (415) 861-6988
www.nctcsf.org
Est. 1981. Response Time: 3-6 mos. Style: no translation. What To Submit: query, synopsis, character breakdown. Author Must Be: resident of US. Material Must Be: un-optioned, Opportunity/Award: 6%-8% royalty. How To Submit: visit website for up to date submission policy.

**New Federal Theatre**
292 Henry St., New York, NY 10002
Woodie King Jr.
Tel: (212) 353-1176; Fax: (212) 353-1088
newfederal@aol.com
www.newfederaltheatre.org
Est. 1970. Equity Showcase. Production: cast limit 5, unit set Response Time: 6 mos. Style: drama. What To Submit: full script, SASE. Material Must Be: unoptioned, unpublished, unproduced, Opportunity/Award: $500 option fee. How To Submit: professional recommendation.

**New Georges**
109 W. 27th St., Suite 9-A,
New York, NY 10001
Emily DeVoti
Tel: (646) 336-8077; Fax: (646) 336-8051
info@newgeorges.org
www.newgeorges.org

Equity Tiered Showcase. Response Time: one year. Style: comedy, drama, heightened aesthetic. What To Submit: full script, submissions returned with SASE. Author Must Be: female. How To Submit: unsolicited.

## New Ground Theatre
2113 E. 11th St., Davenport, IA 52803
Chris Jansen
Tel: (563) 326-7529
cljansen@hotmail.com
www.newgroundtheatre.org
Est. 2001. Production: cast limit 6, unit set, no fly. Response Time: 6 mos. What to Submit: full script. Author Must Be: resident of Iowa, Illinois, quad city area.

## The New Group
410 W. 42nd St., New York, NY 10036
Ian Morgan
Tel: (212) 244-3380; Fax: (212) 244-3438
info@thenewgroup.org
www.thenewgroup.org
Est. 1991. Opportunities incl. workshops and readings. We do not respond to electronic submissions. Response Time: 2 mos for samples, 9 mos for full scripts. What to Submit: query, synopsis, 10-pg sample, resume, SASE. How To Submit: mail.

## New Jersey Repertory Company
179 Broadway, Long Branch, NJ 7740
Suzanne Barabas
Tel: (732) 229-3166; Fax: (732) 229-3167
info@njrep.org
www.njrep.org
Est. 1997. Equity SPT 4. Production: cast limit 4 for plays and musicals. 6-7 Full length plays produced each year. 20-25 staged readings. Theatre Brut Festival of Short Plays. Style: comedy, drama, and musical. What To Submit: Prefers full script via email with cast breakdown and synopsis. Hard copy may be mailed, but will not be returned. For musicals send disk with songs, or email mp3 files. Material Must Be: unproduced and unpublished, Opportunity/Award: royalty. How To

Submit: Email with cast breakdown and synopsis. Deadline: ongoing.

## New Perspectives Theatre Company
456 W. 37th St., New York, NY 10018
Melody Brooks
Tel: (212) 630-9945; Fax: (212) 594-2553
contact@newperspectivestheatre.org
www.newperspectivestheatre.org
Est. 1992. Staged reading workshops and full productions provided to new scripts in development whenever possible. Response Time: 3 mos. Style: comedy, drama, translation. What To Submit: synopsis, 15-pg sample, SASE. Material Must Be: unoptioned, unpublished, unproduced.

## New Repertory Theatre
200 Dexter Ave., Watertown, MA 02472
Bridget Kathleen O'Leary
artistic@newrep.org
www.newrep.org
Est. 1984. Equity. Production: cast limit 12. What to Submit: full-length plays. Author Must Be: agented or local playwright. Material Must Be: unoptioned, Opportunity/Award: 5%-10% royalty. How To Submit: Send to Artistic Associate. Bridgetoleary@newrep.org or mail to 200 Dexter Ave, Watertown, MA 02472.

## New Stage Theatre
1100 Carlisle St., Jackson, MS 39202
Francine Thomas Reynolds
Tel: (601) 948-3533; Fax: (601) 948-3538
mail@newstagetheatre.com
www.newstagetheatre.com
Est. 1965. Production cast limit 8. Response Time: 3 mos query, 6 mos script- no guaranteed response. Style: comedy, drama, musicals. What To Submit: query, synopsis, author's bio. Material Must Be: Typed-fastened in folder or notebook. Opportunity/Award: Eudora Welty New Play Series/Award & Readings. Deadline: December 31, check website for details.

**New Theatre**
4120 Laguna St., Coral Gables, FL 33146
Steven Chambers
Tel: (305) 443-5373; Fax: (305) 443-1642
schambers@new-theatre.org
www.new-theatre.org
> Est. 1986. Equity SPT-4. Production:
> cast limit 6, minimal set. Response
> Time: 2-3 mos. Style: Check history
> of productions on website. All styles,
> small cast/ piano musicals accepted;.
> What To Submit: query, synopsis,
> sample pages, SASE check website
> for full instructions. Material Must
> Be: unpublished, unproduced, second
> and third productions, adaptations
> of Shakespeare are also welcome,
> Opportunity/Award: 5%-7% royalty.
> How To Submit: Check website for
> full instructions. Deadline: Preferably
> Late December.

**New World Theater (NWT)**
100 Hicks Way, #16 Curry Hicks,
Amherst, MA 01003
Andrea Assaf
Tel: (413) 545-1972; Fax: (413) 545-4414
nwt@admin.umass.edu
www.newworldtheater.org
> We host New WORKS for a New
> WORLD every summer & invite up to
> 4 artists for a development residency.
> See website for details. What to
> Submit: query. How To Submit:
> professional recommendation.

**New York Stage and Film (NYSAF)**
315 W. 36th St., #1006,
New York, NY 10018
Johanna Pfaelzea
Tel: (212) 736-4240; Fax: (212) 736-4241
info@newyorkstageandfilm.org
www.newyorkstageandfilm.org
> Est. 1985. Summer season (Jun-Aug)
> in residence as part of Powerhouse
> program at Vasser Coll. Response
> Time: 6 mos. Style: comedy, drama,
> musical. What To Submit: full script,
> SASE. Material Must Be: unpublished,
> unproduced, Opportunity/Award:
> various. How To Submit: no
> unsolicited scripts; unsolicited queries
> and sample synopsis, agent.

**New York State Theatre Institute
(NYSTI)**
37 1st St., Troy, NY 12180
Patricia Di Benedetto Snyder
Tel: (518) 274-3200
nysti@comcast.net
www.nysti.org
> Est. 1974. Equity TYA. Assistance:
> room/board, travel. Response Time:
> 6 mos. What to Submit: full script,
> SASE. Material Must Be: unproduced.
> How To Submit: agent.

**New York Theatre Workshop (NYTW)**
83 E. 4th St., New York, NY 10003
Tel: (212) 780-9037; Fax: (212) 460-8996
info@nytw.org
www.nytw.org
> Est. 1979. Works of innovative form
> & language about socially relevant
> issues. Response Time: 3 mos query,
> 8 mos script. What to Submit: query,
> synopsis, 10-pg sample, resume, SASE.

**Next Act Theatre**
342 N. Water St., Fl. 2,
Milwaukee, WI 53202
David Cecsarini
Tel: (414) 278-7780; Fax: (414) 278-5930
cez@nextact.org
www.nextact.org
> Est. 1990. Equity SPT-8. Production:
> cast limit 8. Response Time: 1 yr.
> Style: contemporary, no musical. What
> To Submit: query, synopsis, 10-pg
> sample, email ok. Deadline: Sept. 1,
> 2010.

**Next Theater Company**
927 Noyes St., Ste. 108,
Evanston, IL 60201
Jason Southerland
Tel: (847) 475-1875; Fax: (847) 475-6767
info@nexttheatre.org
www.nexttheatre.org
> Est. 1981. Equity CAT 1/2.
> Commissions 1 world premiere per
> season. Production: cast limit 10.
> What to Submit: query, synopsis, 10-
> pg sample, SASE.

**North Carolina Black Repertory Company**
610 Coliseum Dr.,
Winston-Salem, NC 27106
Larry Hamlin

**Northern Stage**
Box 4287,
White River Junction, VT 05001
Brooke Ciardelli
Tel: (802) 291-9009
info@northernstage.org
www.northernstage.org
Est. 1997. Equity LORT-D. What to
Submit: query, SASE. How To Submit:
professional recommendation.

**Northlight Theatre**
9501 N. Skokie Blvd., Skokie, IL 60077
Meghan Beals McCarthy
Tel: (847) 679-9501; Fax: (847) 679-1879
bjjones@northlight.org
www.northlight.org
Est. 1975. Equity LORT C. Response
Time: 1 mo query, 8 mos script. What
to Submit: query, 10-pg sample, SASE.

**Northside Theatre Company**
848 E. William St., San Jose, CA 95116
Richard Orlando
Tel: (408) 288-7820
rto@yahoo.com
www.northsidetheatre.com
Equity BAPP. Production: thrust stage,
no fly. Style: no musical. What To
Submit: synopsis, sample, SASE.

**Obsidian Theatre Company**
943 Queen St. East,
Toronto, Ontario M4M-1J6 Canada
Philip Akin
Tel: (416) 463-8444
obsidiantheatre@bellnet.ca
www.obsidian-theatre.com
Check website for submission details.

**Odyssey Theatre Ensemble [CA]**
2055 S. Sepulveda Blvd.,
Los Angeles, CA 90025
Sally Essex-Lopresti
Tel: (310) 477-2055; Fax: (310) 444-0455
ote2@ix.netcom.com

www.odysseytheatre.com
Est. 1969. Equity 99-seat. Response
Time: 2 wks query, 6 mos script. What
to Submit: query, synopsis, 10-pg
sample, SASE.

**Old Globe**
Box 122171, San Diego, CA 92112
Kim Montelibano Heil
Tel: (619) 231-1941; Fax: (619) 231-5879
www.theoldglobe.org
Est. 1935. Equity LORT B, C. 1984
Regional Theater Tony winner.
Response Time: 3 mos query, 6
mos script. What to Submit: query,
synopsis, 10-pg sample, SASE. How
To Submit: agent.

**Old Log Theater**
Box 250, Excelsior, MN 55331
Don Stolz
Tel: (952) 474-5951; Fax: (952) 474-1290
info@oldlog.com
www.oldlog.com
Est. 1940. Equity theater. Production:
cast limit 8. Response Time: 2 wks.
Style: comedy, drama. What To
Submit: full script, SASE. Material
Must Be: all genres welcome,
Opportunity/Award: royalty. How To
Submit: prefer mail.

**Oldcastle Theatre Company**
Box 1555, Bennington, VT 5201
Eric Peterson
Tel: (802) 447-1267; Fax: (802) 442-3704
oldcastle@gmail.com
www.oldcastletheatreco.org
Est. 1972. Equity LOA. Productions
and workshops. What to Submit: full
script, SASE.

**Olney Theatre Center for the Arts**
2001 Olney-Sandy Spring Rd,
Olney, MD 20832
Jim Petosa
Tel: (301) 924-4485; Fax: (301) 924-2654
www.olneytheatre.org
Est. 1937. 4 performance spaces. Does
not accept any unsolicited scripts.
Style: Plays and musicals.

**Omaha Theater Company at The Rose**
2001 Farnam St., Omaha, NB 68102
James Larson
Tel: (402) 502-4618
jamesl@rosetheater.org
www.rosetheater.org
> Est. 1949. Production: cast limti 10, unit set. Response Time: 6 mos. Style: adaptation, comedy, drama. How To Submit: professional recommendation.

**Open Circle Theater (OCT)**
2222 2nd St. Ste. 222, Seattle, WA 98121
Ron Sandahl
Tel: (206) 382-4250
info@octheater.com
www.octheater.com
> Est. 1992. Response Time: 3 mos query, 6 mos script. What to Submit: query, synopsis, 10-pg sample, resume. How To Submit: local professional recommendation.

**Open Eye Theater**
Box 959, Margaretville, NY 12455
Amie Brockway
Tel: (845) 586-1660; Fax: (845) 586-1660
openeye@catskill.net
www.theopeneye.org
> Est. 1972. Readings and productions for a multigenerational audience. Production: small cast, modest set. Response Time: 6 mos. What to Submit: query, synopsis. Material Must Be: unproduced or looking for a second production. How To Submit: professional recommendation.

**OpenStage Theatre & Company**
Box 617, Fort Collins, CO 80522
Denise Burson Freestone
Tel: (970) 484-5237; Fax: (970) 482-0859
denisef@openstagetheatre.org
www.openstagetheatre.org
> Rolling submissions. Est. 1973. Response Time: 1 year. Style: no musicals or one-act plays (unless latter is full evening of entertainment). What To Submit: plot summary; script samples of first 2 pages, 2 pages from the middle, last 2 pagesquery, resume. Material Must Be: full evening of entertainment, Opportunity/Award: staged workshop production, minimal tech. How To Submit: mail submission.

**Opera Cleveland**
1422 Euclid Ave, #1052, Cleveland, OH 44115
Dean Williamson
Tel: (216) 575-0903; Fax: (216) 575-1918
williamson@operacleveland.org
www.operacleveland.org
> Est. 2006 (merger of Lyric Opera Cleveland, Cleveland Opera). Spring-fall season and summer fest of 5 full-length operas. Assistance: room/board, travel. Response Time: 1 mo. Style: opera. What To Submit: query, synopsis, full script, audio, SASE. How To Submit: agent.

**Oregon Shakespeare Festival**
Box 158, Ashland, OR 97520
Lue Morgan Douthit
Tel: (541) 482-2111; Fax: (541) 482-0446
literary@osfashland.org
www.osfashland.org
> Est. 1935. Equity LORT B+. 1983 Regional Theater Tony winner. Response Time: 6 mos. What to Submit: query. Author Must Be: women/minorities encouraged. How To Submit: agent.

**Pasadena Playhouse**
39 S. El Molino Ave., Pasadena, CA 91101
Tel: (626) 797-8672; Fax: (626) 792-7343
www.pasadenaplayhouse.org
> Est. 1917. Equity LORT B. Year-round season in 670-seat and 99-seat theaters. The Pasadena Playhouse does not accept unsolicited manuscripts unless submitted by an agent or by invitation. However, each year from June 1-30, we do accept inquiry letters with a synopsis and 10-page sample. Scripts sent unsolicited will not be read. Please do not call or email to follow up on the status of your submission. If you wish your material returned, please include a SASE with your submission

**Passage Theatre**
P.O. Box 967, Trenton, NJ 08605
Tel: (609) 392-0766; Fax: (609) 392-0318
info@passagetheatre.org
www.passagetheatre.org
> Est. 1985.Production: Modest cast
> size, 4-6 actors, no fly. Response
> Time: 5 mos. Style: Boundary-pushing
> & stylistically adventurous new works
> for the theatre that entertain and
> challenge a diverse audience. What
> To Submit: Full length if professional
> recommendation, sample work
> if unrepresented; see website for
> details. How To Submit: professional
> recommendation, website. Deadline:
> ongoing.

**Paul Robeson Theatre**
350 Masten Avenue, Buffalo, NY 14209
Paulette D. Harris
> Paul Robeson Theatre at the African
> American Cultural Center was
> founded to nurture and showcase the
> artistic talents of African American
> playwrights, producers, directors,
> actors and stage technicians.

**PCPA Theatrefest**
800 S. College Dr.,
Santa Maria, CA 93454
Patricia M. Troxel
Tel: (805) 928-7731; Fax: (805) 928-7506
literary@pcpa.org
www.pcpa.org
> Est. 1964. Response Time: 3 mos
> query, 6 mos script. What to Submit:
> query, synopsis.

**Pegasus Players**
1145 W. Wilson Ave., Chicago, IL 60640
Christopher Schram
Tel: (773) 878-9761; Fax: (773) 271-8057
info@pegasusplayers.org
www.pegasusplayers.org
> Est. 1978. Response Time: 1 mo query,
> 6 mos script. What to Submit: query,
> synopsis.

**Pegasus Theater Company**
Box 942, Monte Rio, CA 95462
Tel: (707) 522-9043

director@pegasustheater.com
www.pegasustheater.com
> Est. 1998.

**Pendragon Theatre**
15 Brandy Brook Ave.,
Saranac Lake, NY 12983
Molly Pietz-Walsh
Tel: (518) 891-1854; Fax: (518) 891-7012
pdragon@northnet.org
www.pendragontheatre.com
> Est. 1980. No musicals please. What
> to Submit: query, 10-pg sample,
> SASE. Material Must Be: unpublished,
> unproduced.

**Penguin Repertory Company**
Box 91, Stony Point, NY 10980
Staci Swedeen
staci@penguinrep.org
www.penguinrep.org
> Est. 1977. Equity Guest Full length
> plays, small sets, four characters
> or fewer. If play is selected for
> reading series, author must be able
> to attend rehearsal and reading. If
> play is selected for production, author
> availability is flexible. Response Time:
> Up To One Year. What to Submit: full
> script, submissions not returned. How
> To Submit: Mail full play to address
> listed above. Cover letter, resume,
> synopsis, SASE and emal address.

**Penumbra Theatre Company**
270 N. Kent St., St. Paul, MN 55102
Dominic Taylor
Tel: (651) 288-6795; Fax: (651) 288-6789
dominic.taylor@penumbratheatre.org
www.penumbratheatre.org
> Est. 1976. Response Time: 9 mos.
> Style: all styles.

**People's Light and Theatre Company**
39 Conestoga Rd., Malvern, PA 19355
Alda Cortese
Tel: (610) 647-1900
cortese@peopleslight.org
www.peopleslight.org
> Est. 1974. Equity LORT. Style:
> adaptation, comedy, drama. What To
> Submit: query, synopsis, 10-pg sample,

full script. Opportunity/Award:
royalty. How To Submit: prefer email.

**Performance Network Theatre**
120 E. Huron St., Ann Arbor, MI 48104
Carla Milarch
Tel: (734) 663-0696; Fax: (734) 663-7367
david@performancenetwork.org
www.performancenetwork.org
   Est. 1981. Production: cast limit 10,
   no fly. Response Time: 6 mos. What
   to Submit: synopsis, 10-pg sample,
   SASE.

**Perseverance Theatre (PT)**
914 3rd St, Douglas, AK 99824
Tel: (907) 364-2421; Fax: (907) 364-2603
info@perseverancetheatre.org
www.perseverancetheatre.org
   Est. 1979. Response Time: 1 mo query,
   3 mos script. What to Submit: query,
   synopsis, sample. Author Must Be:
   resident of AK, women encouraged.

**Philadelphia Theatre Company (PTC)**
230 S. Broad St., Ste. 1105,
Philadelphia, PA 19102
Jacqueline Goldfinger
Tel: (215) 985-1400 ext. 113
Fax: (215) 985-5800
www.philadelphiatheatrecompany.org
   Est. 1974. Equity LORT D. 4
   contemporary US plays/season
   (Sep-July). Production: cast limit 10.
   Response Time: 6 -8 months. Style:
   comedy, drama, musical. What To
   Submit: full script. How To Submit:
   agent or local writers only. Deadline:
   Mar. 1, 2010.

**Phoenix Theatre [AZ]**
100 E. McDowell Rd., Phoenix, AZ 85004
Daniel Schay
Tel: (602) 258-1974
info@phoenixtheatre.net
www.phoenixtheatre.net
   Est. 1920. Assistance: $200. Response
   Time: 6 mos. What to Submit:
   query, full script. Material Must Be:
   unproduced. Deadline: Jan. 15, 2010.

**Phoenix Theatre [IN]**
749 N. Park Ave., Indianapolis, IN 46202
Bryan Fonseca
Tel: (317) 635-7529
bfonseca@phoenixtheatre.org
www.phoenixtheatre.org
   Est. 1983. Production: cast limit
   6. Response Time: 6 mos. What to
   Submit: query, synopsis, 10-pg sample,
   SASE. How To Submit: professional
   recommendation, see website.

**Pier One Theatre**
Box 894, Homer, AK 99603
Lance Petersen
lance@xyz.net
www.pieronetheatre.org
   Est. 1973. Non-Equity community
   theater. Response Time: 6 mos.
   What to Submit: full script, SASE,
   Opportunity/Award: 4% royalty.

**Pillsbury House Theatre**
3501 Chicago Ave. S.,
Minneapolis, MN 55407
Neal Spinler
Tel: (612) 825-0459; Fax: (612) 827-5818
info@pillsburyhousetheatre.org
www.pillsburyhousetheatre.org
   Est. 1992. Production: cast limit
   10. Response Time: 5 mos query, 6
   mos script. Style: no musical. What
   To Submit: Invitation only. How To
   Submit: agent.

**Pioneer Theatre Company**
300 South 1400 East, #205,
Salt Lake City, UT 84112
Elizabeth Williamson
Tel: (801) 581-6356; Fax: (801) 581-5472
www.pioneertheatre.org
   Est. 1962. Equity LORT B. Response
   Time: 1 mo query, 6 mos script. How
   To Submit: agent submissions only at
   this time.

**Pittsburgh Public Theater**
621 Penn Ave., Pittsburgh, PA 15222
Margie Romero
Tel: (412) 316-8200 ext. 707
mromero@ppt.org
www.ppt.org

Est. 1975. Equity LORT B. Style:
comedy, drama, classics and new
plays. Not accepting submissions at
this time.

**Piven Theatre**
927 Noyes St., #110, Evanston, IL 60201
Scott Shallenbarger
Tel: (847) 866-8049
scott@piventheatre.org
www.piventheatre.org
Style: Adaptation, Drama, Translation.
What To Submit: Query, Synopsis or
Treatment, 15 Page Sample.

**Plan-B Theatre Company**
138 W. 300 S., Salt Lake City, UT 84101
Jerry Rapier
Tel: (801) 297-4200; Fax: (801) 466-3840
jerry@planbtheatre.org
www.planbtheatre.org
Est. 1995. Equity SPT-2. Production:
cast limit 5, minimal set. Response
Time: 3 mos. Style: drama. What To
Submit: full script, SASE. Author
Must Be: preference given to plays
by Utah playwrights. Material Must
Be: full script, Opportunity/Award:
royalty. How To Submit: email (PDF)
only.

**Play With Your Food**
PO Box 2161, Westport, CT 06880
Carole Schweid
Tel: (203) 247-4083
carole@playwithyourfood.org
www.playwithyourfood.org
Looking for first rate one-act plays for
popular lunchtime play-reading series.
What to Submit: One Act Play script,
Opportunity/Award: Reading/Royalty.

**Playhouse on the Square**
51 S. Cooper St., Memphis, TN 38104
Jackie Nichols
Tel: (901) 725-0776
info@playhouseonthesquare.org
www.playhouseonthesquare.org
Est. 1968. No longer accepting
submissions.

**PlayMakers Repertory Company**
CB-3235, Center for Dramatic Art,
Chapel Hill, NC 27516
www.playmakersrep.org
Est. 1976. Equity LORT D. Response
Time: 6 mos. Style: no musical.
Submissions not returned. How To
Submit: agent.

**Playwrights' Forum [TN]**
Box 11265, Memphis, TN 38111
Billy Pullen
Tel: (901) 725-2040
www.playwrights-forum.org
Est. 1991. 3-weekend run in 100-
seat theater. Assistance: $300 travel.
Frequency: semiannual. Production:
ages 18-90, cast of 2-6. Response
Time: 8 mos. Style: adaptation,
comedy, drama. What To Submit:
query, 10-pg sample. Material Must
Be: unpublished. How To Submit: mail.

**Playwrights Horizons**
416 W. 42nd St., New York, NY 10036
Adam Greenfield
Tel: (212) 564-1235; Fax: (212) 594-0296
literary@playwrightshorizons.org
www.playwrightshorizons.org
Est. 1971. Equity Off-Broadway
nonprofit dedicated to new American
voices, offering 6 productions/season
and numerous readings. Production:
cast limit 10. Response Time: 6
mos for plays; 9 mos for musicals.
Contacts: Adam Greenfield (plays),
Kent Nicholson (musicals). Style: We
*do not* accept one-acts, one-person
shows, non-musical adaptations,
translations, children's shows,
screenplays, musicals without original
scores or works by non-US writers.
What To Submit: full script, audio,
bio, SASE. Author Must Be: citizen of
US. Material Must Be: unpublished,
unproduced in NYC. How To Submit:
open submission policy.

**Playwrights Theatre of New Jersey**
Box 1295, Madison, NJ 7940
Peter Hays
Tel: (973) 514-1787 ext. 18

Fax: (973) 514-2060
phays@ptnj.org
www.ptnj.org
> Est. 1986. Equity SPT. Works accepted
> through New Play Development
> Program. Production: ages 10 and
> above, casts up to 6. Response Time:
> 1 year. Style: comedy, drama. What
> To Submit: synopsis, 10-pg writing
> sample, submissions returned with
> SASE. Material Must Be: Not
> Optional, unpublished, Opportunity/
> Award: production, reading. How To
> Submit: professional recommendation,
> agent.

**Polarity Ensemble Theatre**
135 Asbury Ave., Evanston, IL 60202
Richard Engling
Tel: (847) 475-1139
richard@petheatre.com
www.petheatre.com
> We only accept scripts when we put
> out a call for submissions. We do not
> read year round. Visit our website
> and register on our auditions list.
> Style: All. What To Submit: Full
> Script. Author Must Be: Chicago
> Area, Opportunity/Award: Workshop/
> Production.

**Porchlight Music Theatre Chicago**
2814 N. Lincoln Ave., Chicago, IL 60657
L. Walter Stearns
Tel: (773) 325-9884
porchlighttheatre@yahoo.com
www.porchlighttheatre.com
> Est. 1994. Response Time: 6 mos.
> Style: musical. What To Submit:
> synopsis, audio, bio, SASE. Material
> Must Be: unoptioned.

**Portland Center Stage [OR]**
128 NW 11th Ave., Portland, OR 97209
Kelsey Tyler
Tel: (503) 445-3792; Fax: (503) 445-3721
www.pcs.org
> Est. 1988. Production: cast limit 12.
> Response Time: 3 mos query, 6 mos
> script. Style: comedy, drama. What To
> Submit: query, 10-pg sample, resume.

**Portland Stage Company [ME]**
PO Box 1458, Portland, ME 04104
Daniel Burson
Tel: (207) 774-1043; Fax: (207) 774-0576
dburson@portlandstage.com
www.portlandstage.com
> Est. 1970. Rolling submissions.
> Response Time: 3 mos query, 6 mos
> script. Must be submitted by literary
> agent. Style: comedy, drama. How To
> Submit: agent.

**Powerhouse Theatre**
3116 Second St., Santa Monica, CA 90405
Jennifer Keller

**Primary Stages**
307 W. 38th St, #1510,
New York, NY 10018
Tessa LaNeve
Tel: (212) 840-9705; Fax: (212) 840-9725
www.primarystages.org
> Est. 1984. Equity Off-Broadway,
> ANTC. In residence at 59E59
> Theaters. Founded to produce new
> plays and develop playwrights.
> Staff: Andrew Leynse (Artistic Dir.).
> Response Time: 1 yr. Material Must
> Be: unproduced. How To Submit: we
> no longer accept unsolicited scripts,
> agent.

**Prime Stage Theatre**
Box 1849, Pittsburgh, PA 15230
Wayne Brinda
Tel: (412) 771-7373; Fax: (412) 771-8585
wbrinda@primestage.com
www.primestage.com
> Literature based youth and adult theatre
> Production: age 12 through senior
> citizen. Style: adaptation. What
> To Submit: query, synopsis, 30-pg
> sample, submissions returned with
> SASE. How To Submit: unsolicited.

**Prince Music Theater**
100 S. Broad St., #1950,
Philadelphia, PA 19110
Tel: (215) 972-1000
info@princemusictheater.org
www.princemusictheater.org

Est. 1984. Formerly American Music Theater Festival. Production: cast of 2-12. Response Time: 8 mos. Style: musical. What To Submit: query, synopsis, 30-pg sample, audio, SASE. Material Must Be: unproduced. How To Submit: professional recommendation.

**Prop Thtr**
3502-4 N. Elston Ave., Chicago, IL 60618
Diane M. Honeyman
www.propthtr.org
Est. 1981.

**Prospect Theater Company**
520 8th Ave., Suite 307, 3rd fl.,
New York, NY 10018
Cara Reichel
Tel: (212) 594-4476; Fax: (212) 594-4478
artistic@prospecttheater.org
www.prospecttheater.org
Est. 1998. Small company of emerging artists, producing a 3-show season OOB under Equity Transition Contract. Style: primarily new musicals. What To Submit: full script, demo CD, SASE, Opportunity/ Award: royalty. How To Submit: for full productions, professional recommendation only. Dark nights series productions applications are available periodically in the summer / fall through our website.

**Public Theater [NY]**
425 Lafayette St., New York, NY 10003
Liz Frankel
Tel: (212) 539-8530; Fax: (212) 539-8505
www.publictheater.org
Est. 1954. Response Time: 6 mos. What to Submit: query, synopsis, 10-pg sample. How To Submit: full submission, agent only/ other submissions send query, synopsis and 10 page sample.

**Puerto Rican Traveling Theatre**
141 W. 94th St., New York, NY 10025
Allen Davis
Tel: (212) 354-1293; Fax: (212) 307-6769
prtt@prtt.org

Est. 1997. Workshops for beginning and professional playwrights.

**Pulse Ensemble Theatre**
266 W 37th St., Fl. 22,
New York, NY 10018
Alexa Kelly
theatre@pulseensembletheatre.org
www.pulseensembletheatre.org
Est. 1989. Only developing new works in Playwrights' Lab. Response Time: up to 1 year. What to Submit: synopsis, 10 pgs. sample, submissions returned with SASE. Material Must Be: unoptioned. How To Submit: invite.

**Purple Rose Theatre Company**
137 Park St., Chelsea, MI 48118
Guy Sanville
Tel: (734) 433-7782; Fax: (734) 475-0802
sanville@purplerosetheatre.org
www.purplerosetheatre.org
Est. 1991. Equity SPT-8. Production: ages 18-80, cast of 2-10. Response Time: 6 mos. What to Submit: synopsis, 15-pg sample, SASE, character sheets. Author Must Be: age 18 or older. Material Must Be: unoptioned, unpublished, unproduced, Opportunity/Award: 6%-8% royalty. How To Submit: agent.

**Queens Theatre in the Park**
Box 520069, Flushing, NY 11352
Rob Urbinati
Tel: (718) 760-0064
urbinati@aol.com
www.queenstheatre.org
Est. 2001. New play development series incl. Immigrant Voices Project and Plays a Mother Would Love. Check our website, www. queenstheatre.org for submission policies. Production: cast limit 6. Response Time: 6 mos. Style: comedy, drama, musical. What To Submit: No unsolicited submissions.

**Rainbow Artist Workshop**
112 S. College St., Santa Maria, CA 93454
Leo Cortez

**Rainbow Dinner Theatre**
Box 56, Paradise, PA 17562
David DiSavino
Tel: (717) 687-4300
david@rainbowdinnertheatre.com
www.rainbowdinnertheatre.com
> Est. 1984. Professional non-Equity
> dinner theater. Production: ages 18 and
> older, cast of 2-12, set limit 2. Response
> Time: 6 mos. Style: mainstream
> comedy. What To Submit: synopsis,
> sample, SASE, Opportunity/Award:
> Production, collaborative revision/
> rewriting, author retains all rights, 3%
> royalty. How To Submit: agent.

**Random Acts of Theater (RAT)**
1220 N. Lawrence St.,
Philadelphia, PA 19122
> Original works, incl. but not limited to
> one-person shows and new approaches
> to classic works.

**Rattlestick Playwrights Theatre**
244 Waverly Pl., New York, NY 10014
Lou Moreno
Tel: (212) 627-2556; Fax: (630) 839-8352
info@rattlestick.org
www.rattlestick.org
> Yearlong development program,
> culminating in annual spring
> Exposure Fest. Production: cast of
> up to 8. Response Time: May 15.
> Style: all styles, Drama, Musical.
> What To Submit: Query, application,
> actor breakdown, 20 page sample,
> full script, no A/V unless musical,
> resume, submissions returned with
> SASE. Material Must Be: unpublished,
> unproduced, still in development. How
> To Submit: unsolicited, professional
> recommendation, Agent.

**Red Bull Theater**
Literary Submission, P.O. Box 250863,
New York, NY 10025
Callie Kimball
Tel: (212) 414-5168
callie@redbulltheater.com
www.redbulltheater.com
> Est. 2003. Red Bull Theater is
> interested in new full-length plays and

adaptations that relate to our mission
of exploring Jacobean themes and
heightened language. Along with letter
of inquiry, please send bio or resume,
a synopsis of play with character
breakdown, the play's production or
development history, and the first ten
pages of your script. Response Time:
6 mos. Enclose a SASE with sufficient
postage for your materials to be
returned. Style: adaptation, translation,
classically inspired. How To Submit:
by regular mail ONLY.

**Red Orchid Theatre**
1531 N. Wells St., Chicago, IL 60610
Kristen Lahey
Tel: (312) 943-8722
literary@aredorchidtheatre.org
www.aredorchidtheatre.org
> Est. 1993. Accepts Synopsis with 10
> page sample or Full Length Plays.
> How To Submit: Electronic preferred.

**Repertorio Espanol**
138 E. 27th St., New York, NY 10016
Tel: (212) 889-2850; Fax: (212) 225-9085
info@repertorio.org
www.repertorio.org
> Est. 1968. Production: small cast.
> Response Time: 6 months. Style:
> adaptation, comedy, drama. What
> To Submit: query, synopsis. Material
> Must Be: unpublished, unproduced.

**Repertory Theatre of St. Louis**
P. O. Box 191730, St. Louis, MO 63119
Susan Gregg
Tel: (314) 968-7340
sgregg@repstl.org
www.repstl.org
> Est. 1966. Equity LORT B, D.
> Production: small cast. Response
> Time: 4 mos query, 2 yrs script. Style:
> comedy, drama. What To Submit:
> query, synopsis.

**Riant Theatre**
The Black Experimental Theatre,
Box 1902, New York, NY 10013
Van Dirk. Fisher
Tel: (646) 623-3488

TheRiantTheatre@aol.com
www.therianttheatre.com
> Opportunities incl. semiannual
> Strawberry One-Act Fest, Core Project
> workshop. Please send query bfore
> submitting work. Style: All types.
> What To Submit: An application
> and play for the Strawberry One-Act
> Festival., Opportunity/Award: Best
> Play Award: $1,500. How To Submit:
> Download an application from our
> website. Deadline: Apr. 30 and Oct.
> 30, 2010.

**Riverside Theatre [IA]**
213 N. Gilbert St., Iowa City, IA 52245
Jody Hovland
Tel: (319) 887-1360; Fax: (319) 887-1362
artistic@riversidetheatre.org
www.riversidetheatre.org
> Est. 1981. Guidelines on website.
> Also accepts submissions for annual
> monologue festival. Production: small
> cast, simple set. Response Time: only
> if interested. Style: all styles. What To
> Submit: synopsis, first 10 pages, bio.
> How To Submit: By post or email.

**Riverside Theatre [FL]**
3250 Riverside Park Dr.,
Vero Beach, FL 32963
Allen D. Cornell
Tel: (772) 231-5860
info@riversidetheatre.com
www.riversidetheatre.com
> Est. 1985. Production: cast limit 10.
> What to Submit: query, synopsis.

**Tracy Roberts Theater**
12265 Ventura Blvd., #209,
Studio City, CA 91604
Nat Christian
Tel: (818) 623-9500
www.tracyroberts.com
> Style: all styles. What To Submit:
> query, synopsis, SASE. Material Must
> Be: unproduced. How To Submit:
> unsolicited.

**Roots & Branches Theater**
315 Hudson St., New York, NY 10013
Arthur Strimling
Tel: (212) 366-8032; Fax: (212) 366-8033

astrimling@fegs.org
> Workshop process, ensemble based
> company. Apply as artist, no script
> submissions. Interested in age theme
> stories/inter-generational stories.

**Rorschach Theatre**
1421 Columbia Rd., NW, #303,
Washington, DC 20009

**Ross Valley Players**
Box 437, Ross, CA 94957
Tel: (415) 456-9555
raw@rossvalleyplayers.com
www.rossvalleyplayers.com
> Opportunities incl. RAW (Ross
> Alternative Works) staged readings.
> All types except children's plays.
> Limited resources for musicals. Author
> Must Be: Greater San Francisco Bay
> Area Playwrights showcased. Material
> Must Be: unproduced.

**Round House Theatre**
Box 30688, Bethesda, MD 20824
Tel: (240) 644-1099; Fax: (240) 644-1090
www.roundhousetheatre.org
> Est. 1978. Literary Works Project in
> Bethesda, and New Works Series in
> Silver Spring. Production: cast limit 8,
> piano only, unit set. Response Time:
> 2 mos query, 1 yr script. What to
> Submit: Letter of inquiry.

**Roxbury Crossroads Theatre**
37 Vine St., Roxbury, MA 02119
Ed Bullins
Tel: (617) 442-0640
rct9@verizon.net
www.roxburycrossroadstheatre.com

**Royal Court Theatre**
Sloane Sq., London, UK
www.royalcourttheatre.com
> Est. 1956. Opportunities incl.
> production and development for both
> international writers (international@
> royalcourttheatre.com) and young
> writers (ywp@royalcourttheatre.com).
> What to Submit: 1/2-page synopsis,
> SASE (intl. reply coupon). How To
> Submit: by snail mail only.

**Ryan Repertory Company Inc.**
2445 Bath Ave., Brooklyn, NY 11214
Barbara Parisi
Tel: (718) 996-4800
ryanrep@juno.com
www.ryanrep.org
Est. 1972. Staff: John Sannuto, Artistic
Dir. What to Submit: full script, audio,
submissions not returned.

**Sacramento Theatre Company**
1419 H St., Sacramento, CA 95814
Peggy Shannon
Tel: (916) 446-7501; Fax: (916) 446-4066
www.sactheatre.org
Est. 1942. Equity LORT D.
Production: cast limit 10. Response
Time: 6 mos. Style: adaptation,
comedy, drama, revue. How To
Submit: agent.

**San Diego Asian American Repertory
Theatre**
PO Box 81796, San Diego, CA 92138
Est. 1995.

**San Diego Repertory Theatre**
79 Horton Plz.,
San Diego, CA 92101-6144
Angela Rasbeary
Tel: (619) 231-3586; Fax: (619) 235-0939
arasbeary@sdrep.org
www.sdrep.org
Est. 1976. What to Submit: full script.
Deadline: rolling.

**San Jose Repertory Theatre**
101 Paseo de San Antonio,
San Jose, CA 95113
Bruce Elsperger
Tel: (408) 367-7276; Fax: (408) 367-7237
www.sjrep.com
Est. 1980. Equity LORT C. Works
begin in New America Playwrights
Fest of mid-career playwrights.
Interested in ethnic plays, plays by
women, and plays with music. Staff:
Rick Lombardo (Artistic Director),
Nick Nichols (Managing Dir).
Response Time: 6-9 mos. How To
Submit: professional recommendation.

**Santa Monica Playhouse**
1211 4th St., Suite #201,
Santa Monica, CA 90401-1391
Cydne Moore
Tel: (310) 394-9779 ext. 623
Fax: (310) 393-5573
theatre@SantaMonicaPlayhouse.com
www.santamonicaplayhouse.com
Est. 1960. Production: cast limit 10.
Response Time:9 mos query, 12 mos
script. Style: no musical. What To
Submit: query, 1-pg synopsis, 10-pg
sample, resume, submissions not
returned.

**Seacoast Repertory Theatre**
125 Bow St., Portsmouth, NH 03801
Craig Faulkner
Tel: (603) 433-4793; Fax: (603) 431-7818
craig@seacoastrep.org
www.seacoastrep.org
Est. 1986. Offers 8 mainstage and
6 youth works each year. Response
Time: 6 mos. Style: all styles. What
To Submit: 1-pg synopsis, 10 page
sample, SASE. Material Must Be:
unoptioned. How To Submit: agent.

**Seattle Children's Theatre**
201 Thomas St., Seattle, WA 98109
Torrie McDonald
Tel: (206) 443-0807; Fax: (206) 443-0442
torriem@sct.org
www.sct.org
Est. 1975. Innovative and professional
theater for family and school
audiences, Sept.-June. Response Time:
6 mos. What to Submit: synopsis, 10-
pg sample, SASE. How To Submit:
No unsolicited works, professional
recommendation only.

**Seattle Repertory Theatre**
155 Mercer St., Box 900923,
Seattle, WA 98109
Braden Abraham
Tel: (206) 443-2210; Fax: (206) 443-2379
bradena@seattlerep.org
www.seattlerep.org
Est. 1963. Equity LORT B+, C. 1990
Regional Theater Tony winner. 8-9
plays/yr on 2 proscenium stages:

850-seat Bagley Wright; 300-seat Leo K. Staff: Jerry Manning (Artistic Dir). Assistance: room/board, travel. Response Time: 6 mos. Style: adaptation, comedy, drama. What To Submit: full script, SASE, Opportunity/Award: royalty. How To Submit: agent.

## Second Stage Theatre
307 W. 43rd St., New York, NY 10036
Sarah Steele
Tel: (212) 787-8302; Fax: (212) 397-7066
ssteele@2st.com
www.2st.com
> Est. 1979. Two Off-Broadway theaters, 6 shows per season. Full-length plays and musicals of heightened realism and sociopolitical issues, particularly by women and minority writers. Prefer work with contemporary setting. No historical biography or one person shows. Staff: Carole Rothman (Artistic Dir), Ellen Richard (Exec Dir). Response Time: 1 mo query, 6 mos script. What to Submit: Only by agents; no queries or unsolicited material accepted.

## Seventh Street Playhouse, LLC
PO Box 15414, Washington, DC 20003
Anthony Gallo
seventheatre@verizon.net
www.webspace.webring.com/people/ta/agallo2368
> Email submissions only. Style: All. What To Submit: Synopsis or Treatment, 10 page sample. Material Must Be: not published, Opportunity/Award: Reading, workshop. How To Submit: prior professional recommendations only.

## ShadowBox: The Sketch Comedy Rock 'n' Roll Club
164 Easton Town Center,
Columbus, OH 43219
Tom Cardinal
Tel: (614) 416-7625; Fax: (614) 416-7600
tomcardinal@earthlink.net
www.shadowboxcabaret.com

Est. 1989. Production: age 15-50, cast of up to 5, minimal set. Response Time: 10 months. Style: comedy / drama / musicals. What To Submit: full script. Scripts will not be returned. How To Submit: unsolicited.

## Shadowlight Productions
22 Chattanooga St.,
San Francisco, CA 94114
Larry Reed
Tel: (415) 648-4461; Fax: (415) 641-9734
info@shadowlight.org
www.shadowlight.org
> Est. 1972. Production: cast limit 15. Response Time: 1 mo. Material Must Be: suitable for shadow theater (puppets and live actors). How To Submit: professional recommendation.

## Shakespeare & Company
70 Kemble St., Lenox, MA 01240
Tony Simotes
Tel: (413) 637-1199 ext. 111
tsimotes@shakespeare.org
www.shakespeare.org
> Est. 1978. Production: cast of 2-8. Response Time: 3 mos. Style: no musical. What To Submit: query, synopsis, 10-pg sample, by post only, SASE. How To Submit: By post only.

## Shakespeare Festival at Tulane
215 McWilliams Hall,
New Orleans, LA 70118
Claire Moncrief
Tel: (504) 865-5105; Fax: (504) 865-5205
brad@tulane.edu
www.neworleansshakespeare.com
> Est. 1993. Production: unit set, no fly. Response Time: 2 mos query, 3 mos script. Style: Shakespeare, adaptation, new plays. What To Submit: query, synopsis, sample, resume, SASE.

## Shakespeare Theatre Company
516 8th St. SE, Washington, DC 20003
Akiva Fox
Tel: (202) 547-3230; Fax: (202) 547-0226
afox@shakespearetheatre.org
www.shakespearetheatre.org

Est. 1986. Classical theatre dedicated to works of Shakespeare and other classical writers in new translations and adaptations. Fees: royalty. Style: adaptation, translation. What To Submit: query, SASE. How To Submit: agent.

### Shotgun Productions Inc.
165 E. 35 St., #7-J, New York, NY 10016
Patricia Klausner
Tel: (212) 689-2322; Fax: (212) 689-2322
literary@shotgun-productions.org
www.shotgun-productions.org
Est. 1989. Equity. 3-step development, incl. staged readings, workshops and full productions. Response Time: 1 yr. What to Submit: query, synopsis. Material Must Be: unoptioned, unproduced. How To Submit: professional recommendation.

### Signature Theatre Company [NY]
630 9th Ave., #1106,
New York, NY 10036
Kirsten Bowen
Fax: (212) 967-2957
kbowen@signaturetheatre.org
www.signaturetheatre.org
Est. 1990. Production: small and large cast shows. Response Time: 4 mos. Style: Premieres and revivals produced in a season of work by one Playwright-in-Residence, as well as work by past Playwrights-in-Residence. How To Submit: Due to the nature of our programming, we do not accept unsolicited submissions.

### SignStage
11206 Euclid Ave.,
Cleveland, OH 44106-1798
William Morgan
Tel: (216) 231-8787 ext. 302
Fax: (216) 231-7141
wmorgan@chsc.org
www.signstage.org
Est. 1975. In-school residencies, educational performances about deaf awareness. Response Time: only if interested. What to Submit: synopsis, SASE.

### SITI Company
520 8th Ave., #310, New York, NY 10018
Megan Szalla
Tel: (212) 868-0860; Fax: (212) 868-0837
inbox@siti.org
www.siti.org
Est. 1992. Staff: Anne Bogart (Artistic Dir).

### Skylight Opera Theatre
158 N. Broadway, Milwaukee, WI 53202
Diana Alioto
Tel: (414) 291-7811 ext. 238
Fax: (414) 291-7815
diana@skylightopera.com
www.skylightopera.com
Est. 1959. Formerly Skylight Opera Theatre. Production: cast limit 22, orchestra limit 18. Response Time: 2 mos query, 1 yr script. Style: musical, revue. What To Submit: query, synopsis, audio.

### Society Hill Playhouse
507 S. 8th St., Philadelphia, PA 19147
Deen Kogan
Tel: (215) 923-0210; Fax: (215) 923-1789
shp@erols.com
www.societyhillplayhouse.org
Production: cast of up to 8. Response Time: 3 months. Style: no adaptation, no translation. What To Submit: query letter (note theme addressed), submissions returned with SASE. How To Submit: no email.

### SoHo Repertory Theatre Inc.
86 Franklin St, Fl. 4,
New York, NY 10013
Daniel Manley
Tel: (212) 941-8632; Fax: (212) 941-7148
sohorep@sohorep.org
www.sohorep.org
Est. 1975. Apply thru Writer/Director Lab. Style: contemporary plays. What To Submit: Application to Writer/Director Lab with required materials. How To Submit: No unsolicited scripts. Writer/Director Lab Application open to all.

**Sonoma County Repertory Theater**
104 N. Main St., Sebastopol, CA 95472
Scott O. Phillips
Tel: (707) 823-0177
www.the-rep.com
    Est. 1993. Staff: Jennifer King (Assoc./
    Art. Dir.), Scott Phillips (Art. Dir),
    Amber Wallen (Managing Director).
    What to Submit: 1-pg synopsis, full
    script, cast list, SASE.

**South Camden Theatre Company**
1739 Ferry Ave., Camden, NJ 08104
Joseph M. Paprzycki
Tel: (856) 456-2850
joep@southcamdentheatre.org
www.southcamdentheatre.org
    Est. 2005. Non-Equity. Opportunities
    incl. one-act fest. Style: drama.
    What To Submit: synopsis, SASE,
    Opportunity/Award: honorarium. How
    To Submit: invite only.

**South Coast Repertory Theatre**
Box 2197, Costa Mesa, CA 92628
Empty Contact
Tel: (714) 708-5500
www.scr.org
    Est. 1964. 1988 Regional Theater
    Tony winner. Mainstage programming
    in 507-seat Segerstrom and 335-seat
    Argyros; family series in Argyros.
    Also NewSCRipts reading series and
    Pacific Playwrights Festival (PPF)
    of new work. Response Time: 2 mos
    query; 6 mos script. What to Submit:
    query, synopsis, 10-pg sample, SASE;
    for more information please see
    submission guidelines on website,
    Opportunity/Award: royalty. How
    To Submit: please see submission
    guidelines on website.

**Springer Opera House**
103 10th St., Columbus, GA 31901
Paul Pierce
Tel: (706) 324-5714; Fax: (706) 324-4461
www.springeroperahouse.org
    Est. 1871. Production: small cast, unit
    set or single set. Response Time: 2
    mos query. Style: comedy, musical.
    What To Submit: query, synopsis.

**Square Mama Productions**
63 El Pavo Real, San Rafael, CA 94903
Randy Warren
Tel: (415) 225-3258; Fax: (415) 444-0766
info@squaremama.com
www.squaremama.com
    We normally produce revivals of
    overlooked plays, but we're always
    ready for a new play offer we can't
    refuse. Email submission is preferred.
    Style: Comedy or Drama. Opportunity/
    Award: Workshop, Production. How
    To Submit: Unsolicited.

**St. Louis Black Repertory Company**
1717 Olive St., Fl. 4, St. Louis, MO 63103
Ronald J. Himes
Tel: (314) 534-3807; Fax: (314) 534-4035
ronh@theblackrep.org
www.theblackrep.org
    Est. 1976. Response Time: 2 mos.
    Style: comedy, drama, musical. What
    To Submit: query, synopsis, 5-pg
    sample, resume.

**Stage One: The Louisville Children's
Theater**
323 W. Broadway, Suite #609,
Louisville, KY 40202
Peter Holloway
Tel: (502) 498-2436; Fax: (502) 588-4344
stageone@stageone.org
www.stageone.org
    Est. 1946. Equity TYA. Classic and
    contemporary tales of childhood with
    strong social and emotional content.
    Production: cast limit 12, touring
    set. Response Time: 3 mos. Style:
    adaptation, comedy, drama. What To
    Submit: query, sample.

**Stages Repertory Theatre [TX]**
3201 Allen Pkwy., #101,
Houston, TX 77019
Tel: (713) 527-0220; Fax: (713) 527-8669
www.stagestheatre.com
    Est. 1978. Production cast limit: 6.
    Response time: 9 mos. Style: comedy,
    drama. What To Submit: full script.

**Stages Theatre Company [MN]**
1111 Main St., Hopkins, MN 55343
Bruce Rowan
Tel: (952) 979-1120; Fax: (952) 979-1124
brow@stagestheatre.org
www.stagestheatre.org
> Est. 1984. Production: ages 10-21.
> Response Time: 3 mos. What to
> Submit: query, synopsis, full script,
> SASE. Material Must Be: with
> children in primary roles.

**Stages Theatre Center [CA]**
1540 N. McCadden Pl.,
Hollywood, CA 90028
Paul Verdier
Tel: (323) 463-5356
stagestheatre@yahoo.com
www.stagestheatrecenter.com
> Est. 1982. Response Time: 1 yr.
> What to Submit: full script. Material
> Must Be: Spanish and French texts
> encouraged.

**Stageworks, Inc.**
120 Adriatic Ave., Tampa, FL 33606
Anna Brennen
Tel: (813) 215-8984
www.stageworkstheatre.org
> For FL playwrights only. Prefer multi-
> racial casts, not to exceed 6. Unit
> set. Stageworks is a minority issues
> driven theatre. Style: Comedy, Drama,
> Variety. What To Submit: Full-Length
> script. Author Must Be: 21 or older. FL
> resident (at least part time). Material
> Must Be: Unproduced, Opportunity/
> Award: Reading with nationally
> known dramaturg. How To Submit:
> Unsolicited. Deadline: May 15, 2010.

**Stageworks/Hudson [NY]**
41-A Cross St., Hudson, NY 12534
Laura Margolis
Tel: (518) 828-7843; Fax: (518) 828-4026
contact@stageworkstheater.org
www.stageworkstheater.org
> Est. 1993. Equity SPT, spring-fall
> season. Production: cast limit 8, unit
> set, no fly. Response Time: 8 mos.
> Style: adaptation, comedy, drama.

> What To Submit: query, synopsis,
> submissions not returned.

**Steppenwolf Theatre Company**
758 W. North Ave., 4th Fl.,
Chicago, IL 60610
Joy Meads
Tel: (312) 335-1888
www.steppenwolf.org
> Est. 1976. 1985 Regional Theater
> Tony winner. Formed by an actors
> collective, Steppenwolf is now an
> ensemble of 41, performing in 3
> spaces: 515-seat Downstairs (CAT-6);
> 299-seat Upstairs (CAT-3, CAT-5);
> 88-seat Garage (CAT-3). Production:
> cast limit 10. Response time is 6-8
> months. Style: adaptation, drama.
> What To Submit: query, synopsis,
> 10-pg sample, resume. Material Must
> Be: unproduced. How To Submit:
> Full scripts via agent only. If not
> represented, follow guidelines posted
> on website.

**Stepping Stone Theatre for Youth
Development**
55 Victoria St. N, St. Paul, MN 55104
Richard Hitchler
Tel: (651) 225-9265; Fax: (651) 225-1225
www.steppingstonetheatre.org
> Est. 1987. Production: youth cast of
> 10-20. Response Time: 6 mos. What
> to Submit: full script, audio. Material
> Must Be: unoptioned, unproduced.

**Stoneham Theatre**
395 Main St, Stoneham, MA 02180
Weylin Symes
weylin@stonehamtheatre.org
www.stonehamtheatre.org
> Est. 2000. Equity theatre located
> 8 miles North of Boston. NEAT
> contract. Production: cast limit 12
> (play) or 18 (musical), orchestra limit
> 7. Response Time: 4 mos. What
> to Submit: query, synopsis, 20-pg
> sample, audio, submissions not
> returned.

**SummerNITE**
NIU School of Theater & Dance,
DeKalb, IL 60115
Alexander Gelman
Tel: (815) 753-1334; Fax: (815) 753-8415
www.niu.edu/theatre/summernite/
playwrights.htm
Premieres (US or Chicago) of
innovative and intellectually
stimulating stage works. How To
Submit: agent.

**Sundog Theatre**
Box 10183, Staten Island, NY 10301
Susan Fenley
Tel: (718) 816-5453
sfenley@sundogtheatre.org
www.SundogTheatre.org
Also looking for six 10 - 15 minute
plays with Staten Island Ferry as
setting. Full length play, production.
cast of 2-10 . orchestra limit 4,
miinimal set. Style: New plays.
Author Must Be: resident or citizen
of US. Material Must Be: unoptioned,
unproduced, Opportunity/Award:
$100 for 6 Staten Island Ferry
plays. How To Submit: professional
recommendation. Deadline: Jan. 18,
2010.

**Sweetwood Productions**
3406 Riva Ridge Rd., Austin, TX 78746
Pat Hazell
Tel: (512) 383-9498; Fax: (512) 383-1680
pat@sweetwoodproductions.com
www.sweetwoodproductions.com
Not accepting submissions at this time.

**Synchronicity Performance Group**
Box 6012, Atlanta, GA 31107
Rachel May
Tel: (404) 523-1009
info@synchrotheatre.com
www.synchrotheatre.com
Est. 1997. Dedicated to strong
women characters, scripts with depth,
meaning and social content, and
powerful stories. Production: cast limit
12, no fly. Response Time: only if
interested. Style: no musical. What To
Submit: query, synopsis, 5-pg sample,
SASE.

**Syracuse Stage**
820 E. Genesee St., Syracuse, NY 13210
Kyle Bass
kebass@syr.edu
www.syracusestage.org
Est. 1974. Production: small cast.
What to Submit: How To Submit:
professional recommendation, agent.

**TADA! Youth Theater**
15 W 28th St, Fl. 3, New York, NY 10001
Emmanuel Wilson
Tel: (212) 252-1619 ext. 17
Fax: (212) 252-8763
jgreer@tadatheater.com
www.tadatheater.com
Est. 1984. Production: teenage cast
(limit 2 adults). Response Time: 6
mos. Style: musical. What To Submit:
full script. Author Must Be: age 19 or
older. Material Must Be: unpublished.

**Teatro Vision**
1700 Alum Rock Ave.,
San Jose, CA 95116
Elisa Marina Alvarado
Tel: (408) 928-5582; Fax: (408) 928-5589
elisamarina@teatrovision.org
www.teatrovision.org
Est. 1984. Equity BAT-2. 3-play
season in 500-seat theater. Production:
age 18 and older, cast limit 12,
orchestra limit 4, flexible set. Response
Time: 1 mo. What to Submit: query,
synopsis, SASE. Author Must Be:
age 18 or older, Opportunity/Award:
royalty.

**Tectonic Theater Project**
204 W 84th St, New York, NY 10024
Jimmy Maize
Tel: (212) 579-6111; Fax: (212) 579-6112
literary@tectonictheaterproject.org
www.tectonictheaterproject.org
Est. 1992. Lab led by Moisés
Kaufman. Response Time: 1 month.
Style: all styles, daring/experimental
in form/structure. What To Submit:
synopsis, full script, SASE. How To
Submit: agent.

**Ten Grand Productions**
123 E 24th Street, New York, NY 10010
Jason Hewitt
Tel: (212) 253-2058; Fax: (917) 591-9398
jhewitt@tengrand.org
www.tengrand.org
> Est. 2003. Style: drama. What To
> Submit: 20-pg sample, SASE.

**Tennessee Repertory Theatre**
161 Rains Ave., Nashville, TN 37203
Rene D. Copeland
Tel: (615) 244-4878
www.tennesseerep.org
> Est. 1985. Production: small cast,
> small orchestra. Response Time: 1
> yr. What to Submit: query, synopsis,
> dialogue sample, audio, SASE.

**Thalia Spanish Theatre**
41-17 Greenpoint Ave.,
Sunnyside, NY 11104
Angel Gil Orrios
Tel: (718) 729-3880; Fax: (718) 729-3388
info@thaliatheatre.org
www.thaliatheatre.org
> Est. 1977. Response Time: 3 mos.
> Style: no musical. What To Submit:
> full script.

**The Theatre @ Boston Court**
Box 60187, Pasadena, CA 91116
Aaron Henne
Tel: (626) 683-6883; Fax: (626) 683-6886
AaronH@BostonCourt.com
BostonCourt.org
> Est. 2003. Equity 99-seat. Production:
> cast limit 12. Response Time: 6 wks
> query, 6 mos script. What to Submit:
> query, synopsis, 10-pg sample, audio,
> SASE. Author Must Be: Southern
> California writers only. We are unable
> to accept unsolicited queries from
> non-local writers. How To Submit:
> professional recommendation, see
> website.

**Theater Alliance**
1365 H St., NE, Washington, DC 20002

**Theater at Monmouth**
Box 385, Monmouth, ME 04259

David Greenham
TAMOffice@TheaterAtMonmouth.org
www.theateratmonmouth.org
> Est. 1970. Only adaptations of popular
> classics for adults and children.
> Response Time: 2 mos. Accepting
> adaptations of classics only or
> adaptation of children's literature
> only. Style: Adaptation or new play in
> classic style. What To Submit: query,
> synopsis. How To Submit: E-mail or
> mail, no phone calls, please. Deadline:
> ongoing.

**Theater Breaking Through Barriers**
306 W. 18th St. #3A,
New York, NY 10011
Ike Schambelan
Tel: (212) 243-4337; Fax: (212) 243-4337
ischambelan@nyc.rr.com
www.tbtb.org
> Est. 1979. LOA. Production: cast
> of 1-6. Response Time: 2 mos.
> What to Submit: full script, SASE,
> Opportunity/Award: $1,500 - $2,000
> honorarium.

**Theatre Exile**
525 S. 4th St., #475,
Philadelphia, PA 19147
Joe Canuso

**Theater for the New City (TFNC)**
155 1st Ave., New York, NY 10003
Crystal Field
Tel: (212) 254-1109; Fax: (212) 979-6570
www.theaterforthenewcity.net
> Est. 1970. Equity Showcase.
> Experimental new works. What to
> Submit: synopsis, 10-pg sample,
> SASE. Material Must Be: unproduced.

**Theater IV**
114 Broad St., Richmond, VA 23220
Janine Serresseque
Tel: (804) 783-1688
TheatreIVandBarksdale@gmail.com
www.theatreiv.org
> Est. 1975.Production: cast of 3-5,
> touring set. Audience: Grades K - 12.
> Response Time: 2 mos query, 2 yrs
> script. Style: fairy tales, folk tales,

fables, history, African American history, safety, outreach, science. What To Submit: query, synopsis. Material Must Be: 50 min. to 1 hour in length. How To Submit: email, regular mail.

**Theater J**
1529 16th St. NW, Washington, DC 20036
Shirley Serotsky
Tel: (202) 777-3228; Fax: (202) 518-9421
shirleys@washingtondcjcc.org
www.theaterj.org
Est. 1991. Offers readings, workshops, and productions. Response Time: 6 mos. What to Submit: synopsis, full script, SASE. Material Must Be: Generally seeking material that relates to our mission: celebrating the distinctive urban voice and social vision that are part of the Jewish cultural legacy.

**Theatre for a New Audience**
154 Christopher St., #3-D,
New York, NY 10014
Jeffrey Horowitz
Tel: (212) 229-2819; Fax: (212) 229-2911
info@tfana.org
www.tfana.org

**Theater of the First Amendment, First Light Discovery Program**
George Mason University, 4400 University Dr., MS 3E6,
Fairfax, VA 22030
Suzanne Maloney
Tel: (703) 993-2195; Fax: (703) 993-2191
smaloney@gmu.edu
www.theateroffirstamendment.org
New play developmental workshops and readings throughout the year. Response Time: 2 wks query, 6 mos script. Style: no restrictions, but rarely develop musicals. What To Submit: query, sample. Material Must Be: unproduced. How To Submit: mail or email. Deadline: Nov. 15, 2010.

**Theater Previews at Duke**
Box 90680, 209 Bivins Bldg.,
Durham, NC 27708
Miriam Sauls

Tel: (919) 660-3346; Fax: (919) 684-8906
mmsauls@duke.edu
www.duke.edu/web/theaterstudies
Est. 1986. Response Time: 3 mos query, 6 mos script. How To Submit: agent.

**Theater Ten Ten**
1010 Park Ave., New York, NY 10028
Judith Jarosz
Tel: (212) 288-3246 ext. 300
theater1010@aol.com
www.Theater1010.com
Est. 1955. Production: small cast, equal roles for men and women. Response Time: 1 yr. What to Submit: synopsis and query. How To Submit: via email.

**Theatreworks/USA [NY]**
151 W. 26th St., Fl. 7,
New York, NY 10001
Michael Alltop
Tel: (212) 647-1100; Fax: (212) 924-5377
info@theatreworksusa.org
www.theatreworksusa.org
Est. 1961. Production: age 20-50, cast of up to 6, piano only, touring set. Response Time: May 15. Style: all styles. What To Submit: query letter (note theme addressed), synopsis, 30-pg writing sample, full script, audio, submissions returned with SASE. Author Must Be: resident of NYC area. How To Submit: professional recommendation, agent submission.

**Theatre Alliance of Michigan**
22323 Cedar St.,
St. Clair Shores, MI 48081
Mary Lou Britton
mellbee@earthlink.net
www.theatreallianceofmichigan.org
Annual contest. Written by adults; performed by children for children. See website for more information and rules. Style: Comedy, Drama, Musical. What To Submit: Full Script. CD/Tape of songs if Musical. Author Must Be: Teen or adult, living anywhere. Material Must Be: Properly typed and formatted, Opportunity/Award: $300;

exposure to members seeking scripts for young audiences. How To Submit: U.S. Mail. See website for details. Award/Grant/Stipend: $300. Deadline: Dec. 31, 2010.

### Theatre at the Center / Lawrence Arts Center

940 New Hampshire St.,
Lawrence, KS 66044
Ric Averill
Tel: (785) 843-2787; Fax: (785) 843-6629
lacdrama@sunflower.com
www.lawrenceartscenter.com
> Est. 1973. Production: cast limit 6 adults or 30 youth. Response Time: 6 wks query, 3 mos script. What to Submit: synopsis, ten page. Material Must Be: original. How To Submit: email.

### Theatre Company

4001 W. McNichols, Detroit, MI 48208
Melinda Pacha
Tel: (313) 993-1130; Fax: (313) 993-6465
pachamj@udmercy.edu
www.libarts.udmercy.edu/dep/thr
> Est. 1972. What to Submit: synopsis, 30-pg writing sample, SASE. How To Submit: unsolicited.

### Theatre in the Square

11 Whitlock Ave., Marietta, GA 30064
Jessica West
Tel: (770) 422-8369; Fax: (770) 422-7436
www.theatreinthesquare.com
> Est. 1982. Equity SPT. Production: cast limit 5, unit set, no fly. Response Time: 6 mos. What to Submit: query, synopsis, 10-pg sample, resume, submissions not returned. Author Must Be: Southern. Material Must Be: unproduced in Southeast.

### Theatre of Yugen

2840 Mariposa St.,
San Francisco, CA 94110
Jubilith Moore
Tel: (415) 621-0507; Fax: (415) 621-0223
info@theatreofyugen.org
www.theatreofyugen.org
> Est. 1978. Non-Equity. Traditional and new works of East-West fusion primarily based on Noh forms. Style: experimental, movement based. What To Submit: query, SASE.

### Theatre Rhinoceros

1360 Mission St. Ste. #200,
San Francisco, CA 94103
John Fisher
Tel: (415) 552-4100 ext. 104
Fax: (415) 558-9044
www.therhino.org
> Est. 1977. Response Time: 6 mos. How To Submit: agent.

### Theatre Three [NY]

Box 512/412 Main St.,
Port Jefferson, NY 11777
Jeffrey Sanzel
Tel: (631) 928-9202; Fax: (631) 928-9120
jsanzel@theatrethree.com
www.theatrethree.com
> Est. 1969. Theatre Three Production Inc. Est. 1997. Festival of One-Act Plays. Each season, festival presents 5 to 6 world premieres on the second stage. Non-equity productions. All plays performed 7-8 times. Frequency: annual. Production: any age, casts from 1 to 8, minimal set. Response Time: 3-6 months. Style: comedy, drama. What To Submit: full script, submissions returned with SASE. Material Must Be: unproduced. Opportunity/Award: $75 award, production. How To Submit: unsolicited.

### TheatreWorks [CA]

PO Box 50458, Palo Alto, CA 94303
Meredith McDonagh
Tel: (650) 463-1950; Fax: (650) 463-1963
www.theatreworks.org
> Est. 1970. LORT B. Staff: Robert Kelley (Artistic Dir.). Response Time: 4 to 6 wks query, 6 mos script. See website for more details. What to Submit: query, synopsis, 10-pg sample, audio, SASE. How To Submit: agent.

### Thick Description

1695 18th St., San Francisco, CA 94107
> Est. 1988.

**Touchstone Theatre**
321 E. 4th St., Bethlehem, PA 18015
Lisa Jordan
Tel: (610) 867-1689
lisa@touchstone.org
www.touchstone.org
> Est. 1981. Only accepts proposals
> for collaborative work with company
> ensemble. Response Time: 8 mos.
> Style: Emsemble theatre, movement-
> based. What To Submit: query.

**Town Hall Theatre Company (THT)**
3535 School St., Lafayette, CA 94549
Clive Worsley
Fax: (925) 283-3481
www.townhalltheatre.com
> Est. 1944. Formerly Dramateurs
> (1944-92). Equity BAT. Response
> Time: 3 mos. Style: comedy, drama,
> musical. What To Submit: query,
> submissions not returned. Author Must
> Be: resident of CA preferred. Material
> Must Be: unpublished, Opportunity/
> Award: TBD.

**Transport Group**
520 Eighth Ave., Ste. 305,
New York, NY 10018
Jack Cummings III
Tel: (212) 564-0333; Fax: (212) 564-0331
info@transportgroup.org
www.transportgroup.org
> What to Submit: Synopsis, 30 page or
> less sample or audio. How To Submit:
> Email preferred.

**Triangle Productions!**
8420 SW Canyon Lane #13,
Portland, OR 97225-3968
Donald L. Horn
Tel: (503) 239-5919
trianglepro@juno.com
www.tripro.org
> Est. 1989. Production: cast limit 4,
> touring set. Response Time: 1 mo
> query, 7 mos. Style: comedy, musical.
> What To Submit: query. How To
> Submit: email.

**TriArts at the Sharon Playhouse**
Box 1187, Sharon, CT 6069
Michael Berkeley

Tel: (860) 364-7469; Fax: (860) 364-8043
info@triarts.net
www.triarts.net
> Est. 1989. Bryan L. Knapp New
> Works series. Production: no fly.
> Response Time: 2 mos query, 6 mos.
> Style: comedy, drama, musical. What
> To Submit: query, synopsis, audio.
> Deadline: January - July is best
> submission period.

**Trinity Repertory Company**
201 Washington St., Providence, RI 02903
Craig Watson
Tel: (401) 351-4242
cwatson@trinityrep.com
www.trinityrep.com
> Est. 1964. Equity LORT. 1981
> Regional Theater Tony winner.
> Staff: Curt Columbus (Artistic
> Dir), MiIchael Gennaro (Exec Dir).
> Response Time: 4 mos. What to
> Submit: query, synopsis, 10-pg sample.

**Trustus Theatre**
Box 11721, Columbia, SC 29211
Sarah Hammond
Tel: (803) 254-9732; Fax: (803) 771-9153
trustus@trustus.org
www.trustus.org
> Est. 1985. Late-night series for open-
> minded audiences. Production: cast
> limit 6, unit set. Style: comedy. What
> To Submit: Application resume, brief
> synopsis and SASE. How To Submit:
> Use application on website. Deadline:
> Dec. 1 through Feb. 1.

**Turtle Shell Productions**
300 W. 43rd St., #403,
New York, NY 10036
John Cooper
Tel: (646) 765-7670
lacoopster@aol.com
www.turtleshellproductions.com
> Equity showcase. Style: Unsolicited.
> What To Submit: Full Script. Material
> Must Be: Not published, not produced,
> Opportunity/Award: Production.
> Deadline: Apr. 9, 2010.

**Two River Theatre Company (TRTC)**
21 Bridge Ave., Red Bank, NJ 7701
Aaron Posner
Tel: (732) 345-1400; Fax: (732) 345-1414
info@trtc.org
www.trtc.org
Est. 1994. Style: adaptation, comedy,
drama. We do not accept unsolicited
materials.

**Ujamaa Black Theatre**
PO Box 4383, Grand Central Sta,
New York, NY 10163
Titus Walker
Tel: (212) 642-8261

**Unicorn Theatre**
3828 Main St., Kansas City, MO 64111
Justin Shaw
Tel: (816) 531-7529 ext. 17
Fax: (816) 531-0421
clevin@unicorntheatre.org
www.unicorntheatre.org
Est. 1974. One new play each year
is developed and produced in the
Unicorn's regular season. Fees:
2% subsidiary rights for 5 yrs.
Production: cast limit 10. Response
Time: 8 mos. Style: comedy, drama,
contemporary. What To Submit: query,
script, bio, cast list, submissions
not returnedclevin@unicorntheatre.
org, cover letter, resume, character
breakdown. Material Must Be:
unpublished, professionally
unproduced, original provocative
plays, Opportunity/Award: $1,000 in
lieu of royalty. How To Submit: by
mail, see address above, see website
for full details. Deadline: ongoing.

**Urban Stages**
17 E. 47th St, New York, NY 10017
Frances Hill
www.urbanstages.org
Frequency: annual. Production: cast
size 7 or less. Response Time: 6
months. Style: adaptation, comedy,
drama, translation. What To Submit:
query, synopsis, 10 pgs. sample, full
script. Material Must Be: unoptioned,
not produced in NY, Opportunity/

Award: $1,000 award, production,
reading. How To Submit: unsolicited,
professional recommendation, agent.

**Valley Youth Theatre (VYT)**
807 N. 3rd St., Phoenix, AZ 85004
Bobb Cooper
Tel: (602) 253-8188; Fax: (602) 253-8282
bobb@vyt.com
www.vyt.com
Est. 1989. Response Time: 2 wks
query, 2 mos script. Style: comedy,
drama, musical. What To Submit:
query, audio.

**Victory Gardens Theater**
2257 N. Lincoln Ave., Chicago, IL 60614
Aaron Carter
Tel: (773) 549-5788; Fax: (773) 549-2779
acarter@victorygardens.org
www.victorygardens.org
Est. 1974. Equity CAT-4. 2001
Regional Theater Tony winner. 6
productions/season. Staff: Dennis
Zacek (Artistic Dir.). Response Time:
6 mos. What to Submit: Chicago area
residents: full script, SASE. All others:
query, synopsis, 10-pg sample, SASE.
Author Must Be: resident of Chicago
area. Material Must Be: original. VG
primarily produces world or regional
premieres. How To Submit: hardcopy.
no electronic submissions. Accepting
submissions January – June only.

**Victory Theatre Center**
3326 W. Victory Blvd.,
Burbank, CA 91505
Maria Gobetti
Tel: (818) 841-4404; Fax: (818) 841-6328
thevictory@mindspring.com
www.thevictorytheatrecenter.org
Est. 1979. Incl. 99-seat Big Victory
and 50-seat Little Victory theaters.
Production: unit set. Response Time: 1
yr. What to Submit: full script, SASE,
Opportunity/Award: royalty. How To
Submit: email.

**Village Theatre**
303 Front St. N., Issaquah, WA 98027
Robb Hunt

Tel: (425) 392-1942; Fax: (425) 391-3242
www.villagetheatre.org
    Est. 1979. Equity LOA. Readings,
workshops, and productions of new
musicals. Production: cast limit
20. Response Time: 6 mos. Style:
musical. What To Submit: full script,
audio, SASE, Opportunity/Award:
royalty. How To Submit: professional
recommendation, agent.

**Vineyard Theatre**
108 E. 15th St., New York, NY 10003
Sarah Stern
Tel: (212) 353-3366 ext. 215
Fax: (212) 353-3803
literary@vineyardtheatre.org
www.vineyardtheatre.org
    Est. 1981. Response Time: 1 yr query.
What to Submit: query, synopsis, 10-
pg sample, audio, resume, submissions
not returned.

**Virginia Premiere Theatre**
PO Box 84, Foster, VA 23056
Robert Ruffin
Tel: (804) 725-3645
info@vptheatre.com
www.vptheatre.com
    Style: all. What To Submit: query,
synopsis or treatment, 10 page sample.
Author Must Be: Not published,
Opportunity/Award: production,
reading, workshop. How To Submit:
unsolicited.

**Virginia Stage Company (VSC)**
Box 3770, Norfolk, VA 23514
Patrick Mullins
Tel: (757) 627-6988 ext. 309
Fax: (757) 628-5958
pmullins@vastage.com
www.vastage.com
    Est. 1979. Equity LORT C.
Production: cast limit 8. Response
Time: 1 mo query, 6 mos script. What
to Submit: query, synopsis. Author
Must Be: resident of VA. Material
Must Be: unproduced.

**Vital Theatre Company**
2162 Broadway, Fl. 4,
New York, NY 10024
Kate Farrington
Tel: (212) 579-0528; Fax: (212) 579-0646
office@vitaltheatre.org
www.vitaltheatre.org
    Workshops, readings, and Showcase
productions. Also invitation
only workshop every other Mon.
Production: csat of 5-8, unit set. What
to Submit: synopsis, 30-pg sample,
SASE. Material Must Be: unpublished,
unproduced.

**Vortex Theater Company**
164 11th Ave., New York, NY 10011
Joshua Randall
Tel: (212) 206-1764; Fax: (212) 206-1765
www.vortextheater.com

**Walnut Street Theatre**
825 Walnut St., Philadelphia, PA 19103
Beverly Elliott
Tel: (215) 574-3550 ext. 515
Fax: (215) 574-3598
literary@walnutstreettheatre.org
www.walnutstreettheatre.org
    Est. 1809. Equity LORT A, D.
Production: cast limit 4 (studio), 14
(Mainstage play) or 20 (Mainstage
musical). Response Time: 3 mos
query, 6 mos script. Please visit WST
website for Mainstage and Studio
production history. Looking for plays
and musicals based on literature.
What to Submit: Cover letter, synopsis
including character breakdown, 10-20
page script, audio, writer/composer,
bio, SASE. How To Submit: Send
synopsis package via mail.

**Watertower Theatre, Inc.**
15650 Addison Rd., Addison, TX 75001
Terry Martin
Tel: (972) 450-6230; Fax: (972) 450-6244
info@watertowertheatre.org
www.watertowertheatre.org
    Est. 1976. Production: medium cast.
Response Time: 4 mos query, 6 mos
script. Style: comedy, musical. What
To Submit: query, synopsis, SASE.

Author Must Be: Represented by an
agent. How To Submit: agent only.

**Wellfleet Harbor Actors Theater**
Box 797, Wellfleet, MA 02667
Daniel Lombardo
Tel: (508) 349-3011 ext. 107
Fax: (508) 349-9082
lombardo.what@gmail.com
www.what.org
Est. 1985. Cast size: 6 maximum
    Response Time: 3 mos query, 6 mos
    script. Style: adventurous. What
    To Submit: synopsis, 20p. excerpt,
    bio. How To Submit: professional
    recommendation.

**West Coast Ensemble**
Box 38728, Los Angeles, CA 90038
Les Hanson
Tel: (818) 786-1900; Fax: (818) 786-1905
www.wcensemble.org
    Est 1982. 99-seat. Response Time:
    9 mos. What to Submit: full script,
    SASE.

**Weston Playhouse**
703 Main St., Weston, VT 5161
www.westonplayhouse.org
    Est. 1935. What to Submit: No
    unsolicited scripts. See website for
    new works programs.

**Westport Arts Center**
51 Riverside Ave., Westport, CT 6880
Tel: (203) 222-7070; Fax: (203) 222-7999
www.westportartscenter.org
    Programs in visual and performing
    arts. Ongoing exhibits. Chamber
    music, jazz and folk concerts, literary
    and film events performed in area
    venues.

**Westport Country Playhouse**
25 Powers Ct., Westport, CT 6880
David Kennedy
Tel: (203) 227-5137
www.westportplayhouse.org
    Est. 1931. 578-seat year-round Equity
    theater with 75-yr summer program.
    Staff: Michael Ross. Production: ages
    12 and older, cast of 2-10, orchestra

of 4-8. Response Time: 9 mos.
What to Submit: full script, SASE,
Opportunity/Award: royalty. How To
Submit: professional recommendation.

**White Horse Theater Company**
205 3rd Ave., #6-N, New York, NY 10003
Cyndy A. Marion
Tel: (212) 592-3706
cymarion@whitehorsetheater.com
www.whitehorsetheater.com
    Est. 2002. Equity Showcase or staged
    reading. Response Time: 4 mos. Style:
    adaptation, comedy, drama. What
    To Submit: SASE. Author Must Be:
    resident of US. Material Must Be:
    unproduced. How To Submit: see
    website for procedure.

**Will Geer Theatricum Botanicum**
Box 1222, Topanga, CA 90290
Ellen Geer
Tel: (310) 455-2322; Fax: (310) 455-3724
info@theatricum.com
www.theatricum.com
    Est. 1973. Production: cast limit 10,
    simple set. Response Time: 1 mo
    query, 6 mos script. What to Submit:
    query, synopsis, 10-pg sample, full
    script, audio. Material Must Be:
    suitable for outdoor space.

**Williamstown Theatre Festival**
229 W. 42nd St. #801,
New York, NY 10036
Justin Waldman
Tel: (212) 395-9090; Fax: (212) 395-9099
jwaldman@wtfestival.org
www.wtfestival.org
    Est. 1955. 2002 Regional Theater
    Tony winner. New Play Staged
    Reading Series offers 7 works/season.
    Frequency: annual. What to Submit:
    query, SASE, Opportunity/Award:
    reading. How To Submit: agent only.

**Willows Theatre Company**
636 Ward Street, Martinez, CA 94553
Alexandra Elliott
Tel: (925) 957-2500
alex@willowstheatre.org
www.willowstheatre.org

Est. 1974. Equity LORT D, LOA.
Frequency: annual. Production: less
than 15. Response Time: 3 mos. Style:
comedy. What To Submit: Summary,
Character Breakdown, Author Bio.
Opportunity/Award: Production. How
To Submit: unsolicited. Deadline:
Ongoing.

**Wilma Theater**
265 S. Broad St., Philadelphia, PA 19107
Walter Bilderback
Tel: (215) 893-9456; Fax: (215) 893-0895
wcb@wilmatheater.org
www.wilmatheater.org
Est. 1979. Equity LORT C.
Production: cast limit 8. Response
Time: 1 yr. Style: Highly theatrical,
poetic, imaginative; politically
evocative (not provocative); arousing,
artful, bold, inventive. What To
Submit: Please check our website for
past seasons and Artistic Statement
to see if your play fits what we do.
How To Submit: agent, otherwise,
professional reccomendation, query,
and 10-pg. sample.

**Women's Project & Productions**
55 West End Ave., New York, NY 10023
Megan Carter
Tel: (212) 765-1706; Fax: (212) 765-2024
megan.carter@womensproject.org
www.womensproject.org
Est. 1978. Equity ANTC contract.
Oldest and largest US theater
dedicated to producing and promoting
theater created by women. Response
Time: 1 yr. Material Must Be:
unproduced in NYC. How To Submit:
agent submission.

**The Women's Theatre Project (TWTP)**
1314 E. Las Olas Blvd., #31,
Ft. Lauderdale, FL 33301
Meredith Lasher
twtp@bellsouth.net
www.womenstheatreproject.com
Est. 2002. Committed to telling
women's stories.

**Woolly Mammoth Theatre Company**
641 D St. NW, Washington, DC 20004
Miriam Weisfeld
Tel: (202) 289-2443
submissions@woollymammoth.net
www.woollymammoth.net
Est. 1980. Equity SPT. Production:
cast limit 6. Response Time: 1 yr.
Style: no musical. What To Submit:
letter of inquiry, synopsis, 10
page sample. How To Submit: No
unsolicited material.

**Working Theater**
520 Eighth Ave., Suite 303,
New York, NY 10018
Mark Plesent
mark@theworkingtheater.org
www.theworkingtheater.org
Est. 1985. Equity LOA. New plays that
appeal to the diverse communities of
working people in NYC. Frequency:
semiannual. Production: 6 max.
Response Time: 6 mos. Style: all
styles. What To Submit: synopsis,
10 page sample. Material Must Be:
unproduced in New York City. How
To Submit: unsolicited, professional
recommendation, agent.

**Writers' Theatre**
376 Park Ave., Glencoe, IL 60022
Jimmy McDermott
Tel: (847) 242-6001; Fax: (847) 242-6011
info@writerstheatre.org
www.writerstheatre.org
Est. 1992. Response Time: 6 mos.
Style: all styles, no musical. What
To Submit: synopsis, 10-pg sample,
SASE. How To Submit: professional
recommendation.

**Yale Repertory Theatre**
Box 208244, New Haven, CT 6520
Ann Boratko
Tel: (203) 432-1591
literary.office@yale.edu
www.yalerep.org
Est. 1965. 1991 Regional Theater Tony
winner. Response Time: 2 mos query,
3 mos script. Style:  What To Submit:
query, SASE. How To Submit: agent.

**Yangtze Repertory Theatre of America**
22 Howard St., #3-B,
New York, NY 10013
Dr. Joanna Chan
Tel: (914) 941-7575; Fax: (914) 923-0733
joannawychan@juno.com
www.yangtze-rep-theatre.org

**York Shakespeare Company**
Box 720, JAF Sta., New York, NY 10116
Submissions
Tel: (646) 623-7117; Fax: (866) 380-7510
info@yorkshakespeare.org
www.yorkshakespeare.org
   Est. 2001. What to Submit: full
   script. Material Must Be: unoptioned.
   How To Submit: professional
   recommendation, unsolicited.

**York Theatre Company**
619 Lexington Ave., New York, NY 10022
Tel: (212) 935-5820; Fax: (212) 832-0037
mail@yorktheatre.org
www.yorktheatre.org
   Est. 1985. Equity Off-Broadway.
   Opportunities incl. developmental
   reading series. Production: cast of 3-6,
   piano only. Response Time: 6 mos.
   Style: musical. What To Submit: full
   script, audio, SASE. Material Must Be:
   unproduced. How To Submit: Mail.

**Young Playwrights Theater (YPT)**
2437 15th St., NW, Washington, DC
20009

---

## THEATERS (*FEE CHARGED*)

**Jewish Ensemble Theatre**
6600 W. Maple Rd.,
West Bloomfield, MI 48322
Christopher Bremer
Tel: (248) 788-2900; Fax: (248) 788-5160
c.bremer@jettheatre.org
www.jettheatre.org
   We are seeking unpublished plays
   for our Festival of New Plays.
   Style: English only - all styles.
   What To Submit: full script, SASE.
   Material Must Be: Cast limited to 8,
   Opportunity/Award: $100 if selected
   for a reading. How To Submit: hard
   copy by mail. Submission/Application
   Fee: $5. Deadline: Sep. 1, 2010.

**Teatro Dallas**
1331 Record Crossing Rd.,
Dallas, TX 75235
Cora Cordona
teatro@airmail.net
www.teatrodallas.org
   Est. 1985. Classical and contemporary
   Latino playwrights. Production:
   cast limit 8, unit set. Style: no
   musical. What To Submit: query,
   synopsis, SASE, will respond if of
   interest. Author Must Be: of any

origin interested in writing about
Latino issues or universal issues. We
give priority to Latino and Iberian
playwrights. Material Must Be:
in English or Spanish. We prefer
structures where if needed actors can
play multiple roles. In other words,
casts of no more than six. Opportunity/
Award: Stage reading of selected
work. TD provides one night hotel.
Airfare must be paid by playwright.
How To Submit: Send script through
regular mail. Submission/Application
Fee: $50. Deadline: Dec. 15, 2010.

**Two Chairs Theater Company**
Box 3390, Grand Junction, CO 81502
James Garland
Tel: (970) 263-7920
submit@twochairs.org
www.twochairs.org
   Acts of Brevity Short Play Fest.
   Production: cast limit 5. What
   to Submit: synopsis, full script,
   production history. Please see
   website for submission details. How
   To Submit: email (pdf, doc, fdr).
   Submission/Application Fee: $10.
   Deadline: March 2010.

# Educational Opportunities

## COLLEGES AND UNIVERSITIES

*Consult websites for specific degrees available.*

**Academy of Art University**
79 New Montgomery St.,
San Francisco, CA 94105
Tel: (800) 544-2787; Fax: (415) 618-6287
info@academyart.edu
www.academyart.edu
Rolling admissions. Undergraduate
and Graduate degree programs.
Certificates, Continuing Art
Education, and Pre-college programs
available online adn on campus. Est.
1929. Staff: Diane Baker, Eduardo
Rufeisen, (Co-Directors Film/TV
School), Jonathon Fung (Assoc.
Director Film/TV School). $670/
unit (undergrad), $770/unit (grad).
What to Submit: application. How To
Submit: Visit www.academyart.edu
or Call 1.800.544.2787. Submission/
Application Fee: $140.

**Agnes Scott College**
141 E. College Ave., Decatur, GA 30030
Dudley Sanders
Tel: (404) 638-6251
info@agnesscott.edu
www.agnesscott.edu

**Angelo State University (ASU)**
Box 10895, ASU Sta.,
San Angelo, TX 76909
Bill Doll
Tel: (915) 942-2146
bill.doll@angelo.edu
www.angelo.edu

**Antelope Valley College (AVC)**
3041 W. Ave. K, Lancaster, CA 93534
Eugenie Trow
Tel: (661) 722-6425
etrow@avc.edu
www.avc.edu

**Arizona State University (ASU)**
School of Theatre and Film,
Box 872002, Tempe, AZ 85287
Guillermo Reyes
Tel: (480) 965-0519; Fax: (480) 965-5351
Guillermo.Reyes@asu.edu
www.asu.edu/clas/english/
creativewriting/

**ART/Moscow Art Institute**
64 Brattle St., Cambridge, MA 02138
Julia Smeliansky
Tel: (617) 496-2000; Fax: (617) 495-1705
information@amrep.org
www.amrep.org
Completion of programs earns
certificate of achievement from
Harvard and an MFA from the
Moscow Art Institute.

**Artistic New Directions**
250 W. 90th St., 15G,
New York, NY 10024
Kristine Niven
Tel: (212) 875-1857
artnewdir@aol.com
www.artisticnewdirections.org
Summer Playwright's Retreat with
Jeffrey Sweet. $500 tution. $320–
$750 room and board.

**Bard College**
Box 5000,
Annandale-on-Hudson, NY 12504
JoAnne Akalaitis
Tel: (845) 758-7957
www.bard.edu

**Bard College at Simon's Rock**
84 Alford Rd.,
Great Barrington, MA 01230

Arthur Hillman
Tel: (413) 528-7289; Fax: (413) 528-7365
ahillman@simons-rock.edu
www.simons-rock.edu

**Bates College**
Schaeffer Theater, #302,
Lewiston, ME 04238
Martin Andrucki
Tel: (207) 786-8294
mandruc@bates.edu
www.bates.edu

**Bethany College**
Fine Arts Dept., Bethany, WV 26032
Herb Weaver
Tel: (304) 829-7000
www.bethanywv.edu

**Boston University**
855 Commonwealth Ave., #470,
Boston, MA 02215
Jim Petosa
Tel: (617) 353-3390
theatre@bu.edu
www.bu.edu/but

**Bowdoin College**
9100 College Sta., Brunswick, ME 04011
Noma Petroff
Tel: (207) 725-3663; Fax: (207) 725-3372
npetroff@bowdoin.edu
www.bowdoin.edu

**Bowling Green State University
(BGSU)**
338 South Hall,
Bowling Green, OH 43403
Ronald E. Shields
Tel: (419) 372-2222; Fax: (419) 372-7186
theatrefilm@bgsu.edu
www.bgsu.edu/theatrefilm

**Brigham Young University**
Dept. of Theatre and Media Arts,
D-581 HFAC, Provo, UT 84602
Elizabeth Funke
Tel: (801) 422-7768; Fax: (801) 422-0654
tmaweb@byu.edu
www.byu.edu

**Brown University**
Box 1852, Waterman St.,
Providence, RI 02912
Spencer Golub
Tel: (401) 863-1955
spencer_golub@brown.edu
www.brown.edu

**California Institute of the Arts (Cal
Arts)**
24700 McBean Pkwy., Valencia, CA 91355
Ellen McCartney
Tel: (661) 253-7853
EMcCartney@calarts.edu
www.calarts.edu

**Campbell University**
Box 128, Buries Creek, NC 27506
Stephen J. Larson
Tel: (910) 893-1507
www.campbell.edu/coas/theatre

**Carnegie Mellon University**
Purnell Center A32, Pittsburgh, PA 15213
Dick Block
Tel: (412) 268-7219
rblock@andrew.cmu.edu
www.cmu.edu/cfa/drama
    MFA, Dramatic Writing. 4 students
    admitted annually plus 2 students
    admitted in screenwriting. Finalists
    invited to campus to visit classes,
    meet students and to interview with
    program coordinator. Applicants
    unable to visit are interviewed by
    phone. Fees: $100 application.

**Catholic Universtiy of America**
Catholic Univ., Dept. of Drama,
620 Michigan Ave. NE,
Washington, DC 20064
Jon Klein
Tel: (202) 319-5360
kleinj@cua.edu
www.drama.cua.edu
    Degrees Offered: MFA in
    Playwriting. Length: 3 years.
    Admitted per year: 2 to 4. Faculty: Jon
    Klein, Guests. Opportunities: Staged
    readings to full thesis production in
    mainstage season, directed by guest
    professional director. Deadline: Mar.
    30, 2010.

**Chapman University**
1 University Dr., Orange, CA 92866
Cyrus Parker-Jeannette
Tel: (714) 997-6891
www.chapman.edu

**College of Charleston (C of C)**
66 George St., Charleston, SC 29424
Franklin Ashley
Tel: (843) 953-8149; Fax: (843) 953-8210
ashleyf@cofc.edu
www.cofc.edu

**College of the Holy Cross**
1 College St., Worcester, MA 01610
Edward Isser
Tel: (508) 793-3490
eisser@holycross.edu

**Collin College**
2800 E. Spring Creek Pkwy.,
Plano, TX 75074
Brad Baker
Tel: (972) 881-5100
www.collintheatrecenter.com

**Columbia College [IL]**
72 E. 11th St., Chicago, IL 60605
Sheldon Patinkin
Tel: (312) 344-6100
theatre@colum.edu
www.colum.edu

**Columbia University School of the Arts
Theatre Program**
2960 Broadway, 601 Dodge Hall,
MC 1807, New York, NY 10027-7021
Julie Rossi
Tel: (212) 854-3408
theatre@columbia.edu
www.arts.columbia.edu/theatre

**Cornish College of the Arts**
1000 Lenora St., Seattle, WA 98121
Richard E. T. White
Tel: (206) 323-1400
www.cornish.edu

**Brooklyn College**
English Dept., 2900 Bedford Ave.,
Brooklyn, NY 11210
Nancy Black
www.brooklyn.cuny.edu

**DePaul University**
2135 N. Kenmore Ave., Chicago, IL 60614
Dean Corrin
Tel: (773) 325-7932
dcorrin@depaul.edu
www.theatreschool.depaul.edu

**Dordt College**
498 4th Ave. NE, Sioux Center, IA 51250
Teresa Ter Haar
Tel: (712) 722-6207
    BA, Liberal Arts.

**Drexel University, Westphal College**
3141 Chestnut St., Philadelphia, PA 19104
Nick Anselmo
Tel: (215) 895-1920; Fax: (215) 895-2452
nick.anselmo@drexel.edu
www.drexel.edu/westphal

**Duke University**
Box 90680, Durham, NC 27708
Sarah Beckwith
Tel: (919) 660-3343
theater@duke.edu; www.duke.edu

**Elmhurst College**
190 Prospect Ave., Elmhurst, IL 60126
Lance Wilcox
Tel: (630) 617-3008
www.public.elmhurst.edu

**Emerson College**
10 Boylston Pl., 5th Fl, Department of
Performing Arts, Boston, MA 02116
Melia Bensussen
Tel: (617) 824-8780
stagedoor@emerson.edu
www.emerson.edu

**Florida International University (FIU)**
Univ. Park Campus, PAC 131,
Miami, FL 33199
Leroy Clark
Tel: (305) 348-1684
www.fiu.edu

**Florida State University (FSU)**
239 Fine Arts Bldg., Tallahassee, FL 32306
Barbara Thomas
Tel: (850) 644-7234; Fax: (850) 644-7246
bgthomas@admin.fsu.edu
www.theatre.fsu.edu

Est. 1973. Undergrad and graduate degree programs. Scholarships and graduate grants available. What to Submit: application.

**Fresno City College (FCC)**
1101 East University Ave.,
Fresno, CA 93741
Tel: (559) 442-4600; Fax: (559) 265-5755
www.fresnocitycollege.edu/finearts/
theatrearts

**Hollins University**
PO Box 9603, Roanoke, VA 24020
Todd Ristau
Tel: (540) 362-6386
tristau@hollins.edu
www.hollins.edu/grad/playwriting/
60 credit hour MFA in Playwriting can be completed in 4-5 annual 6-wk summer sessions (Jun-Jul). Production opportunities at affiliated theatres. Aid available, see website.

**Humboldt State University (HSU)**
1 Harpst St., TA13, Arcata, CA 95521
Margaret Thomas Kelso
Tel: (707) 826-4606; Fax: (707) 826-5494
mtk3@humboldt.edu
www.humboldt.edu

**Illinois State University**
ISU School of Theatre, Box 5700,
Normal, IL 61790
Tom Powers
Tel: (309) 438-2899; Fax: (309) 438-5806
theatre@ilstu.edu
www.cfa.ilstu.edu/theatre
Home of Ill. Shakespeare Festival.

**Indiana University - Purdue University Ft. Wayne (IPFW)**
2101 E. Coliseum Blvd.,
Ft. Wayne, IN 46805
Steven T. Sarratore
Tel: (260)-481-6536
sarrator@ipfw.edu
www.ipfw.edu

**Indiana University**
257 N. Jordan Ave., Rm. A300U,
Bloomington, IN 47405

Charlene McGlashan
Tel: (812) 855-4535; Fax: (812) 856-0698
theatre@indiana.edu
www.indiana.edu

**Johnson County Community College**
12345 College Blvd.,
Overland Park, KS 66210
Beatte Pettigrew
Tel: (913) 469-8500; Fax: (913) 469-2585
bpettigr@jccc.net
www.jccc.net
Produces children's plays and challenging adult short plays. age 15-30, cast of up to 12, unit set. Style: comedy, drama. What To Submit: query letter (note theme addressed), synopsis, submissions returned with SASE. Material Must Be: unoptioned, unpublished. Opportunity/Award: possible future production. How To Submit: unsolicited.

**Johnson State College**
337 College Hill, Johnson, VT 05656
Kenneth Leslie
Tel: (802) 635-1315
www.jsc.vsc.edu

**Juilliard School**
Playwrights Program, 60 Lincoln Center Plaza, New York, NY 10023
Tanya Barfield
Tel: (212) 799-5000; Fax: (212) 875-8437
www.juilliard.edu

**Kansas State University (KSU)**
129 Nichols Hall, Manhattan, KS 66506
John Uthoff
Tel: (785) 532-6875; Fax: (705) 532-3714
jsutd@kus.edu
www.k-state.edu/theatre

**Louisiana Tech University**
PO Box 8608, Ruston, LA 71272
Kenneth Robbins
Tel: (318) 257-2711; Fax: (318) 257-4571
krobbins@latech.edu
www.performingarts.latech.edu

**Loyola University, New Orleans [LA]**
6363 St. Charles Ave., Box 155,

New Orleans, LA 70118
Cheryl Conway
Tel: (504) 865-3840; Fax: (504) 865-2284
theatre@loyno.edu
www.loyno.edu/theatrearts

**James Madison University (JMU)**
JMU, MSC 5601, School of Theatre and
Dance, Harrisonburg, VA 22807
William Buck
Tel: (540) 568-6342
buckwj@jmu.edu
www.jmu.edu/theatre

**Metropolitan State University**
1380 Energy Lane, Suite 207,
St. Paul, MN 55108
Lisa McMahon
Tel: (651) 999-5940
lisaann.mcmahon@metrostate.edu
www.metrostate.edu

**Miami University [OH]**
Miami Univ., CPA 131,
Oxford, OH 45056
Howard Blanning
Tel: (513) 529-3053
blanniha@muohio.edu
www.muohio.edu

**Minneapolis Community and
Technical College**
1501 Hennepin Ave.,
Minneapolis, MN 55403
Michael Robertson
Tel: (612) 659-6410
Michael.Robertson@Minneapolis.edu
www.mctc.mnscu.edu

**Montclair State University**
1 Normal Ave., MSU LI-126G,
Montclair, NJ 07043
Eric Diamond
Tel: (973) 655-7343
diamonde@mail.montclair.edu
www.montclair.edu/Pages/theatredance

**Mount Holyoke College**
50 College St., South Hadley, MA 01075
Vanessa James
Tel: (413) 538-2118; Fax: (413) 538-2838
theatre@mtholyoke.edu
www.mtholyoke.edu/acad/theat/

**Murray State University (MSU)**
MSU, FA 106, Murray, KY 42071
David Balthrop
Tel: (279) 809-4421; Fax: (270) 809-4422
david.balthrop@murraystate.edu
www.murraystate.edu

**Nebraska Wesleyan University**
500 St. Paul Ave., Lincoln, NE 68504
Jay Scott Chipman
Tel: (402) 465-2395
jsc@nebrwesleyan.edu
www.nebrwesleyan.edu

**New School University**
151 Bank St., New York, NY 10014
Frank Pugliese
Tel: (212) 229-5859
studentinfo@newschool.edu
www.drama.newschool.edu
    Offers 3-yr MFA. Each year,
    playwrights work with at least two
    teachers, completing at least one
    full-length play and one screenplay
    by graduation. What to Submit:
    application, sample, interview.

**New York University (NYU) Dramatic
Writing**
721 Broadway, Fl. 7,
New York, NY 10003
David Ranghelli
Tel: (212) 998-1940
www.ddw.tisch.nyu.edu/page/home.html

**New York University (NYU) Musical
Theater Writing**
113-A 2nd Ave., Fl. 1,
New York, NY 10003
Sarah Schlesinger
Tel: (212) 998-1830; Fax: (212) 995-4873
muscial.theatre@nyu.edu
www.gmtw.tisch.nyu.edu/page/home.
html
    Est. 1981. MFA for composers,
    lyricists and bookwriters from Inst.
    of Performing Arts at Tisch School of
    the Arts. Response Time: Decisions
    are made in April for incoming class
    starting in Sept. What to Submit:
    application.

**North Dakota State University (NDSU)**
NDSU Dept. of Theatre, 2336,
P.O. Box 6050, Fargo, ND 58105
Rooth Varland
Tel: (701) 231-7932
rooth.varland@ndsu.edu
www.ndsu.edu

**Northern Kentucky University**
NKU, FA 205-A,
Highland Heights, KY 41099
Ken Jones
Tel: (859) 572-6362; Fax: (859) 572-6057
www.nku.edu/~theatre

**Northwestern University**
Theatre Interpertation Building, 1949
Campus Drive, Evanston, IL 60208
Laura Schelhardt
Tel: (847) 491-3170; Fax: (847) 467-2019
v-valliere@northwestern.edu
www.communication.northwestern.edu/

**Oakland University**
Music, Theater, Dance,
Rochester, MI 48309
Kerro Knox 3
Tel: (248) 370-2030; Fax: (248) 370-2041
knox@oakland.edu
www.oakland.edu/mtd

**Ohio University**
Kantner Hall 307, Athens, OH 45701
Charles Smith
Tel: (740) 593-4818
ohioplaywriting@gmail.com
www.ohioplaywriting.org
    MFA, Playwriting. Response Time:
    by 4/30. What to Submit: full script,
    submissions not returned.

**Ohio Wesleyan University (OWU)**
Chappelear Drama Ctr.,
Delaware, OH 43015
Elane Denny-Todd
Tel: (614) 368-3848
eedennyt@owu.edu
www.theater.owu.edu

**Palm Beach Atlantic University**
Box 24708, West Palm Beach, FL 33416
Deborah McEniry
Tel: (561) 803-2000

timothy_cox@pba.edu
www.pba.edu

**Pensacola Junior College**
1000 College Blvd., Pensacola, FL 32504
Stan Dean
Tel: (850) 484-1847; Fax: (850) 484-1835
sdean@pjc.cc.fl.us
www.pjc.cc.fl.us/lyceum
    Style: no adaptation, no translation.
    What To Submit: query letter
    (note theme addressed), synopsis,
    submissions returned with SASE.
    How To Submit: unsolicited.

**Purdue University**
552 W. Wood Street,
West Lafayette, IN 47907
Richard Stockler Rand
Tel: (765) 494-3074; Fax: (765) 496-1766
theatre@purdue.edu
www.purdue.edu/theatre

**Radford University**
Dance and Theatre, RU Station,
Radford, VA 24142
Carl Lefko
Tel: (540) 831-5207; Fax: (540) 831-6313
clefko@radford.edu
www.theatre.asp.radford.edu

**Regent University**
1000 Regent Univ. Dr.,
Virginia Beach, VA 23464
Michael Kirkland
Tel: (757) 352-4127
www.regent.edu

**Rutgers University (State University of New Jersey)**
Rutgers University/Mason Gross School
of the Arts, Theatre Arts Department,
New Brunswick, NJ 08901
Barbara Harwanko
Tel: (732) 932-4891
www.mgsa.rutgers.edu/theater/thea.html
    MFA. Submission/Application
    Fee: University fee: $60; Theatre
    interview: $75.

**San Francisco State University (SFSU)**
1600 Holloway Ave.,
San Francisco, CA 94132

Roy Conboy
rconboy@sfsu.edu
www.sfsu.edu

**Sarah Lawrence College**
1 Mead Way, Bronxville, NY 10708
Peggy McGrath
Tel: (914) 395-2262; Fax: (914) 395-2666
pmcgrath@slc.edu
www.slc.edu
  MFA. Fee: $60. What to
  Submit: application, letters of
  recommendation, transcript.

**Smith College**
Theatre Dept., Mendenhall Ctr.,
Northampton, MA 01063
Len Berkman
Tel: (413) 585-3206; Fax: (413) 585-3229
lberkman@email.smith.edu
www.smith.edu/theatre
  Est. 1969.

**Southern Illinois University at
Edwardsville (SIUE)**
SIUE Theater/Dance Dept., Dunham
Hall, #1031, Edwardsville, IL 62026
Peter Cocuzza
Tel: (618) 650-2773
www.siue.edu/THEATER

**Southern Illinois University,
Carbondale (SIU)**
Comm. Bldg, #2238,
Carbondale, IL 62901
David Rush
Tel: (618) 453-5747
darush@siu.edu
www.siu.edu/~mcleod
  Est. 1952. BA, MFA, PhD. Material
  Must Be: Original, properly formatted
  and bound. How To Submit: Send
  90 minutes of script, Submission/
  Application Fee: Check the graduate
  school guidelines. Deadline: March.

**Southern Methodist University (SMU)**
Box 750369, Dallas, TX 75275
Gretchen Elizabeth Smith
Tel: (214) 768-2937
gesmith@mail.smu.edu
www.smu.edu

**St. Cloud State University (SCSU)**
Theatre, Film Studies and Dance, PAC
202, St. Cloud, MN 56301
Jeffery Bleam
Tel: (320) 308-3229
www.stcloudstate.edu

**Sul Ross State University (SRSU)**
FAB 203C, Alpine, TX 79832
Dona Roman
Tel: (432) 837-8219; Fax: (432) 837-8376
droman@sulross.edu
www.sulross.edu

**SUNY Purchase**
735 Anderson Hill Rd.,
Purchase, NY 10577
Howard Enders
Tel: (914) 251-6833
howard.enders@purchase.edu
www.purchase.edu

**Texas A&M University, Commerce
(TAMU)**
TAMU PAC, Commerce, TX 75429
Jim Tyler Anderson
Tel: (903) 886-5346
jim-anderson@tamu-commerce.edu
www.tamu-commerce.edu

**Texas State University, San Marcos**
601 University Dr.,
San Marcos, TX 78666
John Fleming
Tel: (512) 245-2147; Fax: (512) 245-8440
jf18@txstate.edu
www.finearts.txstate.edu/theatre

**Texas Tech University (TTU)**
Box 42061, Lubbock, TX 79409
Norman Bert
Tel: (806) 742-3601
bert.norman@ttu.edu
www.theatre.ttu.edu

**The Theatre Lab School of Dramatic
Arts**
733 8th St. NW, Washington, DC 20001
Tel: (202) 824-0449; Fax: (202) 824-0458
contact@theatrelab.org
www.theatrelab.org

Est. 1992. non-profit theatre training organization. offers an honors conservatory, classes for adults, teens and children.

**University of California, Riverside (UCR)**
The Department of Theatre, 900 University Ave., ARTS 121, Riverside, CA 92521
Eric Barr
Tel: (951) 827-4602; Fax: (951) 827-4651
Chrisy@ucr.edu
www.theatre.ucr.edu

**University of California, San Diego (UCSD)**
9500 Gilman Dr., MC0509, La Jolla, CA 92093
Allan Havis
Tel: (858) 534-4004; Fax: (858) 534-8931
ahavis@ucsd.edu
www.theatre.ucsd.edu

**University of California, Santa Barbara (UCSB)**
552 University Rd., Santa Barbara, CA 93106
Ellen K. Anderson
Tel: (805) 893-8303
ellena@silcom.com
www.dramadance.ucsb.edu

**University of Georgia (UGA)**
Univ. of Georgia, Fine Arts Building, Athens, GA 30602
Dr. David Saltz
Tel: (706) 542-2091
saltz@uga.edu
www.drama.uga.edu

**University of Idaho (UI)**
Box 443074, Moscow, ID 83844
Robert Caisley
Tel: (208) 885-6465
rcaisley@uidaho.edu
www.uitheatre.com
	Home of Idaho Repertory Theater.

**University of Iowa**
200 N. Riverside Dr., #107 TB, Iowa City, IA 52242

Art Borreca
Tel: (319) 353-2407; Fax: (319) 335-3568
art-borreca@uiowa.edu
www.uiowa.edu
	Est. 1971

**University of Louisiana, Monroe (ULM)**
700 Univ. Ave., Monroe, LA 71209
Matthew James
Tel: (318) 342-3811; Fax: (318) 342-1599
mjames@ulm.edu
www.ulm.edu

**University of Michigan (UM)**
E.V. Moore Bldg., 1100 Baits Dr., Ann Arbor, MI 48109
Gregory Poggi
Tel: (734) 764-5350; Fax: (734) 647-2297
theatre.info@umich.edu
www.music.umich.edu

**University of Minnesota Duluth (UMD)**
Dept. of Theatre, 141 MPAC, Duluth, MN 55812
Patricia Dennis
Tel: (218) 726-8778
pdennis@d.umn.edu
www.d.umn.edu/finearts/theatre.htm

**University of Missouri**
129 Fine Arts Bldg., Columbia, MO 65211
Clyde Ruffin
Tel: (573) 882-2021; Fax: (573) 884-4034

**University of Missouri, Kansas City**
4949 Cherry St., Kansas City, MO 64110
Frank Higgins
Tel: (816) 235-2702
fhwriter@aol.com
www.cas.umkc.edu/theatre/

**University of New Mexico (UNM)**
1 UNM, MSC04-2570, Department of Theatre & Dance, Albuquerque, NM 87131
Bill Liotta
Tel: (505) 277-4332
wliotta@unm.edu
www.unm.edu/~theatre
	UNM est. 1892; Theater Dept. est. 1930. MFA, dramatic writing.

**University of New Orleans (UNO)**
Film, Theatre and Communication Arts,
2000 Lake Shore Drive-PAC 307,
New Orleans, LA 70148
David Hoover
Tel: (504) 280-6317; Fax: (504) 280-6318
dhoover@uno.edu
www.uno.edu

**University of South Florida (USF)**
4202 E. Fowler Ave., FAH 110,
Tampa, FL 33620
Denis Calandra
Tel: (813) 974-2701
www.theatreanddance.arts.usf.edu/theatre

**University of Southern California (USC)**
University Park, DRC 107,
Los Angeles, CA 90089
Velina Hasu Houston
Tel: (231) 821-2744
thteinfo@usc.edu
www.theatre.usc.edu
    Est. 1945.

**University of Texas, Austin**
Department of Theate and Dance,
The Unversity of Texas At Austin,
Austin, TX 78712
Suzan Zeder
Tel: (512) 232-5325
suzanz@mail.utexas.edu
www.utexas.edu/cofa/theatre

**University of Texas, El Paso (UTEP)**
Fox Fine Arts, Rm. 371,
500 W. Univ. Ave., El Paso, TX 79968
Tel: (915) 747-5746
www.theatredance.utep.edu

**University of Toledo**
2801 W. Bancroft Ave., Toledo, OH 43606
Edmund Lingan
Tel: (419) 530-2855; Fax: (419) 530-5439
theatre@utnet.utoledo.edu
www.utoledo.edu/as/theatrefilm

**University of Tulsa (TU)**
Kendall Hall, 600 S. College Ave.,
Tulsa, OK 74104
Michael Wright
Tel: (918) 631-2566; Fax: (918) 631-5155

michael-wright@utulsa.edu
www.cas.utulsa.edu/writing

**University of Virginia**
PO Box 400128, Department of Drama,
Charlottesville, VA 22903
Doug Grissom
Tel: (434) 924-3326; Fax: (434) 924-1447
drama@virginia.edu
www.virginia.edu/drama

**University of Wyoming**
1000 E. University Ave., Dept. 3951,
Laramie, WY 82071
William Missouri Downs
Tel: (307) 766-2198
www.uwyo.edu

**Virginia Tech (VT)**
250 E. Henderson Hall,
Blacksburg, VA 24061
Patricia Raun
Tel: (540) 231-5335; Fax: (540) 231-7321
praun@vt.edu
www.theatre.vt.edu

**Wabash College**
Box 352, Crawfordsville, IN 47933
Michael S. Abbot
Tel: (765) 361-6448; Fax: (765) 361-6341
abbottm@wabash.edu
www.wabash.edu/academics/theater

**Wayne State University**
4841 Cass Ave., Detroit, MI 48201
David S. Magidson
Tel: (313) 577-6508
d_magidson@wayne.edu
www.wayne.edu

**Western Connecticut State University (WCSU)**
181 White St., Danbury, CT 6810
Sal Trapani
Tel: (203) 837-8259
trapanis@wcsu.edu
www.wcsu.edu/theatrearts/

**Wright State University**
3640 Col. Glenn Hwy.,
Dayton, OH 45435
Victoria Oleen
Tel: (937) 775-3702

victoria.oleen@wright.edu
www.wright.edu

**Yale University School of Drama**
Box 208325, New Haven, CT 06520
Paula Vogel
Tel: (203) 432-0254
http://www.drama.yale.edu

Est. 1924. MFA.: $95 application.
What to Submit: query, application,
full script, resume, letter of
recommendation, transcript,
submissions not returned. Deadline:
Feb 1 2009 12:00AM.

## WORKSHOPS

**Academy for New Musical Theatre
(ANMT)**
5628 Vineland Ave.,
North Hollywood, CA 91601
Scott Guy
Tel: (818) 506-8500; Fax: (818) 506-8500
academy@anmt.org
www.anmt.org
Est. 1981. Supports wide array
of programs to further artistic
creation of new musical stage works,
incl. workshops (Lehman Engel
curriculum), readings, Search for
New Musicals and commercial
development. $100 (Search); $400
(Dramaturgy); $895 (Intro Workshop);
$695 (Lab); $395 (Fast Track Lab):
Ongoing; December 15th for Search
for New Musicals. What to Submit:
query via website. Opportunity/Award:
query via email. How To Submit: Visit
www.anmt.org

**Around the Block Urban Playwriting
Workgroup**
5 E. 22nd St., #9-K, New York, NY 10010
Carlos Jerome
Tel: (212) 673-9187
info@aroundtheblock.org
www.aroundtheblock.org
Est. 2001. Focusing on (but not
restricted to) the life & aspirations
of urban communities, particularly
NYC. Group meets every 2 wks. No
fee. Membership in ATB not required.
See also: Raymond J Flores Short
Play Series. Response Time: 2 wks.
Opportunity/Award: reading. How
To Submit: contact us to arrange
participation.

**ASCAP Musical Theatre Workshop
[NY]**
1 Lincoln Plaza, Fl. 7,
New York, NY 10023
Michael A. Kerker
Tel: (212) 621-6234; Fax: (212) 621-6558
mkerker@ascap.com
www.ascap.com
Directed by Stephen Schwartz,
program of 50-min from works-in-
progress before a panel of professional
directors, musical directors, producers,
critics and fellow writers. All sessions
begin 7pm, May-Jun. What to Submit:
synopsis, audio (4 songs), bios, song
descriptions.

**ASCAP/Disney Musical Theatre
Workshop [CA]**
7920 W. Sunset Blvd., Fl. 3,
Los Angeles, CA 90046
Tel: (323) 883-1000; Fax: (323) 883-1049
mkerker@ascap.com
www.ascap.com
Directed by Stephen Schwartz, 50-min
presentation of works-in-development
before a professional panel. All
sessions begin 7pm, Jan-Feb. What
to Submit: synopsis, audio (4 songs),
bios, song descriptions. Deadline: Apr.
3, 2010.

**Asian American Theater Company
NewWorks Incubator Project**
690 Fifth St., #211,
San Francisco, CA 94107
Sean Lim
Tel: (415) 543-5738; Fax: (415) 543-5638
info@asianamericantheater.org
www.asianamericantheater.org

Est. 2003. Combines SF's best emerging playwrights and actors to create original new plays. Lead by Sean Lim and mentored by Philip Kan Gotanda, the group meets twice monthly to test new material and ideas. After six months, four new plays are presented.

## BMI Lehman Engel Musical Theatre Workshop - Librettists Workshop
320 W. 57th St., New York, NY 10019
Jean Banks
Tel: (212) 830-2508; Fax: (212) 262-2508
jbanks@bmi.com
www.bmi.com
Weekly 2-hr sessions (Sep-May) in NYC.evenings. Occasional special events. Applicants must live within commuting distance or make local residential arrangements. Style: Musical Theatre script. What To Submit: application, sample. Author Must Be: Sole author of all "book" material submitted. (Lyrics and score may be written by or with others). Material Must Be: In standard script form. Short comedy sample (required) may be from another genre. How To Submit: Download application and follow instructions. Deadline: 5/15/2010 postmark.

## BMI Lehman Engel Musical Theatre Workshop - Songwriters Workshop
320 West 57th Street,
New York, NY 10019
Jean Banks
Tel: (212) 586-2000
jbanks@bmi.com
www.bmi.com/genres/theatre
Weekly 2-hr sessions (Sept - May) Monday evenings (First Year) or Tuesday evenings (Second Year) in NYC. Must live within commuting distance or make local residential arrangements. Frequency: Annual. Style: musical. What To Submit: application, sample, audio. How To Submit: Download application from website and follow instructions. Deadline: 8/1/2010.

## Broadway Tomorrow Musical Theatre
191 Claremont Ave., #53,
New York, NY 10027
Elyse Curtis PhD
Tel: (212) 531-2447; Fax: (212) 532-2447
solministry@juno.com
www.solministry.com/bway_tom.html
Est. 1983. New musicals on new age, transformative or spiritual themes with redeeming value given self-contained concert readings with writer/composer involvement. Response Time: 6 mos. Style: adaptation, musical, translation. What To Submit: synopsis, audio or CD (3 songs), SASE. Author Must Be: resident of NYC area.

## Cape Cod Theatre Project
Box 410, Falmouth, MA 02541
Andrew Polk
Tel: (508) 457-4242
andrew@capecodtheatreproject.org
www.capecodtheatreproject.org
Est. 1995. Equity LOA. Style: others. What To Submit: query, synopsis, submissions not returned. Author Must Be: resident or citizen of US. Material Must Be: unpublished, unproduced. Deadline: 3/1/2010.

## Cherry Lane Theatre Mentor Project
38 Commerce St., New York, NY 10014
James King
Tel: (212) 989-2020
company@cherrylanetheatre.org
www.cherrylanetheatre.org
Est. 1997. Pairs young writers with master to work on scripts for full season, ending with Equity Showcase. Annual. Medium cast size, no orchestra. What to Submit: submissions not returned. Material Must Be: unoptioned, unproduced. How To Submit: professional recommendation.

## Chesterfield Writer's Film Project
1158 26th St., Box 544,
Santa Monica, CA 90401
Tel: (213) 683-3977; Fax: (310) 260-6116
www.chesterfield-co.com
Based at Paramount Pictures, WFP began with support of Steven

Spielberg's Amblin Entertainment. It is currently ON HIATUS.

**Colorado New Play Summit**
1101 13th St., Denver, CO 80204
Douglas Langworth
Tel: (303) 893-4000; Fax: (303) 825-2117
www.dcpa.org
> DCTC (est. 1979; 1998 Regional Theater Tony winner) presents the Colorado New Play Summit (est. 2005), which offers rehearsed reading of new work for industry and general audience. room/board, travel: annual. Response Time: 6 mos. What to Submit: full script, SASE. Material Must Be: unoptioned, unproduced. How To Submit: unsolicited (AZ, CO, MT, NM, UT, WY residents only), agent.

**David Henry Hwang Writers Institute**
120 N. Judge John Aiso St.,
Los Angeles, CA 90012
Jeff Liu
Tel: (213) 625-7000 ext. 27
Fax: (213) 625-7111
jliu@eastwestplayers.org
www.eastwestplayers.org
> Est. 1991. 2 workshops/yr (fall, spring). $400. What to Submit: query.

**Frederick Douglass Creative Arts Center Writing Workshops**
270 W 96th St., New York, NY 10025
Kermit Frazier
Tel: (212) 864-3375; Fax: (212) 864-3474
fdcac@aol.com
www.fdcac.org

**Fieldwork**
161 6th Ave, Fl. 14, New York, NY 10013
Michael Helland
Tel: (212) 691-6969; Fax: (212) 255-2053
michael@thefield.org
www.thefield.org
> Est. 1986. 10-wk workshop to create original material, share work, and receive peer feedback. Visit us online for current offerings. Assistance: work-study option. Frequency: quarterly. Style: all styles, all aesthetics.

**Frank Silvera Writers' Workshop**
Box 1791, Manhattanville Sta.,
New York, NY 10027
Garland Lee Thompson
Tel: (212) 281-8832; Fax: (212) 281-8839
playrite@earthlink.net
www.fsww.org
> Est. 1973. Equity Showcase. Playwright development program. Style: Open. What To Submit: full script, SASE. Author Must Be: age 18 or older, resident or citizen of US. Material Must Be: unoptioned, unpublished, unproduced. Opportunity/Award: 6% royalty. How To Submit: US Postage Mail or hand-delivery.

**Hangar Theatre Lab Company Playwriting Residencies**
Box 205, Ithaca, NY 14851
Literary Asst.
literary@hangartheatre.org
www.hangartheatre.org
> We will begin accepting submissions 10/15/09. 4 playwrights offered 2-3 wk residency in Jul-Aug. Full production by Lab Company. The Hangar solicits full-lengths from former winners. Assistance: $200 plus housing and travel. Frequency: annual. Response Time: by 5/15/10. What to Submit: full script, resume/bio, must be submitted electronically, see website for guidelines. Material Must Be: unproduced. How To Submit: online, Submission/Application Fee: $15.00. Deadline: 3/8/10.

**Harold Prince Musical Theatre Program**
311 W. 43rd St., #307,
New York, NY 10036
Tel: (212) 246-5877; Fax: (212) 246-5882
www.thedirectorscompany.org

**Jeffrey Sweet's Improv for Playwrights**
250 W. 90th St., #15-G,
New York, NY 10024
Kristine Niven
Tel: (212) 875-1857; Fax: (501) 643-0322
artnewdir@aol.com

www.artisticnewdirections.org
Est. 1986. Jeffrey Sweet teaches
technique for setting up scenes to
improvise toward first drafts of
one-acts, plus revising, introducing
characters, and using improv for full-
lengths. Monthly sessions: vary per
length of session.

**The Kennedy Center New Visions/New
Voices Festival (NVNV)**
Kennedy Center, P.O. Box 101510,
Arlington, VA 22210
Kim Peter Kovac
Tel: (202) 416-8830; Fax: (202) 416-8297
kctya@kennedy-center.org
www.kennedy-center.org/education/nvnv.
html
Est. 1991. Deadline and applications
available online summer of 2009.
Biennial (even yrs) weeklong residency
in May to encourage and support
creation of new plays and musicals
for young people and families. What
to Submit: application, synopsis,
sample, full script (4 copies), audio,
submissions not returned. Material
Must Be: unproduced. How To Submit:
thru sponsoring theater.

**Manhattan Playwrights Unit (MPU)**
338 W. 19th St., #6-B,
New York, NY 10011
Saul Zachary
Tel: (212) 989-0948
saulzachary@yahoo.com
Est. 1979. Ongoing biweekly inhouse
workshop for professional-level
playwrights and screenwriters.
Informal and intense. Staff: Stacie
Linardos. Style: all styles. What To
Submit: query, resume, submissions
not returned. How To Submit: invite
only.

**Missouri Playwrights Workshop
(MPW)**
129 Fine Arts Bldg., Columbia, MO 65211
David Crespy
Tel: (573) 882-0535
crespyd@missouri.edu
www.theatre.missouri.edu/mpw/index.htm

Est. 1998. Weekly salon for developing
work by Missouri playwrights.
What to Submit: query, synopsis,
submissions not returned. Author
Must Be: resident of MO, and attend
workshop.

**Musical Theatre Lab**
133 Wortham, Houston, TX 77204
Stuart Ostrow
Tel: (713) 743-2912
Est. 1973. Each fall, 3 works
performed by Lab students at Hobby
Center. Recent works incl. 'Twas,
Doll, Coyote Goes Salmon Fishing,
and 1040. Response Time: 1 mo. Style:
musical. What To Submit: full script,
audio, score, SASE. Material Must Be:
unoptioned, original.

**New Directors/New Works (ND/NW)**
520 8th Ave., #320, New York, NY 10018
Roger Danforth
Tel: (212) 244-9494; Fax: (212) 244-9191
www.dramaleague.org
Directors Project program to
support new works by directors and
collaborating artists. Application
must be submitted by the director.
Each team works with a professional
mentor. $1,500 stipend: annual.
What to Submit: application, sample,
production budget, two letters of
recommendation. Author Must
Be: resident of US, Submission/
Application Fee: $25.00. Deadline:
Feb. 1, 2010.

**The New Harmony Project**
Box 441062, Indianapolis, IN 46244
Joel Grynheim
Tel: (317) 464-1103
jgrynheim@newharmonyproject.org
www.newharmonyproject.org
Est. 1986. Development thru
rehearsals and readings in 14 day
conference of scripts that explore
the human journey by offering hope
and showing respect for the positive
values of life. No stipend, room/
board, travel: annual. What to Submit:
2-pg proposal, 10-pg sample, full

script, audio, resume. Opportunity/
Award: reading. How To Submit:
Electronically only. Deadline: Oct. 1,
2010.

**New Musicals Project**
1 Holyoke Ln., Stony Brook, NY 11790

**Pataphysics**
41 White St., New York, NY 10013
Tel: (212) 226-0051; Fax: (212) 965-1808
garyw@theflea.org
www.theflea.org
    Pataphysics workshops are scheduled
    sporadically and occur unexpectedly.
    To receive notification of upcoming
    classes, please email. Recent master
    playwrights have incl Lee Breuer,
    Lisa Kron, Jeffrey M. Jones, Ruth
    Margraff, Lynn M. Thomson, Paula
    Vogel, and Mac Wellman. What
    to Submit: query, 10-pg sample (4
    copies), resume, SASE.

**Penumbra Theatre Company**
270 N Kent St., St. Paul, MN 55102
Dominic Taylor
Tel: (651) 288-6795; Fax: (651) 288-6789
dominic.taylor@penumbratheatre.org
www.penumbratheatre.org
    Style: all styles.

**The PlayCrafters Group**
11 Golf View Rd., Doylestown, PA 18901
James Breckenridge
Tel: (888) 399-2506
hbcraft@att.net
    Professional play script and screenplay
    evaluations and consultations for the
    creative dramatic writer. $175 and up.
    Style: all genres. What To Submit:
    play scripts & screenplays. Material
    Must Be: Any stage of development.
    How To Submit: Please contact by
    phone or e-mail.

**Playwrights' Center of San Francisco
Staged Readings**
588 Sutter St., #403,
San Francisco, CA 94102
Tel: (415) 820-3206
www.playwrightscentersf.org

**Playwrights Gallery**
119 W. 72nd St., #2700,
New York, NY 10023
Deborah Savadge
Tel: (212) 595-2582
www.playwrightsgallery.com
    Est. 1989. Company of professional
    actors reads new work twice monthly.
    Public readings 2-3 times/yr. Meet
    Sep-Jun, alt Wed, noon-2pm..
    Response Time: 9 mos. Style: comedy,
    drama. What To Submit: 20-pg
    sample, SASE. How To Submit: mail.
    Deadline: Jan. 1, 2010 and July 1,
    2010.

**Playwrights Lab**
55 West End Ave., New York, NY 10023
Megan Carter
www.womensproject.org
    2-yr program for playwrights,
    directors, and producers. Each Lab
    has 10 members who collaborate
    with guest artists, WP staff, industry
    professionals, and other Lab
    participants. Competitive application
    for the next Lab will begin spring
    2008. biennial. Material Must Be:
    unproduced. How To Submit: see
    website for submission details.

**Playwrights' Lab**
266 W. 37th St., Fl. 22,
New York, NY 10018
Brian Richardson
Tel: (212) 695-1596
theatre@pulseensembletheatre.org
www.pulseensembletheatre.org
    Develops work of each playwright
    in 4-mo workshop. Group (limit 10)
    meets 3 hrs/wk to read scenes, with
    discussion afterward. Presents two
    showcases of 3 works/year. Some
    plays selected for further development.
    Group is under the leadership of
    Award winning playwright Lezley
    Steele. Fees $100/month. Style: all.
    What To Submit: 30 page sample of
    work. How To Submit: hard copy - not
    email.

**Playwrights' Platform**
398 Columbus Ave #604,
Boston, MA 02116-6008
Kelly DuMar
membership@playwrightsplatform.org
www.playwrightsplatform.org
> Est. 1976. Monthly developmental
> readings in Boston area and annual
> festival in Boston, MA. Fees: $35/
> yr. Response Time: 3 mos. Author
> Must Be: available to attend monthly
> meetings in Boston area. How To
> Submit: member only submissions
> online.

**Primary Stages Playwriting Workshops**
307 W. 38th St., #1510,
New York, NY 10018
Michelle Bossy
Tel: (212) 840-9705; Fax: (212) 840-9725
www.primarystages.org
> Est. 2002. Each wk, 8 writers bring
> 10-15 pgs for instructor feedback and
> group discussion, completing first
> draft of new full-length in 10 wks.
> $600. What to Submit: application,
> please see website.

**PRTT Playwrights Unit**
304 W. 47th St., New York, NY 10036
Allen Davis III
Tel: (212) 354-1293; Fax: (212) 307-6769
allen@prtt.org
www.prtt.org
> Est. 1977. Developmental workshops
> for beginners and for professionals
> (Oct-Apr), with readings and staged
> productions. $150: annual. Response
> Time: 1 mo. What to Submit: query,
> full script (professional unit), SASE.
> Author Must Be: resident of NYC
> area, Latino/minorities preferred.
> Opportunity/Award: production,
> reading.

**Rattlestick Theatre Playwriting School**
244 Waverly Pl., New York, NY 10014
Louise Shannon
Tel: (212) 627-2556; Fax: (212) 627-8481
rattlestic@aol.com
www.rattlestick.org

For playwrights of all levels, including
advanced class with artistic director.
10-week courses, including rehearsed
reading.: $395-$495 program fee.
What to Submit: query letter (note
theme addressed), application,
submissions returned with SASE. How
To Submit: unsolicited.

**Sage Theater**
711 7th Ave., Fl. 2, New York, NY 10036
Diana Blake
Tel: (212) 302-6665; Fax: (212) 302-4661
info@sagetheater.us
sagetheater.us
> Response Time: 4 mos. Style: sketch/
> musical comedy only. What To
> Submit: full script, SASE.

**The Scripteasers**
3404 Hawk St., San Diego, CA 92103
Jonathan Dunn-Rankin
Tel: (619) 295-4040
thescripteasers@msn.com
www.scripteasers.org
> Est. 1948. Writers' development group
> with biweekly readings of original
> plays and facilitated discussion. Staff:
> Jonathan Dunn-Rankin (Sec'y). What
> to Submit: full script, SASE. Author
> Must Be: resident of SoCal. Material
> Must Be: unoptioned, unpublished,
> unproduced.

**Scripts Up!**
355 South End Ave., #5-N,
New York, NY 10280
Janet McCall
Tel: (212) 946-1155
> Est. 1999. Small NFP play-
> development organization specializing
> in professional full-time workshop
> stagings with audience feedback.
> Playwrights should have NYC area
> residency availabilty during entire
> process and it's preferred to have
> playwrights involved in process. Style:
> Any. No one-acts or 10 min plays, no
> musicals. What To Submit: synopsis,
> 15-pg sample, resume. Material
> Must Be: unoptioned, unpublished,
> unproduced.

**Sewanee Writers' Conference**
735 University Ave., 123-D Gailor H,
Sewanee, TN 37383
Cheri B. Peters
Tel: (931) 598-1141
cpeters@sewanee.edu
www.sewaneewriters.org
    Est. 1990. Workshop in late July
    led by two noted playwrights.
    Limited number of scholarships and
    fellowships available on a competitive
    basis. $15 aplication, $1,000 program,
    $560 room/board: fellowship (full
    fee waiver), scholarship (program fee
    waiver): annual. Style: comedy, drama.
    What To Submit: application, 40-pg
    sample, submissions not returned.
    Deadline: May 1, 2010.

**The Simon Studio**
Box 231469, Ansonia Sta. NY 10023
109 Hooker Ave.,
Poughkeepsie, NY 12601,
Roger Simon
Tel: (212) 841-0204
rhsstudio@hotmail.com
www.simonstudio.com
    Development through long distance
    consultation and/or residency
    services of 6-12 weeks or short term
    intensive (1-5) days in NYC and/or
    Poughkeepsie, NY. Writers develop
    and showcase new work for stage, TV/
    Film, radio. Service includes ongoing
    readings and critiques in workshops
    for in-house, public and invited
    industry. What To Submit: Inquiring
    phone call and/or query letter,
    synopsis, 5-10 page sample, audio,
    submissions returned with SASE.

**Southern Writers Project (SWP)**
1 Festival Dr., Montgomery, AL 36117
Nancy Rominger
 Fax: (334) 271-5348
swp@asf.net
www.southernwritersproject.net
    ASF accepts scripts through its
    Southern Writers' Project (est. 1991).
    Up to 6 scripts each year are developed
    in weeklong workshop, with some
    chosen for production next season.:

room/board, travel. Response Time:
6 mos. Style: Southern or African
American themed or from a Southern
writer. What To Submit: full script,
SASE. Material Must Be: unproduced.

**Stage Left Theatre Company**
3408 N. Sheffield Ave., Chicago, IL 60657
Kevin Heckman
Tel: (773) 883-8830 ext. 3
scripts@stagelefttheatre.com
www.stagelefttheatre.com
    Est. 1982. Storefront theatre for plays
    that raise debate on sociopolticial
    issues. program: Downstage Left
    (or DSL) development program.
    work for production consideration or
    for development. Kevin Heckman,
    Literary Manager: travel. Response
    Time: 1 yr. No deadline for script
    submissions. What to Submit:
    application, 1-pg synopsis, full
    script, resume, SASE, development
    and production history of piece.
    Opportunity/Award: royalty.

**Sundance Institute Theatre at White Oak**
8530 Wilshire Blvd., Fl. 3,
Beverly Hills, CA 90211
Christopher Hibma
Tel: (310) 360-1981; Fax: (310) 360-1975
theatre@sundance.org
www.sundance.org
    Est. 2003. Equity Special Agreement.
    2-wk developmental workshop
    focusing on musical theater and
    ensemble-created work. Stipend,
    room/board, travel. Annual. What
    to Submit: synopsis, submissions
    not returned. Material Must Be:
    unproduced. How To Submit: invite.

**Sundance Institute Theatre Program**
8530 Wilshire Blvd., Fl. 3,
Beverly Hills, CA 90211
Ignacia Delgado
Tel: (310) 360-1981; Fax: (310) 360-1975
theatre@sundance.org
www.sundance.org
    Est. 1981. Equity Special Agreement.
    Developmental Jul workshops for

directors and playwrights in Sundance, UT. $35 application: $500, room/ board, travel: annual. Response Time: 4 mos. Style: online at www.sundance. org/theatreapp. What To Submit: application, full script, audio, video, SASE. Material Must Be: unproduced. How To Submit: Online at www. sundance.org/theatreapp, Submission/ Application Fee: $35.00. Deadline: Oct. 1, 2010.

**Theatre Building Chicago Musical Theatre Writers' Workshop**
1225 W. Belmont Ave., Chicago, IL 60657
Allan Chambers
Tel: (773) 929-7367 ext. 222
Fax: (773) 327-1404
jsparks@theatrebuildingchicago.org
www.theatrebuildingchicago.org
Est. 1984. Formerly New Tuners Workshop. 3-tiered workshop: Intro (1st yr), Intermediate (2nd yr), Advanced (ongoing). $25 application, $1,000/yr (Intro/Intermediate), $500/ yr (Advanced). Style: Musical theatre (book, music and lyrics). What To Submit: application, 5-pg sample as detailed on application form available on website. Deadline: Sep. 1, 2010.

**Waldo M. & Grace C. Bonderman Playwriting for Youth National Symposium**
140 W. Washington St.,
Indianapolis, IN 46204
Atth: Paul Hengesteg
Tel: (317) 506-4566; Fax: (317) 278-1025
bonderma@iupui.edu
www.indianarep.com/Bonderman
1 week of development and staged readings. room/board, travel: biennial. Style: musical. What To Submit: application, full script (1 entry per author), submissions returned with SASE. Material Must Be: unpublished, unproduced. Opportunity/Award: $1,000 award to 4 winners. How To Submit: unsolicited, send SASE in fall for application.

**Williamstown Theatre Festival**
229 W. 42nd St., #801,
New York, NY 10036
Michael Ritchie
Tel: (212) 395-9090; Fax: (212) 395-9099
www.wtfestival.org

**Women of Color Productions, Inc.: Writers Development Lab**
163 East 104th Street, Suite 4E,
New York, NY 10029
Jacqueline Wade
Tel: (212) 479-7916
womenofcolorfilm@gmail.com
www.womenofcolorpro.citymax.com

**Women Playwrights Series**
400 Jefferson St., Hackettstown, NJ 7840
Catherine Rust
Tel: (908) 979-0900; Fax: (908) 979-4297
rustc@centenarycollege.edu
www.centenarystageco.org

**Young Playwrights Inc. Advanced Playwriting Workshop**
PO Box 5134, New York, NY 10185
Tel: (212) 594-5440; Fax: (212) 684-4902
admin@youngplaywrights.org
www.youngplaywrights.org
Deadline: Postmarked by 9/20/10. Advanced Playwriting Workshop meets in midtown Manhattan every Tue, 4:30-7:00pm, October–May. Exercises help members develop and revise new plays. Members also attend Broadway and Off-Broadway productions, and receive a staged reading of an excerpt of their work in May. Style: all except musicals and adaptations. What To Submit: application, sample, teacher/mentor recommendation, submissions not returned. Author Must Be: age 18 or younger. Material Must Be: original. How To Submit: Visit our website at www.youngplaywrights.org for application instructions. Deadline: 09/20/10.

# Writer Resources

## EMERGENCY FUNDS

**Authors League Fund**
31 E. 32nd St., Fl. 7, New York, NY 10016
Sarah Heller
Tel: (212) 568-1208; Fax: (212) 564-5363
staff@authorsguild.org
www.authorsleaguefund.org
Interest-free loans for personal
emergencies of immediate need
(rent, medical, etc.). What to Submit:
application. Author Must Be: produced
or published.

**Carnegie Fund for Authors**
1 Old Country Rd., #113,
Carle Place, NY 11514
Tel: (516) 877-2141
Aid to authors (of at least 1
commercially published book) for
financial emergency as a result of
illness or injury to self, spouse or
dependent child, or that has placed
author in pressing and substantial
verifiable need. Author Must Be: age
18 or older.

**Entertainment Industry Assistance
Program (EIAP)**
729 7th Ave., Fl. 10, New York, NY 10019
Tel: (212) 221-7300 ext. 119
info@actorsfund.org
www.actorsfund.org
Helps working entertainment
professionals with: counseling;
advocacy and referrals to social
services; emergency aid for food, rent,
medical care. Chicago: 312-372-0989,
Los Angeles: 323-933-9244 x15.

**Mary Mason Memorial Lemonade
Fund**
870 Market St, #375,
San Francisco, CA 94102
Tel: (415) 430-1140; Fax: (415) 430-1145
dale@theatrebayarea.org
www.theatrebayarea.org/programs/
lemonade.jsp
Mail or fax application from web site.

**PEN Writers Fund**
588 Broadway, #303,
New York, NY 10012
Lara Tobin
www.pen.org
Est. 1921. Emergency fund for
professional writers with serious
financial difficulties. $2,000 limit.
Response Time: 2 mos. What to
Submit: application. Author Must
Be: resident of US. Material Must
Be: produced or published (not self-
published).

## MEMBERSHIP AND SERVICE ORGANIZATIONS

**Actors' Fund of America**
729 7th Ave., Fl. 10, New York, NY 10019
Barbara Davis
Tel: (212) 221-7300
www.actorsfund.org
> Est. 1882. Human services org for
> all entertainment professionals. Also
> makes emergency grants for essential
> needs.

**ACTS Institute Inc.**
Box 30854,
Palm Beach Gardens, FL 33420
Charlotte Plotsky
Tel: (561) 625-2273
actsinstitute@bellsouth.net
> Est. 1981. Nonprofit public foundation
> and membership group for developing
> creative artists and projects as a
> charitable and educational endeavor.
> Current project is public education
> (lectures, workshops, etc.) various
> topics, and publications program.
> What to Submit: query with SASE.

**Alliance for Inclusion in the Arts**
1560 Broadway, #709,
New York, NY 10036
Sharon Jensen
Tel: (212) 730-4750; Fax: (212) 730-4820
info@inclusioninthearts.org
www.allianceinthearts.org
> Est. 1986. Today its mission is to serve
> as expert advocate and educational
> resource for full inclusion and
> diversity in the arts. Author Must Be:
> of color, female or disabled.

**Alliance of Artists Communities (AAC)**
255 South Main St., Providence, RI 2903
Tel: (401) 351-4320; Fax: (401) 351-4507
aac@artistcommunities.org
www.artistcommunities.org

**Alliance of Los Angeles Playwrights
(ALAP)**
7510 Sunset Blvd., #1050,
Los Angeles, CA 90046
Dan Berkowitz, Jonathan Dorf
Tel: (323) 957-4752

info@laplaywrights.org
www.laplaywrights.org
> Service and support org for
> professional needs of LA playwrights.
> Sponsors annual reading series,
> professional symposia, networking
> and social events. Also offers
> phone hotline, email listserv, online
> script catalogue, actor and director
> databases, bimonthly newsletter,
> resource guide to local theater, model
> contracts, and online membership
> directory.: $40/yr dues, $20 students,
> $275 life. Time (tax-deductible).
> What to Submit: application. How To
> Submit: See instructions on website.

**Alternate ROOTS Inc.**
1083 Austin Ave., NE, Atlanta, GA 30307
Shannon Turner
Tel: (404) 577-1079; Fax: (404) 577-7991
shannon@alternateroots.org
www.alternateroots.org
> Service org for playwrights, directors
> & choreographers creating original,
> community-based projects. Services
> incl. newsletter, bulletin, presenters'
> subsidy, annual meeting, and
> professional/artistic training and
> development.: $20/yr (intro), $65/yr
> (voting membership). What to Submit:
> application. Author Must Be: resident
> of the South.

**American Assn. of Community Theatre
(AACT)**
1300 Gendy St., Fort Worth, TX 76107
Rod McCullough
Tel: (817) 732-3177; Fax: (817) 732-3178
www.aact.org
> Est. 1986. Non-producing company.
> How To Submit: See website for
> details.

**American Indian Community House**
11 Broadway, Fl. 2, New York, NY 10004
Jim Cyrus
Tel: (212) 598-0100 ext. 228
Fax: (212) 598-4909

jcyrus@aich.org
www.aich.org
 $25/yr.

## ASCAP (American Society of Composers, Authors & Publishers)

1 Lincoln Plaza, New York, NY 10023
Tel: (212) 621-6234; Fax: (212) 621-6558
mkerker@ascap.com
www.ascap.com
 Est. 1914. Membership org for
 composers, lyricists and publishers
 of musical works. Programs incl.
 winter and spring Musical Theater
 Workshops directed by Stephen
 Schwartz and Songwriters Showcases
 in NY and LA. What to Submit:
 application. Author Must Be:
 published, recorded or performed.

## Association for Jewish Theatre (AJT)

Edward Einhorn
utc61@aol.com
www.afjt.com
 International network of theatres
 and playwrights to enhance Jewish
 theatre. Info and increased visibility of
 Jewish theater, incl. annual newsletter,
 website with member pages, annual
 conference, submissions guide, etc.
 Exec Director- Kayla Gordon: $90/
 yr dues (Sep-Aug). What to Submit:
 application on website.

## Association for Theatre in Higher Education (ATHE)

Box 1290, Boulder, CO 80306
Tel: (888) 284-3737; Fax: (303) 530-2168
info@athe.org
www.athe.org
 Org of individuals and institutions
 promoting excellence in theater
 education thru its publications,
 conferences, advocacy, projects,
 and collaborative efforts with other
 organizations. Membership year runs
 Jun-May.: $230 (organizational), $130/
 yr (indiv), $80/yr (retiree), $65/yr
 (student). What to Submit: application.
 How To Submit: online.

## Association of Authors' Representatives, Inc.

676A 9th Ave., #312, New York, NY 10036
Emily Cullings
aarinc@mindspring.com
www.aar-online.org

## Association of Writers & Writing Programs (AWP)

George Mason Univ., Mail Stop 1E3,
Fairfax, VA 22030
David Fenza
www.awpwriter.org
 Est. 1967.

## Audrey Skirball-Kenis (ASK) Unpublished Play Collection

630 W. 5th St., Los Angeles, CA 90071
Virginia Loe
Tel: (213) 228-7325; Fax: (213) 228-7329
www.lapl.org/central/literature.html
 Service org with over 800 unpublished
 scripts of plays done in L.A. The
 collection, located in the Lit/Fiction
 Dept for reference only, incl. reviews
 and playwright bios. Open Mon-Thu,
 10am-8pm; Fri-Sat, 10am-6pm; Sun,
 1pm-5pm.

## Austin Script Works (ASW)

Box 9787, Austin, TX 78766
Christina J. Moore
Tel: (512) 454-9727
info@scriptworks.org
www.scriptworks.org
 Est. 1997. Austin Script Works
 supports playwrights by providing
 opportunities at all stages of the
 writing process from inception to
 production, through a variety of
 programming. $45/yr, $35/yr (student,
 senior). What to Submit: application.
 How To Submit: online.

## Billy Rose Theatre Division

40 Lincoln Center Plaza, Fl. 3,
New York, NY 10023
Karen Nickeson
Tel: (212) 870-1639; Fax: (212) 870-1868
theatrediv@nypl.org
www.nypl.org/research/lpa
 Research facility with historical
 and current docs of performing arts

and popular entertainment, incl. books, personal papers, scripts and promptbooks from theater, film, TV and radio. Tape archive incl. Broadway, Off-Broadway and regional productions.

**Black Theatre Network**
2609 Douglass Rd., SE, #102, Washington, DC 20020
La Tanya Rees

**BMI (Broadcast Music Inc)**
320 W. 57th St., New York, NY 10019
Tel: (212) 586-2000; Fax: (212) 262-2824
www.bmi.com
> Est. 1939. Performing rights society that collects royalties from radio, TV, web, restaurants, and other businesses that use music on behalf of songwriters, composers, and music publishers.

**Centre for Creative Communities**
118 Commercial St., London, UK
Jennifer Williams
Tel: 44-20-7247-5385
Fax: 44-20-7247-5256
info@creativecommunities.org.uk
www.creativecommunities.org.uk

**Centre for Indigenous Theatre**
401 Richmond St. W., #205, Toronto, Ontario Canada
J.L. Watson
Tel: (416) 506-9436; Fax: (416) 506-9430
citmail@indigenoustheatre.com
www.indigenoustheatre.com
> Est. 1994. The Centre for Indigenous Theatre offers training in the performing arts to students of Indigenous ancestry.

**Chicago Dramatists**
1105 W. Chicago Ave., Chicago, IL 60622
Russ Tutterow
Tel: (312) 633-0630
newplays@chicagodramatists.org
www.chicagodramatists.org
> Est. 1979. Developmental theater and playwright workshop. Programs incl. readings, productions, workshops,

panels, marketing services, and referrals to producers, etc. Classes and quarterly 10-min workshop open to all playwrights. Quarterly bulletins and website announce all events and programs. $125/year (National Associate Membership), $200/yar (Chicago Associate Membership), free (Residency). How To Submit: See "Programs" chapter of web site for full information.

**Circus Theatricals**
Hayworth Theatre Center, 2511 Wilsh, Los Angeles, CA 90057
Jeannine Stehlin
www.circustheatricals.com
> Est. 1983. Membership company of actors, directors and writers who collaborate on new and classic plays, as well as participate in a weekly studio designed to further all aspects of the art.

**Colorado Dramatists**
Box 40516, Denver, CO 80204
Melanie Tem
Tel: (303) 629-9306
www.coloradodramatists.org
> Nonprofit serving theater artists in Colo. and the Rocky Mt. region.

**Educational Theatre Association**
2343 Auburn Ave., Cincinnati, OH 45219
David LaFleche
Tel: (513) 421-3900; Fax: (513) 421-7077
dlafleche@edta.org
www.edta.org
> Fees: $75/yr, $25/yr (student). What to Submit: application, see website.

**The Field**
161 6th Ave., Fl. 14, New York, NY 10013
Michael Helland
Tel: (212) 691-6969 ext. 18
Fax: (212) 255-2053
michael@thefield.org
www.thefield.org
> Founded by artists, for artists. The Field has been dedicated to providing impactful and supportive programs to thousands of performing artists

in New York and beyond since 1986. Please visit us online for seasonal creative opportunities, including: Fieldwork: creative lab for artists to show works-in-progress and exchange feedback; the Field Artist Residency: subsidized rehearsal space with a production-related consultation, and the Emerging Artist Residency. Style: performing arts, all styles/genres: dance, music, theater, performance art, text. What To Submit: Completed application forms and program guidelines online.

**FirstStage [CA]**
Box 38280, Los Angeles, CA 90038
Dennis Safren
Tel: (323) 850-6271
firststagela@aol.com
www.firststagela.org
Work must be 30 min. or less. Est. 1983. Develops new work for stage and screen. Do not have to be a member for work to be considered. If you wish to join, dues are $75 a quarter, $250 per year. No one has to join to have their work submitted for our readings and workshops. Response Time: 6 mos. What to Submit: full script, SASE. Material Must Be: unproduced.

**The Foundation Center**
79 5th Ave., New York, NY 10003
Maggie Morth
Tel: (212) 807-2415; Fax: (212) 807-3677
www.fdncenter.org
Est. 1956. Network of centers with grant info. We do not make grants, do research, consult, make referrals, arrange intros, or write/review proposals. HQ in NY. Regional centers in Atlanta (50 Hurt Plz, #150), Cleveland (1422 Euclid Ave, #1600), DC (1627 K St, NW, 3rd Fl) San Francisco (312 Sutter St, #606).

**Fractured Atlas**
248 W. 35th St., #1202,
New York, NY 10001
Adam Natale
Tel: (212) 277-8020; Fax: (212) 277-8025

support@fracturedatlas.org
www.fracturedatlas.org
Est. 2002. Benefits incl. fiscal sponsorship, low-cost healthcare & Liability insurance, press/publicity services, online classes, calendar, forums, grants. Fees: $75/yr (individual), FREE Associate Membership for Dramatists Guild members. Opportunity/Award: Micro-Grants for creative and organizational development. Includes education and other long-term development to increase artistic ability, business capacity, and/or professional development. How To Submit: Through organization's website., Submission/Application Fee: 10.00. Deadline: June 30th and December 31st, 2010.

**Greensboro Playwrights' Forum**
200 N. Davie St., #2,
Greensboro, NC 27401
Stephen D. Hyers
Tel: (336) 335-6426; Fax: (336) 373-2659
stephen.hyers@greensboro-nc.gov
www.playwrightsforum.org
Est. 1993. Aids area dramatists in publishling, producing, and learning theater writing. Services incl. monthly meetings, workshops, staged readings, newsletter, and studio space. What to Submit: application, Submission/Application Fee: $25/yr.

**Hatch-Billops Collection**
491 Broadway, Fl. 7, New York, NY 10012
James V. Hatch
Tel: (212) 966-3231; Fax: (212) 966-3231
hatchbillops@yahoo.com
www.hatch-billopsarchive.org
Est. 1975. Collection of primary and secondary resource materials in the black cultural arts.

**Helen Hayes Awards**
2233 Wisconsin Ave., NW, #300,
Washington, DC 20007
Est. 1984.

**Hispanic Organization of Latin Actors
(HOLA)**
107 Suffolk St., #302,
New York, NY 10002
Manuel Alfaro
Tel: (212) 253-1015; Fax: (212) 253-9651
holagram@hellohola.org
www.hellohola.org

**Inside Broadway**
630 9th Ave., #802, New York, NY 10036
Michael Presser
Tel: (212) 245-0710 Fax: (212) 245-3018
mpresser@insidebroadway.org
www.insidebroadway.org
   Professional children's theater
   producing classic musicals in NYC
   public schools. Also offer hands-on,
   in-school residencies that enrich core
   curriculum through drama, dance, and
   music.

**Institute of Outdoor Drama**
1700 MLK Jr. Blvd., CB-3240,
Chapel Hill, NC 27599-3240
Rob Fox
Tel: (919) 962-1328; Fax: (919) 843-5455
outdoor@unc.edu
www.outdoordrama.unc.edu
   Public service agency of UNC at
   Chapel Hill for consultation, info,
   publicity, employment advice,
   conferences and symposia, and
   research material on every phase
   of planning and producing outdoor
   theater. What to Submit: query, SASE.

**International Theatre Institute US
Center (ITI/US)**
520 8th Ave., Fl. 24, New York, NY 10018
Emilya Cachapero
Tel: (212) 609-5900; Fax: (212) 609-5901
iti@tcg.org
www.tcg.org
   TCG is the US center of ITI, a
   UNESCO network of over 90 centers
   dedicated to cultural exchange and
   advocacy. TCG/ITI helps intl. theater
   professionals and scholars with info
   about US practice, introductions to
   US professionals, and planning visits.
   Similar help is offered to Americans

traveling and working abroad. $39.95/
year.

**International Women's Writing Guild
(IWWG)**
Box 810, Gracie Sta.,
New York, NY 10028
Hannelore Hahn
Tel: (212) 737-7536; Fax: (212) 737-9469
www.iwwg.org
   Est. 1976. Network for empowering
   women thru writing, incl. workshops/
   courses, submission tip sheet,
   bimonthly newsletter, and dental/
   vision insurance. $45/yr. What to
   Submit: application (name, address
   and phone).

**League of Chicago Theatres/League of
Chicago Theatres Foundation**
228 South Wabash #200,
Chicago, IL 60604
Tel: (312) 554-9800; Fax: (312) 922-7202
info@chicagoplays.com
www.chicagoplays.com
   Est. 1979.

**League of Professional Theatre Women**
New York, NY
Linda Chapman
Tel: (212) 414-8048; Fax: (212) 225-2378
www.theatrewomen.org
   Nonprofit advocacy organization
   promoting visibility and increasing
   opportunities for women in the
   professional theater.

**League of Washington Theatres
(LOWT)**
Box 21645, Washington, DC 20009
Nicola Daval
Tel: (202) 638-4270
   Est. 1982. Association of nonprofit
   professional theaters and related
   organizations in the greater
   Washington metropolitan area.

**Literary Managers & Dramaturgs of
the Americas (LMDA)**
P.O. Box 36.20985, P.A.C.C.,
New York, NY 10129
Danielle Carroll
Tel: (800) 680-2148

lmdanyc@gmail.com
www.lmda.org
> Est. 1985. Volunteer membership
> org w/500 members in US/Canada.
> Current programs and services
> incl. annual conference, regional
> meetings/symposia, LMDA Review
> quarterly journal, Script Exchange
> newsletter, outreach program, univ./
> advocacy caucuses, email network,
> and dramaturgy prize. Annual
> memberships is Jun-May. $60/yr,
> $25/yr (student). What to Submit:
> application. How To Submit: online.

**LA Stage Alliance**
644 S. Figueroa St.,
Los Angeles, CA 90017
Douglas Clayton
Tel: (213) 614-0556; Fax: (213) 614-0561
info@lastagealliance.com
www.lastagealliance.com
> Est. 1975. Formerly TheatreLA.
> Nonprofit service org of groups and
> individuals providing L.A. Stage
> magazine, networking opportunities,
> half-price tickets, Ovation Awards,
> cooperative ads, info and referrals.
> What to Submit: application. How To
> Submit: online.

**National Foundation for Jewish Culture**
330 Seventh Ave., Fl. 21,
New York, NY 10001
Richard A. Siegel
Tel: (212) 629-0500; Fax: (212) 629-0508
nfjc@jewishculture.org
www.jewishculture.org

**The National League of American Pen Women, Inc.**
1300 17th St. NW, Washington, DC 20036
N. Taylor Collins
Tel: (202) 785-1997
nlapw1@verizon.net
www.nlapw.org
> See website for more details. $40/yr.

**National Writers Association Foundation (NWAF)**
Box 4187, Parker, CO 80134
Sandy Whelchel
Tel: (303) 841-0246; Fax: (303) 841-2607

authorsandy@hotmail.com
www.nationalwriters.com
> Est. 1998. One $1,000 scholarship and
> one Conference scholarship which
> includes an opportunity to speak with
> four producers. Annual. Response
> Time: 4 months. Style: all styles. What
> To Submit: application, 10 pg. sample,
> SASE. Material Must Be: unoptioned,
> unpublished, unproduced. Opportunity/
> Award: $1,000. How To Submit:
> unsolicited. Deadline: Dec. 31, 2010.

**New Dramatists**
424 W. 44th St., New York, NY 10036
Emily Morse
Tel: (212) 757-6960 ext. 23
Fax: (212) 265-4738
newdramatists@newdramatists.org
www.newdramatists.org
> Est. 1949. New Dramatists is a non-
> profit center for the development of
> talented, professional playwrights.
> We support our resident playwrights
> through free, seven-year residencies,
> providing access to an array of
> programs and services, primarily
> space and time to grow as artists in
> the company of some of their most
> gifted peers. Other services include
> our Playwrights' Laboratory - i.e.
> readings, workshops and innovative
> studios for new plays and musicals;
> writing space, free copying;
> international exchanges; retreats;
> awards; temporary accommodations
> in 7th Heaven; a full-time support
> staff for casting, dramaturgical
> advocacy; and a vibrant community
> of colleagues. Response Time: 9 mos.
> What to Submit: application, 2 copies
> of full scripts, bio/resume/statement
> of interest. Deadline: between July 15
> and September 15 annually.

**New Playwrights Foundation**
608 San Vicente Blvd., #18,
Santa Monica, CA 90402
Jeffrey Bergquist
Tel: (310) 393-3682 ext. 2
dialogue@newplaywrights.org
www.newplaywrights.org

Est. 1969. Meets every other Thursday in Santa Monica. NPF has produced works for stage, film and video by NPF members. Accepts material from members only. Author Must Be: able to attend workshops in Santa Monica. Material Must Be: submitted by members of NPF. Opportunity/Award: for NPF members only. How To Submit: Become a member and participate in 3 meetings, Submission/Application Fee: $25/year. Deadline: Ongoing.

**NYC Playwrights**
509 E. 85th Street, 3FW,
New York, NY 10028
Nancy McClernan
info@nycplaywrights.org
www.nycplaywrights.org
Est. 2000. Writers and actors meet each Wed., 7-10 PM (location TBD - check web site) free and open to the public. Member writers may reserve a 30 min. slot, on a first-come, first-served basis, up to 8 wks in advance. $60/5 months local / $120/5 months worldwide. What to Submit: application, 10-pg sample.

**North Carolina Playwrights Alliance (NCPA)**
Box 10463, Raleigh, NC 27605
Adrienne Pender
adrienne.pender@rtp.ppdi.com
www.ncplaywrightsalliance.org
Est. 2001. $20/yr. What to Submit: application. Author Must Be: resident of NC. How To Submit: online.

**North Carolina Writers' Network (NCWN)**
P.O. Box 21591,
Winston-Salem, NC 27120
Ed Southern
Tel: (336) 293-8844
ed@ncwriters.org
www.ncwriters.org
Nonprofit to connect, promote and lead NC writers thru conferences, contests, newsletter, website, member pages, member book catalog, critique and

consultation, etc. (some services require addl. fees). $75/yr, $55/yr (senior), $55/yr (student). What to Submit: Membership application. How To Submit: Online at www.ncwriters.org.

**Ollantay Center for the Arts**
Box 720449,
Jackson Heights, NY 11372-0449
Pedro Monge-Rafuls
Tel: (718) 699-6772; Fax: (718) 699-6773
ollantytm@aol.com
Each season Ollantay offers playwright workshops with well-known Latin American authors and play-reading programs to help local playwrights. A literature program is dedicated exclusively to the promotion of local writers through conferences and panel discussions. Creators of Ollantay magazine, a biannual journal in English and Spanish that publishes at least one play in each issue. Ollantay Press publishes books. What to Submit: synopsis, submissions returned with SASE. Opportunity/Award: awards, possible future production, publication, reading. How To Submit: unsolicited.

**OPERA America**
330 7th Ave., Fl. 16, New York, NY 10001
Tel: (212) 796-8620; Fax: (212) 796-8631
frontdesk@operaamerica.org
www.operaamerica.org
National service org promoting creation, presentation and enjoyment of opera. Provides professional development resources for composers, librettists, educators, etc. Composers may subscribe to Opera Source job search ($45/yr, $25/yr for students). Style: National Service org for opera. What To Submit: application.

**Orange County Playwrights Alliance (OCPA)**
412 Emerald Place, Seal Beach, CA 90740
Eric Eberwein
firenbones@aol.com
www.ocplaywrights.org

Est. 1995. Member org. workshop of
Orange Co. dramatists. Develops new
works, staged readings, occasional
productions. $80/yr. What to Submit:
full script.

**Pacific Northwest Writers Assn.**
PMB 2717, 1420 NW Gilman Blvd, St 2,
Issaquah, WA 98027
Dana Murphy-Love
Tel: (425) 673-2665
pnwa@pnwa.org
www.pnwa.org
Est. 1956. $25/year students, $65/year
regular. What to Submit: application.
How To Submit: unsolicited, send
SASE in fall for application.

**Philadelphia Dramatists Center (PDC)**
P.O. 22666, Philadelphia, PA 19104
Walt Vail
dextly3@yahoo.com
www.pdcl.org
Membership org for improving the
craft, opportunities and conditions
of dramatic writers, incl. newsletter,
emails, readings, writers' circles,
workshops, free/discounted space
rental, guest speakers, reading library,
social events, resource books, and
copyright forms. Members may also
list works on PDC's website. $40/
yr, $20/yr (student). What to Submit:
application.

**Playformers**
20 Waterside Plaza, #11H,
New York, NY 10010
Debbie Silverman
Tel: (917) 825-2663
playformers@earthlink.net
Playwright Group. Est. 1987. Monthy
meetings (Sep-May) to read new work
by members. $25/quarter (covering
refreshments for actors and guests).
Response Time: 2 mos. What to
Submit: full script, SASE.

**The Playwrights Center San Francisco
(PCSF)**
131 10th St. Fl. 3,
San Francisco, CA 94113

Laylah Muran
Tel: (415) 626-0453 ext. 119
www.playwrightscentersf.org
Est. 1980. Organization of
playwrights, directors and actors
developing Bay Area writing,
audience development and related arts.
Weekly events incl. staged readings,
scene workshops, classes and panel
discussions. Author provides scripts
for actors. No submission process
for scene nights. $60/yr (full), $30/yr
(student): semiannual for staged and
developmental readings. Response
Time: 3 mos. What to Submit:
application. Author Must Be: resident
of Bay Area.

**The Playwrights' Center**
2301 Franklin Ave. E.,
Minneapolis, MN 55406
Anna Peterson
Tel: (612) 332-7481; Fax: (612) 332-6037
info@pwcenter.org
www.pwcenter.org
Provides services that support
playwrights and playwriting. Programs
incl. listed submission opportunities,
fellowships, workshops, readings,
classes, and online member-to-
member networking services. Fees:
$50/yr. What to Submit: application.
How To Submit: online.

**Playwrights' Forum [MD]**
Box 5322, Rockville, MD 20848
Ernie Joselovitz
Tel: (301) 816-0569
pforum7@yahoo.com
www.playwrightsforum.org
Deadlines: 1/15/2010, 5/15/2010,
9/15/2010. 1991. Tiered options:
Forum 2 professional member; Forum
1 apprentice member; Associate
member.: $120/session (4 mos). What
to Submit: application. Author Must
Be: resident of Mid-Atlantic. How To
Submit: online, regular mail.

**Playwrights Guild of Canada (PGC)**
215 Spadina Ave. Suite 210,
Toronto, Ontario M5T-2C7 Canada

Kevin Gojmerac
Tel: (416) 703-0201; Fax: (416) 703-0059
info@playwrightsguild.ca
www.playwrightsguild.ca
>Est. 1972. Formerly Playwrights Union
of Canada. National nonprofit offering
triannual directory of Canadian plays/
playwrights, contract negotiation
with PACT, amateur/professional
production administration, and
quarterly magazine. $155/yr (full),
$75/yr (assoc), $65/yr (senior 65+).
Response Time: 3 wks. What to
Submit: application, resume. Author
Must Be: citizen or landed immigrant
of Canada.

**Playwrights Theatre of New Jersey**
Box 1295, Madison, NJ 7940
John Pietrowski
Tel: (973) 514-1787; Fax: (973) 514-2060
www.ptnj.org
>Est. 1986. Cast of up to 8, unit set, no
fly space. Response Time: 8 months
letter, 1 year script. Style: comedy,
drama. What To Submit: query,
synopsis, 10-pg sample, development
26 production history, bio.

**The Purple Circuit**
921 N. Naomi St., Burbank, CA 91505
Bill Kaiser
Tel: (818) 953-5096
purplecir@aol.com
www.buddybuddy.com/pc.html
>Service group to promote GLBT
performing arts worldwide. Maintains
Calif. show listings hotline (818-953-
5072), directory of GLBT-friendly
venues, and freelisting of playwrights.
How To Submit: email.

**Rodgers & Hammerstein Theatre
Library**
229 W. 28th St, Fl. 11,
New York, NY 10001

**Rodgers & Hammerstein Theatricals**
229 W. 28th St., Fl. 11,
New York, NY 10001
Tel: (800) 400-8160; Fax: (212) 268-1245
editor@rnh.com
www.rnhtheatricals.com

**Saskatchewan Writers Guild (SWG)**
Box 3986, Regina, SK Canada
Laura Malhiot
Tel: (306) 757-6310
info@skwriter.com
www.skwriter.com
>Est. 1969. Membership is open to
all writers, teachers, librarians,
publishers, booksellers, students, and
others interested in Saskatchewan
writing. $75/yr (regular), $55/yr
(student, senior). Opportunity/Award:
John V. Hicks MS Awards, Short
Manuscript Awards. How To Submit:
See skwriter.com for complete details,
Submission/Application Fee: Hicks
$25; Short MS - free for members, $10
non members. Deadline: Last working
day of June annually.

**Shubert Archives**
149 W. 45th St., New York, NY 10036
Mary Ann Church
Tel: (212) 944-3895; Fax: (212) 944-4139
www.shubertarchive.org
>Est. 1976. Repository for over 6m
docs related to the Shubert brothers
and Shubert Org, incl. costume/set
designs, scripts, music, publicity,
photos, letters, business records, and
architectural plans.

**The Songwriters Guild of America
Foundation (SGAF)**
1560 Broadway, #1306,
New York, NY 10036
Mark Saxon
Tel: (212) 768-7902
ny@songwritersguild.com
www.songwritersguild.com
>Est. 1931. $60/yr (gold), $84/yr
(platinum), $108/yr (diamond).

**StageSource**
88 Tremont St., #714, Boston, MA 02108
Jeremy Johnson
Tel: (617) 720-6066; Fax: (617) 720-4275
info@stagesource.org
www.stagesource.org
>Est. 1985. Alliance of artists and
organizations in New England.
Benefits incl. e-newsletters, group
health insurance, professional

development seminars, job expo, free/ discount tickets, talent bank, and networking events.: $115 (initial), $65/ yr (renewal).

## Theatre Communications Group (TCG)
520 8th Ave., Fl. 24, New York, NY 10018
Teresa Eyring
Tel: (212) 609-5900; Fax: (212) 609-5901
tcg@tcg.org
www.tcg.org
> National service org for nonprofit US professional theater. Services incl. grants, fellowships and awards to artists and institutions; workshops, roundtables and conferences; advocacy; surveys, research and publications, incl. reference, plays and periodicals; US Center for Intl. Theatre Institute. Membership incl. American Theatre magazine subscription, ticket discounts nationwide, savings on TCG resource materials and book discounts from TCG and other select publishers. $39.95/yr, $20/yr (student) How To Submit: online.

## Theatre Bay Area (TBA)
870 Market St., #375,
San Francisco, CA 94102
Brad Erickson
Tel: (415) 430-1140; Fax: (415) 430-1145
tba@theatrebayarea.org
www.theatrebayarea.org
> Nonprofit of Bay Area individuals and theater companies. Services incl. monthly Theatre Bay Area magazine with listing of writer opportunities, grants of $2,500–$5,000 for artists and $10,000 new works fund. Other publications incl. regional theater directory. $70/yr, $60/yr (student). What to Submit: application. Author Must Be: resident of Bay Area.

## Theatre Development Fund (TDF)
520 8th Ave. #801, New York, NY 10018
Tel: (212) 221-0885; Fax: (212) 768-1563
info@tdf.org
www.tdf.org

> Est. 1968. To identify and provide support, including financial assistance, to theatrical works of artistic merit, and to encourage and enable diverse audiences to attend live theatre and dance in all their venues.incl. TKTS discount booths, TDF membership, Theater Access Project (TAP), Costume Collection. $30/yr. What to Submit: application. How To Submit: online.

## Theater Instituut Nederland (TIN)
Box 19304, Amsterdam, Netherlands
Henk Scholten
info@tin.nl
www.tin.nl
> Est. 1992. Houses a museum and library, collects current info and documentation and organizes events such as discussions, conferences, workshops, exhibitions and international presentations. It also publishes books, CDs and other materials and participates in various international networks.

## Theatre Project
45 W. Preston St., Baltimore, MD 21201
Anne Cantler Fulwiler
Tel: (410) 539-3091
office@theatreproject.org
www.theatreproject.org
> Est. 1971. Introduces Baltimore to those experimenting with new forms, incl. both globally recognized and emerging local artists. Small cast, unit set. Response Time: 2 mos. Style: avant garde. What To Submit: synopsis, video, SASE. Material Must Be: original. Opportunity/Award: box office percentage. How To Submit: professional recommendation.

## Theatre for Young Audiences/ USA
Emerald City Theatre Admin. Offices,
2936 N. Southport Ave, 3rd Floor,
Chicago, IL 60657
Caitlin Hansen
Tel: (703) 403-5820; Fax: (773) 529-2693
info@tyausa.org
www.tyausa.org

National service org promoting professional TYA across cultural and international boundaries. Services incl TYA Today subscriptions and frequent bulletins, member directories. American branch of ASSITEJ International. $75/yr, $40/yr (retiree), $35/yr (student) Organizational fees vary. What to Submit: Membership application. Opportunity/Award: Ann Shaw Fellowship, check website for details.

### TRU (Theater Resources Unlimited)
115 MacDougal Street,
New York, NY 10012
Bob Ost
Tel: (212) 714-7628; Fax: (212) 864-6301
trunltd@aol.com
www.truonline.org
> Est. 1992. Support and educational services for producers, theater companies, and self-producing artists, emphasizing the business side of the arts. $60/yr (individual). What to Submit: application, 2 copies each production history, synopsis, script and CD of at least 6 songs. How To Submit: please see guidelines and application at www.truonline.org. Deadline: Jan. 15, 2010 (plays), Aug. 31, 2010 (musicals).

### United States Copyright Office
101 Independence Ave., SE,
Washington, DC 20003
Tel: (202) 707-3000
www.copyright.gov
> Though registration isn't required for protection, copyright law provides several advantages to registration.: $45 (basic claim). What to Submit: application, full script (2 copies), audio (2 copies).

### V&A Theatre and Performance Department
23 Blythe Road, Blythe House,
London, UK W14 0QX
tmenquiries@vam.ac.uk
www.vam.ac.uk

### WomenArts
3739 Balboa St. #181,
San Francisco, CA 94121
Martha Richards
Tel: (415) 751-2202; Fax: (650) 244-9136
info@womenarts.org
www.womenarts.org
> Founded to ensure women have full access to the resources they need, by challenging stereotypes and increasing opportunities.

### Women's Theatre Alliance (WTA)
2936 N. Southport Ave., Chicago, IL 60657
Brenda E. Kelly
Tel: (312) 408-9910
wtachicago@gmail.com
www.wtachicago.org
> Est. 1992. $25/yr (Jan-Dec).

### Writers Guild of America, East (WGAE)
555 W. 57th St., #1230,
New York, NY 10019
www.wgae.org
> Est. 1954.

### Writers Guild of America, East (WGAE)
555 W. 57th St., New York, NY 10019
Adrine Stephens-Gordon
Tel: (212) 767-7800
www.wgaeast.org

### Writers Guild of America, West (WGAW)
7000 W. 3rd St., Los Angeles, CA 90048
Corinne Tippin
Tel: (323) 782-4532
www.wga.org

### Writers' Guild of Great Britain
40 Rosebery Avenue,
London, UK EC1R 4RX
Anne Hogben
Tel: (420)-783-3077; Fax: (420)-783-3477
anne@writersguild.org.uk
www.writersguild.org.uk
> TUC-affiliated union for professional writers living or working in UK. £100 yr (candidate), £180/yr (full).

**The Writers Room**
740 Broadway, Fl. 12,
New York, NY 10003
Donna Brodie
Tel: (212) 254-6995
writersroom@writersroom.org
www.writersroom.org
Est. 1978. Large loft with 44 work
stations, library, storage area, kitchen/
lounge and phone room. Open 24/7. 1
month list for full-time membership;
no wait list for part-time. $75
application, $450/6 mos. (6pm-6am),
$550/6 mos. (6pm-11:30am), $650/6
mos. (27/7). See website for full
submission application details. What
to Submit: application. Opportunity/
Award: Reading series.

**Young Playwrights Inc. (YPI)**
P.O. Box 5134, New York, NY 10185
Sheri Goldhirsch
Tel: (212) 594-5440; Fax: (212) 684-4902
admin@youngplaywrights.org
www.youngplaywrights.org
Est. 1981 by Stephen Sondheim and
Dramatists Guild members, YPI
identifies and develops young US
playwrights by involving them as
active participants in the highest
quality professional productions
of their plays. Style: All except
musicals or adaptations. Submissions
not returned. Author Must Be: age
18 or younger. Material Must Be:
original. Opportunity/Award: Winning
playwrights receive a trip to New
York City to participate in the Young
Playwrights Conference and an off-
Broadway staged reading of their
work. How To Submit: Check Website
for details. Deadline: Jan. 2, 2009.

# Special Interests

## TEN-MINUTE AND SHORT PLAY OPPORTUNITIES

Because of the popularity of the ten-minute play, we thought it might serve a lot of you to list those opportunities that are particular for short plays and ten-minute plays. *If the submission is in italics, review dates and submission procedures on the website of the sponsoring organization; at press time, we weren't able to verify the information posted.*

### General Sites

http://www.burryman.com/submissions.html#sub
http://www.aact.org/cgi-bin/webdata_contests.pl?cgifunction=Search
http://enavantplaywrights.yuku.com/forums/3/t/Opportunities-10-Minute-amp-Other-Short-Plays.html

### Publishers Of Ten-Minute Plays

**Brooklyn Publishers** - www.brookpub.com please send a query letter and sample pages either via email to submissions@brookpub.com (preferred) or via postal mail to: Brooklyn Publishers, Attn: Editor, 1841 Cord St., Odessa, TX 79762. Please provide a brief description of the play, cast size and gender breakdown, running time, and any production history or awards. As a writing sample, feel free to attach the first 10 pages of the play (5 pages for plays with running times of 10 minutes or less) in PDF or Microsoft Word format.

**Big Dog Plays** - www.bigdogplays.com "We publish short plays (under 30 minutes) only as collections. Therefore, the playwright should send several short plays together as one submission. We prefer produced works. We need to see the entire script. Also, we like playwrights to include a cover letter, production history, all music for musicals (CD and score), and a SASE. We don't accept email submissions. Response time is 2-3 months."

**Meriweather** – a query letter is suggested, but ten-minute plays should be appropriate for the school or church market and most should be in a collection of plays. Production tested plays are encouraged. Editor, Contemporary Drama Service, 885 Elkton Drive, Colorado Springs, CO 80907. Or e-mail query letters (no attachments) to: editor@meriwether.com www.meriwetherpublishing.com/school.aspx

**NewPlays -** All plays to be considered for publication must have been successfully produced for their intended audience, directed by someone other than the author. A simple cover letter with a production history, and perhaps a program or review, is appropriate. Multiple submissions are acceptable; and should be so noted in your cover letter. Patricia Whitton Forrest, Editor and Publisher, NEW PLAYS INCORPORATED, Box 5074, Charlottesville, VA 22905.

**Pioneer Drama Service** - www.pioneerdrama.com/playwrights/submit.asp - A query letter or email is suggested: http://www.pioneerdrama.com//contactus.asp?ID=5 . Plays must be accompanied by a Synopsis/Description, Cast List and Breakdown (i.e. 5M, 6W), Running Time, Set Design, Prop List, Recording of Music (when applicable). All plays received will be considered for publication and will usually be accepted or rejected within four months. Send submissions to: Editor Pioneer Drama Service, Post Office Box 4267, Englewood, CO 80155-4267

## CALENDAR LISTINGS

### JANUARY

**Inspirato Festival, Toronto Ten Minute Play Festival**
Inspirato Festival
www.inspiratofestival.ca
http://www.inspiratofestival.ca/write-a-play.php
> **Consideration.** Remuneration: $100, production. **Preference.** Length: 10 minutes. Content/Subject Matter: Sense of touch must be an important element in the play (see website). **Application.** See website for online submission. **Deadline:** January 2 (midnight).

### FEBRUARY

*Premiere One-Act Competition*
*Moving Arts*
*www.movingarts.org/submission_guidelines.html*
> *Consideration. $10 entry fee\* per script (made out to Moving Arts). Remuneration: $200. Preferences: One-Acts, unproduced in L.A. Application. Submit script, cover letter, SASE to Moving Arts, Premiere One-Act Competition, P.O. BOX 481145, Los Angeles, CA 90048. Playwright's name should appear only on the cover letter and nowhere on the script. Scripts must be three-hole punched, preferably with a cover-- please do not send loose sheets or spiral bound scripts. Deadline: February 1).*

**10-minute Play Festival**
Heartland Theatre Company
P. O. Box 1833, Bloomington, IL 61702
309.452.8709
www.heartlandtheatre.org
> playfest@heartlandtheatre.org
> **Consideration.** Production. **Preference.** Length: 10-Minute. No 10-minute monologues accepted. **Content/Subject Matter:** Theme. Inns & Outs: The Hotel Lobby (see website). **Material Must Be**: unproduced. **Application.** Submit play by e-mail or a hard copy to Heartland Theatre Company, P. O. Box 1833, Bloomington, IL 61702, (Attention: Play Fest 2008) and see online entry form at: www. heartlandtheatre.org/tenminute_rules.html.**Deadline:** February 1, 2010.

**Theatre Oxford 10-Minute Play Contest**
Theatre Oxford
10 Minute Play Contest
P. O. Box 1321, Oxford, MS 38655
Dinah Swan, Contest Director: 662-236-5052
www.10minuteplays.com
> **Consideration:** production, contest. **Fees:** $10 made out to Theatre Oxford. **Remuneration:** $1000 prize. **Preference.** Length: max 10 pages. Material Must

Be: unproduced. **Application.** Assemble script as follows: Optional cover letter; a title page with the play's title, author's name, address, phone number, and email address. (This is the only place the author's name should appear.) The second page should contain a cast of characters list and time and place information. The third page will be the first page of the script. The other pages of the play follow. Name of play and page numbers on every page. Do NOT use binders or folders of any kind. Plays cannot be returned. Enclose a SASP if you want assurance that your play was received. Submit to: Theatre Oxford 10 Minute Play Contest, P. O. Box 1321, Oxford, MS 38655. **Deadline:** February 16, postmarked.

## 10 by 10 in the Triangle
The Arts Center
300-G East Main St., Carrboro, NC 27510
(919) 929-2787
www.artscenterlive.org
infor@artscenterlive.org

> **Remuneration:** $100 plus travel stipend. **Preference.** 10-minute plays. No 10-minute monologues. Musicals accepted. **Application.** For each play, send two separate emails to theatre@artscenterlive.org. The first e-mail regards playwright contact information, and the second regards contents of the play. **E-mail 1** – the subject line and the attached file retain the same name, which is the title of the play followed by the phrase "contact info." For example, if the name of the play is *Poker Face*, the subject line and attached file would read "Poker Face contact info". The attached file only contains the title page with contact information. Please use the full title of the play as numerous plays with similar titles are often received. **Email 2** – the subject line and the attached file retain the same name, which is the title of the play. For example, the subject line of this email is Poker Face and the attached file is Poker Face. This file contains cast, set requirements, and script. No contact information, please. If you are submitting two scripts, please send four separate emails. Please do not zip the files. **Submission period:** January 8-February 15.

## MARCH

## 10-Minute International Play Competition
Fire Rose Productions
11246 Magnolia Blvd., NoHo Theatre & Arts District, CA 91601
(818) 766-3691
www.fireroseproductions.com
info@fireroseproductions.com

> **Consideration.** Fees: $5 each play. **Remuneration:** production, $200. Youth Award: $100 gift certificate. **Preference.** Length: 8-12 minutes. **Application.** Submit unbound play, fee, and application form (see website) to 10-Minute Play Competition, Fire Rose Productions, 11246 Magnolia Blvd., NoHo Theatre & Arts District, CA 91601. **Deadline:** March 30, postmarked

## *Ten-Minute Play Contest*
*Princeton University Ten-Minute Play Contest*
*Theater and Dance Program*
*185 Nassau St., Princeton University, Princeton NJ 08544*
*(609) 258-8562*
*http://www.princeton.edu/arts/lewis_center/high-school-contests/ten-minute-play-contest/*

*Consideration: Juniors in high school only. **Remuneration:** First Prize: $500.00; Second Prize: $250.00; Third Prize: $100.00. **Preference.** Length: 10-Minute. Author Must Be: Any student who is in the eleventh grade. **Application.** Submit one copy of play, include name, address, and phone number on submission and online form. Submit to: Princeton Ten-Minute Play Contest, Theater and Dance Program, 185 Nassau Street, Princeton University, Princeton NJ 08544. **Deadline:** March 1, postmarked.*

### Estrogenius Short Play Showcase
EstroGenius/Manhattan Theatre Source
177 MacDougal St., New York, NY 10011
(212) 260-4698
www.estrogenius.org
estrogenius.festival@gmail.com

**Preferences.** Only new short plays about women, no monologues. Female writer preferred but not required. Length: 10-15 minutes. Simple production values. **Application:** see website for "cover sheet." Submit play, completed cover sheet, and character breakdown to Manhattan Theatre Source, Attn: ESTROGENIUS SHORT PLAY SHOWCASE - play selection, 177 MacDougal Street, NY, NY 10011. **Deadline:** March 2, postmarked.

### *Festival of Originals*
*Theatre Southwest*
*944 Clarkcrest, Houston, Texas 77063*
*www.theatresouthwest.org*
*http://www.theatresouthwest.org/foorules.html*

*Consideration. Remuneration: production, $100. **Preference.** No Monologues. Length: 20 minutes. Material Must Be: unproduced. **Application.** Submit script, fee, plot summary to Theatre Southwest, 944 Clarkcrest, Houston, Texas 77063,Attention: Festival Submissions; or email mimi@theatresouthwest.org. **Deadline:** March 15.*

### *Salute UR Shorts New Play Festival*
*Rapscallion Theatre Collective*
*2064 46th St 2nd Floor, Astoria, NY 11105*
*www.rapscalliontheatrecollective.com*
*rapscalliontheatre@gmail.com*

***Consideration:** production. **Preference.** Length: 10-15 minutes*
*Application. Submit play to rapscalliontheatre@gmail.com (preferred method), or mail to Reynold Malcolm Hewitt, Rapscallion Theatre Collective, 2064 46th St 2nd Floor, Astoria, NY 11105. **Deadline:** March 25.*

## APRIL

### *Moments of Play: A Festival of One-Acts*
*Salem Theatre Company*
*Catherine Bertrand*
*978-790-8546*
*info@salemtheatre.com*
*salemtheatre.com*

*Consideration. Remuneration: production only. Preference. Length: not be longer than 10 minutes. Minimal scene set up. Application. Submit the play, brief synopsis not exceeding one page, and character breakdown to: info@salemtheatre.com; or mail to P.O. Box 306, Salem, MA 01970. Deadline: April 2*

## MAY

**The Seven: New Works Fest**
FUSION Theatre
700 1st St. NW, Albuquerque, NM 87102
jeng@fusionabq.org
www.fusionabq.org/theseven.htm
>    **Consideration:** production, award. Fees: $5. Disclosure: offset printing costs, Remuneration: jury prize. **Preference.** Length: 10 pages or less, Content/Subject Matter: see website. **Material Must Be:** unproduced, not previously submitted. **Application.** Play with title page and contact info, fee with e-submission at: http:// thecell.fatcow.com/store/page6.html, or mail to: FUSION Theatre Co., Attn: Jen Grigg, 700 1st Street NW, Albuquerque, New Mexico 87102. **Deadline:** May 1. Theme announced in February; check website.

*New Rocky Mountain Voices Competition*
*The Westcliffe Center for the Performing Arts*
*Steve Miller, New Rocky Mountain Voices Program Coordinator*
*(719) 783-9344*
*smiller012@centurytel.net*
*www.jonestheater.com/NRMV-2008.htm*
>    *Consideration. Fees: $5.00 for each play submitted (check out to "WCPA"). Preference. Length: not exceed 30 minutes. 6 or fewer actors. Author Must Be: currently residing in or attending an educational institution in Arizona, Colorado, or New Mexico.. Material Must Be: unpublished. Application. Send four copies of the manuscript with no mention of the author's name or contact information anywhere in the manuscript, Fee, Cover letter to include a summary of the author's theater and playwriting experience and goals, mailing address, email address, telephone number and other pertinent contact information. Send to: New Rocky Mountain Voices, C/O Custer County Library, PO Box 689, Westcliffe, CO, 81252 (for United States Postal Service); or New Rocky Mountain Voices, C/O Custer County Library, 209 Main Street, Westcliffe, CO, 81252 ( for UPS or FEDEX). Deadline: May 1, postmarked.*

## JUNE

**The Actors' Theatre 15th Annual Ten-Minute Play Contest**
The Actors' Theatre
1001 Center St., Suite 12, Santa Cruz, CA 95060
(831) 425-1003
www.actorssc.org
www.actorssc.org/contests.php#810s
>    **Consideration.** Fees: $10 per play. **Preference.** Length: 10 pages maximum. Minimal set requirements. Material Must Be: unproduced, unpublished. **Application.** Submit 5 copies of your play (securely bound, preferably in a soft

cover). Two types of cover pages: 1) a separate cover letter, which includes your name, address, phone number, e-mail and the play title. 2) the play title on each copy. No identifying information on the script other than the title. Submission: mail five hard copies (see address above) to TEN-MINUTE PLAY CONTEST. **Deadline:** June 1.

## JULY

### Future 10
Future Tenant
Stacey Vespaziani
Future 10 Play Submissions
3251 Pinehurst Ave., Pittsburgh, PA 15216
svespaz@mac.com
www.futuretenant.org

> Consideration. Production. Preference. Length: approx 10 pages. Theme: "Life in Pittsburgh." Production: Cast size 2-6, limited set/prop requirements. Application. Submit four copies of play, plus a cover letter with all contact info and title of play. No contact info or name should be on submitted scripts. **Deadline:** July 15

## AUGUST

### *Pick of the Vine*
*Little Fish Theatre*
*www.littlefishtheatre.org*

> **Preference.** *Minimal set requirements, 6 or fewer characters.* **Application.** *Email script with contact info to melanie@littlefishtheatre.org or mail hard copy to: Melanie Jones , Little Fish Theatre, 619 West 38th St, San Pedro CA 90731. http:// www.littlefishtheatre.org/scripts.html*

## SEPTEMBER

### *One Act Play Festival*
*Circus Theatricals*
*info@circustheatricals.com*
*310 226-6144 ext. 1*
*www.circustheatricals.com/playwrights.html*
*www.circustheatricals.com*

> **Preference.** *Length: 15 pages or less, simple production value.* **Application.** *Submit three copies of full script, typed and securely bound. No contact info on script/ separate title page with contact info. Short bio. Previous productions must not have been in L.A. or Southern CA. Submit to: Circus Theatricals, Attn: One Act Plays Festival 2008, PO Box 586, Culver City , CA 90232.* **Deadline:** *September 1.*

### Festival of One-Act Plays
Theatre Three
P.O. Box 512, Port Jefferson, NY 11777-0512
(631) 928-9202
www.theatrethree.com
www.theatrethree.com/oneactsubmissionguidelines.htm

**Consideration.** Remuneration: small stipend, production. **Preference.** Length: 40 minutes maximum. Simple set, 8 actors or less. Material Must Be: unproduced, no adaptations, musicals, or children's plays. **Application.** Submit a cover letter, a synopsis, and a resume along with one copy of the play. Cover sheet of play should have title, author, author's address, author's telephone number, and author's email address (if available). Plays should be neatly bound or stapled on the left-hand corner. (No loose pages and no binders, please.) All submissions must include a standard SASE for correspondence. Submit to The 13th Annual Festival of One-Act Plays, Attn: Jeffrey Sanzel, Artistic Director, THEATRE THREE, P.O. Box 512, Port Jefferson, NY 11777-0512. **Deadline:** September 30 (postmark).

## OCTOBER

*Kansas City Women's Playwriting Festival*
*Potluck Productions*
*7338 Belleview, Kansas City, MO 64114*
*www.kcpotluckproductions.com*
   *Consideration. Remuneration: production. Preference. Length: 10-20 minutes. Author Must Be: female. Material Must Be: unpublished. Application. Send two (2) paper copies of your script (bound), a show synopsis, resume, and cover letter. Enclose two (2) SASE envelopes or postcards. Submit to: Potluck Productions, 7338 Belleview, Kansas City, MO 64114. Deadline: Oct. 15.*

**ShowOff! Camino Real International Playwriting Festival**
Camino Real Playhouse
ShowOff!
Camino Real Playhouse
31776 El Camino Real, San Juan Capistrano, CA 92675
info@city-theater.org; pantheater@comcast.net
www.caminorealplayhouse.org/ShowOffs.html
   **Consideration:** Contest, production. Fees: A $10.00 per play. Disclosure: for use as winner stipends. Remuneration: not specified. **Preference.** Length: 10 minutes. Comedy or drama. **Application.** Submit plays unbound (stapled is OK) with your full contact info on the cover or title page to: ShowOff!, Camino Real Playhouse, 31776 El Camino Real, San Juan Capistrano, CA 92675. **Deadline:** October 15.

**Queer Shorts**
StageQ
Queer Shorts, c/o StageQ, PO Box 8876, Madison, WI 53708-8876
www.stageq.com
   **Preference.** Length: 5-15 minutes. Content/Subject Matter: queer lifestyle.
   **Application.** Email play, paragraph synopsis, production requirements, cast breakdown, and if there are any queer characters, or nudity to QueerShorts@stageq. com, or mail to: Queer Shorts, c/o StageQ, PO Box 8876, Madison, WI. 53708-8876. **Deadline:** October 30, received by. check website for details

### National Ten-Minute Play Contest
Actors Theatre of Louisville
www.actorstheatre.org
www.actorstheatre.org/humana_contest.htm
> **Consideration.** Remuneration: $1000, production. **Preference.** Length: 10 pages
> or less. Author Must Be: US citizen. Material Must Be: unproduced, not previously
> submitted. **Application.** Submit play with contact info to: National Ten-Minute Play
> Contest, Actors Theatre of Louisville, 316 West Main Street, Louisville, KY 40202-
> 4218. **Deadline:** November 1, check website for details.

### Snowdance 10 Minute Comedy Festival
Over Our Head Players
SNOWDANC
c/o Sixth Street Theatre, 318 6th St., Racine, WI 53403
www.overourheadplayers.org
> **Consideration.** production, prize. Remuneration: A cash award of $300.00, $100.00
> to second and third place. **Preference.** Length: 10 minutes. Content/Subject Matter:
> comedy. Material Must Be: unpublished. **Application.** Submit play with contact
> info to SNOWDANCE, c/o Sixth Street Theatre, 318 6th St.,Racine, WI, 53403.
> **Deadline:** November 1, check website for details.

### Ten-Minute Play Contest
Lakeshore Players
Outreach Committee
4820 Stewart Ave., White Bear Lake, MN  55110
www.lakeshoreplayers.com
> **Consideration.** Remuneration: production, $10 per performance. **Preference.**
> Length: 10 minutes. High school students also encouraged to submit. Production:
> 5 or fewer characters **Application.** Submit two copies of script (One with contact
> information, one with title only)to: Lakeshore Players Outreach Committee, 4820
> Stewart Ave. White Bear Lake, MN  55110. **Deadline:** November 11, received by.
> Check website for details

### Source Festival
1835 14th St., NW, Washington, DC 20009
(202) 315-1305
www.sourcedc.org
> **Consideration.** Remuneration: production. **Preference.** Length: 10 minutes.
> Material Must Be: unpublished. **Application.** Submit play online at theatre's website.
> Include contact info on title page and submission form found on website. Plays
> only accepted in following formats: .doc, .pdf, or .rtf. All pages must have number
> and include title of play and name of playwright. One submission per applicant.
> **Deadline:** November 13, midnight. Check website for details.

### EATfest
EATheatre, Emerging Artists Theatre
464 W. 25th St. #4, New York, NY 10001-6501
(212) 247-2429
EATheatre.org
EATheatre.org/submissions.php

**Consideration.** Remuneration: production. **Preferences.** No monologues. **Length:** 10 to 50 minutes. **Material Must Be:** unproduced in NYC, unpublished. **Application.** Submit online via website (preferred), or send play to Emerging Artists Theatre, Attention: Playwrights Manager, 464 W. 25th St. #4, New York, NY 10001-6501. Include play and a letter including your name, telephone number, address and e-mail address. **Deadline:** November 30.

## DECEMBER

### IN10 National Play Competition
*UMBC Department of Theatre*
*1000 Hilltop Circle, Baltimore, MD 21250*
*www.umbc.edu/theatre/In10.html*

> **Consideration.** *Remuneration: $1,000 prize and a staged reading.* **Preference.** *Length: 10 minutes. Content/Subject Matter: Mostly female cast ages 16-35. Male characters permitted, but major characters should be female. No monologues.* **Application:** *See website. Submit play and application to: Professor Susan McCully, 10-Minute Play Competition, UMBC Department of Theatre, 1000 Hilltop Circle, Baltimore, MD 21250.* **Deadline:** *December 1.*

### 6 Women Play Festival
c/o Pikes Peak Arts Council
PO Box 1073. Colorado Springs, CO 80901
www.sixwomenplayfestival.com
www.sixwomenplayfestival.com/guidelines.html

> **Remuneration:** $100.00 and a travel stipend to attend the festival. **Preference**. Length: 10 pages. Content/Subject Matter: See website for theme. Author Must Be: female. Material Must Be: unpublished, unproduced. **Application:** Submit three copies of play (bound with staple only) with title only. Include one unbound sheet which includes title of play, author's name and address, email, and phone number. **Submission period:** July 1-October 31 (postmarked by).

## ROLLING DEADLINE

### Annual Jersey Voices Festival
Chatham Playhouse
23 North Passaic Ave., Chatham, NJ 07928
(973) 635-7363
chathamplayers.org/jerseyvoices.html
jerseyvoices@chathamplayers.org

> **Preference**. Length: 20 minute or less. Musicals accepted. Author Must Be: New Jersey playwright. **Application.** Submit play to Jersey Voices c/o CCP, P.O. Box 234, Chatham, NJ 07928 or email (in Word of PDF format) to jerseyvoices@ chathamplayers.org. **Deadline:** rolling

**Chester Horn Short Play Festival**
TheatreRats
www.theatrerats.com
> **Consideration.** Remuneration: production. **Preference.** Length: no more than 15 pages. Any style/genre accepted. **Application.** Submit script (PDF or Word) to scripts@theatrerats.com. **Deadline:** rolling.

**Quickies - the annual festival of shorts**
Live Girls! Theater
www.livegirlstheater.org
> **Consideration:** production or reading. **Preferences.** Small cast and low production requirements. Length: 10-minute. Author Must Be: Female. **Application.** Email plays and include your bio\resume, production history for plays submitted to: submissions@livegirlstheater.org. Attach plays as Word docs. **Deadline:** ongoing.

## OPPORTUNITIES FOR PEOPLE OF COLOR

### AFRICAN AMERICAN

**African American Children's Theatre**
Milwaukee Youth Arts Center
325 West Walnut Street, Milwaukee WI 53212
Tel: 414 461 5771; Fax: 414 461 5771
Constance Clark, Founder
www.aact.us americanplays@aol.com
> Youth theater, primarily musicals. For submissions information, contact the theater directly. Call before faxing.

**African American Drama Company**
The Plaza of San Jose
30 E. Julian #218, SJ, CA 95112-4076
Tel: (408) 216 9877; VM: (415) 378-0064
www.africanamericandramacompany.org
DRAMART@comcast.net
> Dedicated exclusively to African-American history. For submission, contact theater directly.

**African American Theater Program**
Department of Theatre Arts
University of Louisville, Louisville, KY 40292
Tel: 502-852-8442
Dr. Lundeana Thomas, Director
> Accepts full-length plays for mainstage productions. For submission information, contact theater directly.

**African American Performing Arts Community Theater**
(AAPACT)
P.O. Box 472451 Miami, FL 33247
Teddy Harrel, Jr., Founder, Board Chair
www.aapact.com
aapact@yahoo.com

**African –American Shakespeare Company**
762 Fulton Street, Suite 306, San Francisco, CA  94102
Tel: (415) 762-2071
Victoria Irvil, Artistic Director
www.african-americanshakes.org
> Register on website for opportunities newsletter.

**African Continuum Theatre Company**
3523 12th Street, NE, 2nd Floor, Washington, DC 20017
Benny Sato Ambush, Acting Artistic Director
Tel: 202-529-5763; Fax: 202-529-5764
info@africancontinuumtheatre.com
www.africancontinuumtheatre.com
> Est. 1996. **Preference.** Fresh Flavas Reading Series: staged readings of three-works-in-progress per year.

**AfroSolo Theatre Company**
762 Fulton Street, Suite 307, San Francisco, CA 94102
www.afrosolo.org; afrosolo@afrosolo.org
Thomas R. Simpson, Artistic Director
Tel: 415-771-2376; Fax: 415-771-2312
   **Preference.** Solo work only, usually to be performed by the writer. Send up to 10pg
   synopsis, bio and photo.

**American Negro Playwrights Theatre**
Tennessee State University's Professional Theater-in-Residence
P.O. Box 24976, Nashville TN 37202
Tel: 615-403-5635; Fax: 615-862-6731
www.myspace.com/anpt
wbscott@tnstate.edu
Barry Scott, Producing Artistic Director
   New Play Series. For submissions information, contact the theater directly.

**Arena Players**
801 McCulloh Street
Baltimore, MD 21201
Tel: 410-728-6500
Donald Owens, Artistic Director

**Bay Area Repertory Theater**
Malonga Casquelourd Center for The Arts
1428 Alice Street, Suite #306 Oakland, CA 94612-4082
Tel: (510) 464-3086
info@bayarearep.org or valerie.allums@bayarearep.org;
www.bayart.us

**b current**
601 Christie St., Suite 251
Toronto, ON, Canada M6G 4C7
Tel: 416.533.1500; Fax: 416.533.1560
www.bcurent.ca; info@bcurrent.ca
   Toronto-based arts company based that presents and support performance works
   emerging from the Canadian and international Black Diaspora. B current hosts an
   annual themed festival. See website for details.

**The Billie Holiday Theatre**
Restoration Plaza
1368 Fulton Street, Brooklyn, NY 11216
Mailing Address: PO Box 470131, Brooklyn NY 11247-0131
Tel: (718) 636-0918; Fax: (718) 636-0919
www.Thebillieholiday.org

**Black Ensemble Theatre**
4520 N Beacon, Chicago, IL 60640
Tel: (773) 769-4451; Fax: (718) 636-0919
Jackie Taylor, Artistic Director
www.blackensembletheatre.org
blackensemble@aol.com
> **Subject:** African American. Musicals only, except for Black Playwrights Festival.
> No children's theatre. **Preference:** Year-round open submissions. Black Playwrights
> Initiative: 21 playwrights are chosen for development, education and workshopping
> in pairs with professionals who serve as mentors. The group meets twice per month.
> Open to year-round submissions. Clearly note that the script is for the festival.

**Black Rep**
1717 Olive Street, Fourth Floor, St. Louis, MO 63103
Tel: 314-534-3807; Fax: 314-534-4035
www.theblackrep.org
info@theblackrep.org
Ronald J. Himes, Founder and Producing Director
> Est. 1976. **Preference.** Length:full-length. Subject: African American. Production:
> reading. **Application:** Synopsis, three-five-page sample, resume and letter of inquiry
> to Ameer Harper, Assistant to the Executive Director. (ameerh@theblackrep.org)

**The Black Spectrum Theatre**
Roy Wilkins Park
177 Street and Baisley Blvd. Entrance
119-07 Merrick Blvd. (For Mailing Only)
Jamaica, NY 11434
Tel: 718-723-1800; Fax: 718-723-1806
www.blackspectrum.com;
info@blackspectrum.com
> Mail scripts and contact information directly to theater.

**The Black Theatre Troupe**
P.O. Box 13349, Phoenix, Arizona 85002-3349
**Offices:**
514 West Roosevelt St., Phoenix, Arizona 85003
Tel: (602) 258-8128; Fax: 602-253-3690
David J. Hemphill, Executive Director
www.blacktheatretroupe.org
info@blacktheatretroupe.org

**Blacken Blues Theater of African American Life**
PO Box 151334, Dallas, TX 75315
Tel: 214-618-4522
Willie Holmes, Founder
info@blackenblues.com
www.blackenblues.org

**The Carpetbag Theatre**
100 S. Gay St., Knoxville, TN 37902
865-544-0447
info@carpetbag.org
Linda Parris-Bailey, Executive/Artistic Director
> Does not accept unsolicited scripts. Community-based ensemble that creates its own work.

**The Classical Theatre of Harlem**
520 8th Avenue, Suite 313, New York, NY 10018
Tel: (212) 564-9983; Fax: (212) 564-9109
Alfred Preisser, Artistic Director
www.classicaltheatreofharlem.org
info@ClassicalTheatreofHarlem.org
> Est. 1999 **Future Classics Reading Series:** The festival accepts plays in early stages of development and workshops them with professional playwrights, actors and directors, culminating in a free public reading. The play should deal with one of the following: 1) an expansive view of the classical, 2) classical subjects and themes, 3) the history of African Americans, 4) the history, culture and community of Harlem. Contact the theatre for further submission information.

**Cincinnati Black Theatre Company**
5919 Hamilton Ave., Cincinnati, OH 45224
Tel: 513-241-6060 Fax: 513-241-6671
Don Sherman, Artistic Director
www.cincyblacktheatre.org
> **Subject:** African American. **Materials:** full length plays. Musicals, children's theater. Year round. Open submissions. Annual **Black Theatre Festival**: year round open submissions.

**Congo Square Theatre Company**
2936 Southport, #210, Chicago, IL 60657
Derrick Sanders, Artistic Director
Tel: 773-296-1108; Fax: 773-472-6634
www.congosquaretheatre.org
atdouglas125@congosquaretheatre.org
> **Subject**: Theatre spawned from the African. Full-length, translations, adaptations, musicals and performance art are all accepted. **August Wilson New Play Initiative:** Must be submitted in one of three ways 1. Through a literary agent. 2. Accompanied by a recommendation letter from a theatre professional. 3. A 10-15 page sample as well as a cover letter and detailed description. All submissions should be sent Attention To: Daniel Bryant, Assistant Artistic Directior. No e-mail or fax submissions. **Best Time To Send:** Open submissions accepted year round. Before March is preferable for the reading series.

**Crossroads Theatre Company**
P.O. Box 238, 7 Livingston Ave., New Brunswick, NJ 08901
Tel: (732) 545-8100; Fax: 732 907-1864
Marshall Jones, Executive Director,
www.crossroadstheatrecompany.org
info@crossroadsthetrecompany.org
> Est. 1978. **Subject:** African American. No unsolicited scripts. Send through agent, attorney or manager. Genesis Festival: unsolicited scripts accepted. Send before Dec. 31st. Full script with contact info and writer bio.

**Cultural Odyssey**
762 Fulton St., San Francisco, CA
Mailing Address:
PO Box 156680, San Francisco, CA 94115-6680
Idris Ackamoor, Executive Director
idris@culturalodyssey.org
Rhodessa Jones, Co-Artistic Director
rhodessa@culturalodyssey.org
Tel: 415-292-1850; Fax: 415-346-9163
www.culturalodyssey.org

**The Ensemble Theatre**
3535 Main St., Houston, TX 77002
Tel: (713) 520-0055; Fax: 713-520-1269
Eileen J. Morris, Artistic Director
www.ensemblehouston.com
ejmorris@ensemblehouston.com
> Est. 1976. **Submission:** send 10-pg synopsis, cover letter and contact information to the Artistic Director.

**Essential Theatre**
Florida A&M University
www.essentialtheatre.us; www.famu.edu
Valencia.matthews@famu.edu
Valencia E. Matthews, PhD, Director of Theatre & Assistant Dean
Tel: (850) 599-3430

**The Essential Theatre**
1112 11th Street NW, Suite 100, Washington DC, 20001
Tel: 202-328-0569; Fax: 301-292-6188
www.theessentialtheatre.org
info@thessentialtheatre.org
S. Robert Morgan, Founder/Artistic Director

**eta Creative Arts Foundation**
7558 S. South Chicago Ave., Chicago, IL 60619-2644
Tel: (773) 752-3955; Fax: (773) 752-8727
Runako Jahi, Artistic Director
www.etacreativearts.org
email@etacreativearts.org
> **Preference.** Subject: African American. **Submission:** send best material and SASE, contact info and bio. Submissions accepted year round. **Playwrights Speak Reading**

**Series:** Staged readings followed by discussion with playwright, cast and audiences. Plays considered for mainstage productions.

**Evelyn Graves Drama Productions**
P.O. Box 5416, 5447 Chester Ave., Philadelphia, PA 19143
Tel: 215.727.7796
Egdrampro@aol.com
evelyngravesdramaproductions.com

**Forbidden Fruit Theatre Company**
5042 Wilshire Blvd., #565, Los Angeles, CA 90036
www.forbiddenfruittheatre.org
info@forbiddenfruittheatre.org
Tonya Jones; Artistic Director
    Annual short play festival.

**The Hansberry Project at ACT (A Contemporary Theatre)**
Kreielsheimer Place
700 Union St., Seattle WA 98101-4037
Tel: (206) 292-7660 ext 1225; Fax: (206) 292-7670
valviv@hansberryproject.org
www.hansberryproject.org

**The Hadley Players**
207 W. 133rd St., New York, NY 10030
Tel (212) 368-9314; Fax (212) 368-9314
www.hadleyplayers.org
    Please call before faxing. **Preference.** Subject: African American or Hispanic-American. **Submissions:** send 10pg synopsis with contact info and SASE. Submissions accepted year-round.

**Harlem Stage at The Gatehouse**
150 Convent Ave., New York, NY 10031
Tel: 212-281-9240; Fax: 212-281-9318
www.harlemstage.org
    **Preference.** Subject: new works by artists of color. **Sunday Works** reading series. **Fund for New Work**: grants and other funds for emerging artists. Download application on website.

**Hattiloo Theatre: A Black Repertory**
656 Marshall Ave., Memphis, TN 38103
(901)-502-3486
Hattilootheatre.org
ekundayo@hattilootheatre.org
Ekundayo Badele, Executive Director
    **Hattiloo Faith-Based Playwriting Contest:** Hattiloo Faith-Based Playwriting Contest is open to all current and former residents of Shelby County, TN and immediate surrounding counties who are 18 years or older. Scripts must be; focused on the African-American experience from a faith-based perspective; full-length (1-hour 20-minute read); submitted in English; contain no more than 6 principal characters; submitted as an unbound hard copy (3 copies); no musicals or adaptations; Unpublished original work only. Scripts will not be returned. Please

send 3 copies of a completed script, a 1-page synopsis double-spaced, in 12-point font and a completed entry form. Send an SASE if you would like confirmation. **ALL ENTRIES DUE: January 30th, 2009, 5:00p.m.** The winner will be announced in April 2009. **Remuneration:** $150 - Staged production in Hattiloo Theatre's next season. Submissions should be mailed with Attention To: Hattiloo Faith-Based Playwriting Contest at the address above.

**InterAct Productions**
138 South Oxford St. Suite 2C, New York, NY 11217
718-230-1323
mail@inneractpd.com
www.inneractpd.com
Dr. John Shévin Foster, Artistic Director
   **Subject:** African American. Submissions in synopsis form. A full script may be requested. PC, MSWORD. Attachments accepted. One-acts, full lengths and musicals are accepted. We do not accept musical revues.

**Jomandi Productions**
City Hall East
675 Ponce De Leon, 8th Fl., Atlanta, GA 30308
Tel: 404-876-6346; Fax: (404) 872-5764
jomandiproductions@yahoo.com
www.jomandi.com
Carol Mitchell-Leon, Artistic Director
   Est. 1978. Black Diamond Reading Series. Send one copy of best script.

**Jubilee Theatre**
506 Main St., Fort Worth, TX 76102
Tel: (817) 338-4204; Fax: (817) 338-4206
Ed.smith@jubileetheatre.org
www.jubileetheater.org
   Please include a letter of intent (no more than 500 words) addressing how the work reflects the African-American experience; your resume, including contact information; a 10-page sample of the play.(This sample need not be from the beginning of the play or all one scene.  Please do not submit full scripts at this time, as they will not be read in entirety.); and a stamped, self-addressed post card if you want to receive acknowledgment of receipt. Send only the above materials to the address above. The best time to submit is the beginning of the year. Applicants may be contacted and asked to supply completed scripts, other plays they have written, references, and/or other materials. No phone calls please.

**Juneteenth Legacy Theatre**
www.juneteenthlegacytheatre.com
juneteenthlegacy@aol.com
Lorna Littleway, Founder and Producing Director
**New York**
605 Water St., #21B, New York, NY 1002
Tel: 212-964-1904
**Louisville**
P.O. 3463, Louisville, KY 40201-3463
Tel: 502-636-4200

**Subject:** 19th century African American experience; pre- and Harlem Renaissance era; Caribbean and Native American influences on African Americans; contemporary issues and African American youth; images of women. **Juneteenth Jamboree of New Plays:** Open Submission. **Best Time to Send:** December 15th through March 15th. There is a $15 script reading/ processing fee, payable by money order to Juneteenth Legacy Theatre. Kentucky writers should send three (3) hard copies of their scripts (no electronic transfers) to: Kristi Papailler, JLT Founding Associate Producer, 3723 Bashford Ave., Louisville, KY 40218 and 1 hard copy to: 605 Water St. #21B, N.Y. N.Y. 10002. All other authors should send three (3) hard copies of their scripts (no electronic transfers) to: JLT, c/o Lorna Littleway, 323 W. Broadway, #505, Louisville KY. 40202 and 1 hard copy to: 605 Water St. #21B, N.Y. N.Y. 10002. Lorna Littleway, Founder and Producing Director.

**Karamu House**
2355 E. 89th St., Cleveland, OH 44106-9990
Tel: (216) 795-7070 x.240; Fax: (216) 795-7073
Terrence Spivey, Artistic Director
www.karamuhouse.org
performingarts@karamu.com
Arena Festival of New Plays, Youth Theatre

**Kuntu Repertory Theatre**
University of Pittsburgh
Dept. of Africana Studies
4140 Wesley W. Posvar Hall
230 South Bouquet St., Pittsburgh, PA 15260
Dr. Vernell A. Lillie, Artistic Director
Tel: 412-648-7547
vawl@pitt.edu
www.kuntu.org
Est. 1974. **Subject:** African American and relevant social issues. **Materials:** full length script.

**Lorraine Hansberry Theatre**
777 Jones St., San Fransisco, CA 94109
Tel: (415) 345-3980; Fax: (415) 345-3983
www.lhtsf.org
stanley@lhtsf.org
Stanley Williams, Artistic Director
**Subject:** African American and people of color. **Materials:** full length script. Accepted year-round. Tomorrow Today Play Reading Series.

**The M-Ensemble**
12320 West Dixie Highway, North Miami, FL 33168
Mailing Address:
P.O. Box 1175 Miami, FL 33168
Patricia E. Williams, Producer & General Manager
Shirley Richardson, Executive Director
www.themensemble.com; info@themensemble.com
Tel: (305) 895-8955; Fax: (305) 895-8945
Open submission. Year-Round. Please call either the General Manager or the Executive Director before submitting.

**Negro Ensemble Company**
303 West 42nd Street Suite 501, New York, NY 10036
Tel: 212.582.5860; Fax: 212.582.9639
necstaff@necinc.org
www.negroensemblecompany.org
Charles Weldon, Artistic Director
    **Subject:** African American. Unsolicited scripts accepted year-round. Send hard copy
    of full script with contact info, including email address.

**New Federal Theatre**
292 Henry St., New York, NY 10002-4804
Tel: 212-353-1176; Fax: 212-353-1088
info@newfederaltheatre.org
www.Newfederaltheatre.org
    **Subject:** African American. **Materials:** full length plays. No musicals. Preference
    given to cast with eight or fewer. **Reading Series:** considered for full production.
    Send full length scripts with contact information.

**New Freedom Theatre**
1346 N. Broad St., Philadelphia, PA 19121
Walter Dallas, Producing Artistic Director
Tel: 215-765-2793
Freedomtheatre.org

**New World Theater**
100 Hicks Way, Room 16 Curry Hicks,
University of Massachusetts, Amherst, MA 01003
Andrea Assaf, Artistic Director
Tel: 413.545.1972; Fax 413-545-4414
www.newworldtheater.org
nwt@admin.umass.edu
    We host New WORKS for a New WORLD every summer where we invite in 4
    artists/projects for a development residency. **Submissions:** New WORLD Theater
    produces and presents new work by artists of color in both our fall and spring
    seasons. Additionally, we support the creation and development of new work through
    the New WORKS for a New WORLD Summer play lab. Because of the increasingly
    high volume of scripts received and the limitations of staffing, we are unable to
    accept unsolicited scripts or inquiries. All submissions must be accompanied by
    a recommendation from a professional colleague. We welcome submissions in a
    range of forms, including (but not limited) to project descriptions, scripts, and/or
    video. We appreciate your patience, as our average response time is 9-12 weeks.
    Send submissions and letters of recommendation to Priscilla Page, Program Curator.
    Lastly, as a part of our summer playlab, we accept dramaturgy AND production
    interns for a six week in residence program. We offer housing, meals, and a
    modest stipend. Anyone interested in this internship should check our website for
    applications and more information.

**Obsidian Theatre Company**
943 Queen St. East, Toronto, Ontario, Canada M4M 1J6
Tel: 416-463-8444
www.obsidian-theatre.com
obsidiantheatre@bellnet.ca
Philip Akin, Artistic Director

**Subject:** primarily African Diaspora, though plays by writers of non-African descent that can be adapted to a black cast will be considered. Material: full length. Open submission. Year-round. Please check website for types of shows before sending.

**Opera Ebony**
2109 Broadway, Suite 1418, New York, NY 10023
Tel: 212. 877. 2110; Fax: 212. 877. 2110
www.operaebony.org
info@operaebony.org

**Penumbra Theatre Company**
270 North Kent St., St. Paul, MN 55102
Tel: 651-224-3180; Fax: 651-288-6789
Lou Bellamy, Founder and Artistic Director
www.penumbratheatre.org
lou.bellamy@penumbratheatre.org

**People's Theatre, Inc.**
511 W. South St., Suite 211 Orlando, FL 32805
Mailing Address:
P.O. Box 678910 Orlando, FL 32867-8910
Tel: (407) 426-0545
Canara Price, Founder & Artistic Director
www.peoplestheatre.org;
mail@peoplestheatre.org

**Pin Points Theatre Company**
4353 Dubois Place S.E., Washington DC 200019
Tel: (202) 582-0002
Ersky Freeman, Executive Director
www.pinpoints.org
pinpoints@aol.com

**Providence Black Repertory Company**
276 Westminster St., Providence, RI 02903
Tel: 401-351-0353; Fax: 401-621-7136
Donald W. King, Artistic Director
www.blackrep.org
elephant@blackrep.org
The Providence Black Repertory Company accepts solicited and unsolicited scripts for consideration for development and/or performance. Before submitting, playwrights should review the Black Rep's mission and core aesthetic values and organizational history on the website. The Black Rep is only interested in reviewing plays that align clearly with our mission and core aesthetic values. Unsolicited manuscripts may be submitted in hard copy only. Please include: 1) one copy of the script with numbered pages; bound copies are preferred. 2) a short synopsis and production history (if applicable) for the play 3) a bio and/or resume for the playwright 4) supporting materials as needed (photographs, reviews, music, etc.) 5) if you would like any materials returned, please include an SASE with the appropriate postage. All submissions receive a response. However, due to the high volume of scripts received, response time is often lengthy. We do our best to get a response out between three and eight months from when the script is submitted. Feel free to

contact Associate Director Megan Sandberg-Zakian (megan@blackrep.org) with any questions or for further information.

**The Riant Theatre**
P.O. Box 1902, New York, NY 10013
T: (646) 623-3488
Van Dirk Fisher, Artistic Director
www.therianttheatre.com
therianttheatre@aol.com

> **Submissions:** The Riant has many opportunities for play submissions. **The Strawberry One-Act Festival:** A play competition in which the audience and the theatre's judges cast their votes to select the best play of the season. Plays move from the 1st round to the semi-finals and then the finals. The playwright of the winning play receives a grant and the opportunity to have a full-length play developed by the Riant. **The Core Project**, an ongoing workshop for playwrights, actors and directors to collaborate and develop new plays. **The International Lesbian & Gay Theatre Festival** and **The Riant Play Reading Series**. Information as well as application forms for all of the above can be found on the website.

**Rites and Reason Theatre**
The Arts Component of the Africana Studies Department
Brown University
PO Box 1148, 155 Angell St., Churchill House, 2nd Fl., Providence, RI 02912
Tel: (401) 863-3558; Fax: (401) 863-3559
Elmo Terry-Morgan, Artistic Director
www.brown.edu/Departments/Africana_Studies/rites_reason/

**Robey Theater Company**
514 S. Spring St., Los Angeles, CA 90013
Tel: 213-489-7402; Fax: 213-489-4520
Bennet Guillory, Producing Artistic Director
www.robeytheatrecompany.com
robeytc@sbcglobal.net

> Est. 1996. Also produces a Playwright Workshop Series.

**Shadow Theatre Company**
1468 Dayton St., Aurora, CO. 80010
Tel: 720-857-8000
www.shadowtheatre.com
info@shadowtheatre.com
Jeffrey Nickelson, Founder, Executive/Artistic Director

**Take Wing and Soar Productions**
Administrative Offices
45 Tiemann Place, New York, NY 10027-3322
Tel: 212-696-6575
Production Offices
Take Wing And Soar Productions, Inc., c/o National Black Theatre, Inc.
2031 Fifth Ave., Harlem, NY 10035
www.twasinc.xbuild.com
info@takewingandsoar.org

**Theatre North**
PO Box 6255, Tulsa, Ok 74148
Tel: 918-596-1611
Maybelle Wallace, Executive Director
theatrenorthmw@hotmail.com
theatrenorth.net

**Towne Street Theatre**
5215 Rosemead Blvd. #C, San Gabriel, CA 91776
Tel: 213-624-4796
V. Thompson
www.townestreet.org
info@townestreet.org
   Est. 1993. **Application:** Resume and 5 pg sample. Ten Minute Play Festival.

**True Colors Theatre Company**
Studioplex
659 Auburn Avenue, Suite 257, Atlanta, Georgia 30312
Tel: 404-588-0308; Fax 404-588-0310
Kenny Leon, Artistic Director
www.truecolorstheatrecompany.com
info@truecolorstheatre.org
   **Submissions:** no unsolicited submissions.

**Ujima Company**
545 Elmwood Ave., Buffalo, New York, 14222
Tel: 716-883-4232; Fax: 716-882-4960
www.ujimatheatre.org
ujimacoinc@aol.com

**Unity Theatre Ensemble**
P.O. Box 2466, St. Louis, MO 63031
http://utensemble.org
Tel: 314-355-3586
Ralph E. Greene, Producing Artistic Director
   **Submissions:** Unity Theatre Ensemble develops and performs scripts centered on
   special themes and occasions as requested by sponsoring organizations. Email or call
   the UTE office for further details.

**Youth Ensemble of Atlanta**
881 Ponce de Leon Ave., Atlanta, GA 30306
Debi Barber, Executive Director
Tel: 404.756.2184; Fax: 404.756.2182
touring@youthensemble.org
www.fhyea.org

## FESTIVALS

### Alabama Shakespeare Festival
1 Festival Dr., Montgomery, AL 36117
T: 334-271-5379
www.asf.net
swp@asf.net
Nancy Rominger, Artistic Associate
   **Southern Writer's Project**: The Southern Writers' Project of the Alabama
   Shakespeare Festival accepts original scripts and adaptations, not professionally
   produced, that meet one or more of the following criteria: 1. You are a Southern
   Writer. 2. Your script is set in the South, or deals specifically with Southern issues,
   characters, or themes. 3. Your script deals with African-American themes or
   characters. Submissions that meet these criteria are considered for the Southern
   Writers' Project Festival of New Plays, an annual weekend of readings of new
   work. These plays are then considered for production in subsequent ASF seasons.
   If your play is an adaptation, please secure the permission to the underlying rights
   prior to submission. Full length plays only, please. Submissions are limited to one
   play per author per season. Musicals and theatre for young audiences should send a
   letter of inquiry first. Due to the large volume of submissions, please allow up to six
   months for response. If you wish your materials returned to you, please include an
   appropriate SASE. Plays submissions may be mailed or emailed.

### Hip-Hop Theater Festival
442-D Lorimer St. #195, Brooklyn, NY 11206
T: 718.497.4282 ; F: 718.497.4240
Clyde Valentin, Executive Director
www.hhtf.org

### National Black Arts Festival
Promenade II
1230 Peachtree St. NE, Suite 500, Atlanta, GA  30309
Stephanie S. Hughley, Executive Producer
www.nbaf.org
info2@nbaf.org
   Est. 1987. Yearly festival including film, literature, visual art and theater.
   **Application:** Best Material

### National Black Theatre Festival
610 Coliseum Drive, Suite 1, Winston-Salem, NC 27106
Tel: (336) 723-2266
Larry Leon Hamlin, Producer and Artistic Director
nbtf@bellsouth.net
www.nbtf.org
   Main Stage Productions, Fringe, Reader's Theater of New Works, Workshops &
   Seminars

**The Annual Theodore Ward Prize for African-American Playwriting**
Columbia College Theater Dept.
72 E. 11th St., Chicago, IL 60605
Tel: 312-344-6136; Fax: 312-344-8077
Chuck Smith, Contest Facilitator
www2.colum.edu/undergraduate/theater/department.php
> **Material:** Full-Length Plays by African American Playwrights. **Eligibility:** of African-American descent and permanent US residents. **Submission:** Full-length plays addressing the African-American experience. One-acts and musicals are not accepted (with the exception of a play-with-music). Adaptations and translations are not eligible unless from works in the public domain. All rights for music or biographies must be secured by entrant prior to submission. One completed script per playwright will be accepted. Scripts that have received professional productions are ineligible. "Professional" Includes Equity Showcase and Waiver productions, but does not include amateur and college productions. All manuscripts must be typed and bound. Please include a brief personal resume (phone number please), a short synopsis and a script history. The script history should include information about any prior productions or readings. Staff and faculty of Columbia College Chicago are not eligible. Winners cannot win within five successive years.

## RESOURCES, ETC.

**AAPEX – African American Playwrights Exchange**
Jaz Dorsey, Dramaturg
Blog of African American theater news
www.africanamericanplaywrightsexchange.blogspot.com

**Black Women's Playwright Group**
3523 12th St. NE 2nd Floor, Washington, DC 20017
Tel: 202-635-BWPG (2974)
www.blackwomenplaywrights.org

**Black Theater Network**
2609 Douglass Rd SE, Unit102, Washington DC, 20020
Tel: 202-419-9968
www.blackthreatrenetwork.org
info@blacktheatrenetwork.org
Luther D. Wells, President
> Est. 1986. **Black Theater Network** publishes several publications for the African American theater community including: Black Theater Network Newsletter (quarterly); the Black Theater Directory; Black Theater Connections, a job listing (quarterly); and Black Voices, a catalog of work being made by black theater professionals. ($20). Annual dues: $75 for individuals, $35 for students and retirees, $110 for organizations.

## ASIAN AMERICAN

**Asian American Theatre Company (AATC)**
c/o 55 Teresita Blvd., San Francisco, CA 94217
Jeannie Barroga, Artistic Director
www.asianamericantheater.org
info@asianamericantheater.org

**East-West Players**
120 Judge John Aiso St., Los Angeles, CA 90012
Tel: 213-625-7000 x29; Fax: 213-625-7111
Jeff Liu, Literary Manager
www.eastwestplayers.org
jliu@eastwestplayers.org
info@eastwestplayers.org
 East-West offers many opportunities including the **David Henry Hwang Writers Institute** as well as unsolicited scripts and competitions. **Submissions:** Most of the new works we produce revolve around Asian Pacific American (as opposed to Asian) characters and/or themes. We are looking for both comedy and drama, in English and financially viable (which includes considerations such as cast size, number of sets, etc.), and they don't necessarily have to be "issue-oriented," in that race can be an unspoken component in the work. Writers are strongly encouraged to browse through our production history, which can be found on the website. Manuscripts should be bound, preferably with brads and three-hole punch paper, with a title page containing all contact information for the author. Please also include cover letter and resume. If you'd like to send a SASP (self-addressed stamped postcard) for confirmation of receipt, we'll send it back to you when we receive your materials. If you'd like us to return your script, please send a manuscript-sized SASE with the appropriate postage. We typically keep all plays for our archives; please let us know if you would NOT like us to do so. If you have Internet access and prefer to be notified via email, we can do that as well. Please allow 3 - 9 months for consideration. All scripts are read by our Literary Committee and a single script is read by a minimum of 2 readers, sometimes more, before we make a recommendation. PLEASE DO NOT EMAIL SCRIPTS. Good luck!

**Lodestone Theatre Ensemble**
PO Box 1072, Studio City, CA 91614
Tel: 323-993-7245
Philip W. Chung, Artistic Director
Chil Kong, Artistic Director
www.lodestonetheatre.org
info@lodestonetheatre.org
 Not currently accepting admissions.

**Mu Performing Arts**
2700 NE Winter Street, Suite 4, Minneapolis, MN 55413
612-824-4804
Rick Shimoi, Artistic Director
info@muperformingarts.org
www.muperformingarts.org
 Primarily focuses on new work.

**National Asian American Theatre Company**
520 8th Avenue, Suite 316, New York, NY 10018
Tel: (212) 244-0447; Fax: (212) 244-0448
www.naatco.org
info@naatco.org
> NAATCO performs European and American classics as written with all Asian
> American casts; adaptations of these classics by Asian American playwrights; and
> new plays - preferably world premieres - written by non-Asian Americans, not for or
> about Asian Americans, but realized by an all Asian American cast.

**Rasaka Theatre Company (South Asian American Artists)**
2936 N Southport Ave., Chicago, IL 60657
Tel (312) 777-1070
www.rasakatheatre.org
info@rasakatheatre.org
> Season features some new work.

**ReOrient**
Golden Thread Productions
131 10th St., San Francisco, CA 94103
Tel: 415-626-4061; Fax 415-626-1138
Torange Yeghiazarian, Artistic Director
www.goldenthread.org
information@goldenthread.org

**Silk Road Theatre Project**
680 South Federal Street, Suite 301, Chicago, IL 60605
Jamil Khoury, Artistic Director
www.srtp.org
info@strp.org
> Season focuses on new work.

---

**National Asian American Theatre Festival**
520 Eighth Ave., Suite 308, New York, NY 10018
Tel: 646-522-0931
Jeff Mousseau, General Manager
jmousseau@naatf.org
www.naatf.org
info@naatf.org

## LATINO-AMERICAN

**Aguijón Theater Company of Chicago**
2707 N. Laramie Ave., Chicago, Illinois 60639
Tel: (773) 637-5899; Fax: (773) 637-5040
info@aguijontheater.org
www.aguijontheater.org
Rosario Vargas, Artistic Director

**Company of Angels**
501 S. Spring St. 3rd Floor, Los Angeles, CA 90013
Tel: 323-883-1717
Armando Molina, Artistic Director
amolina@companyofangels.org
Ricardo Brach, Literary Liaison
angeliclee@gmail.com
www.companyofangels.org;
    Their season primarily focuses on new work

**El Centro Su Teatro**
4725 High St., Denver, CO 80216
Tel: 303-296-0219; Fax: 303-296-4614
www.suteatro.org
staff@suteatro.org

**GALA Hispanic Theatre**
P.0. Box 43209, Washington, DC 20010
Tel: 202-234-7174
Hugo Medrano, Producing Artistic Director
info@galatheatre.org
www.galatheatre.org
    Primarily focuses on new work

**Repertorio Español**
138 East 27th St., New York, NY
Tel: 212-225-9920; Fax: 212-225-9085
www.repertorio.org

**Teatro Familia Aztlan**
(Artists In Residence at SJMAG)
San Jose Multicultural Artists Guild, Inc. (SJMAG)
1700 Alum Rock Ave., Suite 265, San Jose, CA 95116
Tel: (408) 272-9924; Fax: (408) 928-5597
info@sjmag.org; sjmag.org

**Teatro Luna**
P.O. Box 47256, Chicago, IL 60647
Tanya Seracho, Co-Artistic Director
www.teatroluna.org
info@teatroluna.org
    Season features new work and offers new play development program.

**Teatro Vista**
3712 North Broadway, Suite 275, Chicago, IL 60613
Tel: 312-666-4659
Edward F. Torres, Artistic Director/Founder
www.teatrovista.org
info@teatrovista.org

## MIDDLE-EASTERN / ARAB-AMERICAN

**Ajyal Theater Group**
20250 Dubois Street, Clinton Township, MI 48035
Tel: 248-341-3383; Fax: 586-792-6888
Najee Mondalek, Artistic Director
www.arabamericantheater.com
ajyal@comcast.net
ajyal@arabamericantheater.com

**Arab Theatrical Arts Guild**
www.arabtheater.org
info@arabtheater.org
    Please email scripts.

**ReOrient**
    See listing under "ASIAN-AMERICAN"

**Silk Road Theatre Project**
    See listing under "ASIAN-AMERICAN"

FESTIVALS

**National Asian American Theatre Festival**
    See listing under "ASIAN-AMERICAN"

**New York Arab-American Comedy Festival**
338 E. 70th St., Suite 3A, New York, NY 10021
www.arabcomedy.org
info@arabcomedy.org
    **Deadline:** February (check website for specific date). **Comedic theater:** We are
    seeking comedic theater pieces written or co-written by Arab-Americans which
    do not exceed 30 minutes in length. The works can be one acts or excerpts from a
    longer work. The pieces do not have to be Arab themed. Please include with your
    submission: contact information and short bio, script, with character breakdown, and
    a one-paragraph blurb about the play. If the play has been staged already, you can
    submit a DVD of the play. Due to time constraints, any submissions received after
    the deadline will not be considered for this year's Festival. Submissions of scripts
    should be sent via email to submissions@arabcomedy.org

## RESOURCES, ETC.

**Middle East America: A National New Plays Intitiative**
Three Participating Theatres:
**Golden Thread Productions** (listed under "ASIAN- AMERICAN")
**Lark Play Development Center** (listed under "MINORITY FRIENDLY")
**Silk Road Theatre Project** (listed under "ASIAN-AMERICAN")
    CURRENTLY NOT ACCEPTING SUBMISSIONS UNTIL 2010. Middle
    East America: A National New Plays Initiative is a first-of-its-kind tri-coastal
    collaboration involving San Francisco's Golden Thread Productions, New York's
    Lark Play Development Center, and Chicago's Silk Road Theatre Project. This
    initiative was designed to encourage and support the development of Middle
    Eastern American playwrights and Middle Eastern American plays, of the highest
    artistic caliber, and to enrich the canon of American dramatic literature. We aim
    to challenge both the lack of representation and the one-dimensional stereotypical
    representation of persons of Middle Eastern descent on America's stages. The goal
    of this initiative is to provide additional opportunities for writers of Middle Eastern
    backgrounds, to expand cultural representation of Middle Eastern Americans, and to
    integrate Middle Eastern American plays into the American theatre repertoire. The
    initiative will provide $10K to commission a Middle Eastern American playwright
    to develop a new work. The commission will be awarded to a playwright selected
    by application process and will include in-depth development support at the Lark
    Play Development Center in collaboration with Golden Thread Productions and Silk
    Road Theatre Project. This initiative also includes a development phase that will be
    designed with an eye towards production at Golden Thread Productions and/or Silk
    Road Theatre Project.

## NATIVE AMERICAN

**Algonkuin Theatre Company**
1231 Pulaski Blvd., Bellingham, MA 02019
Telephone: 508-883-1808
Marty BlackEagle-Carl, Artistic Director
www.Algonkuintheatre.org
eaglesweyr@comast.net
    Season features new work.

## MINORITY FRIENDLY

**Amas Musical Theater**
115 MacDougal Street, Suite 2B, New York, NY 10012
tel: (212) 563-2565; fax (212) 239-8332 fax
amas@amasmusical.org
amasmusical.org
Donna Trinkoff, Producing Artistic Director
    Founded 1968. Promotes American diversity and minority perspectives. Amas
    Six O'Clock Musical Theatre Lab: development series for writers, lyricists and
    composers to mount staged readings of new musicals. Presented for three consecutive
    evenings in hour-long concert versions. (Fall and Spring). Amas Workshop Program

gives composers and lyricists opportunity to continue work on a polished and complete version of their new work. Including a two-week rehearsal culminating in a series of performances using minimal costumes, lighting and sets. Focus remains on the writing and the music. Amas Mainstage Program Select musicals given a full off-Off Broadway run of four weeks under an equity showcase of LOA contract.

### Centerstage
700 North Calvert St., Baltimore, MD 21202
tel: (410) 986-4000; fax (410) 539-3912
access@centerstage.org
www.centerstage.org
Donna Trinkoff, Producing Artistic Director
> Founded 1963. Commitment to diversity. No unsolicited scripts. Send a brief cover letter or letter of introduction, synopsis, cast breakdown,10-pg excerpt all to Gavin Witt, Resident Dramaturg. If you want your material confirmed or returned, please indicate and include an SASE. For musicals, please include recordings of songs or music. You may also send your bio or resume and reviews of any productions of the work. First Look: readings and development wrokshops for emerging writers. Some plays considered for future Centerstage seasons. First Look: Special Edition: New Play Reading Festival.

### Cornerstone Theater Company
708 Traction Ave., Los Angeles, CA 90013
Tel: 213-613-1700; Fax: 213-613-1714
Michael John Garces, Artistic Director
www.cornerstonetheater.org
mgarces@cornerstonetheater.org

### Detroit Repertory Theatre
13103 Woodrow Wilson , Detroit, MI 48238
Tel: (313) 868-1347; Fax (313) 868-1705
Bruce E Miller, Artistic Director
DetRepTh@aol.com ;www.detroitreptheatre.com
> **Subject:** Multi-racial. Open submissions year-round. Selections made in June of each year. **Application:** Issue oriented plays (comedic is fine); 5 to 7 characters. No one-acts. No musicals. No double casting. No children. Include SASE for return of materials. Submissions must be bound in a folder, and include a cast list.

### Eden Theatrical Workshop
1570 Gilpin St., Denver, CO 80218
Tel: (303) 321-2320

### Hollywood Thespian Company
8443 Vicksburg Ave., Westchester, CA  90045
Renita Thomas-Franklin, Artistic Director
info@hollywoodthespiancompany.com
www.hollywoodthespiancompany.com

**Kelly-Strayhorn Theater**
5941 Penn Ave., Pittsburgh, PA 15206
Tel: 412-363-3000; Fax: 412-363-3416
Robert Neu, Executive Director - ext. 101
www.kelly-strayhorn.org
info@kelly-strayhorn.org
　　Performing arts venue promoting diverse artistic representation in culturally diverse
　　Pittsburgh. Performance spaces open for rental.

**Lark Play Development Center**
c/o Literary Wing Submission
939 Eighth Ave., Suite 301, New York, NY, 10019
www.larktheatre.org
submissions@larktheatre.org
　　The Lark is committed to providing access to all writers, regardless of age, ethnicity,
　　experience, or whether they have agent representation. The Open Access Program
　　ensures that the Lark's programming reflects both global and U.S. ethnic diversity.
　　The Lark distributes a call for submissions to the industry-at-large, seeking new plays
　　and new voices, and the work is then carefully reviewed by a volunteer committee of
　　readers, the Literary Wing, and the highest-ranking work is showcased in an annual
　　Playwrights' Week Festival. A submission to this annual festival is the ONLY way
　　that the Lark is able to support unsolicited play submissions. We are seeking works
　　that are ambitious, fresh, playful, engaging, energizing, provocative, powerful and
　　theatrical, works that reveal unheard and vital perspectives and authors with clear
　　goals about their writing who are open to the Lark's developmental process. See the
　　website for more information about submission deadlines and guidelines.

**Mixed Blood Theatre Company**
1501 South 4th St., Minneapolis, MN 55454
Tel: 612-338-0937
Jack Reuler, Artistic Director
　　junior@mixedblood.com
　　www.mixedblood.com
　　Partial season devoted to new work.

**Pangea World**
711 West Lake St., Suite 101, Minneapolis, MN 55408
Tel: 612-822-0015; Fax: 612-821-1070
Meena Natarajan, Literary Director
www.pangeaworldtheater.org
meena@pangeaworldtheater.org
　　Offers a play development program and is devoted to new works

**San Jose Multicultural Artists Guild, Inc. (SJMAG)**
1700 Alum Rock Ave., Suite 265, San Jose, CA 95116
Tel: (408) 272-9924; Fax: (408) 928-5597
info@sjmag.org
www.sjmag.org
　　SJMAG is home to artists in residence: Tabia African American Theater Ensemble
　　and Teatro Familia Aztlan.

**The Watts Village Theater Company**
1827 E. 103rd St., Los Angeles, CA 90002
Tel: 818-919-9705
Guillermo Aviles-Rodriguez, Artistic Director
slapdrama@yahoo.com
www.wattsvillagetheatrecompany.org

## FELLOWSHIPS

**New York Theatre Workshop – Artists of Color Fellowships**
79 E. 4th St., New York, NY 10003
Tel: 212-780-9037; Fax:212-460-8996

**Emerging Artists of Color Fellows:** The Emerging Artists of Color Fellowship program grew out of NYTW's fundamental belief that diversity of thought, experience, and culture is crucial to continued theatrical innovation. Emerging Artist Fellows hold a 16-18 month part-time appointment, and include directors, playwrights, and designers. During their fellowship, these artists are provided with valuable tools to support them through the delicate and often vulnerable process of developing new work. Activities include participation in our Mondays @ 3 reading series, which take place regularly throughout the year and are attended by NYTW artistic staff and members of the Usual Suspects, the Workshop's community of affiliated artists.

**Resident Artists of Color Fellows:** The Resident Artists of Color Fellowship program expands on the principles of the Emerging Artists Fellowship program and allows artists to develop a longer, more in-depth relationship with NYTW. Resident Artist Fellowships last for two years, and the recipients are hired as full-time NYTW staff members. Each Fellow focuses on one particular area of interest, such as literary management or casting which allows for immersion in NYTW's artistic and operational model. Many Resident Fellows maintain working relationships with NYTW, and some have assumed permanent staff positions. The 2007-09 Creative Resident Fellow, Jorge Ignacio Cortiñas, divides his time between working with NYTW education programs and developing a new play about the process of social change in Venezuela. The 2008-10 Artistic Leadership Fellowship was awarded to Rafael Gallegos, who is focusing on producing while working closely with the Artistic Department. Both Jorge and Rafael began their relationships with NYTW as Emerging Artist Fellows.

## AVANT-GARDE / EXPERIMENTAL THEATRE

Avant-garde theatre and experimental theatre are terms that are often used interchangeably with each other. These are general terms for innovative theatre that is active in the invention and application of new techniques. The terms continually shift over time, as the mainstream theatre world adopts many forms that were once considered radical.

The theatre companies that are listed follow these loose guidelines. Some companies produce work that poses questions to audiences, urging them to think. Socially- and politically-driven theatre, theatre that speaks for specific groups, and theatre that uses non-traditional applications, such as new technologies, puppetry and various aspects of physical theatre, such as acrobatics and miming, are included in these examples.

**Annex Theatre**
PMB 1440
1122 East Pike St., Seattle, WA 98122-3934
Tel: 206-728-0933; Fax: 206-774-6083
www.annextheatre.org
Artistic Director: Bret Fetzer
    "Annex Theatre is dedicated to creating bold new work in an environment of improbability, resourcefulness and risk ..."

**Big Art Group**
P.O. Box 1034, New York, NY 10276
Tel: 646-808-3046
info@bigartgroup.com
www.bigartgroup.com
Caden Manson
    Est. 1999. The company uses the language of media and blended states of performance in a unique form to build culturally transgressive and challenging new works, presented through use of technology, often as installations [company produced pieces]

**Bread and Puppet Theater**
753 Heights Rd., Glover, VT 05839
Tel: 802-525-3031 or 802-525-1271; Fax: 802-525-3618
breadpup@together.net
www.breadandpuppet.org
Artistic Director: Peter Schumann
    Est. 1962. All **Bread and Puppet Theater** shows, created and designed by **Peter Schumann** with input from the company, use music, dance and slapstick to get their point across. Their distinctive imagery — featuring puppets (of all kinds and sizes), masks, costumes, paintings, buildings, and landscapes — seemingly breathe with Schumann's distinctive visual style of dance, expressionism, dark humor and low-culture simplicity. Most shows are morality plays; overall theme is universal peace.

**Bricolage Production Company**
P.O. Box 42336, Pittsburgh, PA 15222
Tel: 412-381-6999
Artistic Director: Jeffrey Carpenter

Producing Artistic Director: Tami Dixon
jeff@webbricolage.org; tami@webbricolage.org
www.webbricolage.org

> Mission: Making artful use of what's at hand, Bricolage uses the distinctive resources of the Pittsburgh region to create theatrical events that stimulate a heightened sense of involvement for the audience. "Play-in-a-day" Series. Produces a lot of new work.

**Brooklyn Lyceum**
227 4th Ave., Brooklyn, NY 11215
Tel: 866-gowanus; Fax: 718-398-7301
www.gowanus.com

> SwampKing: A Brooklyn Vaudville, A Ten-Minute Play Tournament Wrapped In A Variety Show. Monthly ten-minute play competition, which presents the work of playwrights from all five boroughs to standing-room-only crowds in intimate 60 seat Geloscopic Theatre.

**Clubbed Thumb**
312 East 23rd Street #4B, New York, NY 10010-4700
Tel: 212-802-8007; Fax: 212-533-9286
www.clubbedthumb.org
info@clubbedthumb.org

> Clubbed Thumb will consider for production plays that fall within the following guidelines: Unproduced in New York City, Running time: between 1 hr. and 1:30 hr. Intermissionless. Must have a reasonable representation of women, both in quantity and quality of roles. At least 3 characters - we prefer medium sized ensemble casts. Director of the piece will be chosen by mutual consent of playwright and Clubbed Thumb. Clubbed Thumb is committed to play development, and therefore produces only plays that are actively being worked on with the expectation that the rehearsal process will prove beneficial to the playwright's writing process. If you would like to submit a play, please send it to: Clubbed Thumb, c/o Maria Striar, 141 East Third St. #11H, New York, NY 10009. Please do not bind scripts; pages should be loose or clipped with a binder clip. Scripts will not be returned. Sorry, electronic submissions are not accepted. If you send us a play between now and June, you probably won't get a response from us before July. Thanks for your patience.

**Dad's Garage Theatre Company**
280 Elizabeth St., Suite C-101, Atlanta, GA 30307
Tel: 404.523.3141; Fax: 404.688.6644
www.dadsgarage.com
Artistic Director: Kate Warner

> Est. 1995. Original Mainstage shows, "Top Shelf" premieres (created by their company), year-round improv

**Double Edge Theatre**
948 Conway Rd., Ashfield, MA 01330
Tel: 413-628-0277; Fax: 831-307-6159
office@doubleedgetheatre.org
www.doubleedgetheatre.org
Artistic Director: Stacy Klein

> Est. 1982. Company uses physical training and improvisation to create original performances. [company produced pieces]

**Frank Theatre**
3156 23rd Ave. South, Minneapolis, MN 55407
Tel: 612-724-3760
www.franktheatre.org
> Frank Theatre is a professional theatre company committed to producing unique work that stretches the skills of the artists who create the work while simultaneously challenging the everyday perceptions of the audience through the exploration of ideas and issues of social, political and/or cultural concern. Frank Theatre was founded with the desire to produce work that provides opportunities for artists to grow, to stretch, to work outside of and beyond the typical opportunities provided by theatres with a greater commercial interest. The theatre has successfully pursued this goal through the consistent staging of works that require the actors, designers, and director to challenge themselves and each other. [unsure if they accept new plays from outside sources]

**InterAct Theatre Company**
2030 Sansom St., Philadelphia, PA 19103
Tel: 215-568-8077; Fax: 215.568.8095
www.interacttheatre.org
Producing Artistic Director: Seth Rozin
> InterAct is a theatre for today's world, producing new and contemporary plays that explore the social, political, and cultural issues of our time. InterAct strives to produce plays that explore issues of social, cultural and political relevance. InterAct uses the unique power and magic of the theatre to ask difficult questions about the world we live in, examining the forces that influence what we believe and why. InterAct dares to dramatize complex and controversial issues with artistic integrity and fairness.

**Kitchen Dog Theater**
3120 McKinney Ave., Dallas, TX 75204
www.kitchendogtheater.org; admin@kitchendogtheater.org
Co-Artistic Directors: Christopher Carlos, Tina Parker
> Est. 1990. Mission: to provide a place where questions of justice, morality, and human freedom can be explored. We choose plays that challenge our moral and social consciences, invite our audiences to be provoked, challenged, and amazed. We believe that the theater is a site of individual discovery as well as a force against conventional views of the self and experience. It is not a provider of answers, but an invitation to question. New Works Festival: new play submission: Scripts must be received by March 1, 2008 to be considered for the 2008 Festival. Each year, Kitchen Dog Theater selects one original script to receive: A fully staged production (as part of our regular season – a five-week run), Paid travel to Dallas, TX (if necessary) to work with the Director, Cast and Crew, Royalty stipend (amount TBD). Seven other original scripts will be selected for staged readings as part of the Festival (travel not included). Prospective scripts must meet the following guidelines: Full-length plays only (preferably one hour or longer), Submitted scripts must be type-written, Completed scripts only, Do not include a synopsis and/or reviews (if any) of the play, Ideally have between one and five actors (character doubling acceptable). There are no restrictions on play content. Only one script per playwright may be submitted. All unproduced scripts will be recycled. Please send your script with cover letter to: Attn: Tina Parker, Co-artistic Director, Kitchen Dog Theater
> 3120 McKinney Avenue, Ste. 100, Dallas, TX 75204. DO NOT EMAIL SCRIPTS. ONLY COMPLETE SCRIPTS WILL BE ACCEPTED. **DEADLINE for 2008 New Works Festival: received by March 1, 2008**

**La MaMa E.T.C.**
74A East 4th St., New York, NY 10003
Tel: 212-475-7710
www.lamama.org
Founder and Artistic Director: Ellen Stewart
> Est. 1961. For 46 years La MaMa has passionately pursued its original mission to develop, nurture, support, produce and present new and original performance work by artists of all nations and cultures.

**Mabou Mines**
150 First Ave., New York, NY 10009
Tel: 212-473-0559; Fax: 212-473-2410
office@maboumines.org
www.maboumines.org
Artistic Directors: Lee Breuer, Ruth Maleczech, Fred Neumann, Terry O'Reilly, Sharon Fogarty, Julie Archer
> Est. 1970. Today, the work is at the forefront of experimentation with technology, international collaboration, multi-disciplinary creations with visual artists, puppeteers and composers.

**Mixed Blood Theatre Company**
1501 South Fourth St., Minneapolis, MN 55454
Tel: 612-338-0937
www.mixedblood.com
> Est. 1976. Mixed Blood Theatre Company is a professional, multi-racial theatre promoting cultural pluralism and individual equality through artistic excellence. They produce plays ranging from intimate chamber theater to irreverent political satires to technical extravaganzas. Member of Theatre Communications Group (TCG). Member of the National New Play Network (NNPN)

**The Necessary Theatre**
Kentucky Center for the Arts
501 West Main St., Louisville, KY 40202
www.tntky.org
Artistic Director: Tad Chitwood
> Est. 1991. The Necessary Theatre is a company of theater artists whose primary mission is to produce new, and rarely seen, works for the stage.

**Neo-Futurists**
5153 N. Ashland Ave. 2nd Floor, Chicago, IL 60640
Tel: 773-275-5255
www.neofuturists.org
Artistic Director: Jay Torrence
> The Neo-Futurists are a collective of wildly productive writer/director/performers who create: Theater that is a fusion of sport, poetry, and living-newspaper; non-illusory, interactive performance that conveys our experiences and ideas as directly and honestly as possible; immediate, unreproducable events at headslappingly affordable prices. [company produced pieces]

**Ontological-Hysteric Theater**
St. Mark's Church
131 East 10th St., New York, NY 10003
Tel: (212) 420-1916

info@ontological.com; www.ontological.com
Artistic Director: Richard Foreman
> The Ontological-Hysteric Theater (OHT) was founded in 1968 by Richard Foreman
> with the aim of stripping the theater bare of everything but the singular and essential
> impulse to stage the static tension of interpersonal relations in space. The OHT seeks
> to produce works that balance a primitive and minimal style with extremely complex
> and theatrical themes. The core of the company's annual programming is Richard
> Foreman's theater pieces, of which he has made over 50 in the last 40 years.

**PUSH Physical Theatre**
Rochester, NY
ChitChat@pushtheatre.org; www.pushtheatre.org
Founded by Darren & Heather Stevenson
> Intensely physical theatre hard to define as one art form. [unsure if they use much
> text in their pieces]

**Ridge Theater**
141 Ridge Street, #8, New York, NY 10002
Tel/Fax: 212-674-5485
ridgetheater@earthlink.net (Artistic Director)
http://www.ridgetheater.org
Artistic Director: Bob McGrath
> "Ridge Theater has established itself as one of America's premiere creators of avant-
> garde theater, opera, and new music performance. Ridge productions are epic visual
> and aural works that typically position performers within film and video projections,
> redefining traditional theatrical boundaries."

**Theatre de la Jeune Lune**
105 North First St., Minneapolis, MN 55401
Tel: (612) 332-3968; Fax: (612) 332-0048
info@jeunelune.org
www.jeunelune.org
Artistic Director: Dominique Serrand
> Est. 1978 in France. "Our name - *"Theatre of the New Moon"* - reflects our
> commitment to finding theatrical sustenance by looking for the new in the old. The
> name comes from a little poem by Bertolt Brecht: "As the people say, at the moon's
> change of phases / The new moon holds for one night long / The old moon in its
> arms." The strong and tender care that the future shows for the past describes the
> dialectic that informs all of Jeune Lune's work: striving to link a past heritage of
> popular performance traditions - from circus and classical farce to commedia dell'arte
> and vaudeville - to a present function within the local community and the larger
> international community of cultural production. While embracing the 'old moon' of
> theatrical tradition, Jeune Lune seeks to create an entirely new kind of theatre that is
> immediate, high spirited, passionately physical, and visually spectacular.

**Woolly Mammoth Theatre Company**
641 D St. NW, Washington DC 20004
Tel: 202-289-2443
www.woollymammoth.net
> Est. 1980. Submissions: Woolly Mammoth's literary department does not accept
> unsolicited manuscripts. If you would like your play to be considered for production,
> please send an inquiry letter as well as a synopsis and ten-page sample to the address
> below. Materials will not be returned. We are grateful for your interest in our company.

## BOOKS ON WRITING FOR THE STAGE: ART, CRAFT, THEORY, AND BUSINESS

The following list was designed to aid writers in selecting the scriptwriting craft and business books that best fit their individual needs. Readers can generally assume that playwriting craft books will explore action, character, and dialogue. Specific aspects of craft that are emphasized by the author are listed under Features. Chapter or section titles that suggest further distinguishing features are listed in quotes.

**The 2009 Screenwriter's and Playwright's Market**
By Chuck Sambuchino
Publisher: Writers Digest Books (January 7, 2009)
ISBN-10: 1582975523 - ISBN-13: 978-1582975528
    Features: Business strategies, Business resources

**The Art and Craft of Playwriting**
By Jeffrey Hatcher
Publisher: F W Publications
ISBN-13: 9781884910463 - ISBN-10: 1884910467
    Features: Aristotle's theories, Interviews, "Space, Time, and Causality," Structure

**The Art of Dramatic Writing**
By Lajos Egri
Publisher: Simon and Schuster (June 1st, 1960)
ISBN-13: 9780671213329 - ISBN-10: 0671213326
    Features: Character behavior, Dialectics, "Orchestration," Premise, "Unity of Opposites"

**The Art of the Playwright - Creating the Magic of Theatre**
By William Packard
Publisher: Thunder's Mouth Press; 2nd edition (May 5, 1997)
ISBN-10: 1560251174 - ISBN-13: 978-1560251170
Features: Business resources, "Contemporary and Avant Garde Playwrights," "Dramatic Versus Narrative"

**The Art of Writing Drama**
By Michelene Wandor
Publisher: A&C BLACK (September 2008)
ISBN: 9780413775863

**Blunt Playwright: An Introduction to Playwriting**
By Clem Martini
Publisher: Consortium Book (September 30th, 2007)
ISBN-13: 9780887548949 - ISBN-10: 0887548946
    Features: Exercises, Play Analyses, Rewriting, Workshopping

**Collaborative Playwright: Practical Advice for Getting Your Play Written**
By Bruce Graham, Michele Volansky
Publisher: Heinemann (March 30th, 2007)
ISBN-13: 9780325009957 - ISBN-10: 0325009953
    Features: Collaboration, Interviews, "Prewriting and outlines," Rewriting

**The Crafty Art of Playmaking**
By Alan Ayckbourn
Publisher: Palgrave Macmillan (September 30th, 2008)
ISBN-13: 9780230614888 - ISBN-10: 0230614884
  Features: Directorial perspectives

**Creating Unforgettable Characters**
By Linda Seger
Publisher: Henry Holt (July 1st, 1990)
ISBN-13: 9780805011715 - ISBN-10: 0805011714
  Features: Character psychology, "Creating Nonrealistic Characters," Research

**Developing Story Ideas**
By Michael Rabiger
Publisher: Elsevier Science (October 21st, 2005)
ISBN-13: 9780240807362 - ISBN-10: 0240807367
  Features: Artistic Identity, Exercises, Generating ideas

**Dramatic Writer's Companion: Tools to Develop Characters, Cause Scenes and Build Stories**
By Will Dunne
Publisher: University of Chicago Press (April 15th, 2009)
ISBN-13: 9780226172538 - ISBN-10: 0226172538
  Features: Character development, Structure

**Dramatists Toolkit: The Craft of the Working Playwright**
By Jeffrey Sweet
Publisher: Heinemann (November 1st, 1993)
ISBN-13: 9780435086299 - ISBN-10: 0435086294
  Features: "Negotiations," "Violating Rituals"

**The Elements of Playwriting**
By Louis E. Catron
Publisher: Waveland Press (November 1st, 2001)
ISBN-13: 9781577662273 - ISBN-10: 157766227X

**A More Perfect Ten: Writing and Producing the Ten Minute Play**
By Gary Garrison
Publisher: Focus Publishing (2008)
ISBN-10: 1585103276 - ISBN-13: 978-1585103270
  Features: Specific "how to" instructions for how to write a ten-minute play; six published ten-minute plays.

**Musical Theatre Writer's Survival Guide**
By David Spencer
Publisher: Heinemann (July 1st, 2005)
ISBN-13: 9780325007861 - ISBN-10: 0325007861
  Features: Musical Writing, Collaboration, Business Strategies, "Presentation, Formatting and Packaging," "The Spirit of the Thing, or: Adaptation"

**Naked Playwriting: The Art, the Craft, and the Life Laid Bare**
By Robin U. Russin and William M. Downs
Publisher: Silman-James Press (December 15th, 2004)
ISBN-13: 9781879505766 - ISBN-10: 1879505762
    Features: Business strategies, Generating ideas, Rewriting

**New Playwriting Strategies: A Language-Based Approach to Playwriting**
By Paul C. Castagno
Publisher: Theatre Arts Book
ISBN-10: 0878301364 - ISBN-13: 978-0878301362
    Features: "On Multivocality and Speech Genres," Play analyses

**Notes from a Practicing Writer: The Craft, Career, and Aesthetic of Playwriting**
By Ed Shockley
Publisher: Lightning Source (January 30th, 2007)
ISBN-13: 9780972690638 - ISBN-10: 0972690638
    Features: Business strategies, "Compression," "The Magic What-If," "Projection,"
    Play analyses, "Reduction"

**Playwright's Guidebook**
By Stuart Spencer
Publisher: Farrar Straus and Grioux (April 1st, 2002)
ISBN-13: 9780571199914 - ISBN-10: 0571199917
    Features: Exercises, Generating ideas, Rewriting, Structure, "High Stakes and High
    Hopes," "Writing from an Image"

**The Playwright's Handbook**
By Frank Pike, Thomas G. Dunn
Publisher: Plume; Rev Upd Su edition (April 1, 1996)
ISBN-10: 0452275881 - ISBN-13: 978-0452275881
    Features: Rewriting, Business Strategies, Workshops, "Sight, Hearing, Touch, Taste,
    Smell," "Understanding the Relationship of Ritual and Dram"

**The New, Improved Playwright's Survival Guide: Keeping the Drama in Your
Work and Out of Your Life**
By Gary Garrison
Publisher: Heinemann Books (2005)
ISBN-10: 0325008167 - ISBN-13: 978-0325008165
    Features: More of a book on how to be a playwright more than how to write

**The Playwright's Workbook**
By Jean-Claude Van Itallie
Publisher: Applause (1997)
ISBN: 1557833028
    Features: Exercises, Play analyses, Images, Various forms and genres

**The Playwright's Workout**
By Liz Engelman, Michael Bigelow Dixon
Publisher: Smith and Krause Publishers
ISBN-13: 9781575256177 - ISBN-10: 1575256177
    Features: Exercises

**The Playwright's Process - Learning the Craft from Today's Leading Dramatists**
By Buzz McLaughlin
Publisher: Back Stage Books (May 1, 1997)
ISBN-10: 0823088332 - ISBN-13: 978-0823088331
   Features: Interviews, Rewriting, Development, "The Play Idea Worksheet," "The
   Short-form Biography," "The Long-form Biography".

**Playwrights Teach Playwriting**
By Joan Harrington (editor) and Brian Crystal (editor)
Publisher: Smith & Kraus (September 30, 2006)
ISBN-10: 1575254239 - ISBN-13: 978-1575254234
   Features: Essays, Interviews, Teaching methods

**Playwriting: A Practical Guide**
By Noel Greig
Publisher: Routledge (February 28th, 2005)
ISBN-13: 9780415310444 - ISBN-10: 041531044X
   Features: Generating ideas, Rewriting

**Playwriting, Brief and Brilliant**
By Julie Jensen
Publisher: Smith & Kraus (October 30, 2007)
ISBN-10: 1575255707 - ISBN-13: 978-1575255705

**Playwriting in Process: Thinking and Working Theatrically**
By Michael Wright
Publisher: Heinemann (August 4th, 1997)
ISBN-13: 9780435070342 - ISBN-10: 0435070347
   Features: Exercises, Process, Writer's Block

**Playwriting : The Structure of Action**
By Norman A. Bert, Sam Smiley
Publisher: Yale University Press (October 30th, 2005)
ISBN-13: 9780300107241 - ISBN-10: 0300107242
   Features: Aristotle's principles, Generating ideas

**Playwriting: Writing, Producing and Selling Your Play**
By Louis E. Catron
Publisher: Waveland Press (July 1990)
ISBN-10: 0881335649 - ISBN-13: 978-0881335644
   Features: Business strategies, Aristotle's principals, Workshops

**The Power of the Playwright's Vision: Blueprints for the Working Writer**
By Gordon Farrell
Publisher: Heinemann Drama (September 6, 2001)
ISBN-10: 0325002428 - ISBN-13: 978-0325002422

**Reminiscence Theatre : Making Theatre from Memories**
By Glenda Jackson, Pam Schweitzer
Publisher: Jessica Kingsley Publishers (January 15th, 2006)
ISBN-13: 9781843104308 - ISBN-10: 184310430X
   Features: Community building, Documentary, Teaching methods, Therapy

**Script is Finished, Now What Do I Do: The Scriptwriter's Resource Book and Agent Guide**
By K. Callan
Publisher: SCB Distributors (January 15th, 2007)
ISBN-13: 9781878355188 - ISBN-10: 187835518X
     Features: Business resources, Business strategies

**Solving Your Script : Tools and Techniques for the Playwright**
By Jeffrey Sweet
Publisher: Heinemann (February 15th, 2001)
ISBN-13: 9780325000534 - ISBN-10: 0325000530
     Table of Contents: "Negotiation Over Objects," "Different Relationships, Different Roles," "Disruption of a Ritual"

**So You Want to Be a Playwright? : How to Write a Play and Get It Produced**
By Tim Fountain
Publisher: Nick Hern Books (April 1, 2008)
ISBN-10: 1854597167 - ISBN-13: 978-1854597168

**Stage Writers Handbook: A Complete Business Guide for Playwrights, Composers, Lyricists and Librettists**
By Dana Singer
Publisher: Theatre Communications Group (May 1, 1996)
ISBN-10: 1559361166 - ISBN-13: 978-1559361163
     Features: Business resources, Business strategies

**Strategies for Playbuilding : Helping Groups Translate Issues into Theater**
By Will Weigler
Publisher: Heinemann (March 15th, 2001)
ISBN-13: 9780325003405 - ISBN-10: 0325003408
     Features: Community building, Documentary, Teaching methods

**Teaching Young Playwrights**
By Gerald Chapman, Lisa A Barnett
Publisher: Heinemann (November 26th, 1990)
ISBN-13: 9780435082123 - ISBN-10: 0435082124
     Features: Exercises, Teaching methods

**Teach Yourself Writing a Play**
By Ann Gawthorpe, Lesley Brown
Publisher: McGraw-Hill (October 26th, 2007)
ISBN-13: 9780071496971 - ISBN-10: 0071496971
     Features: Business strategies, Generating ideas, Genres, Rewriting

**To Be a Playwright**
By Janet Neipris
Publisher: Theatre Arts Book; New edition (September 28, 2005)
ISBN-10: 0878301887 - ISBN-13: 978-0878301881
     Features: "Twelve Habits of Successful Playwrights," "Adapting from Fact and Fiction," "Critics"

**Way of Story: The Craft & Soul of Writing**
By Catherine Ann Jones
Publisher: Ingram Publisher Services (August 1st, 2007)
ISBN-13: 9781932907322 - ISBN-10: 1932907327
    Features: Dialogue Structure, Rewriting, Generating ideas,

**"Writer's Block" Busters : 101 Exercises to Clear the Deadwood and Make Room for Flights of Fancy**
By Velina Hasu Houston
Publisher: Smith & Kraus (September 16, 2008)
ISBN-10: 1575255979 - ISBN-13: 978-1575255972
    Features: Exercises

**The Writer Got Screwed (but didn't have to): Guide to the Legal and Business Practices of Writing for the Entertainment Industry**
By Brooke A. Wharton
Publisher: Harper Paperbacks (March 14, 1997)
ISBN-10: 0062732366 - ISBN-13: 978-0062732361
    Features: Business strategies

**The Writer's Journey: Mythic Structure for Writers**
By Christopher Vogler
Publisher: Ingram Publisher Services (November 1st, 2007)
ISBN-13: 9781932907360 - ISBN-10: 193290736X
    Features: Mythic Structure, Mythic Characters

**Writing 45-minute One-act Plays, Skits, Monologues, & Animation Scripts for Drama Workshops : Adapting Current Events, Social Issues, Life Stories, News & Histories**
By Anne Hart
Publisher: ASJA Press (March 14, 2005)
ISBN-10: 0595345972 - ISBN-13: 978-0595345977
    Features: One-Act Plays, Documentary

**Writing Dialogue for Scripts: Effective Dialogue for Film, TV, Radio, and Stage**
By Rib Davis
Publisher: A&C Black; 3rd edition (January 1, 2009)
ISBN-10: 1408101343 - ISBN-13: 978-1408101346
    Features: Dialogue

**Writing the Broadway Musical**
By Aaron Frankel
Publisher: Perseus Books Group (August 17th, 2000)
ISBN-13: 9780306809439 - ISBN-10: 0306809435
    Features: Musical writing

**Writing Musical Theatre**
By Allen Cohen, Steven L. Rosenhaus
Publisher: St. Martins Press (February 7th, 2006)
ISBN-13: 9781403963956 - ISBN-10: 1403963959
    Features: Musical writing, adaptations, business strategies

**Writing Your First Play**
By Stephen Sossaman
Publisher: Prentice Hall (August 11, 2000)
ISBN-10: 013027416X - ISBN-13: 978-0130274168

**Writing: Working in the Theatre**
By Robert Emmet Long (Editor), Paula Vogel (Foreword)
Publisher: Continuum (January 15, 2008)
ISBN-10: 0826418074 - ISBN-13: 978-0826418074

**You Can Write a Play!**
By Milton E. Polsky
Publisher: Applause Books; Revised edition (February 1, 2002)
ISBN-10: 1557834857 - ISBN-13: 978-1557834850

**Young At Art : Classroom Playbuilding in Practice**
By Christine Hatton and Sarah Lovesy
Publisher: David Fulton Publish; 1 edition (November 24, 2008)
ISBN-10: 0415454786 - ISBN-13: 978-0415454780
    Features: Exercises, Teaching methods

# INDEX OF SPECIAL INTERESTS

## THEATER FOR YOUNG AUDIENCES (T.Y.A.)

## WOMEN

## Writers of Color

# Submission Calendar

These opportunities accept submissions year-round. Consult the company website for the most up to date information. Also, consult the Dramatists Guild website for new opportunities, changes in rules and deadlines, and for ongoing opportunities not listed in this year's directory.

## JANUARY

| | | |
|---|---|---|
| 01/01/10 | Carnegie Mellon University | 160 |
| 01/01/10 | Kitchen Dog Theater (KDT) New Works Festival | 54 |
| 01/01/10 | Towngate Theatre Playwriting Contest | 78 |
| 01/01/10 | Women's Work Lab | 48 |
| 01/02/10 | Young Playwrights Inc. National Playwriting Competition | 79 |
| 01/03/10 | Yale University School of Drama | 168 |
| 01/04/10 | Hawai'i Prize | 69 |
| 01/04/10 | Pacific Rim Prize | 74 |
| 01/04/10 | Resident Prize | 75 |
| 01/12/10 | Camargo Foundation | 43 |
| 01/15/10 | Ashland New Plays Festival | 60 |
| 01/15/10 | CEC ArtsLink | 89 |
| 01/15/10 | Last Frontier Theatre Conference | 54 |
| 01/15/10 | Perishable Theatre Women's Playwriting Festival | 63 |
| 01/15/10 | Phoenix Theatre [AZ] | 138 |
| 01/15/10 | Premiere Stages Play Festival | 57 |
| 01/15/10 | Ragdale Foundation | 47 |
| 01/15/10 | Southern Playwrights Competition | 76 |
| 01/15/10 | Summerfield G. Roberts Award | 76 |
| 01/15/10 | TRU Theater Resources Unlimited | 187 |
| 01/15/10 | Virginia Center for the Creative Arts (VCCA) | 48 |
| 01/15/10 | Wichita State University (WSU) New Play Competition | 79 |
| 01/15/10 | WordBRIDGE Playwrights Laboratory | 98 |
| 01/16/10 | PEN/Laura Pels Foundation Awards for Drama | 74 |
| 01/18/10 | Helene Wurlitzer Foundation of New Mexico | 44 |
| 01/18/10 | Sundog Theatre | 149 |
| 01/30/10 | Bakers Plays High School Contest | 66 |
| 01/31/10 | Dubuque Fine Arts Players One Act Play Contest | 81 |
| 01/31/10 | Lionheart Theatre's Make the House Roar Prize | 83 |
| 01/31/10 | PEN Center USA Literary Awards | 85 |
| 01/19/11 | Jewel Box Theatre Playwriting Competition | 82 |

## FEBRUARY

| | | |
|---|---|---|
| 02/01/10 | Blue Mountain Center | 43 |
| 02/01/10 | Centre Stage South Carolina New Play Festival | 51 |
| 02/01/10 | Envision Retreat | 43 |
| 02/01/10 | Kentucky Arts | 92 |
| 02/01/10 | Moving Arts Premiere One-Act Competition | 84 |
| 02/01/10 | New Directors/New Works (ND/NW) | 171 |
| 02/01/10 | New York University Musical Theater Writing | 163 |
| 02/01/10 | North Dakota Council on the Arts | 95 |

| 02/01/10 | Trustus Playwrights' Festival | 64 |
| 02/01/10 | Trustus Theatre | 153 |
| 02/01/10 | United States / Japan Creative Artists' Program | 97 |
| 02/01/10 | Vermont Playwrights Award | 78 |
| 02/14/10 | Penobscot Theatre | 56 |
| 02/15/10 | Djerassi Resident Artists Program | 43 |
| 02/15/10 | Fresh Fruit Festival | 52 |
| 02/15/10 | Jane Chambers Playwriting Award | 70 |
| 02/15/10 | Jane Chambers Student Playwriting Award | 70 |
| 02/16/10 | Isle Royale National Park Artist-in-Residence | 45 |
| 02/16/10 | Theatre Oxford 10-Minute Play Contest | 86, 190 |
| 02/19/10 | Artist Trust | 88 |
| 02/28/10 | Attic Theatre One-Act Marathon | 49 |
| 02/28/10 | Beverly Hills Theatre Guild Youth Theatre Marilyn Hall Award | 66 |
| 02/28/10 | Francesca Primus Prize | 81 |
| 02/28/10 | McLaren Memorial Comedy Playwriting Competition | 83 |
| 02/01/11 | Indiana Arts Commission (IAC) | 91 |
| 02/15/11 | Travel & Study Grant Program | 97 |

## MARCH

| 03/01/10 | Alabama State Council on the Arts | 87 |
| 03/01/10 | Byrdcliffe Arts Colony Artist-in-Residence (AIR) | 42 |
| 03/01/10 | Cape Cod Theatre Project | 169 |
| 03/01/10 | Edward Albee Foundation | 43 |
| 03/01/10 | Golden Thread Festival | 53 |
| 03/01/10 | Kimmel Harding Nelson (KHN) Center for the Arts | 45 |
| 03/01/10 | Louisiana Division of the Arts | 92 |
| 03/01/10 | Old Opera House Theatre Company  New Voice Play Festival | 63 |
| 03/01/10 | Philadelphia Theatre Company (PTC) | 138 |
| 03/01/10 | South Dakota Arts Council | 97 |
| 03/01/10 | Southern Illinois University, Carbondale (SIU) | 165 |
| 03/01/10 | Two Chairs Theater Company | 158 |
| 03/01/10 | Ucross Foundation Residency Program | 48 |
| 03/01/10 | Write a Play! NYC Contest | 79 |
| 03/08/10 | Hangar Theatre Lab Company Playwriting Residencies | 170 |
| 03/11/10 | Colorado Council on the Arts | 89 |
| 03/15/10 | Arts & Letters Prize in Drama | 80 |
| 03/15/10 | Barnstormers Theater | 50 |
| 03/15/10 | Blank Theatre Company Young Playwrights Festival | 50 |
| 03/15/10 | Juneteenth Legacy Theatre | 62, 205 |
| 03/15/10 | Laity Theatre Company | 71 |
| 03/15/10 | Short Attention Span PlayFEST | 57 |
| 03/19/10 | Baldwin New Play Festival | 50 |
| 03/31/10 | Appalachian Festival of Plays and Playwrights | 49 |
| 03/31/10 | Fire Rose Prods. 10-Min. Play Festival | 61 |
| 03/31/10 | Intersection for the Arts James D. Phelan Literary Award | 70 |
| 03/31/10 | Princess Grace Foundation USA Playwriting Fellowship | 96 |
| 03/01/11 | Arthur W. Stone New Play Award | 65 |
| 03/02/12 | Anna Zornio Memorial Children's Theatre Playwriting Award | 65 |

## APRIL

| | | |
|---|---|---|
| 04/01/10 | Actors' Playhouse National Children's Theatre Festival | 60 |
| 04/01/10 | Aurand Harris Fellowship | 80 |
| 04/01/10 | Baltimore Playwrights Festival | 60 |
| 04/01/10 | National Childrens Theater Festival | 84 |
| 04/01/10 | New Hampshire State Council on the Arts | 94 |
| 04/01/10 | New Rocky Mountain Voices | 84 |
| 04/01/10 | Pittsburgh New Works Festival (PNWF) | 63 |
| 04/01/10 | Rhode Island State Council on the Arts | 96 |
| 04/03/10 | ASCAP/Disney Musical Theatre Workshop [CA] | 168 |
| 04/09/10 | Turtle Shell Productions | 153 |
| 04/10/10 | McKnight Theatre Artists Fellowship | 93 |
| 04/15/10 | John Gassner Memorial Playwriting Award | 82 |
| 04/15/10 | Montana Artists Residency | 47 |
| 04/15/10 | VSA arts Playwright Discovery Program | 79 |
| 04/23/10 | Essential Theatre Playwriting Award | 68 |
| 04/30/10 | Riant Theatre | 142, 209 |

## MAY

| | | |
|---|---|---|
| 05/01/10 | Aurand Harris Memorial Playwriting Award | 80 |
| 05/01/10 | Don and Gee Nicholl Fellowships | 90 |
| 05/01/10 | Lewis Galantiere Award | 71 |
| 05/01/10 | LiveWire Chicago Theatre | 71 |
| 05/01/10 | Page 73 Productions | 95 |
| 05/01/10 | Sewanee Writers' Conference | 174 |
| 05/01/10 | W. Keith Hedrick Playwriting Contest | 87 |
| 05/15/10 | BMI Lehman Engel Musical Theatre Workshop–Librettists Workshop | 169 |
| 05/15/10 | Community Theatre Association of Michigan | 80 |
| 05/15/10 | Ragdale Foundation | 47 |
| 05/15/10 | Stageworks, Inc. | 148 |
| 05/15/10 | Virginia Center for the Creative Arts (VCCA) | 48 |
| 05/15/10 | Writer's Digest Writing Competition | 87 |
| 05/31/10 | Award Blue | 65 |
| 05/31/10 | Das Goldkiel | 80 |
| 05/31/10 | Naples Players ETC | 72 |
| 05/31/10 | Prix Hors Pair | 85 |

## JUNE

| | | |
|---|---|---|
| 06/01/10 | Chicano / Latino Literary Prize in Drama | 66 |
| 06/01/10 | California Young Playwrights Contest | 67 |
| 06/01/10 | Charles M. Getchell Award, SETC | 67 |
| 06/01/10 | Christopher Brian Wolk Award | 67 |
| 06/01/10 | Jackie White Memorial National Children's Play Writing Contest | 82 |
| 06/01/10 | Met Life Nuestras Voces Playwriting Competition | 72 |
| 06/01/10 | New Professional Theatre Writers Festival | 55 |
| 06/15/10 | Institute of Gunnar Gunnarsson - Klaustrid | 45 |
| 06/15/10 | L. Arnold Weissberger Award | 70 |
| 06/15/10 | Towson University Prize for Literature | 78 |
| 06/30/10 | Canadian Jewish Playwriting Competition | 67 |
| 06/30/10 | Walt Disney Studios / ABC Entertainment Writing Fellowship | 98 |
| 06/30/10 | Firehouse Theatre Project's Festival of New American Plays | 52 |
| 06/30/10 | Fractured Atlas | 180 |
| 06/30/10 | Hawthornden Retreat for Writers | 45 |

| 09/30/10 | Baltimore Playwrights Festival | 60 |
| 09/30/10 | Boomerang Theatre Company | 50 |
| 09/30/10 | Long Beach Playhouse New Works Festival | 62 |
| 09/30/10 | Theatre Three [NY] One-Act Play Festival | 58 |

## OCTOBER

| 10/01/10 | Millay Colony for the Arts | 46 |
| 10/01/10 | National Playwrights Conference (OPC) | 62 |
| 10/01/10 | New Harmony Project | 171 |
| 10/01/10 | Radcliffe Institute Fellowships | 96 |
| 10/01/10 | Rhode Island State Council on the Arts | 96 |
| 10/01/10 | South Carolina Arts Commission | 97 |
| 10/01/10 | Sundance Institute Theatre Program | 174 |
| 10/01/10 | Theatre Building Chicago | 58 |
| 10/01/10 | U.S. Dept. of State Fulbright Program for US Students | 97 |
| 10/05/10 | American Antiquarian Society Fellowships | 87 |
| 10/15/10 | Artists' Fellowships | 88 |
| 10/15/10 | Playwrights First Award | 75 |
| 10/15/10 | ShowOff! Playwriting Festival | 64 |
| 10/30/10 | Riant Theatre | 142, 209 |
| 10/31/10 | 6 Women Playwriting Festival | 49 |
| 10/31/10 | Cultural Conversations | 51 |
| 10/31/10 | FutureFest | 52 |
| 10/31/10 | GAYFEST NYC | 61 |
| 10/31/10 | Irish American Theatre Co. | 82 |
| 10/31/10 | Mildred & Albert Panowski Playwriting Award | 72 |
| 10/31/10 | Reva Shiner Full-Length Play Contest | 86 |
| 10/31/10 | Southern Appalachian Playwrights' Conference | 57 |
| 10/31/10 | Stanley Drama Award | 86 |

## NOVEMBER

| 11/01/10 | Beverly Hills Theatre Guild Julie Harris Playwright Award | 66 |
| 11/01/10 | Black Box New Play Festival | 61 |
| 11/01/10 | City Theater [FL] Summer Shorts | 112 |
| 11/01/10 | Coe College Playwriting Festival & Symposia | 51 |
| 11/01/10 | David Mark Cohen Playwriting Award | 80 |
| 11/01/10 | Hodder Fellowship | 90 |
| 11/01/10 | John Cauble Short Play Awards Program | 83 |
| 11/01/10 | Musical Theater Award | 84 |
| 11/01/10 | National Ten-Minute Play Contest | 73, 196 |
| 11/01/10 | Year End Series (YES) New Play Festival | 59 |
| 11/01/10 | Summer Play Festival | 58 |
| 11/01/10 | Ten Minute Play Festival | 77 |
| 11/01/10 | Tennessee Williams/New Orleans Literary Festival | 64 |
| 11/02/10 | American-Scandinavian Foundation (ASF) | 88 |
| 11/02/10 | Richard Rodgers Awards for Musical Theater | 75 |
| 11/05/10 | Fiscal Sponsorship | 90 |
| 11/15/10 | Beverly Hills California Musical Theatre Award | 66 |
| 11/15/10 | Boston Theater Marathon | 50 |
| 11/15/10 | Lark Play Development Center: Playwrights' Week | 54 |
| 11/15/10 | Nebraska Arts Council | 94 |
| 11/15/10 | Theater of the First Amendment, First Light Discovery Program | 151 |
| 11/20/10 | Ledig House Writers Residency Program | 46 |

| 11/25/10 | FirstStage One-Act Play Contest | 81 |
| 11/30/10 | Bay Area Playwrights Festival (BAPF) | 60 |
| 11/30/10 | Edgar Allan Poe Award for Best Play | 68 |
| 11/30/10 | International Mystery Writers' Festival | 53 |
| 11/30/10 | Poems & Plays | 40 |
| 11/30/10 | Raymond J. Flores Short Play Festival | 63 |
| 11/30/10 | Rome Prize | 96 |

## DECEMBER

| 12/01/10 | American College Theater Festival (ACTF) | 60 |
| 12/01/10 | George Bennett Fellowship | 90 |
| 12/01/10 | Georgia College and State University | 81 |
| 12/01/10 | High School New Play Award | 82 |
| 12/01/10 | Jean Kennedy Smith Playwriting Award | 82 |
| 12/01/10 | Lavender Footlights Festival | 54 |
| 12/01/10 | National Music Theater Conference (OMTC) | 62 |
| 12/01/10 | One-Act Playwriting Competition | 74 |
| 12/01/10 | Rocky Mountain National Park Artist-in-Residence Program | 47 |
| 12/03/10 | Ruby Lloyd Apsey Award | 76 |
| 12/15/10 | Collaboraction: Sketchbook Festival | 61 |
| 12/15/10 | Michener Center for Writers | 93 |
| 12/15/10 | New York City 15-Minute Play Fest | 55 |
| 12/15/10 | Next Generation Playwriting Contest | 85 |
| 12/15/10 | PEN Translation Prize | 85 |
| 12/15/10 | Reverie Productions | 86 |
| 12/15/10 | Teatro Dallas | 158 |
| 12/16/10 | Burning Coal Theatre Company | 109 |
| 12/17/10 | Cincinnati Fringe Festival | 61 |
| 12/31/10 | Dorothy Silver Playwriting Competition | 68 |
| 12/31/10 | Fractured Atlas | 180 |
| 12/31/10 | Genesis Festival | 53 |
| 12/31/10 | Inspirato Festival | 53, 190 |
| 12/31/10 | Little Festival of the Unexpected | 54 |
| 12/31/10 | Mountain Playhouse Playwriting Contest | 72 |
| 12/31/10 | Nathan Miller History Play Contest | 72 |
| 12/31/10 | National Writers Association Foundation (NWAF) | 182 |
| 12/31/10 | New Stage Theatre | 133 |
| 12/31/10 | Ohioana Career Award | 73 |
| 12/31/10 | Ohioana Citations | 73 |
| 12/31/10 | Ohioana Pegasus Award | 74 |
| 12/31/10 | Robert J. Pickering Award for Playwriting Excellence | 76 |
| 12/31/10 | Seven Devils Playwrights Conference | 64 |
| 12/31/10 | Theatre Alliance of Michigan | 150 |
| 12/31/11 | Goshen College Peace Playwriting Contest | 69 |
| 12/31/11 | Theatre in the Raw Play Writing Contest | 86 |

# INDEX

Join over 6,000
    Playwrights
    Composers
    Lyricists
    Librettists

# Dramatists Guild of America

in the only professional association established to protect your rights.

ANYONE writing for the stage can apply and enjoy the privileges of membership, which include:

A subscription to *The Dramatist* magazine

A bimonthly e-Newsletter listing upcoming events, ticket offers, member news, and the latest business affairs news items

An annual *Dramatists Guild Resource Directory*, a guide to the theatrical marketplace, with comprehensive lists of opportunities and resources

Model Contracts for all levels of production, plus collaboration agreements and more

Free business adivce and assistance on many theatre and career-related matters

Free admission to symposia, seminars, and other events around the country

Access to the Members Lounge section of the Dramatists Guild website, where you can order contracts, download articles, search the database of resources, view videos and stream audio from past seminars and events

## AND MORE!

---

## CATEGORIES OF MEMBERSHIP

The Dramatists Guild of America offers membership to all dramatic writers, including playwrights, librettists, lyricists and composers, regardless of their production or publication history.

### Active Members ($150/yr)
Have been produced on a First- Class/Broadway or Off-Broadway contract, or on the main stage of a regional LORT theatre. Applications must be accompanied by a copy of a review or program from the qualifying production.

### Associate Members ($95/yr)
Authors of all theatrical works, including plays, librettos, lyrics and musical compositions written for the stage. Applications must be accompanied either by a complete theatrical work of any length written by the applicant or by a program or a review of a stage production.

### Student Members ($35/yr)
Must be enrolled in a course of dramatic writing instruction at the time of their application for membership. Applications must be accompanied by a letter from the program's senior administrator, or other proof of enrollment, indicating the expected date of graduation.

College/University

Graduation Date

### Estate Members ($125/yr)
The the executors of estates of deceased theatrical writers who would have qualified as Active or Associate Members during their lifetime. To become an Estate Member, please call the office at 212-398-9366 and speak with the membership department.

### Subscribers
If you are not a theatrical writer, you can still obtain certain Guild publications as an Individual Subscriber, an Institutional Subscriber, or a Professional Subscriber. For more information on the various levels of subscription, please call the office 212-398-9366.

## MEMBERSHIP APPLICATION

Please check all that apply:

☐ Playwright  ☐ Composer  ☐ Lyricist  ☐ Librettist

(Mr./Mrs./Ms.) _____
(Name you use professionally. Please print or type)

Pseudonym(s) _____

Address _____

City _____  State _____  Zip _____

Phone _____

Email _____

Social Security Number _____

Date of Birth _____

(If Applicable) Agent/Agency _____

Agent Address/Phone _____

☐ I authorize the release of my personal information

☐ Enclosed is my check to The Dramatists Guild of America, Inc.

☐ Please bill my credit card:  ☐ MC  ☐ VISA  ☐ AMEX  ☐ DISCOVER

Card Number _____  Exp. Date _____

Signature _____

Unlike other guilds and unions, there is no initiation fee. Residents of Canada, please add $10 to the membership fee. Other residents outside the United States, please add $20 to membership fee. All payments must be in U.S. funds or payable through a U.S. bank.

Mail to: The Dramatists Guild of America
Attn: Membership Department
1501 Broadway, Suite 701, NY, NY 10036.

For more information: 212.398.9366